MW01448085

For Joey, one of the very best arrangements of stardust in the cosmos
—Isabel Thomas

For my dad, Bryan Gillingham, now at peace with the universe
—Sara Gillingham

Dear Reader,

It's often difficult to see the stars when the night sky is so brightly lit from below. I have a small telescope at home, but the only object I can see well is the Moon. Gazing at its craters and mountains never gets boring, but nothing compares to my first experience of a truly dark sky, aged 22, in the Chilean Atacama Desert. What I had thought was only possible to see in photographs—nebulae, galaxies, the great glowing band of the Milky Way—was suddenly spread across the sky, making Earth seem almost empty in comparison. I lay for hours on the ground, unable to look away from the universe.

Since then, I have sought out dark skies whenever possible. I've carried binoculars up North American volcanoes and Spanish mountains, and into the Amazon rainforest, India's Thar Desert, and Welsh national parks. But one of the most amazing experiences came far closer to home. One night in 2024, I stepped outside my house in Cambridge, UK, and realized the sky was pink. A burst of energy on our nearest star had delivered the Northern Lights to my doorstep. Astronomy is about patience, but also preparation. Reading about the universe helps you better understand the mind-boggling wonder of what you are seeing, which makes it all the more exhilarating. I hope this book helps to get you ready for the exciting aurorae, asteroid, and comet visits, eclipses, meteor showers, planet parades, and other astronomical marvels to come.

Isabel Thomas

NAMING ASTRONOMICAL OBJECTS
The International Astronomical Union (IAU) is the body that oversees the naming of objects inside and outside our solar system, as well as the definitions of each category of object. It is the source of the names and designations used in this book. In some instances, ancient or traditional names are also provided, for information. Find out more at https://www.iau.org/.

EXPLORING THE UNIVERSE

A COMPLETE GUIDE TO THE COSMOS

WORDS BY ISABEL THOMAS   PICTURES BY SARA GILLINGHAM

6
INTRODUCTION
FROM EARTH TO THE EDGE OF THE UNIVERSE

16
SECTION 1
THE VIEW FROM EARTH

34
SECTION 2
NEAR-EARTH SPACE

126
SECTION 4
STARS

68
SECTION 3
OUR SOLAR SYSTEM

CONT

ENTS

168
SECTION 5
GALAXIES

188
SECTION 6
THE UNIVERSE

208
CONCLUSION
ASTRONOMICAL DATA AND OTHER RESOURCES

216
GLOSSARY AND FIND OUT MORE

220
INDEX

FROM EARTH TO THE EDGE OF THE UNIVERSE

THE UNIVERSE INCLUDES EVERYTHING THAT EXISTS, FROM THE STARS SCATTERED ACROSS THE NIGHT SKY TO THE BUILDING BLOCKS OF YOUR BODY.

THE BIGGEST QUESTION

We know our own corner of the universe well, with its spectacular landscapes and extraordinary living things. But **star** maps painted in prehistoric caves suggest that humans have always gazed up at the night sky and wondered: what lies beyond?

Answering this question has been one of humanity's greatest technological and conceptual challenges.

This book is your guide to what we know about the universe beyond Earth's surface, and how we know it. Beginning with the view from our **planet**, it takes you on a journey through our cosmic neighborhood and far beyond. One of the most mind-boggling insights of **cosmology** is that the universe contains far more than we can see with our eyes, or even detect with our instruments. Exploring the universe means stepping outside your everyday understanding of reality to explore phenomena beyond your senses.

WHEN WE LOOK UP AT THE NIGHT SKY, WE SEE OBJECTS SO DISTANT THAT VIEWING THEM IS A FORM OF TIME TRAVEL.

You'll see objects so alien that we can't yet fully understand how they work, and so distant that seeing them is a form of time travel. At the same time, you'll learn how our curiosity about the universe has helped us better understand the most familiar cosmological objects of all: planet Earth, and the living things that call it home.

OUR PLACE IN SPACE

It took a huge leap of imagination to recognize that we live on a ball-shaped planet that is spinning on its axis, and speeding around the Sun. This leap wasn't made in the mind of a single scientist. It took centuries of careful observation, ideas, and arguments, with each step building on the work of those who had come before. Isaac Newton—whose **theory** of **gravity** helped explain why Earth is **spherical** and why it **orbits** the Sun—described this as "standing on the shoulders of giants."

Some of the earliest "giants" were Ancient Greek thinkers such as Aristotle, who argued that only a spherical Earth could cast a round shadow on the Moon during a lunar **eclipse**. Other evidence was found by watching ships sail away from the coast. Rather than vanishing to a point (as they would on a flat Earth) their tall masts gradually disappeared below the horizon—something that could only happen if they were sailing across the surface of a giant sphere.

The most **massive** objects in the universe are spherical, thanks to a balance between their outward pressure and the inward force of gravity.

INTRODUCTION: FROM EARTH TO THE EDGE OF THE UNIVERSE

MEASURING OUR PLANET

How do you measure the size of a giant ball while you are standing on it?

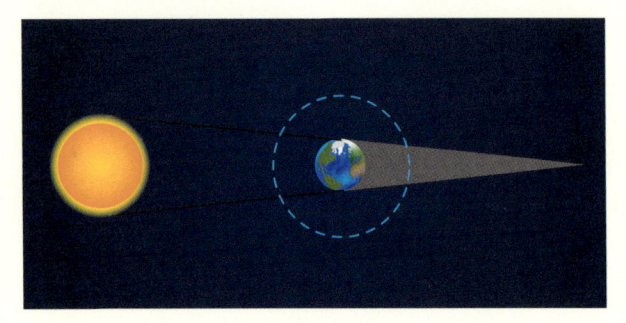

Ancient Greek **astronomer** Aristarchus tried measuring the size of Earth's shadow on the Moon during a lunar eclipse. He didn't get the right answer, but only because instruments of the time were not very precise.

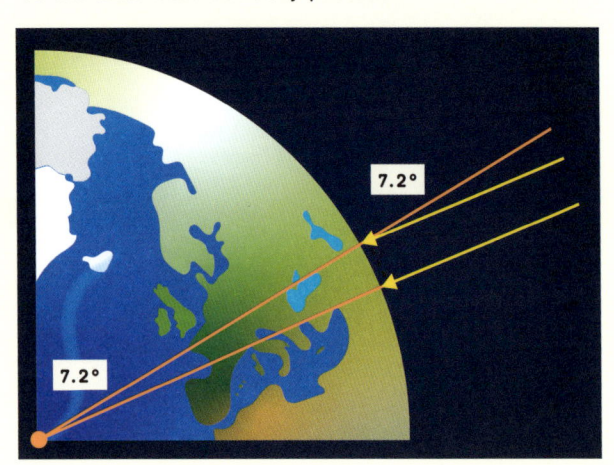

In 240 BCE, Ancient Greek librarian Eratosthenes measured the angle of shadows cast in two different places on Earth's surface, and used simple math to figure out the size of the sphere. His answer of 25,010 miles was almost exactly right.

THE VIEW FROM EARTH

Watching the Sun, Moon, and stars change position in the sky, it's easy to imagine that these objects are moving around Earth. Ancient Greek scientists came to the same conclusion, and went a step further to declare that Earth lies at the center of the universe. This geocentric model was so well explained by Ancient Greek astronomer Ptolemy, it was accepted for more than a thousand years. However, as later astronomers observed the skies, they discovered Ptolemy's model couldn't describe everything they saw.

Section 1 tells the story of a huge shift in scientific thought that began in the 1500s, with its roots in earlier astronomical observations. Over the course of a century, scientists proved that Earth is just one of several planets in our solar system, all orbiting the Sun. This completely changed the way people understood our place in the universe, marking the beginning of modern cosmology.

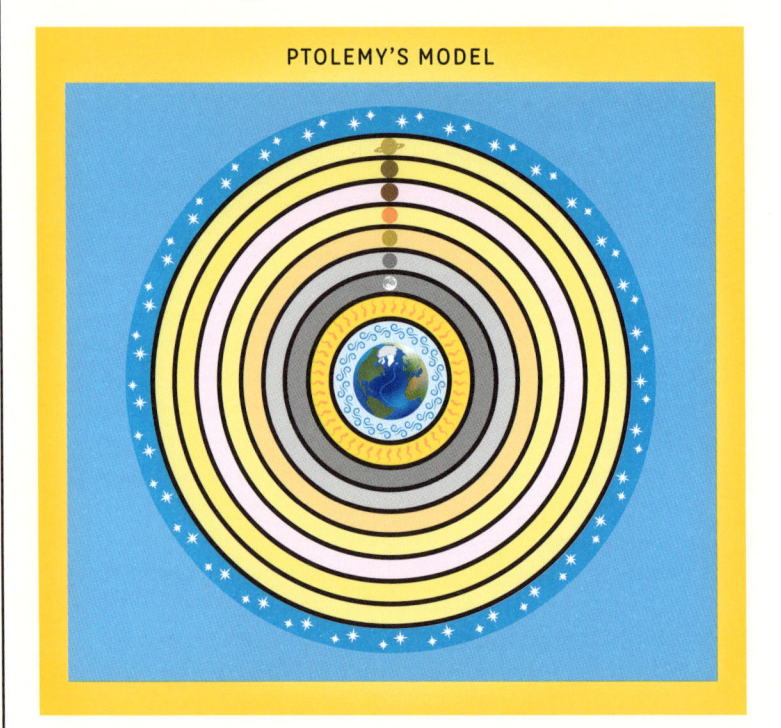

PTOLEMY'S MODEL

NEAR-EARTH SPACE

In the 1600s, the invention of **telescopes** revealed that the universe is crowded with far more objects than we can see with our eyes alone. For the next three centuries, telescopes allowed astronomers to gather reams of information about distant objects in space, allowing **cosmologists** to build better models of the universe. But it wasn't until the mid-1900s that humans got the chance to gaze down on our own planet from space.

Section 2 is the story of how we got off the ground. Space is not far away: the official boundary lies just 60 miles away—an hour's drive for a fast car. But our planet's far-reaching gravity makes this the hardest journey of all.

Exploring near-Earth space has helped us to understand our planet much better. Putting humans into orbit around Earth—and sending them to the Moon—captivated the world in the 1960s, and is still thought of as one of the greatest technological achievements in human history.

Getting off the ground also gives us a much better view of the wider universe, and the different kinds of **light** streaming toward us from every direction in space.

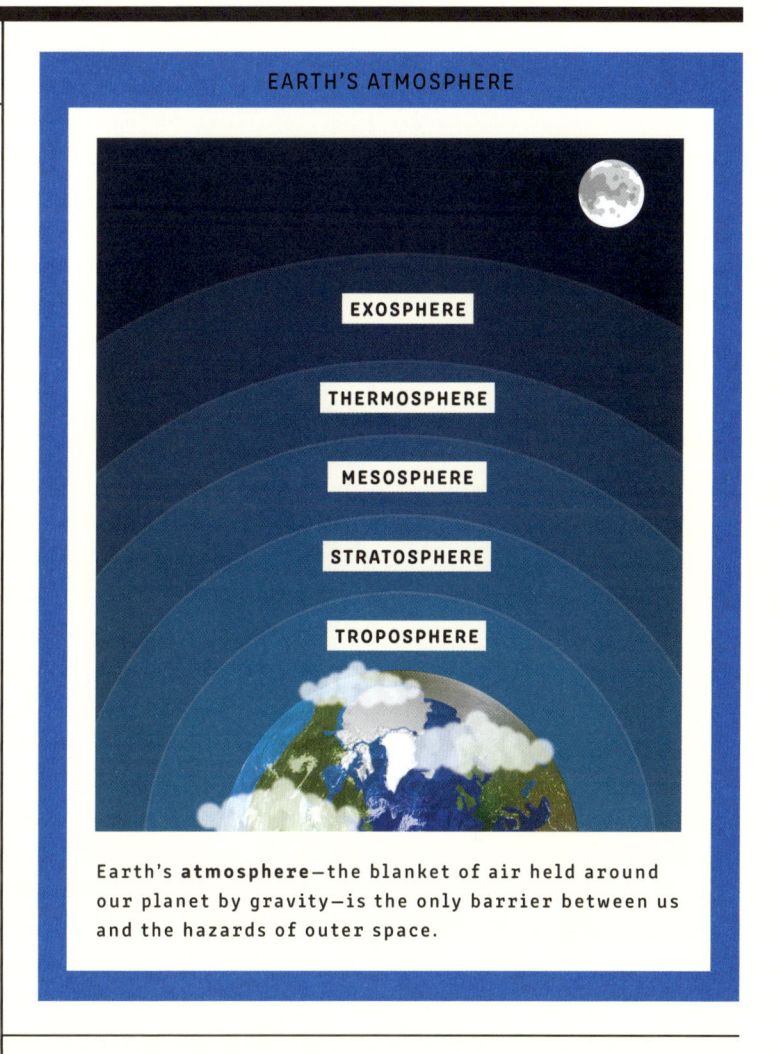

EARTH'S ATMOSPHERE

EXOSPHERE

THERMOSPHERE

MESOSPHERE

STRATOSPHERE

TROPOSPHERE

Earth's **atmosphere**—the blanket of air held around our planet by gravity—is the only barrier between us and the hazards of outer space.

COSMOLOGICAL WORDS

Certain words have different meanings in cosmology (and in this book). For example, in science, **mass** is a measure of how much "stuff" or **matter** something is made from. A "massive" object in space is not an object that is very large, but one that packs in lots of mass. Some of the most massive objects in the universe—such as **black holes**—are actually very small. You'll find a glossary of cosmological words on page 216.

INTRODUCTION: FROM EARTH TO THE EDGE OF THE UNIVERSE

OUR SOLAR SYSTEM

Long before we left the ground, astronomers had discovered that a wide variety of objects orbit the Sun, from planets and their moons to **asteroids** and **comets**. However, it was the space age that transformed exploration of our cosmic neighborhood—the solar system.

Beginning in the 1960s, scientists have sent robotic spacecraft to fly past or orbit every planet in the solar system, as well as moons, **dwarf planets**, asteroids, and comets. **Landers** have touched down on other worlds, and **rovers** have rolled across the surface of some. **Probes** have even returned samples of extraterrestrial rock and soil to Earth.

In Section 3 you will be able to explore each major solar system object in turn, and the most exciting features discovered by probes, **orbiters**, impactors, landers, and rovers. Cosmologists have interpreted these details to figure out how our solar system formed, and how it might change in the future. This section also explores the hunt for life in our solar system, which could hold the key to understanding how life came to be on Earth.

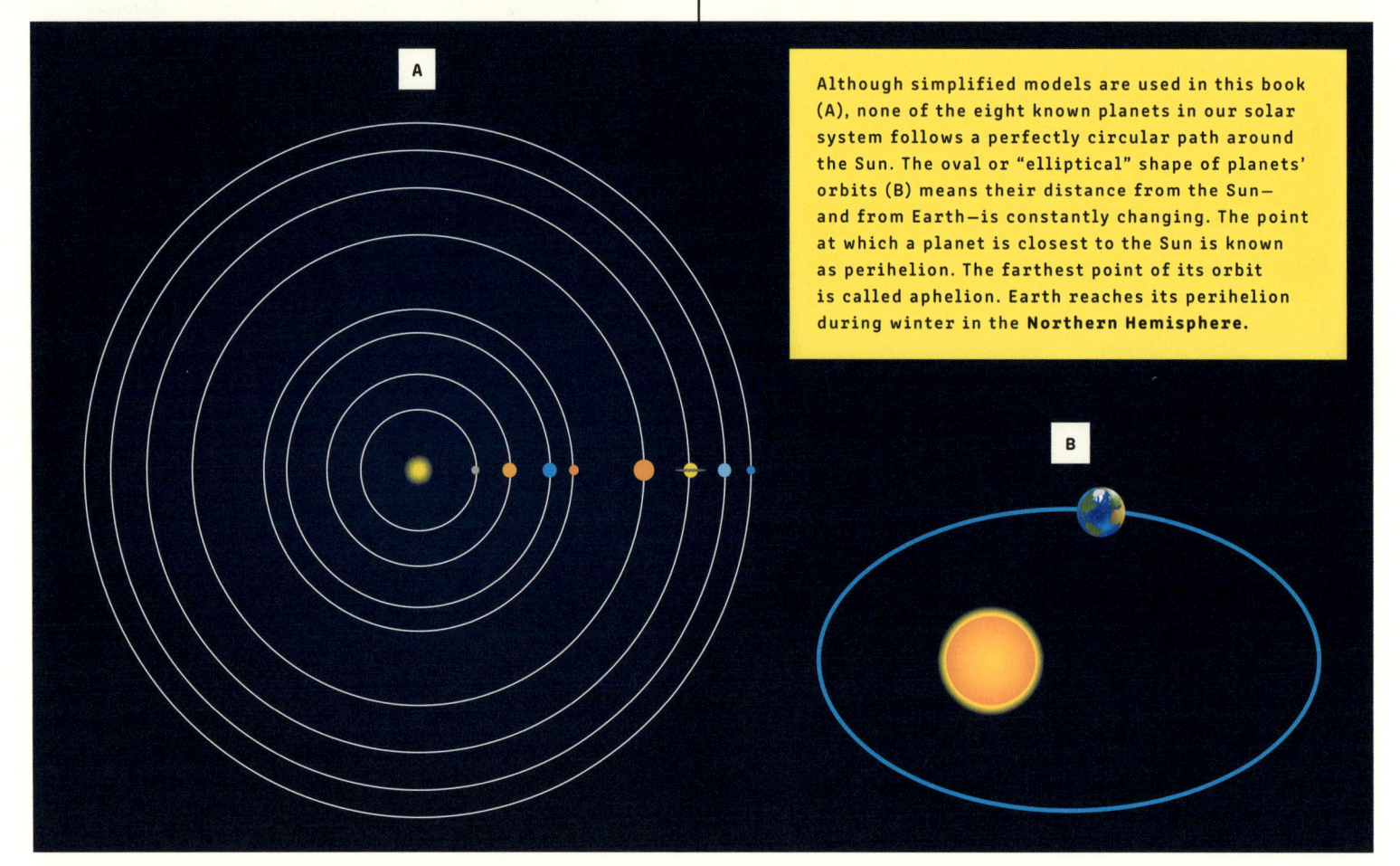

Although simplified models are used in this book (A), none of the eight known planets in our solar system follows a perfectly circular path around the Sun. The oval or "elliptical" shape of planets' orbits (B) means their distance from the Sun—and from Earth—is constantly changing. The point at which a planet is closest to the Sun is known as perihelion. The farthest point of its orbit is called aphelion. Earth reaches its perihelion during winter in the **Northern Hemisphere**.

INTRODUCTION: FROM EARTH TO THE EDGE OF THE UNIVERSE

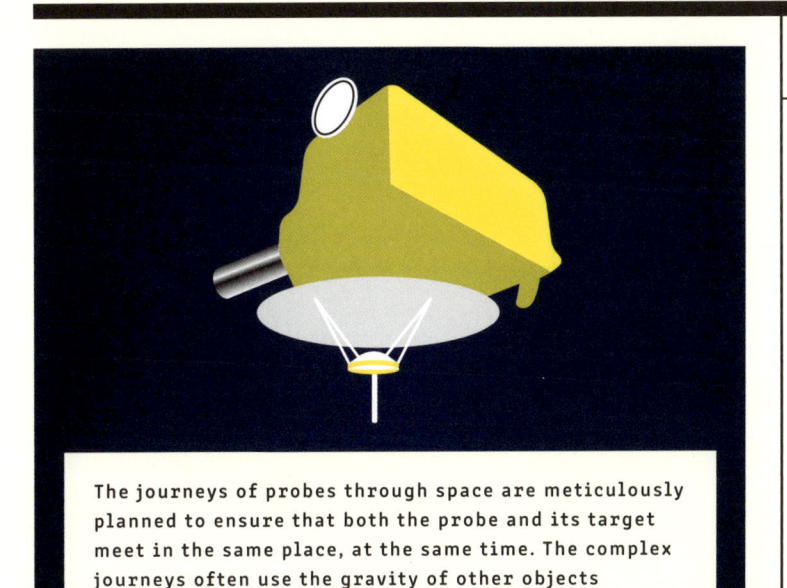

The journeys of probes through space are meticulously planned to ensure that both the probe and its target meet in the same place, at the same time. The complex journeys often use the gravity of other objects to change the speed or direction of a probe.

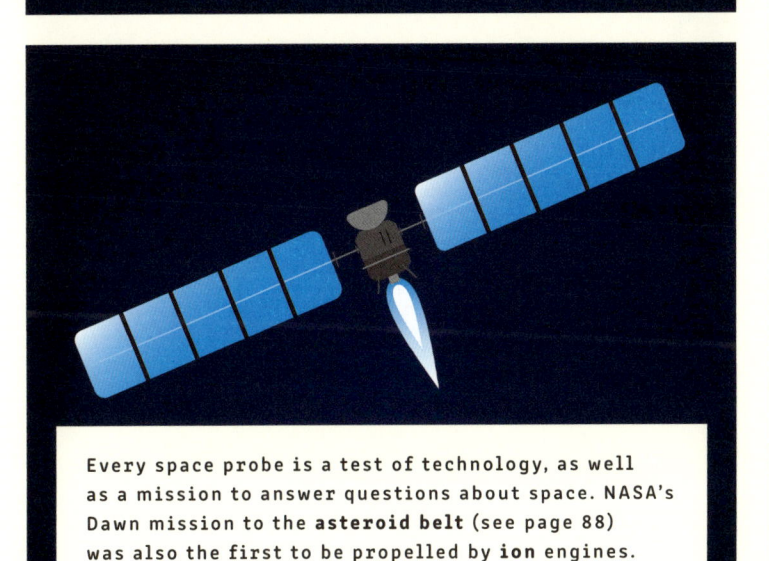

Every space probe is a test of technology, as well as a mission to answer questions about space. NASA's Dawn mission to the **asteroid belt** (see page 88) was also the first to be propelled by **ion** engines. The technology had previously been tested on NASA's Deep Space 1 mission to photograph a comet.

MODERN ASTRONOMY

Modern **astronomy** is a story of cooperation and teamwork. It involves high-tech, precision instruments based on Earth and in space, built and operated by huge international teams of scientists and engineers. More than ever before, discoveries do not come by chance or from flashes of inspiration. They arise from the careful work of thousands of people over decades. In this book, you'll come across the names of the space agencies and other organizations at the heart of this work.

Agenzia Spaziale Italiana (Italy)—ASI
Asia-Pacific Space Cooperation Organization—APSCO
China National Space Administration—CNSA
Canadian Space Agency—CSA
European Space Agency—ESA
Indian Space Research Organisation—ISRO
Inter-Agency Space Debris Coordination Committee—IADC
International Astronomical Union—IAU
Japan Aerospace Exploration Agency—JAXA
National Aeronautics and Space Administration (USA)—NASA
Russian Federal Space Agency—Roscosmos
Space program of the former Soviet Union (USSR)—CCCP/SSSR

STARS

At the center of our solar system lies our nearest star, the Sun. Section 4 explores how our proximity to the Sun has helped **astrophysicists** to understand how stars work, transforming matter into light energy. Though humanity has only been around for a blink of an eye compared to the age of cosmological objects, observations of more distant stars have helped scientists piece together the entire **stellar** life cycle.

The sky seems to change little from night to night, but every few seconds, a dying star explodes somewhere in the universe, while new stars are constantly born. Powerful, wide-field telescopes help astronomers detect these sudden energy bursts, so that other telescopes can be pointed at the right part of the sky.

The forces and the fury of stars are key to understanding everything else in the universe. They provide the building blocks not only for new stars, but for planets and people. Section 4 considers the likelihood that life exists on **exoplanets** orbiting other stars, and the ongoing hunt for evidence.

TYPES OF LIGHT

Carrying instruments above the atmosphere revealed that the Sun—and other stars—give out far more kinds of light than the type we can detect with our eyes (see page 138). Today's spectacular astronomical images are often made with data collected by many different kinds of telescopes, showing us what space would look like if we were able to see the entire **spectrum**.

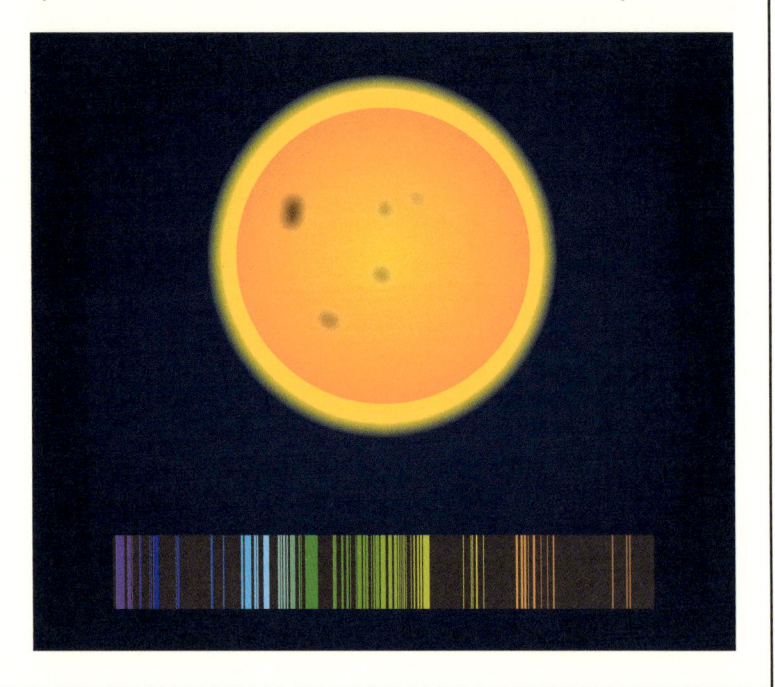

GALAXIES

To us, the space between stars looks empty. In fact, much of the visible matter in the universe is not part of stars or planets, but found between them as gas and dust. Gravity pulls it together to form **nebulae**—huge clouds in which new stars form.

Over the last century, we've come to understand the many kinds of nebulae associated with stars. The biggest breakthrough was the realization in the 1920s that some of these "clouds" are actually **galaxies** outside our own. Section 5 tells the story of the momentous discovery of the true scale of the universe.

Like stars, galaxies form due to gravity, and have their own life histories and life cycles. Studying galaxies is key to understanding how the universe works.

INTRODUCTION: FROM EARTH TO THE EDGE OF THE UNIVERSE

ASTRONOMY IS TIME TRAVEL

Light is the fastest thing in the universe (traveling around 186,000 miles per second) but it does not reach its destination instantly. Because light takes time to travel, we see galaxies, stars, and other space objects not as they are now, but as they were when the light arriving at our eyes or telescopes left their surface. When we look at distant galaxies, we are looking back in time at a much younger universe.

The speed of light never changes. This makes it useful for measuring huge distances in space. We know light always travels a constant distance of 10 **trillion** km (6 trillion miles) in a year, so instead of writing that the center of our galaxy is 260 trillion km (about 160 trillion miles) away, we can say it is 26 light-years away. A light-year is the distance light travels in a year.

THE OBSERVABLE UNIVERSE

The scale of galaxies is almost beyond imagination, but the final section of this book asks you to take an even bigger leap and begin to imagine how galaxies are arranged in a **cosmic web** that stretches across the entire universe.

Understanding the large-scale structure of the universe relies on theory (figuring out underlying laws using mathematics) just as much as it does on astronomy (experiments and observations). Many phenomena, such as black holes and **gravitational waves**, were predicted by theory long before they were detected by astronomers. Other phenomena, such as **dark energy** and **dark matter**, have been predicted but have so far proven impossible to detect. Section 6 delves into these current challenges in exploring the universe.

We haven't finished exploring the universe. At every stage, it has proven to be bigger and stranger than anyone had imagined before. There is no reason to suspect this will stop, but this is what makes astronomy and cosmology so exciting. It's satisfying to answer questions about the objects we can see in the sky, but it's even more exciting to catch a glimpse or hint of something entirely unknown.

INTRODUCTION: FROM EARTH TO THE EDGE OF THE UNIVERSE

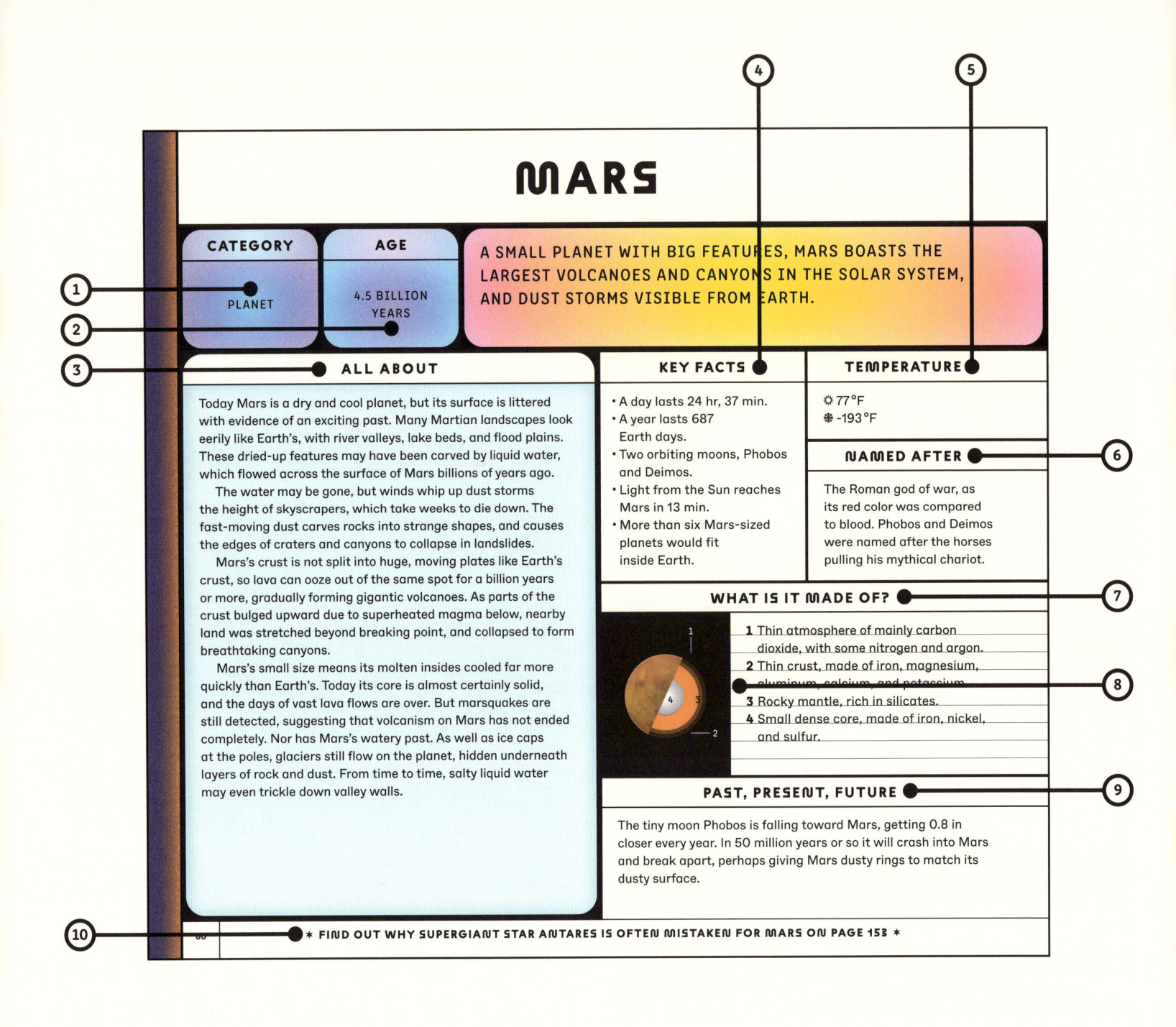

MARS

CATEGORY	AGE	
PLANET	4.5 BILLION YEARS	A SMALL PLANET WITH BIG FEATURES, MARS BOASTS THE LARGEST VOLCANOES AND CANYONS IN THE SOLAR SYSTEM, AND DUST STORMS VISIBLE FROM EARTH.

ALL ABOUT

Today Mars is a dry and cool planet, but its surface is littered with evidence of an exciting past. Many Martian landscapes look eerily like Earth's, with river valleys, lake beds, and flood plains. These dried-up features may have been carved by liquid water, which flowed across the surface of Mars billions of years ago.

The water may be gone, but winds whip up dust storms the height of skyscrapers, which take weeks to die down. The fast-moving dust carves rocks into strange shapes, and causes the edges of craters and canyons to collapse in landslides.

Mars's crust is not split into huge, moving plates like Earth's crust, so lava can ooze out of the same spot for a billion years or more, gradually forming gigantic volcanoes. As parts of the crust bulged upward due to superheated magma below, nearby land was stretched beyond breaking point, and collapsed to form breathtaking canyons.

Mars's small size means its molten insides cooled far more quickly than Earth's. Today its core is almost certainly solid, and the days of vast lava flows are over. But marsquakes are still detected, suggesting that volcanism on Mars has not ended completely. Nor has Mars's watery past. As well as ice caps at the poles, glaciers still flow on the planet, hidden underneath layers of rock and dust. From time to time, salty liquid water may even trickle down valley walls.

KEY FACTS

- A day lasts 24 hr, 37 min.
- A year lasts 687 Earth days.
- Two orbiting moons, Phobos and Deimos.
- Light from the Sun reaches Mars in 13 min.
- More than six Mars-sized planets would fit inside Earth.

TEMPERATURE

☀ 77°F
❄ -193°F

NAMED AFTER

The Roman god of war, as its red color was compared to blood. Phobos and Deimos were named after the horses pulling his mythical chariot.

WHAT IS IT MADE OF?

1 Thin atmosphere of mainly carbon dioxide, with some nitrogen and argon.
2 Thin crust, made of iron, magnesium, aluminum, calcium, and potassium.
3 Rocky mantle, rich in silicates.
4 Small dense core, made of iron, nickel, and sulfur.

PAST, PRESENT, FUTURE

The tiny moon Phobos is falling toward Mars, getting 0.8 in closer every year. In 50 million years or so it will crash into Mars and break apart, perhaps giving Mars dusty rings to match its dusty surface.

* FIND OUT WHY SUPERGIANT STAR ANTARES IS OFTEN MISTAKEN FOR MARS ON PAGE 153 *

INTRODUCTION: FROM EARTH TO THE EDGE OF THE UNIVERSE

HOW TO USE THIS BOOK

This book mirrors the journey that began when Stone Age humans first mapped the stars in the night sky. Starting with our view from Earth, each section moves farther out in space and time: stepping out from near-Earth space to our solar system neighborhood, from the stars of the Milky Way to galaxies outside our own, and finally, delving into the entire **observable universe**.

But you don't have to read these sections in order. This book allows you to build your own journey across the universe, with "wormholes" and page references throughout to discover linked topics as well as a fact-filled section on astronomical data at the back.

HOW TO READ EACH ENTRY

1. The object or structure's official scientific category.
2. The estimated time since the object or structure formed, or the age it is expected to reach.
3. Key information about the object or structure and its significance in understanding the wider universe.
4. Comparisons to help you understand the scale of this object or structure within the universe.
5. The object or structure's average surface temperature. Where it makes sense, maximum (☼) and minimum (❄) surface temperatures are given.
6. How the object or structure got its name, or how far the nearest example is from Earth.
7. A summary of each object or structure's physical and chemical composition.
8. A simple diagram to help you see beneath the surface.
9. Insights into how the object came to be, or how it might change in the future.
10. Follow these "wormholes" to discover linked topics.

Each entry also includes a gallery of illustrations and captions, highlighting some of the most amazing features, discoveries, missions, or people linked to the object or structure.

LOOK OUT FOR THESE FOUR TYPES OF ENTRIES

OBJECTS AND STRUCTURES 
From tiny asteroids to **supermassive** black holes, these entries provide key facts and figures to help you understand the object's place in space. You'll also find tables of astronomical data for key objects at the back of the book.

EXPLORATION 
Find out how humans have gathered knowledge about each object from its discovery to the present day. These entries feature exploration timelines, profiles of key space scientists, and insights into how these discoveries have helped humans beyond space science.

PHENOMENA AND IDEAS 
These pages provide essential background knowledge. Discover the different types of energy and matter that make up our universe, and the key theories and approaches we use to understand them. Join the search for extraterrestrial life in our solar system and beyond.

TECHNOLOGY 
Delve deeper into the instruments and tools that have helped scientists see the unseeable. These entries highlight key technological achievements in the history of space exploration, from the invention of the first telescopes to space probes and artificial intelligence (AI).

INTRODUCTION: FROM EARTH TO THE EDGE OF THE UNIVERSE

THE VIEW FROM EARTH

BY DAY, OUR VIEW OF SPACE IS OBSCURED BY AN OPAQUE BLUE SKY THAT BORROWS ITS GLOW FROM THE BRIGHT SUN. BY NIGHT, THIS SKY BECOMES A TRANSPARENT WINDOW OUT IN TO THE UNIVERSE.

To our ancestors, objects seen in the sky were just as important as those on the ground. The Sun, moving slowly across the sky, provided heat and light, and a way to track time. The Moon, stars, and planets proved just as useful, helping people track the seasons and find their way. The oldest records of Moon phases, star constellations, and even **supernovae** are painted on the walls of prehistoric caves.

From the ground it looks as if the Sun and stars travel around Earth, like the Moon. All ancient cultures believed this was the case, since Earth also felt so solid and still underfoot. However, thousands of years of observation revealed patterns that couldn't be explained if Earth stood still at the center of the universe. In the last 400 years, technology has helped prove that it's Earth that's moving.

Today we understand the rules that guide the movements of the Sun, Moon, stars, and planets. We also have the knowledge and technology to view far more distant objects, and venture into space ourselves. But the rhythms of life on the ground—sunrise and sunset, the Moon's phases, and the seasons—are still defined by the changing skies our ancestors recognized so many thousands of years ago.

OUR VIEW OF THE SUN

THE SUN IS BY FAR THE BRIGHTEST OBJECT IN EARTH'S SKY. OUR VIEW OF IT DEFINES DAY AND NIGHT, AND IT IS THE SUN'S ENERGY THAT POWERS LIFE ON OUR PLANET.

ALL ABOUT

Ancient peoples celebrated the Sun as a source of warmth and light, and recognized its enormous significance for life on Earth. Its most obvious influence was day and night, caused by the Sun rising due east every morning and setting due west in the evening.

Many cultures began to track the way the Sun moved across the sky. They noticed patterns, and used them to predict changes in the seasons and set important dates for farming and festivals. The length of shadows cast by the Sun was used to help measure the length of a year, long before anyone knew that one year marks one orbit of Earth around the Sun. Indeed, for most of human history, people assumed that the Sun orbited Earth!

The Ancient Greek astronomer Ptolemy used these old ideas to publish a model of the "heavens" that put Earth at the very center of the universe. This model became so popular, it was accepted as fact for 1,400 years. In the 1500s, Nicolaus Copernicus joined a handful of astronomers who had realized that planets actually orbit the Sun. However, he was reluctant to share his ideas at first. They challenged beliefs at the time, and he felt foolish claiming that the object we live on is both spinning and speeding through space.

Only when telescopes were invented in the early 1600s did astronomers collect enough evidence to convince the world that Earth orbits the Sun, and that it's Earth's movement—not the Sun's—that causes day and night. The next big leap was understanding that the Sun is a star like any other, but so near to Earth that its light can damage our eyes and burn our skin.

SUNLIGHT HOURS

Over the course of a year, each square foot of Earth's surface gets an average of 12 hours of sunlight per day. However, the number of daylight hours increases in summer and decreases in winter as you move closer to the poles. The effect is most extreme at the North and South Poles themselves, where the Sun doesn't set at all during the summer months.

SUNLIGHT ENERGY

Over the last 300 years, scientists have figured out details of what ancient cultures appreciated from the start: that the Sun's energy drives Earth's weather, climate, seasons, and ocean currents, and powers most life on our planet. We are learning to harness solar energy directly, as part of the move toward a fossil fuel-free future.

THE SUN'S PATH IN THE SKY

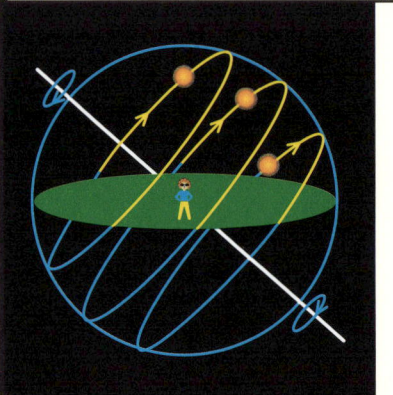

As Earth spins on its axis, the Sun appears to move across Earth's sky, as if it was orbiting our planet. The path the Sun takes across the sky varies through the year. It appears to rise higher in the sky in summer, and lower in the winter.

WHERE DOES THE SUN GET ITS POWER? FIND OUT ON PAGE 128

#	Topic	Description
1	**SUN CLOCKS**	The Ancient Egyptians built tall structures called obelisks to track shadows cast by the Sun. The movement of these shadows was used to measure the progress through days and years.
2	**LIFE ON EARTH**	Green plants and certain microbes can capture sunlight energy and store it as food—a process called photosynthesis. This stored energy is then passed along food chains, meaning the Sun powers most life on Earth. We also release stored sunlight energy when we burn wood or fossil fuels.
3	**SCATTERED SUNLIGHT**	Sunlight is white (a mixture of every color) but as it passes through Earth's atmosphere blue light is scattered more than red light. This makes the sky look blue and the Sun look yellow, orange, or red.
4	**SOLAR ECLIPSES**	These happen when the Moon moves directly in front of the Sun as seen from Earth. A total eclipse (when the Sun's disc is entirely hidden by the Moon) happens somewhere on Earth around every 18 months. Annular and partial eclipses are more common, happening two to five times every year.

OUR VIEW OF THE MOON

THE MOON'S APPARENT SHAPESHIFTING IN THE NIGHT SKY HAS SHAPED OUR CALENDARS. LESS OBVIOUS BUT EVEN MORE IMPORTANT IS THE MOON'S INFLUENCE ON ALL LIFE ON EARTH.

ALL ABOUT

The Moon is the brightest object in the night sky, and is often visible in the daytime too. Before humans discovered methods for lighting fires, it was the main source of light at night.

Like the Sun, the Moon rises due east and seems to move across the sky each night. This led people to deduce (correctly) that it orbits Earth. Unlike the Sun, the Moon appears to change shape each night, waxing and waning in a cycle that lasts almost 30 days—a period of time that became known as a month. Stories throughout history have linked a full Moon with strange events, and mythical creatures such as werewolves.

The Ancient Greek thinker Anaxagoras was one of the first people to suggest a scientific explanation—that the Moon is a sphere that reflects the Sun's light. Moonlight is just sunlight reflected by the Moon toward Earth, and can be bright enough to cast shadows on Earth.

Understanding this also helped to explain the Moon's phases: it's not the Moon's actual shape that changes each month, but our view of its sunlit side. Earth also reflects sunlight back into space. During a crescent moon it is sometimes possible to see part of the Moon's disc lit by this Earthshine.

The Moon's surface looks smooth from Earth, with dark areas that the Ancient Greeks assumed were water. Even Galileo Galilei, viewing the Moon through a telescope for the first time, thought he saw lakes and oceans alongside its mountains and craters. As a result, early maps of the Moon gave these dark patches watery names such as the Sea of Tranquility and the Marsh of Decay.

TIMING OF PHASES

Half of the Moon is lit by the Sun at any one time. As the Moon orbits Earth, we see different amounts of the sunlit side and the Moon seems to change shape. The different shapes are known as phases. It takes the Moon 27.3 days to orbit Earth once. However, both Earth and the Moon are also moving around the Sun at the same time, so the full cycle of phases takes 29.5 days.

PAST, PRESENT, FUTURE

The Moon's regular patterns have shaped calendars around the world. The Islamic calendar has 12 lunar months. The Chinese calendar is based on both the Moon's phases and the solar year, while the Gregorian calendar used in most parts of the world has adapted the length of months to fit the solar year.

THE VIEW FROM EARTH

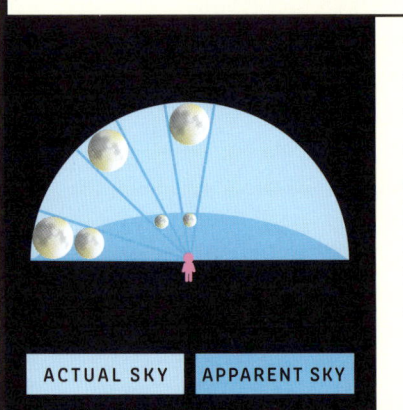

The Moon looks larger when it's close to the horizon, but this is just an optical illusion caused by the way the sky appears from Earth's surface. However, the Moon really does loom larger in the sky when it is closest to Earth in its oval-shaped orbit.

ACTUAL SKY | APPARENT SKY

★ EXPLORE THE MOON'S SURFACE ON PAGES 44 AND 48 ★

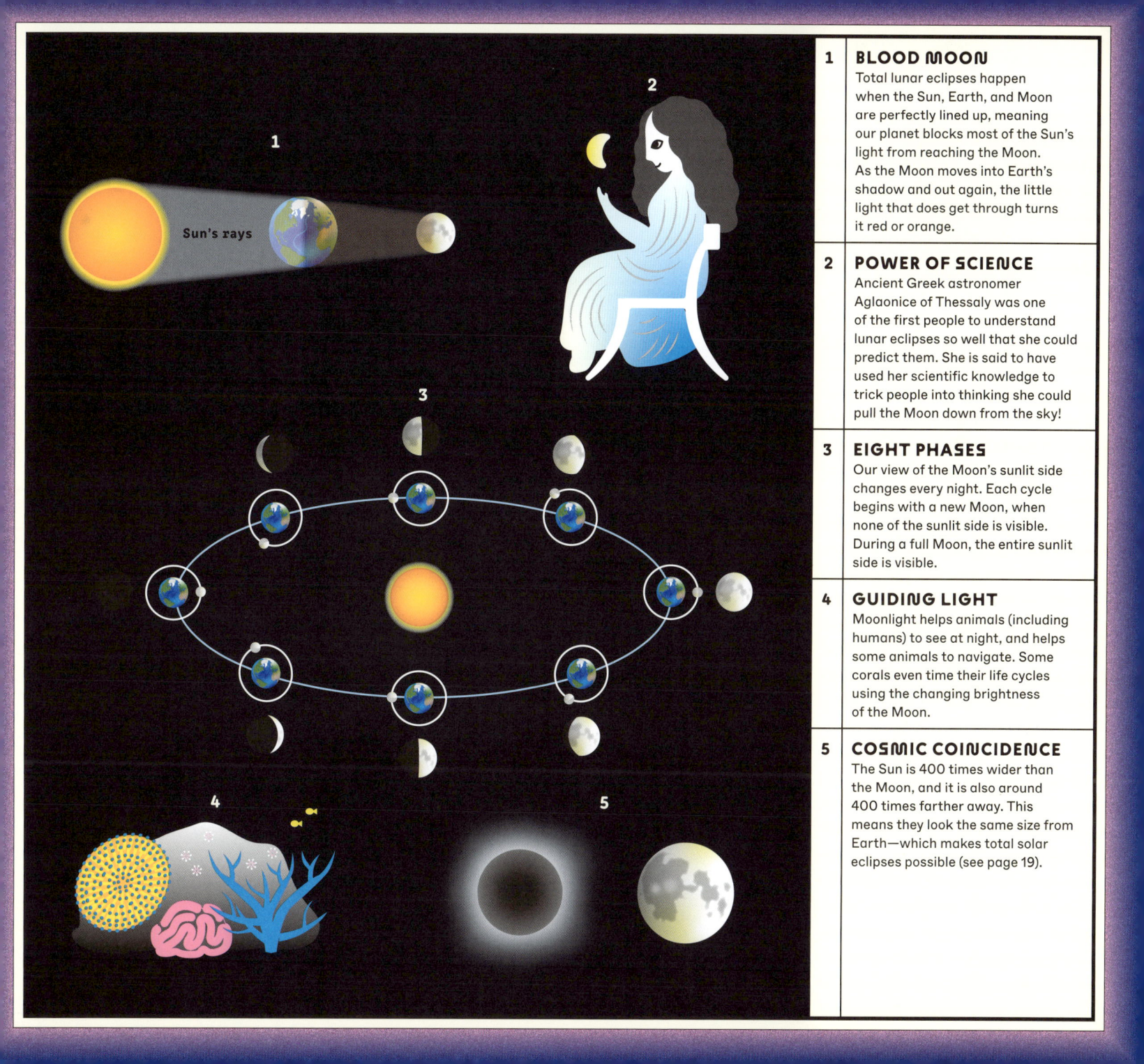

1	**BLOOD MOON**	Total lunar eclipses happen when the Sun, Earth, and Moon are perfectly lined up, meaning our planet blocks most of the Sun's light from reaching the Moon. As the Moon moves into Earth's shadow and out again, the little light that does get through turns it red or orange.
2	**POWER OF SCIENCE**	Ancient Greek astronomer Aglaonice of Thessaly was one of the first people to understand lunar eclipses so well that she could predict them. She is said to have used her scientific knowledge to trick people into thinking she could pull the Moon down from the sky!
3	**EIGHT PHASES**	Our view of the Moon's sunlit side changes every night. Each cycle begins with a new Moon, when none of the sunlit side is visible. During a full Moon, the entire sunlit side is visible.
4	**GUIDING LIGHT**	Moonlight helps animals (including humans) to see at night, and helps some animals to navigate. Some corals even time their life cycles using the changing brightness of the Moon.
5	**COSMIC COINCIDENCE**	The Sun is 400 times wider than the Moon, and it is also around 400 times farther away. This means they look the same size from Earth—which makes total solar eclipses possible (see page 19).

OUR VIEW OF THE STARS

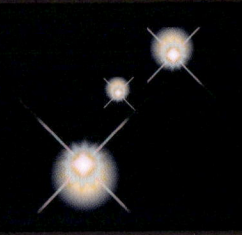

FROM EARTH, STARS CAN SEEM A TRUE MYSTERY, APPEARING AS TINY, TWINKLING LIGHTS EMBEDDED IN A SHELL THAT SLOWLY ROTATES AROUND THE PLANET. THE TRUTH COULD NOT BE MORE DIFFERENT—OR ANY MORE STRANGE.

ALL ABOUT

At night, when the Moon is not too bright, thousands of twinkling stars can be seen by eye. With no artificial lights to drown out this faint starlight, ancient peoples would have been able to see around 3,000 stars from a single spot on Earth.

As stars move across the night sky, their positions remain fixed compared to each other. Ancient peoples connected stars like dot-to-dot images, to create the shapes of animals, people, and objects. These imaginary pictures are known as constellations. They helped people to divide up the vast sky, and to recognize patterns in the appearance and movement of certain stars.

Simple star patterns were first painted on cave walls around 40,000 years ago. Over thousands of years, the collection of constellations grew. Ancient Greek astronomers linked the constellations to religion and named them after their gods and goddesses. We still use many of those names for the 88 constellations recognized today.

After thousands of years of stargazing, astronomers came to understand that stars only appear to move across the sky because Earth spins. But they still didn't know what stars were made of, or why they shine. The first clues came with the invention of telescopes and then cameras, which allowed astronomers to see fainter stars—and begin to see differences between them.

Another important breakthrough came in the late 1800s, when **spectroscopy** was first used to split starlight into its different colors (see page 138). This helped astronomers to unlock the secrets of the stars—including the fact that our Sun is among their number!

MAPPING THE STARS

One of the world's oldest known star maps was painted on the ceiling of an ancient Egyptian tomb around 3,500 years ago. The world's oldest complete star map (showing all the stars visible from a certain place on Earth) was made by Ancient Greek mathematician Hipparchus in 129 BCE. He is known as the father of scientific astronomy.

PAST, PRESENT, FUTURE

Records of the night sky reach back over thousands of years, added to by many different cultures through history. At first, these records were kept for practical reasons: to set dates for farming or religious festivals, or to help sailors figure out how far they'd traveled. Instruments and methods developed to help with these tasks laid the groundwork for today's astronomy.

THE VIEW FROM EARTH

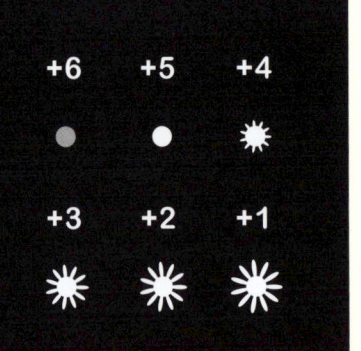

Hipparchus invented a system to describe the brightness, known as the **apparent magnitude**, of stars in the sky. We still use a version of his system. The brightest star visible from Earth is Sirius, with a magnitude of -1.47. The faintest stars visible by eye have a magnitude of +7.2.

★ HOW DID SCIENTISTS FIND OUT WHAT STARS ARE MADE OF? FIND OUT ON PAGE 130 ★

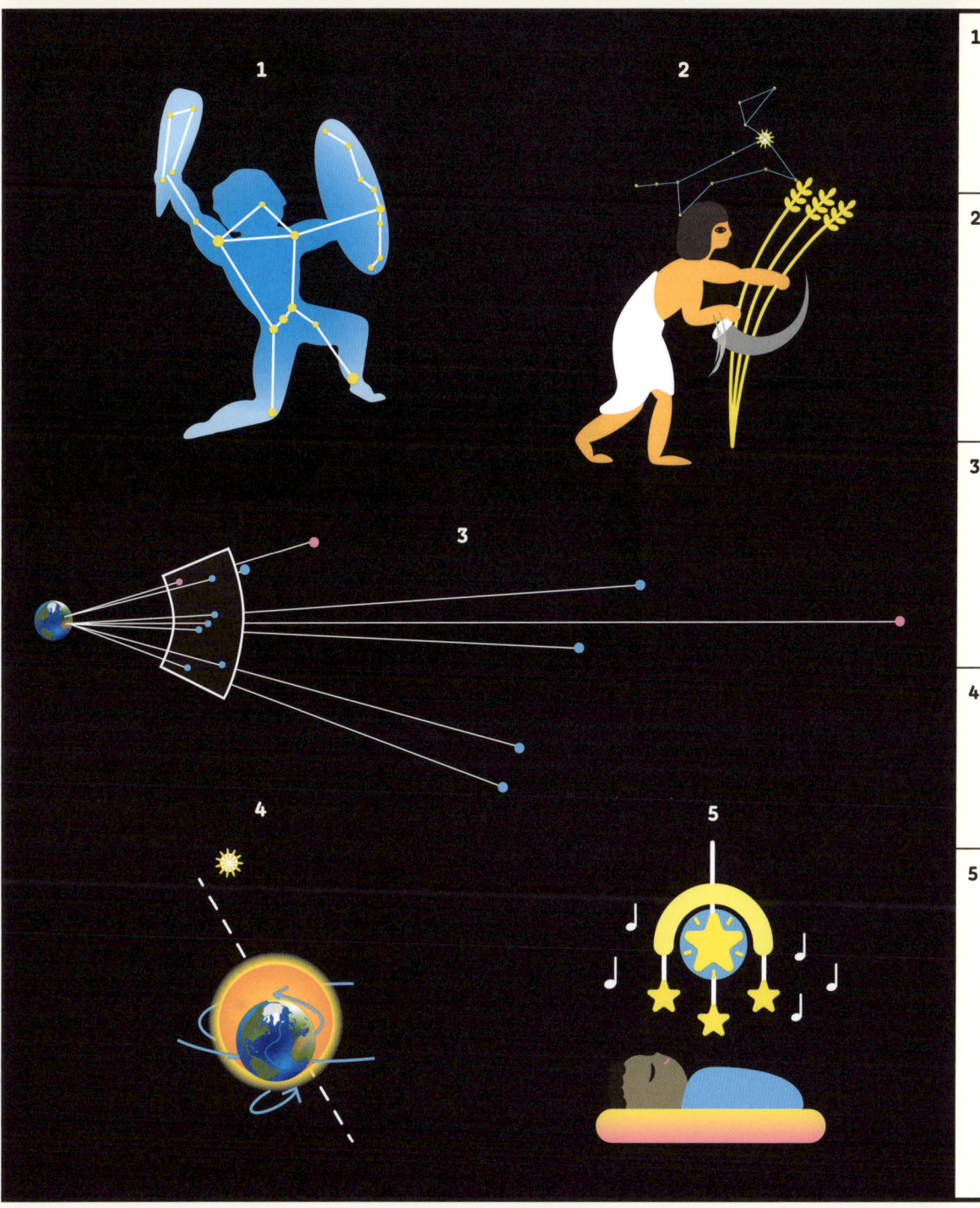

1	**ORION**	This well-known constellation can be seen from most parts of the world. Early Arabic astronomers saw it as the figure of a giant, but its modern name comes from the hunter in Ancient Greek myth.
2	**CONSTELLATIONS**	The positions of stars and constellations change during the year. Many early cultures used these predictable changes as a calendar. For example, Sirius appearing just before the River Nile's annual flood helped Ancient Egyptians harvest crops at the right time.
3	**SHELL OF STARS**	Early astronomers imagined stars were all the same distance away, embedded in a shell slowly rotating around Earth. However, stars in a constellation only look close together because they all lie in the same direction when seen from Earth.
4	**LODE STAR**	Unlike other stars, the North Pole Star (Polaris) seems to stay in the same position all night. Early sailors relied on it to find north, and figure out their latitude (how far they were from the equator).
5	**TWINKLE, TWINKLE**	It may have inspired a famous lullaby, but stars don't really twinkle. This is an effect of starlight traveling through Earth's thick and shifting atmosphere—like seeing pebbles through rippling water.

OPTICAL TELESCOPES

OPTICAL TELESCOPES DETECT THE SAME KIND OF LIGHT THAT OUR EYES DO, BUT COLLECT MORE OF IT—THEY MAKE DISTANT SPACE OBJECTS LOOK BIGGER AND BRIGHTER.

On a cloud-free, moonless night, human eyes can detect up to 3,000 stars from a single spot on Earth's surface. Early astronomers made plenty of discoveries by tracking the movement of these "naked-eye" stars across the night sky. But around 400 years ago, the invention of telescopes revealed a much more crowded universe.

The first telescopes were made using the types of lenses used in reading glasses. By fitting two lenses into a tube, exactly the right distance apart, faraway objects could be made to look closer.

At first, these "spyglasses" were used to look over long distances on Earth. Italian astronomer Galileo Galilei heard about the invention in 1609 and made his own, improved version. Turning it toward the night sky, he saw thousands of stars that had not been known to exist. He spied mountains on the Moon, the line dividing night and day on Venus, and moons around Jupiter. His discoveries changed astronomy—and ideas about the solar system—forever.

The race was soon on to make new discoveries. In the late 1600s, James Gregory and Isaac Newton improved the basic design of telescopes, using curved mirrors rather than lenses to focus the light. Most modern telescopes are reflecting telescopes like these. The largest are often built on mountains, where there is less light pollution, and less air between the telescope and space. This means the stars "twinkle" less and images are sharper.

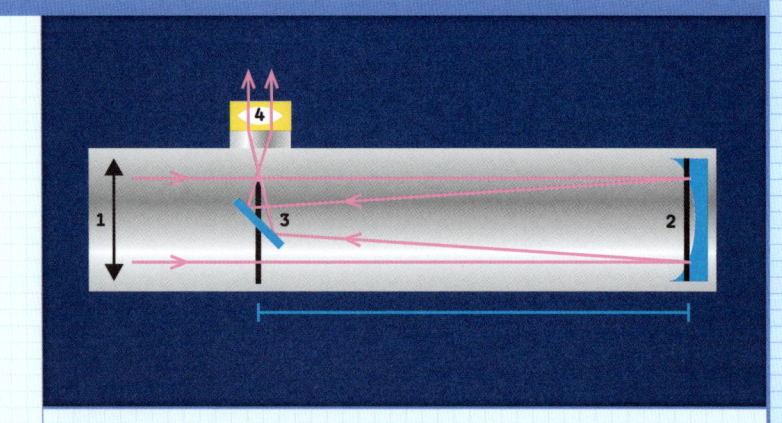

1. Light enters the telescope through a wide opening called an aperture.
2. The light is reflected by a curved primary mirror, focusing it onto a smaller mirror.
3. Light reflects off the smaller mirror toward the eyepiece.
4. Before it reaches the eye, it travels through a curved lens that magnifies the image.

Bigger primary mirrors gather more light, to see fainter objects. The mirror in Newton's telescope was 1-in wide.

BINOCULARS

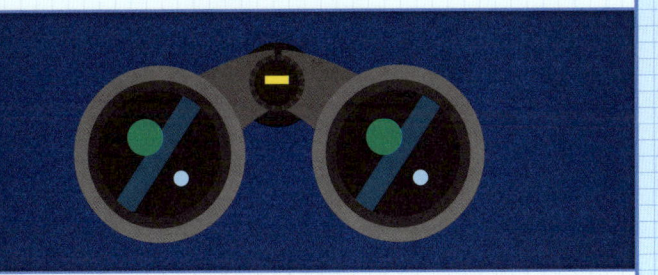

A pair of **binoculars** is just two refracting telescopes (the kind used by Galileo) mounted side-by-side. This allows you to use both eyes when viewing distant objects. Slovakian astronomer Ľudmila Pajdušáková and her team discovered 18 comets using giant binoculars.

MOUNTAINS AND DESERTS

Most large optical telescopes are built on mountains. For example, the Extremely Large Telescope (ELT) is being built in Chile's Atacama Desert, almost two miles above sea level. Here there is less light pollution to drown out faint light from the stars, and less air between the telescope and space.

UNSEEN STARS

More stars were in Galileo's sketches of famous constellations than are visible to the naked eye. He was also the first to see that the glow of the Milky Way was made up of thousands of previously unseen stars.

HOOKER TELESCOPE

Mount Wilson Observatory in California, USA, is home to the Hooker telescope, which was the world's largest optical telescope from 1917 to 1948. Famously, it was used by Edwin Hubble to change our understanding of the universe (see page 180).

EXTREMELY LARGE

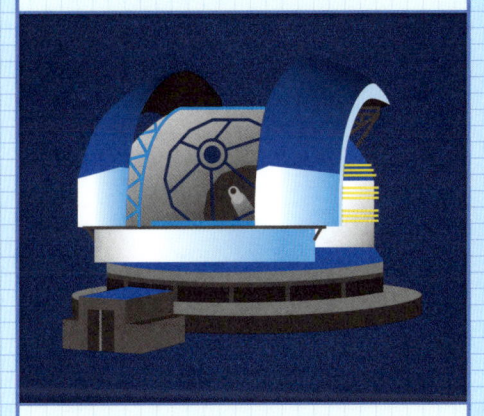

The European Southern Observatory (ESO) is building the biggest optical telescope ever. With a 128-foot main mirror, the ELT will gather 100 **million** times more light than the human eye.

OUR VIEW OF THE PLANETS

FIVE "WANDERING STARS" HAVE BEEN TRACKED IN THE SKY SINCE ANCIENT TIMES, BUT IT WAS THOUSANDS OF YEARS BEFORE ASTRONOMERS REALIZED THEY ARE PLANETS LIKE OUR OWN, AND SPOTTED MORE TO ADD TO THE LIST.

ALL ABOUT

Early stargazers noticed bright points that didn't move across the sky in fixed positions like stars, but wandered in patterns much harder to predict. Many ancient cultures tracked the positions of these "wandering stars" carefully, often linking them to religious events. Their common names—Mercury, Venus, Mars, Jupiter, Saturn—are those of Greek and Roman gods and goddesses.

Two planets—Mercury and Venus—can only be spotted at dusk and dawn. Venus was at first thought of as two separate stars: the Morning Star and the Evening Star. The Ancient Greek astronomer Pythagoras was the first to realize they were the same object, and to suggest that all the planets are spheres.

From the 600s, Arabic astronomers such as al-Battani studied the Ancient Greek ideas and improved on them, building huge observatories and making accurate instruments to track the movement of planets. All this data helped Nicolaus Copernicus make a huge breakthrough in the 1500s, when he suggested that the planets, including Earth, travel around the Sun. Though not accepted immediately, it was the beginning of modern astronomy.

The invention of telescopes in the 1600s revolutionized our understanding of planets. Suddenly it was possible to see them as discs, like tiny versions of the Moon, while stars were still just points of light. Observing the disc of Venus, Galileo saw it has phases like the Moon. This was proof that planets orbit the Sun.

However, the seemingly erratic movements of planets in the night sky remained hard to explain, until Johannes Kepler devised his laws of planetary motion. These explained how planets move through space, and could be used to predict where they will be in the future—the ultimate test of a scientific model.

COUNTING PLANETS

The invention of telescopes led to the discovery of many more objects in space. By the 1800s, more than 40 "planets" had been named. This list changed as astronomers argued about which ones deserved the label. From 1930 to 2006, a book like this one would have counted nine planets in our solar system. The number dropped to eight when Pluto was recategorized as a dwarf planet (see page 116).

PAST, PRESENT, FUTURE

Tracking the motion of planets allowed astronomers to calculate the distance between Earth and the Sun, the size of the solar system, and even the mass of the Sun itself. In the 1600s, Jupiter's moons were used to help figure out how long light from the Sun takes to reach Earth.

THE VIEW FROM EARTH

-2.48 MERCURY
-4.92 VENUS
-2.94 MARS
-2.94 JUPITER
-0.55 SATURN
+5.38 URANUS
+7.67 NEPTUNE

These figures show the minimum brightness of each planet in the night sky. Their apparent magnitudes change as they move around the Sun. The distance between each planet and Earth changes, and different portions of their sunlit sides become visible.

★ EXPLORE THE PLANETS OF OUR SOLAR SYSTEM IN SECTION 3 (PAGE 68) ★

1	**RETROGRADE MOTION**	Seen from Earth, planetary movements are complex compared to stars. It took thousands of years for astronomers to understand why Venus sometimes appears to stop and move backward in our sky.
2	**GREAT STAR**	For the Ancient Maya, the Great Star Nohock Ek (Venus) was as important as the Sun. They kept records of its cycles to plan important events.
3	**KEPLER'S LAWS**	Johannes Kepler solved the puzzle of planetary motion when he realized planets travel around the Sun on an oval rather than circular path. Kepler also explained that planets change speed during their orbits, and those farther from the Sun take longer to orbit it.
4	**GALILEO GALILEI**	The first person to peer at planets through a telescope, Galileo found proof they were not stars, and even spotted **satellites** around Jupiter, which became known as the Galilean moons (see page 94).
5	**PLANET PARADE**	During a planetary alignment, up to seven planets are visible in a small area of Earth's sky at once. Astronomers now understand the rules that govern orbits so well that they can predict these alignments hundreds of years from now.
6	**TRANSIT OF VENUS**	In 1716, British astronomer Edmond Halley realized we could measure the distance to the Sun by watching Venus pass between Earth and the Sun from different places.

EARTH'S PLACE IN SPACE

WE CAN EXPLORE OUR PLANET AT GROUND LEVEL, BUT TO TRULY UNDERSTAND EARTH'S PLACE IN THE UNIVERSE, ASTRONOMERS HAD TO SPEND THOUSANDS OF YEARS GAZING UP AT THE STARS.

ALL ABOUT

Almost 3,000 years ago, astronomers in ancient India proposed that Earth was traveling around the Sun. However, the idea that Earth was at the center of the universe was hard to shake.

Some of the blame can be pinned on the *Almagest*, a manual written by Ancient Greek astronomer Ptolemy almost 2,000 years ago. It spread the view that planets and stars orbit Earth. Popular but wrong, this geocentric model was taught for more than a thousand years.

Gradually, the list of things that *couldn't* be explained by Ptolemy's model grew too long to ignore. In the 1500s, Nicolaus Copernicus suggested that a heliocentric model was more accurate—with Earth, the other planets, and the stars orbiting the Sun. However, Copernicus felt foolish claiming Earth was moving, and didn't share his ideas for 35 years. It was another 100 years before Galileo Galilei pointed a telescope toward the skies, and immediately found proof that Copernicus was right. As other astronomers began using telescopes, the evidence grew.

Tycho Brahe was one of these astronomers. He made instruments so accurate they helped him measure the length of Earth's orbit around the Sun to within one second. He also figured out how much our planet wobbles on its axis as it spins.

In the 1660s, Isaac Newton explained *why* Earth orbits the Sun: due to gravity (see page 30). This helped people accept that Earth is just one planet among many, governed by the same natural laws. Newton also explained how the speed of an orbiting object is linked to its distance from the point it is orbiting. Newton's work on gravity and momentum, along with accurate data about planets, led to new ideas about how they formed in the first place.

EXPLORATION TIMELINE

800s BCE	Ancient Indian astronomers propose that Earth and other planets orbit the Sun.
200s BCE	Ancient Greek astronomer Aristarchus suggests Earth orbits the Sun, but the idea is not accepted.
150 CE	Ptolemy publishes his astronomy manual *Almagest*, which supports Aristotle's geocentric model.
1543	Copernicus publishes his heliocentric model.
1609	Galileo uses an optical telescope to collect evidence to support Copernicus's ideas.
1619	Johannes Kepler publishes his laws of planetary motion.
1687	Isaac Newton publishes his ideas about gravity in *Principia*, beginning a new age of physics and cosmology.

STRANGE BUT TRUE

In 1798, Henry Cavendish became the first person to "weigh the world," using an experiment so sensitive he had to watch it through a telescope from outside so his breathing didn't mess it up!

HELPING HUMANS

It took a giant leap of imagination to recognize that Earth is a ball-shaped planet, speeding around the Sun. This took centuries, each small step building on the work of people who had come before. Newton described this as "standing on the shoulders of giants."

FIND OUT WHEN HUMANS GAZED DOWN AT EARTH FROM SPACE FOR THE FIRST TIME (PAGE 52)

#	
1	**PTOLEMY'S MODEL** The geocentric model was a version of earlier Ancient Greek ideas. Aristotle had said that the Sun, Moon, planets, and stars were embedded in shells that rotated around Earth.
2	**NEW IDEAS** Ptolemy's model could be used to predict certain things, which made it popular. However, Islamic astronomer and mathematician Naīr al-Dīn al-Ṭūsī carefully measured the strange movements of planets in the night sky, and showed it was possible to explain them using a different model.
3	**COPERNICUS'S SYSTEM** Copernicus's heliocentric model put the Sun at the center of the solar system, orbited by Earth, the other planets, and the "fixed stars." This wasn't entirely correct, but Copernicus was able to put the planets in the correct order (leaving out Uranus and Neptune, as they hadn't been discovered yet).
4	**EARTH'S MAGNETISM** Scientists in ancient China began exploring Earth's magnetism at least 2,600 years ago. In 1600, English scientist William Gilbert used everything that was known about magnetism to put forward his theory that Earth is a giant magnet.
5	**EARTH'S FORMATION** In 1796, French astronomer and mathematician Pierre-Simon Laplace suggested that the Sun and planets all formed in the same spinning disc of dust and gas. They formed as matter was drawn together by gravity and began to spin faster as it contracted—just as a figure skater spins faster when they pull in their arms.

GRAVITY

THROW AN APPLE UP, AND YOU CAN EASILY PREDICT THAT IT WILL FALL BACK DOWN. EXPLAINING WHY IT FALLS IS MUCH HARDER. WE USE TWO THEORIES OF GRAVITY TO MODEL THE EFFECTS OF THIS MYSTERIOUS PHENOMENON.

NEWTON'S THEORY OF GRAVITY

Isaac Newton published his theory of gravity almost 350 years ago, and it's still taught in schools around the world. Newton said that we can think of gravity as a force that attracts objects to each other. The strength of this attraction depends on two things: the mass of the objects and their distance apart.

Newton's ideas about gravity changed the way we understand the universe. They allow us to predict how objects will move when they are thrown or dropped, helping to launch satellites, telescopes, and astronauts into Earth's orbit and beyond. However, as scientists explored more of the universe, they noticed many things that Newton's ideas *can't* explain.

EINSTEIN'S THEORY OF GRAVITY

In the early 1900s, Albert Einstein put forward a completely different idea: that gravity is not a force, but a side effect! Every object in the universe—from tiny **atoms** to massive stars—distorts the "fabric" of space all around it, a bit like a trampoline bends when you stand on it (but in 3D). The more massive an object is, the greater the "bend." The effects we call gravity are the result of planets, stars, spacecraft—and even light—moving through an area of space that has been bent out of shape.

Both Newton's and Einstein's theories are extremely useful in predicting the effects of gravity, but neither of them completely explains *how* gravity happens. Scientists continue to come up with new ideas. In the meantime, we can continue to count on gravity to keep our feet on the ground.

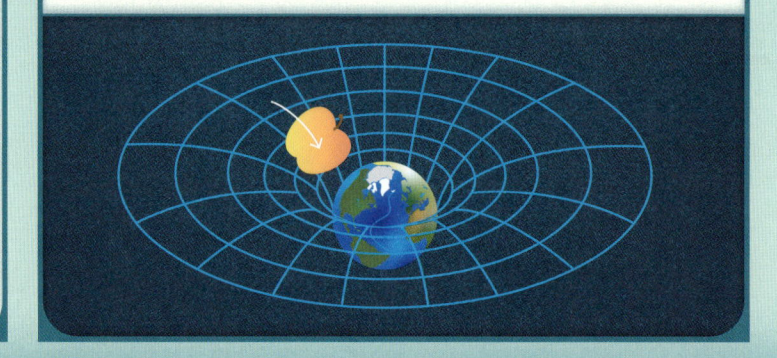

GRAVITY INCREASES WITH MASS

Mass is a measure of how much matter an object is made from—how many **particles**, and which kinds. The more mass an object has, the stronger its overall gravitational field—the region of space where an object's gravity is felt. Another way to think of it is that every particle of Earth attracts every particle of you, and vice versa. As there are many more Earth particles, Earth's gravitational field is much stronger. You fall *toward* Earth rather than the other way around.

GRAVITY WORKS OVER (VERY) LONG DISTANCES

Compared to the strong nuclear force, which stops working as soon as you move two particles even just a few nanometres apart, gravity works over enormous distances. About 250 miles above Earth's surface, the gravitational attraction between the International Space Station and our planet is around 90 percent as strong as it is on the surface. An object's gravitational field is practically infinite.

GRAVITY WEAKENS WITH DISTANCE

The closer two objects are together, the stronger the gravitational attraction between them. Although you are being attracted by the Moon's gravity and the Sun's gravity right now, Earth is much closer, so its **gravitational force** has a much more noticeable effect on your body, keeping your feet on the ground.

GRAVITY GIVES OBJECTS WEIGHT

Mass doesn't change as an object moves around the universe. A person would have the same amount of matter in their body on Earth, the Moon, or Jupiter. However, their **weight** would change in each place. Weight is the force on an object caused by gravitational attraction. The size of the force depends on the mass of the object and not its overall size. **Denser** objects have more stuff packed inside for gravity to pull on, so they are heavier. The direction of the force is toward an object's center of gravity. For ball-shaped objects like Earth, it's toward the center of the planet.

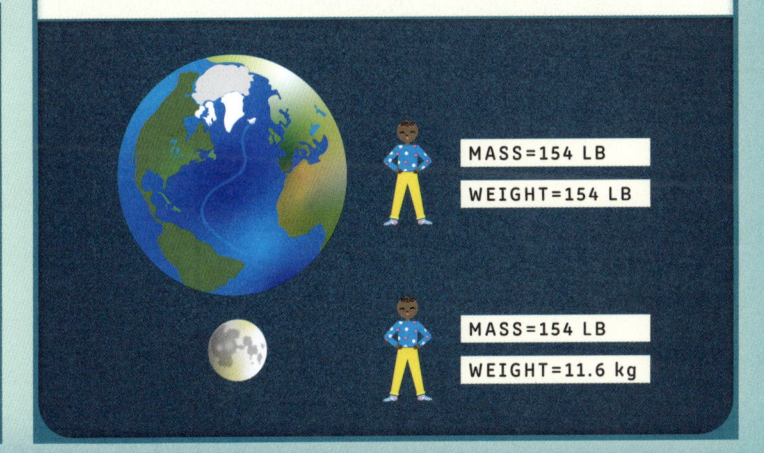

GRAVITY IS A (VERY) WEAK FORCE

An insect crawling up a wall is overcoming the gravity of our entire planet! This is because gravity is the weakest of the four main forces of nature (the other three are strong nuclear, weak nuclear, and electromagnetic). For example, the "strong nuclear force" that holds atoms together is 100 trillion trillion trillion times stronger than the gravitational attraction between those particles.

MASS = 154 LB
WEIGHT = 154 LB

MASS = 154 LB
WEIGHT = 11.6 kg

OTHER OBJECTS IN THE SKY

EARLY STARGAZERS ALSO RECORDED A HOST OF LESS COMMON SIGHTS, FROM "SHOOTING STARS" TO FUZZY CLOUDS. THEY CAME UP WITH ALL KINDS OF EXPLANATIONS, BUT THE TRUTH WOULD TURN OUT TO BE EVEN WEIRDER AND EVEN MORE WONDERFUL.

ALL ABOUT

Alongside the Sun, Moon, stars, and planets, there are plenty of other things to spot in the skies. Some of the most regular spectacles are "shooting stars," visible from all around the world. The oldest written record of this phenomenon, from 687 BCE, describes stars that "fell like rain." Many ancient cultures saw "shooting stars" as omens. Today we know they are **meteors**—rocks from space that glow as they plunge through Earth's atmosphere.

Like meteors, comets were once seen as signs of good or bad events to come. They became better understood in the late 1600s, when Isaac Newton calculated a comet's orbit and showed it was just another object orbiting the Sun. In the 1700s, Edmond Halley proved that certain comets return to the sky time and time again.

Even more attention-grabbing was the sudden appearance of super-bright stars in the night sky. Records of supernovae date back more than 6,000 years. One was so bright that French astronomer Charles Messier mistook it for a comet.

Astronomers also recorded glowing "clouds" dotted across the sky. They were larger than stars, but far fainter. Messier famously made a list of more than 100 of these "nebulae" to avoid any more mistakes in his comet hunting.

The Messier objects have turned out to include many different cosmological wonders, from the remains of supernovae to entire galaxies. Largest of all is the glowing heart of our own galaxy, a spectacular streak of hazy light known as the Milky Way.

MYSTERIOUS METEORS

Around a million "shooting stars" are visible from Earth's surface each year. Yet people only started tracking them properly after a dazzling meteor shower in the Leo constellation captured the world's attention in the 1800s. In 1861, Daniel Kirkwood figured out that the "Leonids" and other regular meteor showers happen as Earth passes through the debris from comet trails.

PAST, PRESENT, FUTURE

Beautiful and mysterious objects in the night sky evoke wonder and inspire the astronomers of the future. Early records of these events are also helpful for today's astronomers, helping them to identify short-period comets (see page 124) or date supernova remnants (see page 154).

THE VIEW FROM EARTH

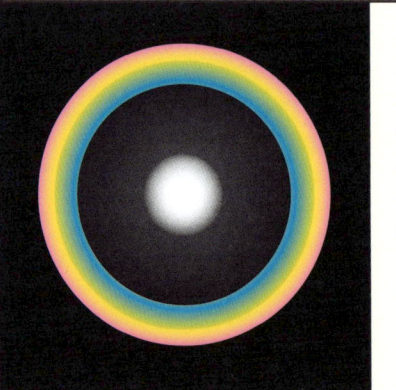

Wispy clouds high in Earth's atmosphere can split sunlight and moonlight into a rainbow of colors. This creates moonbows (rings around a full Moon, as shown) and sun dogs (small sections of rainbow on either side of the Sun).

★ WHAT CAUSES COLORFUL AURORAE? FIND OUT ON PAGE 38 ★

#		
1	**FAMOUS COMET**	A sighting of Halley's comet in 1066 was seen as an omen of change in medieval Europe, especially after the Normans conquered England later that year. The comet is included in the Bayeux Tapestry, a famous 11th-century embroidered cloth that tells the story of the conquest.
2	**SHOOTING STARS**	Every November, the Leonids meteor shower appears in the night sky like a natural firework display. The "shooting stars" are tiny fragments of comet 55P/Tempel-Tuttle, burning up in Earth's atmosphere each time our planet crosses the comet's trail.
3	**FUZZY CLOUDS**	Ancient peoples noticed many nebulae in the night skies. The Maya described the Orion Nebula as a glowing fire, while in 964 CE Persian astronomer al-Sufi called Andromeda the "Little Cloud."
4	**SPACE WEATHER**	Glowing aurorae often ripple and dance across polar skies. Ancient cultures connected these northern and southern lights to their religions. For example, the Vikings described them as reflections from the shields of the Valkyries, female warriors from Norse mythology.
5	**TWO SUNS**	The first record of a supernova is a rock carving found in the Himalayas, from 4,300 BCE. It shows hunters and a bull, with two "suns" in the sky. This tells us the supernova was so bright, it was visible in the daytime alongside the Sun.

NEAR-EARTH SPACE

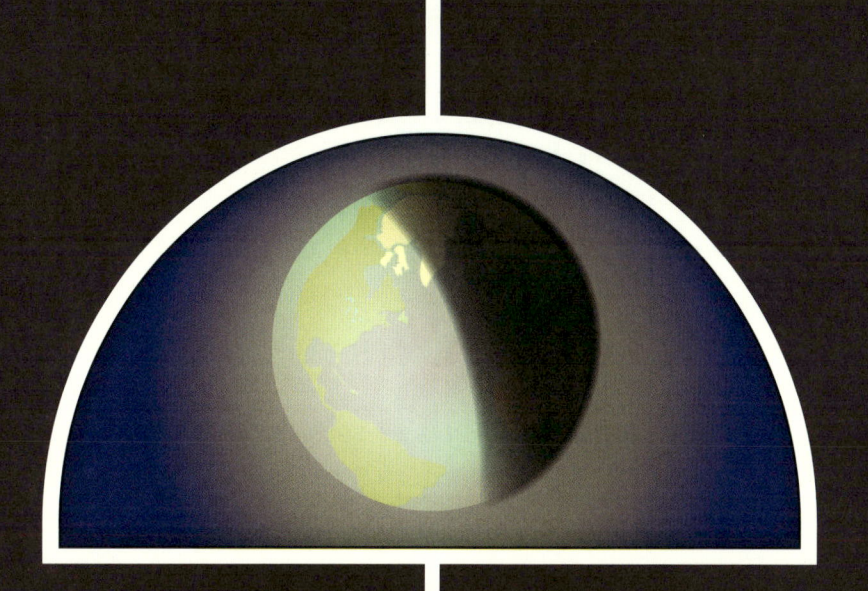

WHERE DOES EARTH'S ATMOSPHERE END AND OUTER SPACE BEGIN? PHOTOS TAKEN FROM ORBIT REVEAL A THIN BLANKET OF AIR AROUND OUR PLANET THAT SEEMS TO MARK THE BOUNDARY.

But Earth's atmosphere reaches much farther than this glowing halo. While heavier gases gather near the surface, the atmosphere does not end abruptly but thins out gradually over many thousands of miles. Earth's gravity holds on to a thin but vast cloud of hydrogen, which stretches 390,000 miles into space. As the Moon orbits Earth, it travels through this geocorona, meaning that even lunar astronauts have never really left Earth's atmosphere.

Although the geocorona is the closest area of space, we are still discovering its secrets. For example, it includes two enormous dust clouds that orbit Earth at roughly the same distance as the Moon.

More than 11,000 human-made satellites orbit our planet, too. These include space stations, where humans live and work for months at a time. The view of Earth from space is helping us to understand our planet better. Views of outer space are clearer from Earth's orbit too.

However, with seven new satellites launched on an average day, near-Earth space is becoming crowded, making human-made space junk a planet-sized problem.

EARTH

CATEGORY	AGE
PLANET	4.54 BILLION YEARS

DESPITE ITS NAME, MOST OF EARTH'S SURFACE IS COVERED WITH LIQUID WATER. THIS WATER MAKES LIFE POSSIBLE—AND LIVING CREATURES HAVE SHAPED THE PLANET IN RETURN.

ALL ABOUT

Four things make Earth very different from the other rocky planets in our solar system. The first is Earth's distance from the Sun, making Earth a "Goldilocks" planet: neither too hot nor too cold for liquid water to gather on the surface. The largest pool of water is the world ocean, which covers 71 percent of the planet.

The second special feature is Earth's powerful **magnetic field**, created by swirling molten metals in the planet's hot outer core. Earth's invisible **magnetosphere** acts as a protective shield, deflecting the invisible but dangerous particles streaming toward us from the Sun (see page 132). Interaction between these particles, Earth's magnetic field, and Earth's air causes phenomena known as space weather—including the spectacular polar lights. Mercury is the only other rocky planet with a magnetic field, but it's far weaker.

Our planet's constantly changing surface is also unusual. Earth's rocky crust and top part of the mantle, known as the lithosphere, are broken up into large pieces called plates. These plates move about on a slushier layer of mantle that is also moving, stirred up like bubbling stew as it is heated from deep within the planet. Where the edges of plates meet, Earth's crust is constantly being reshaped: new crust is formed in volcanic eruptions, mountain ranges are forced upward as areas of the crust crumple, and old crust is forced down into the mantle where it is melted and destroyed.

All these quirks play a part in Earth's most unusual feature of all: life. It is still a mystery how the basic building blocks of a planet rearranged themselves into complex living things. However, scientists *have* been able to trace how living creatures have reshaped Earth over the last 4 billion years.

KEY FACTS

- A day lasts 23.9 hr.
- A year lasts 365.25 days.
- One natural satellite: the Moon.
- Light from the Sun reaches Earth in 8.35 min.
- 1.3 million Earths would fit inside the Sun.

TEMPERATURE

☼ 134 °F (air at the surface)
❄ -135.8 °F (air at the surface)

NAMED AFTER

The Anglo-Saxon word *ertha*, meaning "the ground."

WHAT IS IT MADE OF?

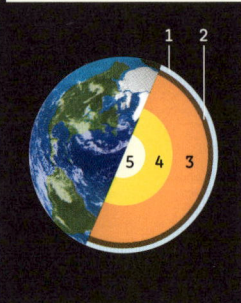

1. Thin atmosphere, mainly nitrogen and oxygen.
2. Solid crust made of many different rocks and **minerals**.
3. Semisolid mantle, rich in silicon, oxygen, magnesium, and iron.
4. Liquid metal outer core (iron and nickel).
5. Solid metal inner core (iron and nickel).

PAST, PRESENT, FUTURE

Just 240 million years ago (a short time in the life of a planet), all Earth's land was part of one supercontinent known as Pangaea. Continental crust is still on the move. Scientists predict a new supercontinent will form 200 to 250 million years from now.

★ WHAT MAKES WATER SO SPECIAL? FIND OUT ON PAGE 40 ★

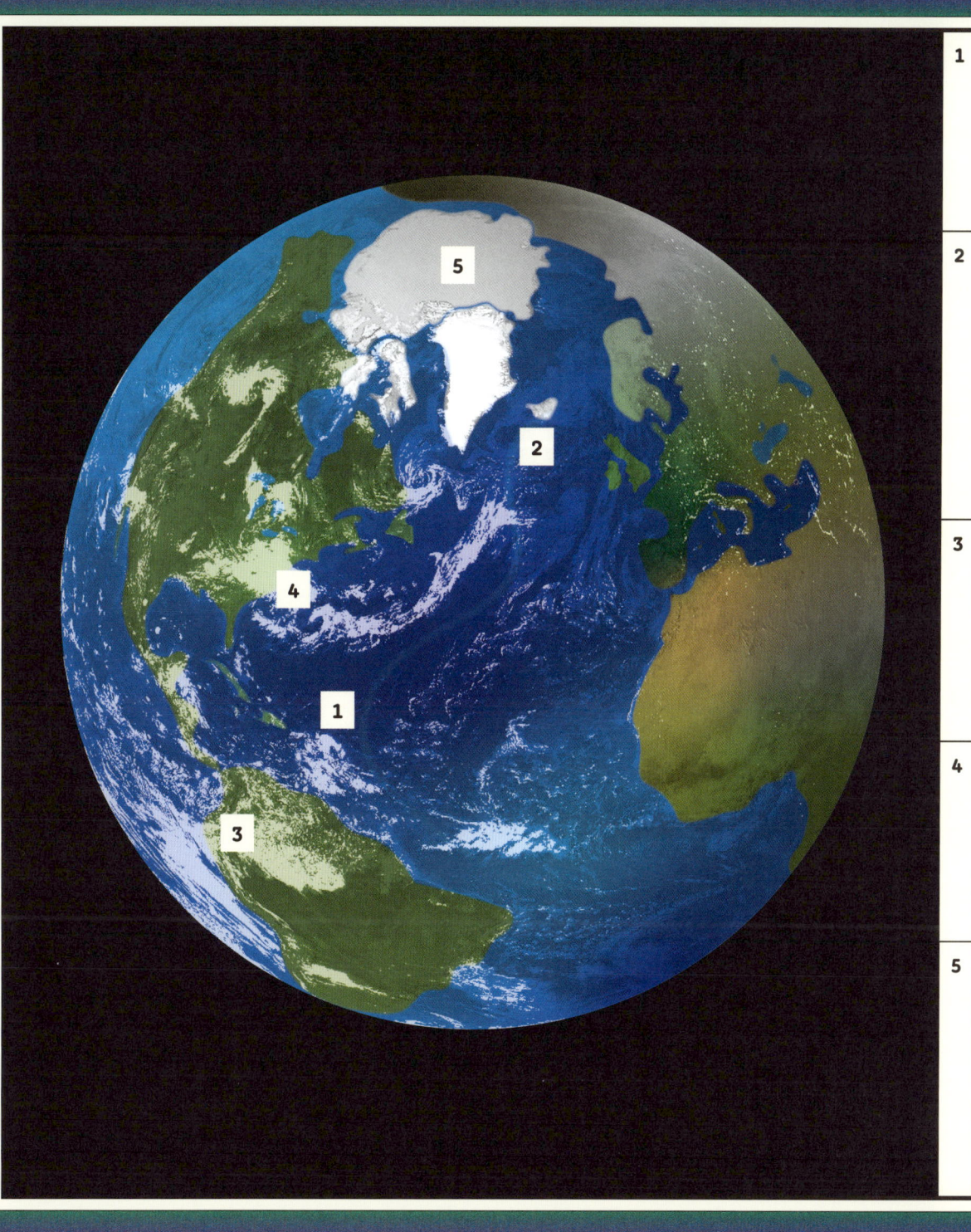

#	
1	**WORLD OCEAN** Seen from space, Earth is a blue planet. The world ocean holds 97 percent of the planet's water. The rest is found as fresh water underground, or in rivers and lakes; as ice in glaciers and ice sheets; and as water vapor in the atmosphere.
2	**OCEANIC CRUST** Earth's crust is thinnest under the ocean. In places, just about 2 miles of rock separates the seabed and the slushy mantle. It's easier for molten rock from the mantle to burst through thinner crust, so three-quarters of Earth's volcanic eruptions happen underwater. They form volcanic mountain ranges like the mid-ocean ridge.
3	**THICKEST CRUST** Mount Everest towers more than 29,000 feet above sea level. However, the peak of Mount Chimborazo in Ecuador is 6,500 feet farther from Earth's core! It lies near the equator, where the land bulges an extra 13 miles from the core, compared to land at the poles.
4	**CONSTANT CHANGE** Weather happens in Earth's atmosphere, but it reshapes the surface, too. Moving wind and water wear down mountains, carve gorges and valleys, deposit new land in the form of deltas, and cause coastlines to crumble.
5	**ICE CAPS** Earth's North and South Poles are covered in frozen water. The Antarctic ice sheet at the South Pole is Earth's biggest glacier. Its ice is almost 3 miles thick in places, squishing the rocky crust below by up to 16,000 feet.

EXPLORING EARTH'S ATMOSPHERE

THE BLANKET OF GASES SURROUNDING EARTH REACHES MANY THOUSANDS OF MILES ABOVE OUR HEADS. OUR URGE TO EXPLORE THIS ATMOSPHERE LED TO THE INVENTION OF SPACE TRAVEL.

ALL ABOUT

We can dive into Earth's oceans and drill into its rocky crust, but exploring its atmosphere is more difficult. Scientists in the 1600s began this process by hauling heavy instruments up a mountain. This is how we discovered Earth's air does not go on forever, and that the vacuum of space lies somewhere above our heads.

In the 1700s, scientists took to attaching instruments to kites, and flying them on strings many miles long. "Aeronauts" also began exploring the atmosphere in person, traveling in balloons lifted by hot air or hydrogen. However, just 3.5 miles off the ground, the air becomes too thin for humans to breathe properly. It would be another century before uncrewed weather balloons were developed to get around this problem.

Weather balloons are filled with gas that is lighter than air. Like a buoy in water, they float to the top of the atmosphere. Eventually the balloon bursts, and the instruments on board fall back to Earth, along with the data they have collected. The first weather balloons helped scientists to name different layers of the atmosphere, based on the temperature at different **altitudes**.

In the 1900s, new ground- and aircraft-based technologies such as radar helped scientists to understand the atmosphere and its weather better. The invention of sounding rockets allowed scientists to send instruments into the outer atmosphere. Soaring far above the 60-mile Kármán line (an imaginary line where space is said to begin) these small, simple rockets were the first space vehicles. They let us peer down at our planet from above, and gave us a better view of outer space, too. Rockets soon became powerful enough to put satellites, people, and entire space stations into orbit around Earth, and to escape our planet's gravity altogether.

EXPLORATION TIMELINE

1648	First record of weather instruments being carried up a mountain (France).
1749	First weather kite used (Scotland).
1780s	Aeronauts carry out the first successful hot air balloon flight (France).
1890s	Weather instruments now routinely attached to uncrewed balloons.
1925	Powered aircraft begin flying instruments into the atmosphere.
1940s	Radar is first used to monitor weather conditions.
1945	Sounding rockets carry instruments higher into the atmosphere.
1957	Sputnik 1 is the first satellite in orbit.
1971	Salyut 1 is the first space station in orbit.

ARE WE THERE YET?

- A car traveling at top speed would take more than 5 hours to reach the top of the thermosphere.
- Rockets can deliver satellites into the thermosphere in around 8 minutes.

HELPING HUMANS

The ozone layer is a region of the stratosphere that absorbs the most dangerous **ultraviolet (UV)** light from the Sun, which would otherwise harm life on Earth. In the 1970s, scientists raised the alarm that the ozone layer was being destroyed by certain chemicals used by humans. The world came together to ban these and the ozone layer is healing.

★ FIND OUT HOW ROCKETS WORK ON PAGE 50 ★

EXOSPHERE

THERMOSPHERE

MESOSPHERE

STRATOSPHERE

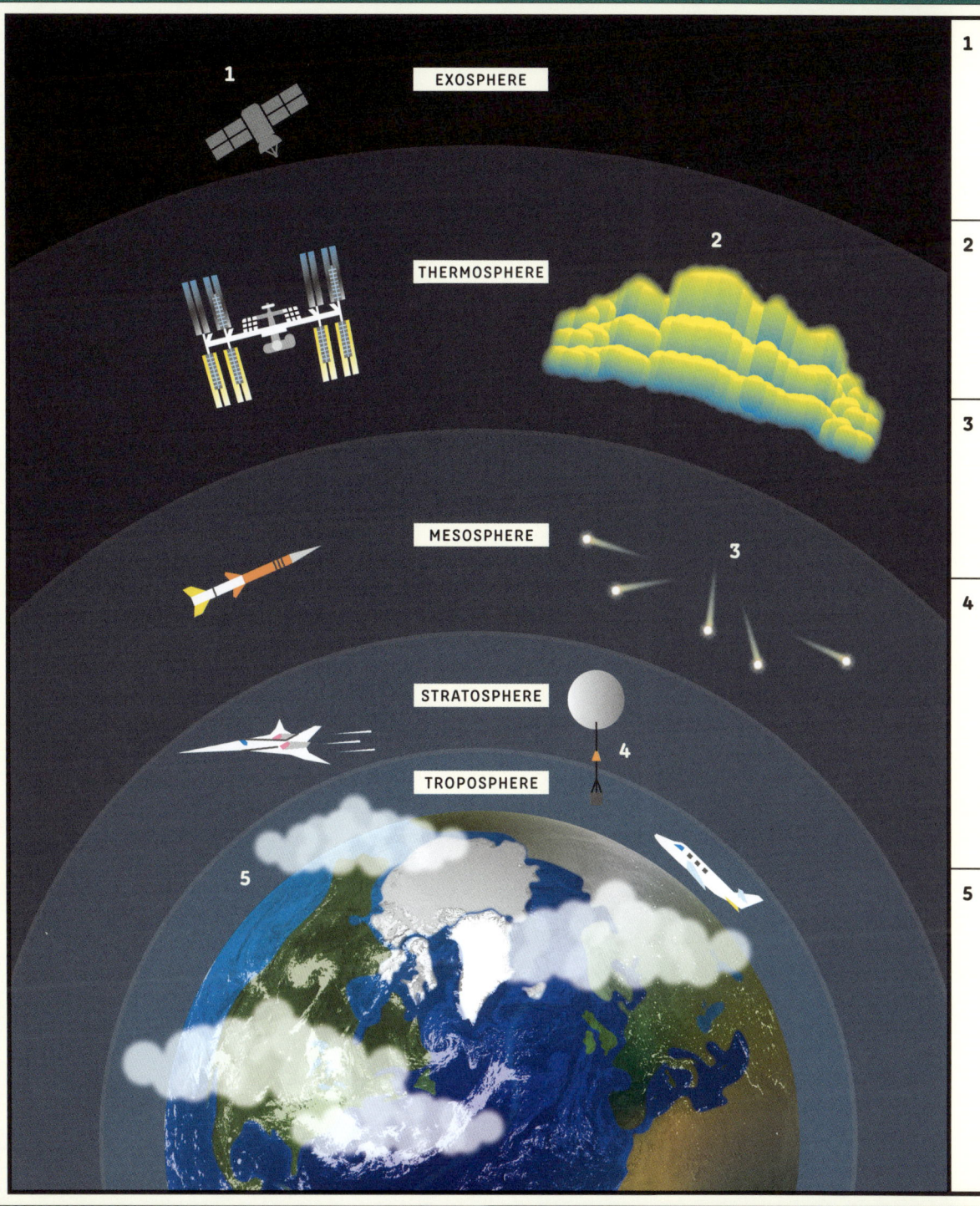

TROPOSPHERE

1	**THIN AIR** In the outermost layer of Earth's atmosphere, the air is extremely thin. Satellites in Medium, Geosynchronous, and High Earth Orbit are placed in the exosphere because there is very little air resistance to slow them down.
2	**DANCING LIGHTS** Air in the thermosphere soaks up lots of energy from incoming sunlight. Colorful aurorae form over Earth's poles, as high-energy particles from the Sun collide with the air and cause it to glow brightly.
3	**SHOOTING STARS** In the mesosphere, the air is thick enough to slow meteors—some as small as a grain of sand. This friction causes them to heat up so much that they glow, giving them the name "shooting stars."
4	**WEATHER BALLOONS** These are still the best tools for exploring the stratosphere, as this layer is too high for aircraft to work, too low for satellites to orbit, and rockets zoom through too quickly. Today's balloons are filled with helium, which expands as the balloons float higher and higher, stretching the balloons to around the height of the Eiffel Tower!
5	**WEATHER** Almost all of Earth's weather happens in the lowest layer of its atmosphere, the troposphere, where there is enough water vapor to form clouds. Below 3.75 miles, clouds are made up of tiny droplets of liquid water gathered around specks of dust. Above 3.75 miles, they are made up of tiny ice crystals.

WATER

WATER IS WEIRD... AND WONDERFUL! ITS UNIQUE PROPERTIES HELP SHAPE EARTH'S SURFACE, ATMOSPHERE, AND CLIMATE, AND SEEM TO BE A KEY REASON THAT EARTH IS HOME TO LIVING THINGS.

The universe is awash with water. In fact, the building blocks of water—hydrogen and oxygen—are two of the most abundant elements. Great clouds of water vapor are found throughout space. Ice caps, watery atmospheres, and vast underground oceans have been spotted on many planets and moons, including some within our own solar system.

What makes Earth unique is that water sticks around on the surface as a liquid, instead of instantly evaporating or freezing. In fact, at the narrow range of temperature found on Earth's surface, it's possible to find water in all three states of matter: as a solid, a liquid, and a gas. Water also moves between the three states in a process called the water cycle.

About 97 percent of Earth's water is sloshing around in seas and oceans. This water is famously salty, due to water's amazing ability to dissolve minerals as it flows over rocks, trickles through soil, and washes over the seabed. When water evaporates, any dissolved substances are left behind. This is how Earth's oceans became salty, over a long period of time. Water that has evaporated from the oceans rains down on the land, constantly topping up Earth's supply of fresh water.

Water's power as a solvent is vital for living things. Watery fluids like blood and sap dissolve substances such as oxygen and food and transport them around a plant or animal. Water even helps to form the structure of living things. The "jelly" that fills living cells is mostly water. By pushing on the inside, it helps cells—and entire living creatures—keep their shape against the outside force of air or water pressure. Inside cells, water helps bring substances together to take part in the unique chemistry of life. Watery fluids then carry waste away.

CHANGING STATE

Many substances can change from solid, to liquid, to gas as they are heated, but only water is found in all three states of matter at typical temperatures on Earth's surface: as solid ice, liquid water, and gaseous water vapor.

POWERFUL SOLVENT

Water dissolves more substances than any other liquid. Dissolving is a special kind of mixing, in which a substance gets broken up into particles so tiny, they seem to disappear into the other substance.

BUILDING BLOCKS

Water forms slowly in the space between stars, as drifting atoms of hydrogen and oxygen "bump" into one another and react. A water **molecule** is made of two hydrogen (H) atoms bonded to one oxygen (O) atom, written as H_2O for short.

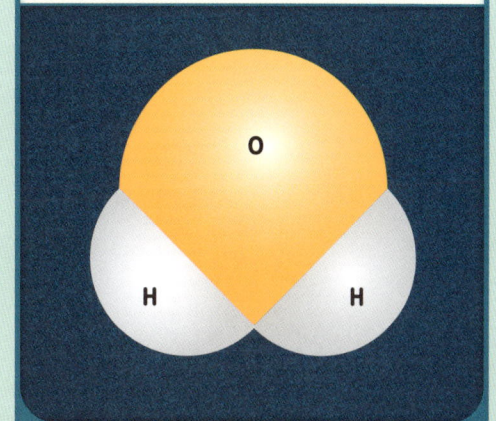

STRONG BONDS

Water has an amazing ability to stick to itself. This happens because the hydrogen atoms in a water molecule are strongly attracted to the oxygen atoms in other water molecules. It's why water forms drops and flows as a liquid.

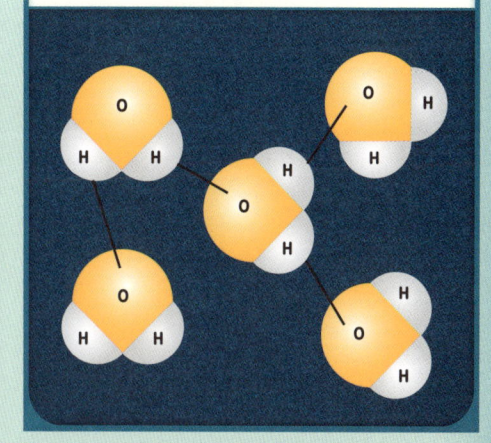

HEAT TRAP

Water heats up and cools slowly compared to other substances, allowing for more stable temperatures—both at Earth's surface, and inside living things.

BEATING GRAVITY

Water will also stick strongly to other substances. The attraction between water molecules and the walls of a narrow tube are powerful enough for water to flow upward against the downward pull of gravity. This is called capillary action. Thanks to capillary action, water can travel from the roots of a plant to the leaves with no mechanical pump.

LIFE ON EARTH

SPECIES
AT LEAST 8.7 MILLION LIVING SPECIES

AGE
AT LEAST 3.7 BILLION YEARS

EARTH'S LIVING SPECIES ARE THE CURRENT LEAVES ON A TREE OF LIFE THAT SPROUTED AROUND 4 BILLION YEARS AGO. CONDITIONS ON OUR PLANET BOTH SHAPE AND ARE SHAPED BY ITS INCREDIBLE BIODIVERSITY.

ALL ABOUT

Our knowledge of past life on Earth comes from traces left in the planet's crust. Patterns made by microbes found inside 3.7-billion-year-old rocks—the world's oldest fossils—tell us that life on Earth is almost as old as the planet.

We don't yet understand how life began—Earth's changing surface has wiped away any record of conditions 4 billion years ago (though Moon rocks offer clues). Yet we know Earth then wasn't the lush planet of today. Its surface was boiling, heated by the core and by frequent comet and asteroid impacts. These very meteors may have delivered the initial building blocks of life.

As Earth cooled and the first rains fell, minerals from partly melted rocks washed into newly forming oceans. In these hot pools full of dissolved chemicals, a spark of energy somehow brought about life: complex chemicals that can make copies of themselves. The first creatures were simple, yet each time they copied themselves, there was a chance for changes. We see these billions of years of change in today's huge variety of living things.

Life on Earth is now found everywhere that water, energy, and carbon are available. It hasn't just adapted to our planet. It has reshaped it into something far more spectacular. Phytoplankton add oxygen to the atmosphere. Plants alter the flow of water across Earth's surface. Certain rocks are the remains of living things.

Humans are living things like any other. However, our activities are having an unusually large impact on the planet, causing rapid changes to Earth's oceans, land, air, and climate.

KEY FACTS

- Earth's smallest living creature is Nanoarchaeum, a microbe so small that 2,500 could line up across a period.
- Earth's largest species is a fungus that spreads underground to cover the area of 1,665 football fields.

BIODIVERSITY

Each unique type of living thing is known as a species. Scientists have named at least 2 million living species, but estimate there are millions more left to discover. They are all descendants of a last universal common ancestor, known as LUCA.

WHAT IS IT MADE OF?

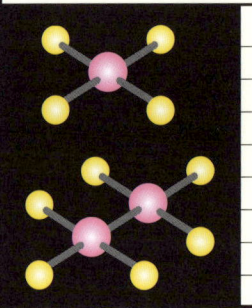

Four elements—carbon, hydrogen, nitrogen, and oxygen—make up 96.5 percent of a living thing's mass. This is very different from the composition of nonliving things. Life on Earth is often described as carbon-based. Carbon's chemical properties allow the complex building blocks of living things to form.

COMPARING TOTAL MASS OF EARTH'S LIVING THINGS

- VIRUSES
- ANIMALS
- PROTISTS
- ARCHAEA
- FUNGI
- BACTERIA
- PLANTS

★ COULD THERE BE LIFE ELSEWHERE IN THE UNIVERSE? FIND OUT ON PAGES 98 AND 166 ★

#	
1	**OXYGEN SOURCE** Phytoplankton are tiny ocean microbes that can capture carbon from their surroundings, using the energy in sunlight. As they make their food, phytoplankton release oxygen as a waste gas. Over millions of years, they have contributed at least half of the oxygen in Earth's air.
2	**CARBON CAPTURE** Land plants share the carbon-capturing power of phytoplankton, and the immense size and coverage of many tree species make forests one of Earth's biggest oxygen providers and carbon stores.
3	**AS LARGE AS LIFE** Earth's largest living structures are the reefs built by tiny animals called corals, over thousands of years. The Great Barrier Reef near the coast of Australia covers 135,000 square miles—an area around the size of Germany. It provides habitats and food for a vast range of other living things.
4	**SEEN FROM SPACE** Antarctic penguins live in remote and harsh habitats, making them hard to track and study. However, penguin colonies are so large, their guano (poop) leaves stains on the ice that are visible from space! Photos taken by satellites are helping scientists to count penguins and discover new colonies.
5	**LIFE AT EXTREMES** Chile's Atacama Desert is so dry that, in places, no animals or plants could possibly survive. Even here, there are microbes that make the most of tiny traces of water trapped inside rocks. Extremophiles like these help us better understand how life began, and what it might look like elsewhere in the universe.

THE MOON

CATEGORY	AGE
PLANETARY SATELLITE	4.46 BILLION YEARS

THE MOON IS OUR NEAREST NEIGHBOR, AND THE BRIGHTEST OBJECT IN THE NIGHT SKY. SCIENTISTS THINK IT COULD BE A DRY AND DUSTY CHUNK OF OUR OWN PLANET, LOCKED IN A GRAVITATIONAL SLOW DANCE WITH EARTH.

ALL ABOUT

The Moon's story began 4.46 billion years ago, when the young Earth is thought to have collided with a smaller planet named Theia. Earth survived the giant impact, but vast chunks of both planets were thrown into space. Trapped by Earth's gravity, much of the debris settled into a doughnut of gas, dust, and rock orbiting our planet.

Each piece of this rubble had its own gravitational pull, and in as little as 40 years it gathered itself into one large lump—the Moon. As for the fate of Theia, scientists recently found evidence that it's still lodged inside Earth's mantle in two huge pieces, each twice the mass of the Moon.

At first the Moon was molten rock, which slowly cooled to form a solid, granite-like crust. Over billions of years, this crust has been pounded by **meteorite** strikes, covering the Moon in craters and a thick layer of powdery dust and rocky rubble, known as regolith.

Meteorite bombardment cracked the Moon's crust, creating fissures up to 15.5 miles deep. In the past, lava oozed up through these cracks, collecting in the lowest-lying craters and basins. It has cooled to form the darker areas of the surface. As there is no atmosphere—and therefore no weather—on the Moon, craters and regolith are only ever disturbed by new meteorite strikes.

The Moon spins so slowly on its axis that two Earth weeks pass between sunrise and sunset. During these long "days," part of the surface heats up beyond 248 °F. During the two-week night that follows, temperatures plummet far below the freezing point of water. Near the Moon's South Pole, some craters are always in shadow. At -400 °F, they are some of the coldest places in the solar system.

KEY FACTS

- Spins on axis every 27 Earth days, 7 hr, 43 min.
- Orbits Earth every 27 days, 7 hr, 43 min.
- Orbits Earth at 0.5 mi/s.
- 50 Moons would fit inside Earth.
- The Moon's surface area is the combined size of Europe and Africa.

TEMPERATURE

☼ 253 °F
❄ -400 °F

NAMED AFTER

The Moon was known as *mōna* in Old English, based on Latin words for measuring and months.

WHAT IS IT MADE OF?

1. Dusty, rocky regolith.
2. Solid crust, mainly anorthosite and basalt.
3. Rocky mantle, mainly olivine and pyroxene.
4. Small iron core, mainly iron and nickel.

PAST, PRESENT, FUTURE

Giant meteorite strikes can send chunks of the Moon flying off into space. Some have landed on Earth, as lunar meteorites. Scientists believe that the Ferris wheel-sized asteroid Kamo`oalewa is also a Moon chunk. Every April, its orbit brings this "mini-moon" close enough to Earth to spot with a telescope.

★ EXPLORE THE MOON'S IMPACT ON EARTH (PAGE 46) ★

#	
1	**SOLID "SEAS"** People once thought the dark areas of the Moon's surface were water. Today we know they are areas of solidified lava from ancient volcanic eruptions that happened billions of years ago.
2	**ANCIENT HIGHLANDS** The brightest areas of the Moon's surface are also its highest, oldest, and roughest parts. They formed early in its history, as minerals floated to the top of the Moon's ancient magma ocean and cooled quickly to form anorthosite rock.
3	**TYCHO CRATER** The Moon's largest craters are easy to see with binoculars. Tycho Crater was formed 100 million years ago, when dinosaurs roamed Earth. It is around 53 miles wide, with steep walls towering almost 3 miles above the crater floor, and jets of debris all around.
4	**IN SYNC** The time it takes the Moon to orbit Earth once matches the time it takes for the Moon to spin once on its own axis. This is not a coincidence, but a result of gravitational forces. It means that the same side of the Moon always faces Earth.
5	**MOON MOUNTAINS** Meteorite strikes have carved such giant craters and basins on the Moon that their rims form mountain ranges. The Apennine range has more than 3,000 peaks, including the Moon's highest mountain, *Mons Huygens*, which is just over half the height of Earth's Mount Everest.

THE EARTH-MOON SYSTEM

CATEGORY	AGE
PLANET-MOON SYSTEM	4.53 BILLION YEARS

ALIENS PEERING INTO OUR SOLAR SYSTEM FROM A DISTANCE WOULD THINK OF EARTH AND THE MOON AS A DOUBLE PLANET. IT'S USEFUL FOR SCIENTISTS TO STUDY THIS "EARTH-MOON SYSTEM" TOO.

ALL ABOUT

The Moon is so large and spherical that it would easily count as a planet if it were orbiting the Sun directly. The gravitational pull from such a large neighbor is responsible for many of Earth's features, including the ocean tides.

The Moon's gravity tugs Earth's liquid oceans out of shape, causing water levels to rise on the side of the planet facing the Moon. A similar bulge forms on the opposite side, as Earth itself is pulled away from its watery covering. As Earth spins on its axis, the two bulges of water sweep around the planet, causing sea levels to continuously rise and fall.

Earth's gravity also causes tidal bulges on the Moon, pulling the crust out of shape on the side facing Earth (with a matching bulge on the opposite side). The forces involved in warping solid rock have caused the Moon to spin more slowly over time. Its rotation now matches the speed of its orbit around Earth—so the same side of the Moon always faces Earth. This synchronous rotation means the Moon's bulge also remains in the same part of the crust, rather than being dragged across the rocky surface.

The Moon's gravity is also gradually slowing Earth's rotation. In 43,500 years, days will last a second longer and, over the long lifespan of a planet, this makes a big difference. Clues from ancient corals reveal that 370 million years ago, Earth spun so much faster on its axis that prehistoric beasts waited 400 days between birthdays.

Earth wobbles as it spins, like a spinning top. In the past, these tiny wobbles have caused significant climate change, including ice ages. They would be more extreme without the Moon's gravity acting as an anchor, reducing the wobble and making Earth's climate more stable. This has helped life on Earth to flourish.

KEY FACTS

- On Earth, high tide comes once every 12 hr and 25 min.
- Around 30 Earth-sized planets could fit in the gap between Earth and the Moon.

DAY LENGTH

When Earth first formed, it rotated so quickly that sunset came three hours after sunrise. The Moon has slowed Earth's spin, so there are now 12 hours between sunset and sunrise at the equator.

DANCE PARTNERS

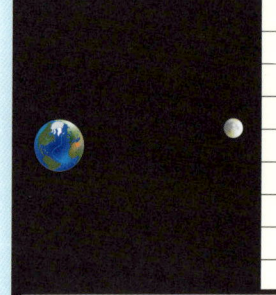

We think of the Moon as orbiting Earth, but really the two objects are orbiting their shared center of gravity—a point inside Earth, but about 2,900 miles from the center. Like whirling dance partners, both Earth and the Moon experience a centrifugal force flinging them outward. This explains why they don't fall toward each other and collide.

PAST, PRESENT, FUTURE

The Moon was much closer to Earth when it first formed. It would have looked ten times larger in the sky and caused tides a thousand times higher! The Moon is still moving away from Earth at around 1.5 inches per year. When humans first landed on the Moon in 1969, it was more than 6 feet closer.

★ EXPLORE MOONS OF OTHER PLANETS IN SECTION 3 (PAGES 94 AND 102) ★

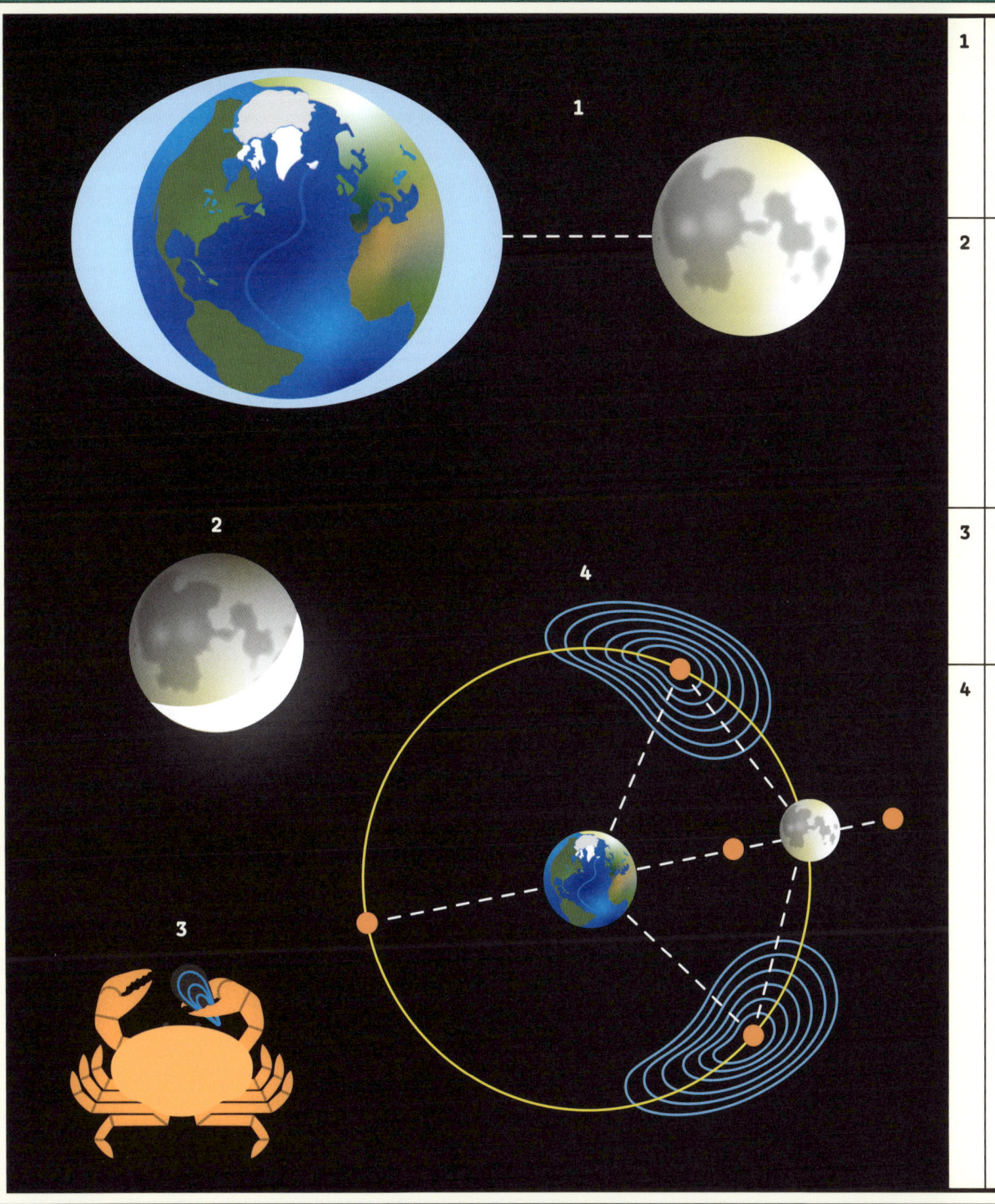

#	
1	**OCEAN TIDES** In the ocean's deeper parts, tidal bulges only raise the water level by a fraction of an inch. Nearer coastlines, the effect is amplified. In the Bay of Fundy, Canada, the difference between high and low tide can be up to about 55 feet!
2	**EARTHSHINE** Moonshine (the Sun's light reflecting off the Moon) can be bright enough to cast shadows on Earth. The Moon's surface can also be brightly lit by Earthshine—when a "full Earth" acts like a giant mirror and reflects lots of sunlight toward the Moon. With a crescent moon, Earthshine sometimes allows us to see the part of the Moon's disc that is not bathed in sunlight.
3	**TIDAL LIFE** Creatures in coastal areas are adapted to make the most of tidal changes. The tides may have even helped life to move from water to land, billions of years ago.
4	**PARKING SPOTS** When two large objects orbit one another, their combined gravity affects the space around them too. The Earth-Moon system has five Lagrange points, where their gravity balances out to create "parking spots" in space, holding smaller objects in place. Two of the Earth-Moon system's Lagrange points contain huge dust clouds. They are known as Kordylewski clouds after the astronomer who first detected them by spotting the faint glow of sunlight reflecting off the dust. Each cloud takes up about 20 to 30 Moons' worth of sky when seen from Earth.

EXPLORING THE MOON

WE HAVE MAPPED THE MOON IN MORE DETAIL THAN EARTH'S OWN OCEANS, AND EVEN WALKED, LEAPT, AND DRIVEN ON ITS SURFACE. BOTH CREWED AND ROBOTIC MISSIONS HAVE RETURNED SAMPLES OF LUNAR ROCK TO EARTH.

ALL ABOUT

The Moon is so large and so close, we can see surface details with our eyes alone. The invention of telescopes in the 1600s revealed further delights—landscapes with mountain ridges, narrow valleys, vast plains, and countless craters.

Beginning in the 1960s, spacecraft were sent to photograph the Moon, land on its surface, and return samples of lunar rock and soil to Earth. The USSR's uncrewed Luna missions were the first to reach, photograph, and land on the Moon. The most famous journeys are NASA's nine crewed Apollo missions. In total, 24 astronauts made the journey to the Moon and back, and 12 explored its dusty surface on foot and in a battery-powered "Moon buggy." In a few days, they completed tasks it would take months for a remote-controlled rover to achieve, including collecting hundreds of pounds of lunar rocks and soil, and returning them to Earth.

Sending people so far from Earth—and returning them safely home—was one of the hardest technological challenges. It took ten years for dozens of robotic and crewed missions to photograph potential landing sites, chart conditions, and practice complex maneuvers such as landing and docking in space.

Although people have not yet returned to the Moon, the world's space agencies have continued to explore its secrets using robotic probes, landers, and rovers. One of the most exciting discoveries is frozen water in deep craters at the Moon's poles and scattered through its soil. This precious resource will be a key focus for future crewed visits and could one day make it possible to establish a permanent scientific base on the Moon.

EXPLORATION TIMELINE

1610	Galileo Galilei uses a telescope to view the Moon.
1959	Luna 1 carries out the first lunar flyby.
1959	Luna 2 crash-lands on the Moon.
1966	Luna 9 touches down on the Moon in a controlled landing.
1966	Luna 10 becomes the Moon's first **orbital probe**.
1968	First robotic Moon rover.
1968	Apollo 8 carries the first crew to the Moon and back.
1969	Apollo 11 is the first crewed mission to land on the Moon.
1970	Lunokhod 1 (Moonwalker 1) is the first robotic Moon rover.

ARE WE THERE YET?

- A car traveling 60 mph would take around five months to reach the Moon.
- The first crewed missions reached the Moon in three days.
- The New Horizons probe zoomed past the Moon after just 8 hours, and 35 minutes, on its way to Pluto.

HELPING HUMANS

Many new technologies invented for the Apollo program are now used in everyday life. They include fire-resistant suits used by firefighters and race car drivers, the tiny cameras in smartphones, and the fabric used to build the roofs of huge sport stadiums.

★ FIND OUT MORE ABOUT LUNAR ROVERS ON PAGE 84 ★

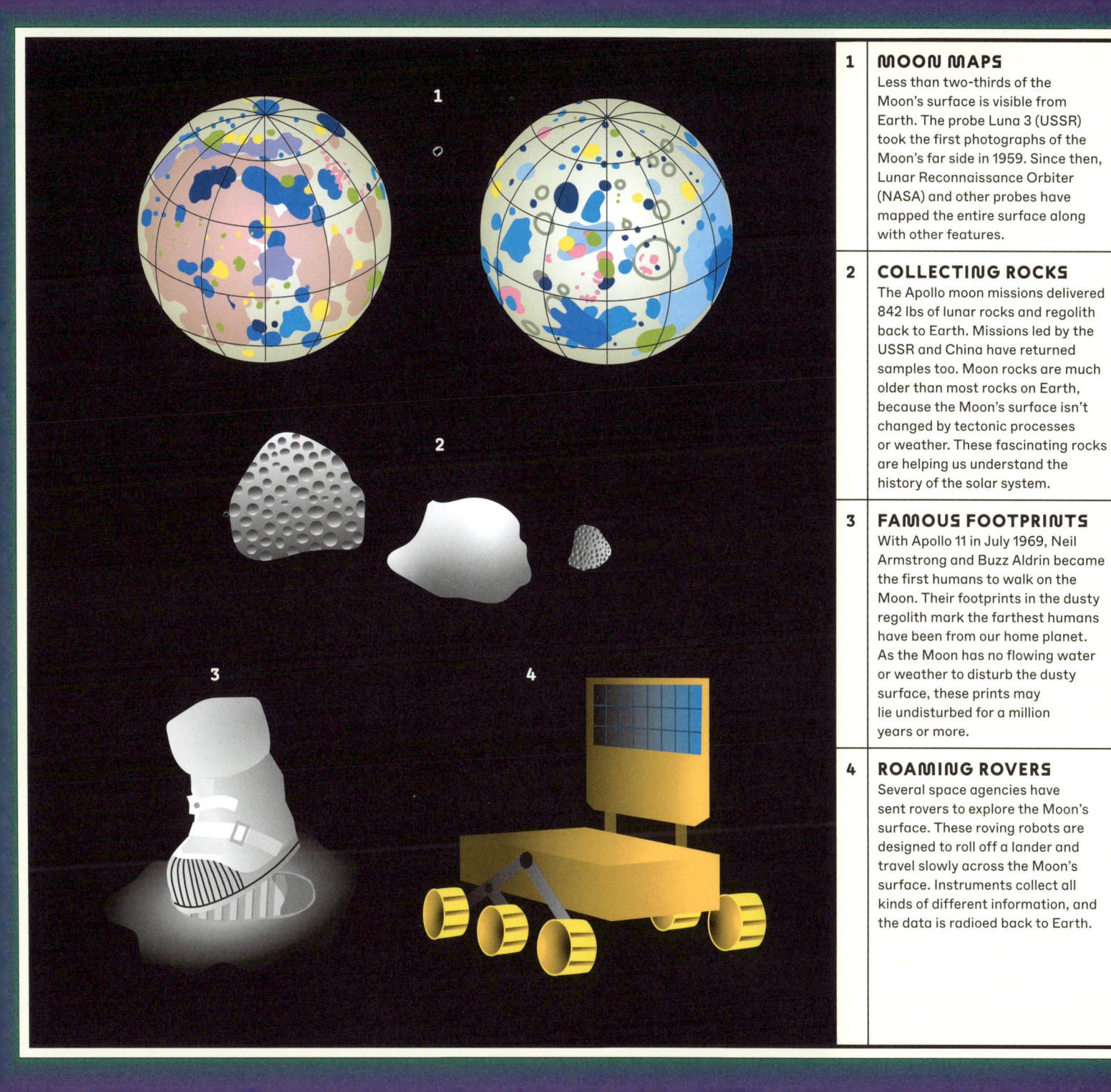

#	
1	**MOON MAPS** Less than two-thirds of the Moon's surface is visible from Earth. The probe Luna 3 (USSR) took the first photographs of the Moon's far side in 1959. Since then, Lunar Reconnaissance Orbiter (NASA) and other probes have mapped the entire surface along with other features.
2	**COLLECTING ROCKS** The Apollo moon missions delivered 842 lbs of lunar rocks and regolith back to Earth. Missions led by the USSR and China have returned samples too. Moon rocks are much older than most rocks on Earth, because the Moon's surface isn't changed by tectonic processes or weather. These fascinating rocks are helping us understand the history of the solar system.
3	**FAMOUS FOOTPRINTS** With Apollo 11 in July 1969, Neil Armstrong and Buzz Aldrin became the first humans to walk on the Moon. Their footprints in the dusty regolith mark the farthest humans have been from our home planet. As the Moon has no flowing water or weather to disturb the dusty surface, these prints may lie undisturbed for a million years or more.
4	**ROAMING ROVERS** Several space agencies have sent rovers to explore the Moon's surface. These roving robots are designed to roll off a lander and travel slowly across the Moon's surface. Instruments collect all kinds of different information, and the data is radioed back to Earth.

ROCKET SCIENCE

OVERCOMING THE GRAVITATIONAL PULL OF A PLANET REQUIRES AN ENORMOUS PUSH IN THE OPPOSITE DIRECTION. ROCKETS ARE THE ONLY INVENTION THAT CAN MAINTAIN A BIG ENOUGH PUSH TO LAUNCH THINGS INTO ORBIT AND BEYOND.

People have been experimenting with rockets for over a thousand years—as fireworks and weapons, tools to explore the atmosphere, and as launch vehicles for space travel.

A rocket's job is to lift things into space. The item, known as a payload, might be a satellite, a space probe, or a spacecraft full of cargo or astronauts. The rocket must get the payload traveling fast enough in the right direction to stop gravity from pulling it back down to the ground.

Rocket science can be explained using the three simple laws of motion written down by Isaac Newton more than 300 years ago. Building a working space rocket is much harder. Fireworks and weapons are designed to explode, but a space rocket must **accelerate** a payload to at least 17,000 mi/h in the right direction, without roasting or crushing everything inside.

Unlike an airplane's jet engines, a rocket engine does not need to suck in air to burn its fuel. Rockets carry their own oxidizer, which allows them to keep burning fuel above 11 miles, when the air becomes too thin for a jet engine to work. In fact, a rocket works much better in space because the exhaust gases don't need to push air out of the way as they stream out of a rocket. Together, a rocket's fuel and oxidizer are known as propellants.

Most of a rocket's mass at launch is the propellants, so large rockets are built in several parts, called stages. Each stage has its own propellant tanks and engines, and they are fired one at a time. Once the propellants for each stage have been used up, the stage is jettisoned, either into space or to fall back to Earth, and the next stage fires up. This means fuel is not wasted hauling empty tanks into space.

An inflated balloon is full of air under pressure. If you let go, the air rushes out through the neck of the balloon. The balloon experiences an equal and opposite force that sends it whizzing off across the room.

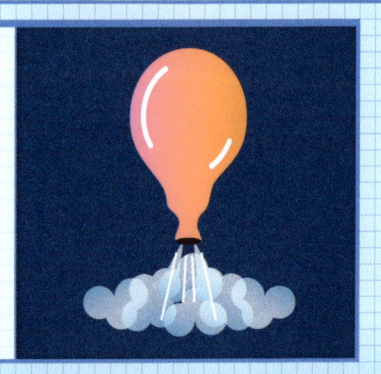

A rocket works in the same way. Gas under pressure rushes out through a nozzle, propelling the rocket in the opposite direction. The exhaust gas that streams out of a rocket is made by burning fuel in the rocket's huge engines.

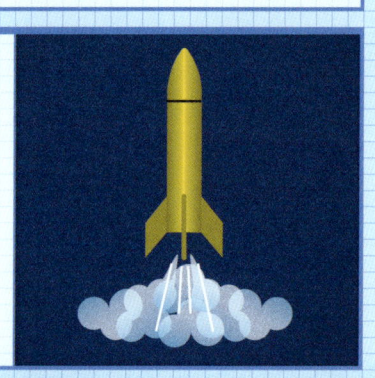

To put a payload into orbit around Earth, a rocket must reach 4.9 mi/s (more than 20 times the speed of sound). This is known as orbital velocity.

To break free of Earth's gravitational pull altogether, a rocket must accelerate to at least 7 mi/s. This is known as escape velocity.

NEWTON'S THREE LAWS OF MOTION (AND WHAT THEY TELL US ABOUT ROCKETS)

Forces always come in pairs. For every action there is an opposite and equal reaction.

The escape of exhaust gases from the engine is the action. The movement of the rocket is the reaction. For a rocket to travel upward, the exhaust gases must escape downward.

The acceleration of an object depends on the mass of the object and the force applied.

The force on a rocket is equal to the force on the exhaust gases. The rocket accelerates more slowly than the exhaust gases because its mass is much greater. As propellants are used up, the rocket's mass decreases and its acceleration increases. Rocket scientists must calculate the perfect balance. If the rocket accelerates too quickly, air resistance will tear it to pieces.

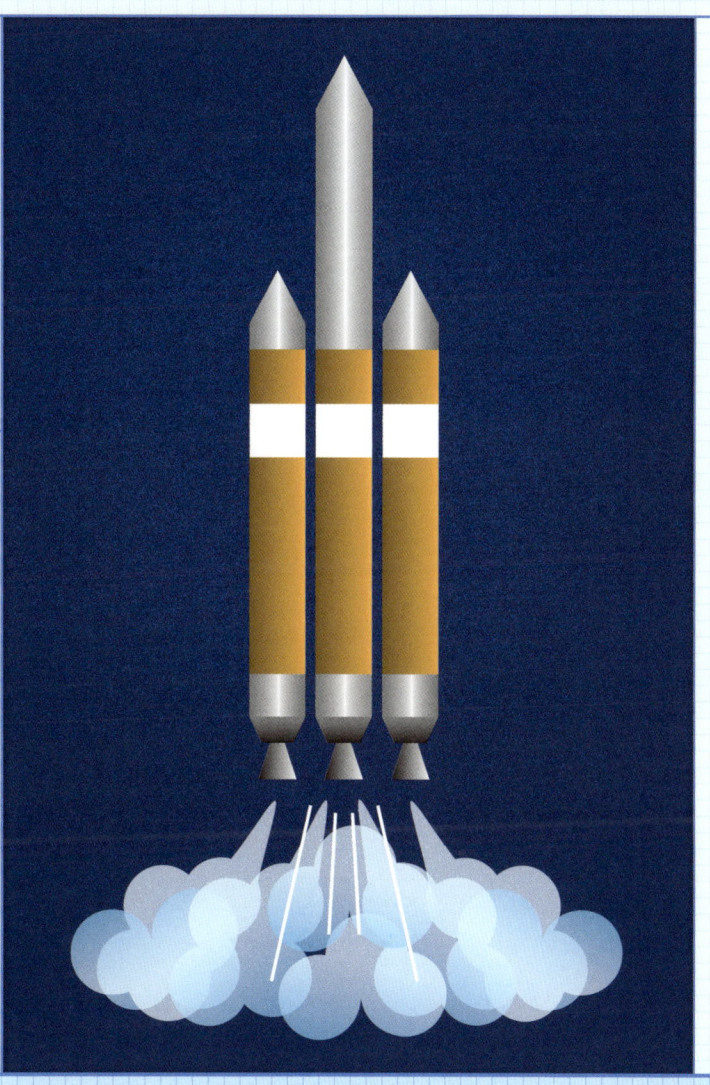

Objects at rest will stay at rest and objects in motion will stay in motion at constant speed and in a straight line unless acted upon by an unbalanced force.

While a rocket is burning fuel, the upward force, or thrust, on the rocket is greater than the downward force due to gravity. Because the forces are unbalanced, the rocket accelerates upward. Once the rocket stops burning fuel, the payload will keep traveling at its final speed and direction, for as long as the forces on it remain balanced.

INTO ORBIT

ORBITS ARE THE CURVED PATHS THAT OBJECTS IN SPACE TAKE AROUND ONE ANOTHER, DUE TO GRAVITY. WE HAVE PLACED HUMAN-MADE OBJECTS INTO ORBIT AROUND MANY DIFFERENT PLANETS AND MOONS, AND AROUND THE SUN ITSELF.

If gravity attracts objects toward one another, why don't Earth and the Moon crash into each other? Isaac Newton used his laws of motion to explain how moons and planets stay in orbit. He explained that the Moon is falling toward Earth, but is moving so quickly that it effectively falls all the way around the planet!

Over 250 years later, engineers used this idea to put the first artificial satellite in orbit. Artificial satellites are accelerated to tremendous speeds by a rocket (see page 50). The job of the rocket is to get the satellite traveling very quickly, parallel to Earth's surface. When the rocket fuel runs out, the satellite begins to fall back to Earth due to gravity. But if it's traveling fast enough, the curved path of its fall will exactly match the curve of Earth's surface. It will fall all the way around the planet. With no air resistance to slow a satellite down, it will just keep going.

In reality, satellites do encounter some air on their journey through the thin upper atmosphere. Over time this causes them to lose speed. Without additional boosts from small rockets, satellites eventually fall out of orbit.

NEWTON'S CANNONBALL

To explain how gravity causes planets to orbit the Sun, Newton asked people to imagine a cannonball fired from a cannon on a mountaintop. The ball would start off traveling sideways. Earth's gravity would immediately start pulling it downward, but because of the ball's sideways motion, it would fall in a curved path to the ground.

With a bigger push from a more powerful cannon, the cannonball would travel faster and cover more distance before it hit the ground.

With a big enough push, the curved path could reach all the way around the planet, returning the cannonball back to where it started!

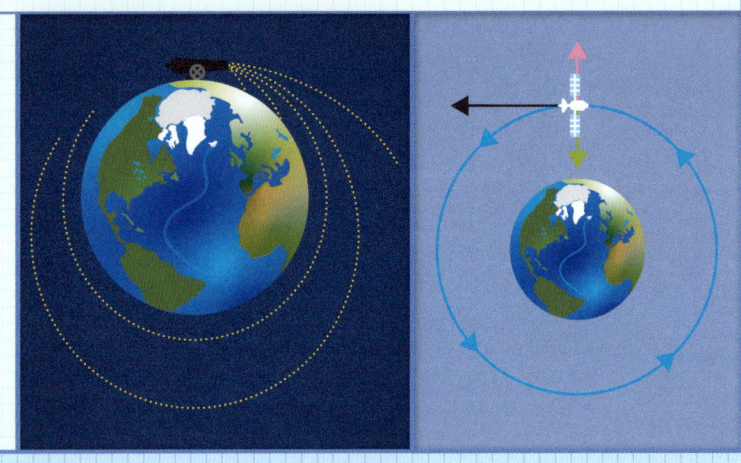

ORBITAL HEIGHTS AND TYPES

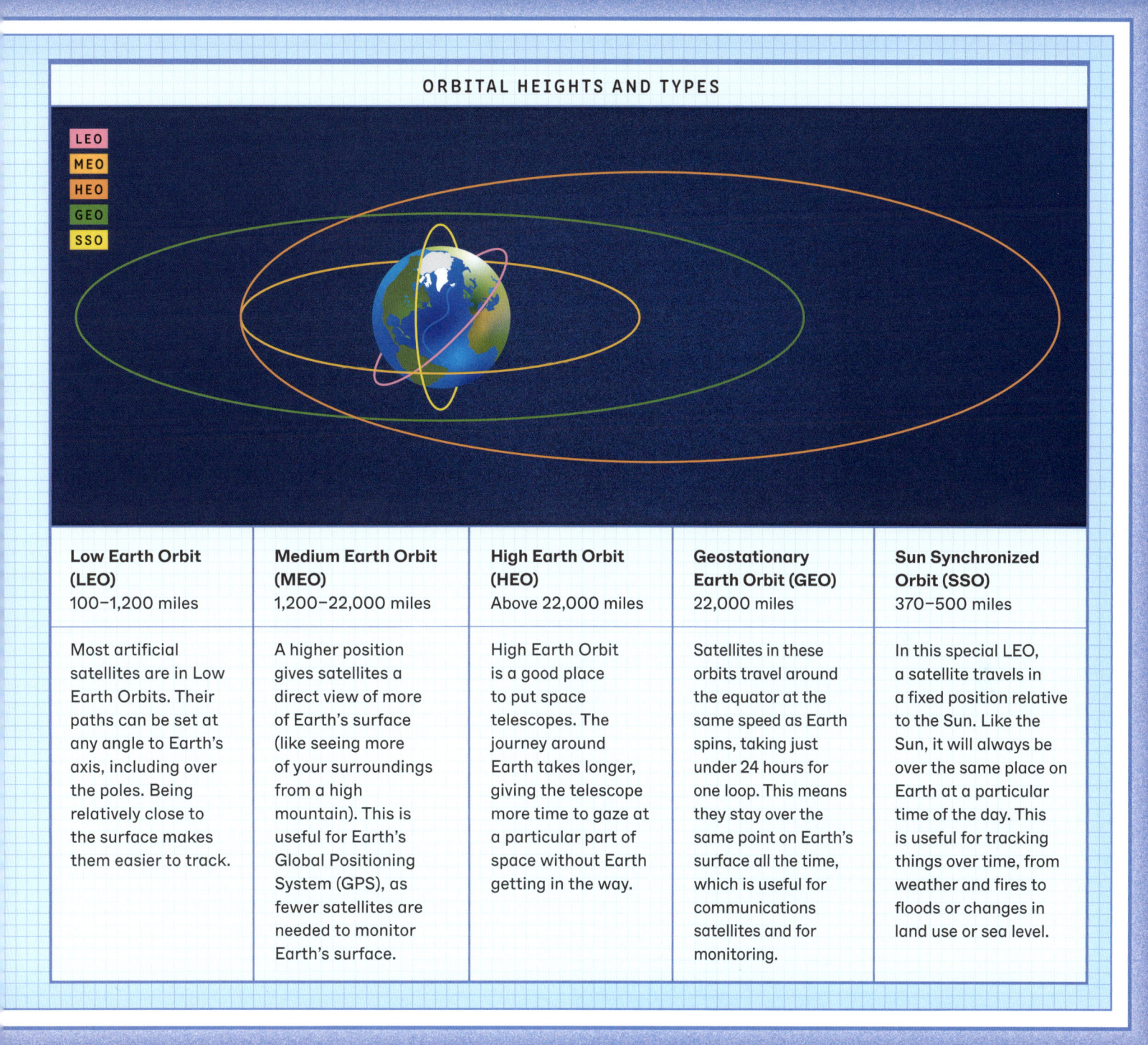

- LEO
- MEO
- HEO
- GEO
- SSO

Low Earth Orbit (LEO) 100–1,200 miles	**Medium Earth Orbit (MEO)** 1,200–22,000 miles	**High Earth Orbit (HEO)** Above 22,000 miles	**Geostationary Earth Orbit (GEO)** 22,000 miles	**Sun Synchronized Orbit (SSO)** 370–500 miles
Most artificial satellites are in Low Earth Orbits. Their paths can be set at any angle to Earth's axis, including over the poles. Being relatively close to the surface makes them easier to track.	A higher position gives satellites a direct view of more of Earth's surface (like seeing more of your surroundings from a high mountain). This is useful for Earth's Global Positioning System (GPS), as fewer satellites are needed to monitor Earth's surface.	High Earth Orbit is a good place to put space telescopes. The journey around Earth takes longer, giving the telescope more time to gaze at a particular part of space without Earth getting in the way.	Satellites in these orbits travel around the equator at the same speed as Earth spins, taking just under 24 hours for one loop. This means they stay over the same point on Earth's surface all the time, which is useful for communications satellites and for monitoring.	In this special LEO, a satellite travels in a fixed position relative to the Sun. Like the Sun, it will always be over the same place on Earth at a particular time of the day. This is useful for tracking things over time, from weather and fires to floods or changes in land use or sea level.

EARTH'S ARTIFICIAL SATELLITES

NUMBER

IN 2020, THE NUMBER OF SATELLITES LAUNCHED IN A YEAR PASSED THE 1,000 MARK FOR THE FIRST TIME.

MORE THAN 10,000 HUMAN-MADE SATELLITES ORBIT EARTH. MANY ARE THERE TO OBSERVE OUR PLANET FROM SPACE, HELPING US UNDERSTAND FEATURES THAT ARE HARD TO SEE FROM THE GROUND.

ALL ABOUT

Humans have been exploring Earth's surface for at least 300,000 years, but only in the last century have we gained the ability to look down on our planet from space. This view has helped us discover features of the land, oceans, and atmosphere that are hard to see or study from the surface.

Eyes in the sky are a particularly powerful way to explore Earth's enormous oceans. Satellites with powerful cameras can detect underwater volcanoes, pollution, and illegal fishing. Instruments can also monitor the health of the ocean, taking the temperature of seawater on a huge scale and measuring how its chemistry is changing.

From high in the atmosphere, satellites can monitor cloud formation, helping with day-to-day weather forecasting. They can watch storms and help predict extreme weather so people can get to safety. Information collected by satellites is also vital for understanding longer-term climate change.

Satellites give us a better view of the land beneath the weather, too. They can monitor the size of ice sheets and glaciers and take the temperature of overheated cities. They can track wildfires and watch forests change over time.

Satellites haven't only changed the way we collect scientific data. They have changed the way that we live. Modern communications, entertainment, and navigation all rely on signals beamed to and from satellites in orbit.

KEY FACTS

- More than 10,000 active satellites are in orbit around Earth.
- Most are in Low Earth Orbits, with more than 6,000 between 300 and 370 miles from the ground.
- By 2030, there could be more than 60,000 active satellites in space.

TEMPERATURE

☼ 257°F (in LEO)
❄ -85°F (in LEO)

NAMED AFTER

Artificial objects in space are identified with a unique code, assigned by the International Science Council's Committee on Space Research (COSPAR).

ELLIPTICAL ORBITS

None of the planets in our solar system move around the Sun on a perfectly round path. Instead their orbits are elliptical, which means they are shaped like stretched ovals. The Moon's path around Earth is also elliptical. This means that the distance between Earth and the Moon is constantly changing. The point in the Moon's orbit where it is farthest from Earth is known as its apogee. Its perigee is the point where it is closest.

Artificial satellites may be put into elliptical orbits around Earth, too. One example is a transfer orbit. A rocket carries a satellite into Low Earth Orbit. When it reaches apogee, a small boost of power from a built-in engine helps it skip into a higher orbit. The launch vehicle doesn't need to travel all the way to the higher orbit, saving energy overall.

★ EXPLORE A SPACE STATION ON PAGE 60 ★

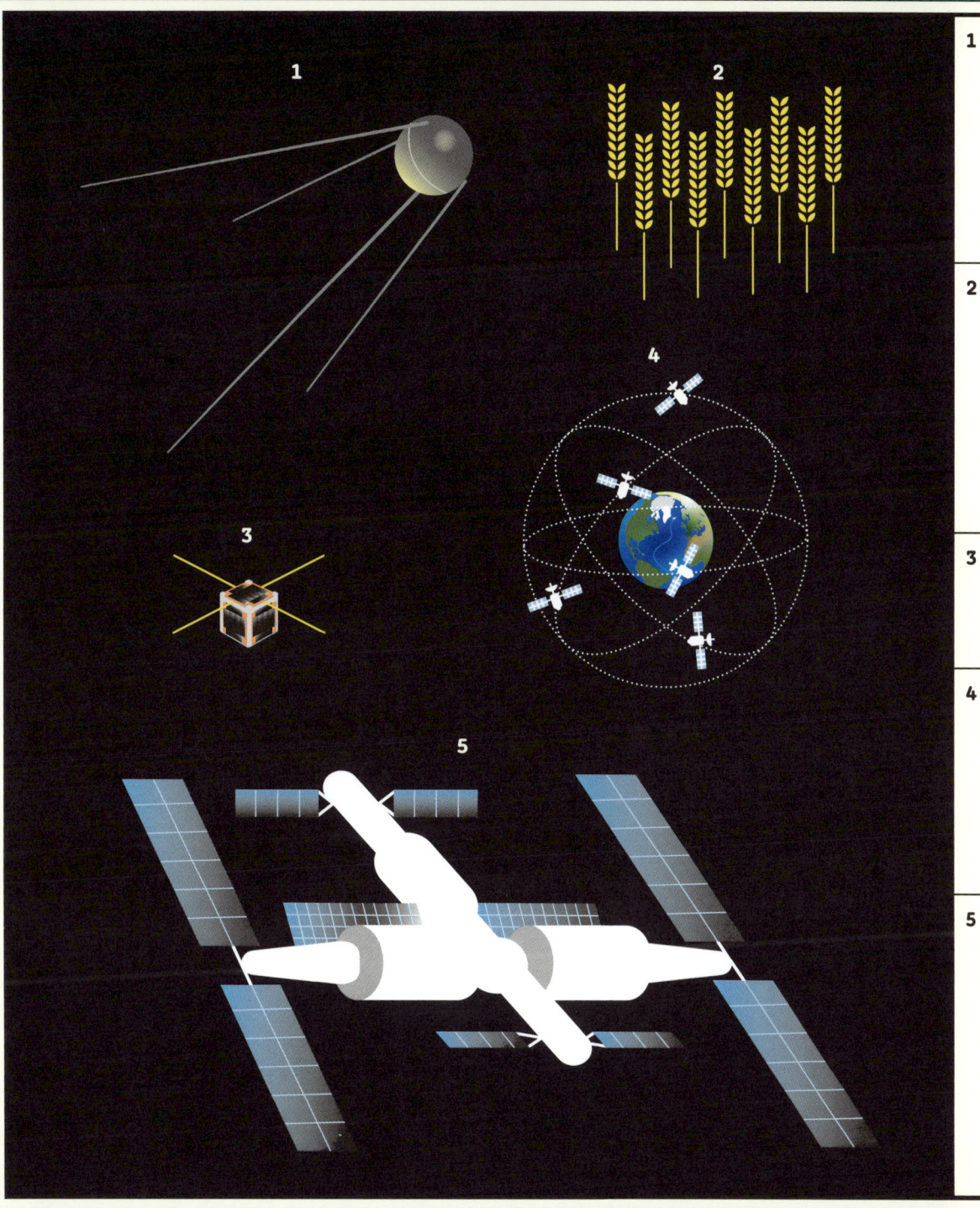

#		
1	**SPUTNIK 1**	Sputnik 1 (USSR) was the first satellite to orbit Earth. Twice the size of a basketball, it had long antennas to beam radio signals back to Earth. Sputnik 1 orbited Earth for three months, traveling 43 million miles, before falling out of orbit and burning up in our atmosphere.
2	**HEALTH CHECK**	ESA's CHIME satellites will carry powerful instruments to "taste" soil from many thousands of miles away. The data will be radioed back to Earth to help scientists monitor how healthy that particular soil is, and how fertilizers, pesticides, and water are being used. This will help to safeguard food production for a growing world population.
3	**SMALLER SATELLITES**	Most satellites launched today are not bus-sized space telescopes, but nanosatellites small enough to hold in your hand.
4	**SATELLITE CONSTELLATIONS**	As satellites get smaller and cheaper to launch, commercial companies have begun launching constellations of tens, hundreds, or thousands of small satellites. These satellites then work together to form communications networks.
5	**SPACE STATIONS**	The largest human-made satellites are space stations, with room for crews of scientists to live and work. At present, there are two permanent space stations in Low Earth Orbit—China's Tiangong space station (CNSA) and the International Space Station (ISS).

SPACE TELESCOPES

THANKS TO OUR PROTECTIVE ATMOSPHERE, GROUND-BASED TELESCOPES CAN ONLY DETECT A SMALL PROPORTION OF THE LIGHT STREAMING TOWARD EARTH. THE ABILITY TO LAUNCH TELESCOPES ABOVE EARTH'S ATMOSPHERE SOLVED THIS PROBLEM, TOTALLY CHANGING OUR VIEW OF THE UNIVERSE.

By night Earth's atmosphere looks completely transparent, but only because it lets **visible light** through—the kind of light detected by our eyes. Stars and other space objects also release types of light energy we can't see (see page 138). These include **infrared** and ultraviolet (UV) light, some of which also make their way through the atmosphere.

Around half of the sunlight reaching Earth's surface is infrared light, also known as heat. Invisible to us, it is what warms our skin on a sunny day. Just over 8 percent of the sunlight reaching Earth's surface is UV light. We can't detect it, but it can damage our eyes and cause sunburn.

Most of the infrared and UV light from the Sun and other stars is absorbed or reflected by Earth's atmosphere long before it can reach the surface. The atmosphere filters out more dangerous kinds of light energy altogether, including **X-rays** and **gamma rays**.

This protective blanket around our planet is good news for living things, but it limits what ground-based telescopes can see. For a long time, the only space objects visible to astronomers were those that gave out or reflected lots of visible light, infrared light, or radio waves.

Rockets changed this, allowing astronomers to carry telescopes and light detectors above Earth's atmosphere, to see the entire spectrum of light streaming toward Earth. We discovered new objects, and gained new understanding of familiar objects.

MOTHER HUBBLE

American astronomer Nancy Grace Roman was NASA's first Chief of Astronomy. In this role, she secured funding for Earth's most famous telescope, the Hubble Space Telescope. One of Hubble's most famous discoveries was dark energy, and a new space observatory to study dark energy has been named in Nancy's honor. The Roman Space Telescope is due to launch in the late 2020s.

HUBBLE SPACE TELESCOPE

Hubble (NASA and ESA) was the world's first optical space telescope. It was launched into orbit around Earth in 1990, and is expected to keep operating until at least the 2030s.

Hubble detects visible light, as well as some infrared and UV light. Because this light has not traveled through hundreds of miles of air, the pictures are much sharper and more detailed than any that could be taken on Earth.

Hubble's 8-foot primary mirror can gather 40,000 times more light than our eyes. The 1-foot secondary mirror focuses the light through a hole in the primary mirror and on to Hubble's cameras and other scientific instruments.

Hubble gave us a new view of the universe, capturing incredible images of almost every kind of space object, from star-forming nebulae and planet-forming discs around new stars (see page 142), to supernovae and distant galaxies.

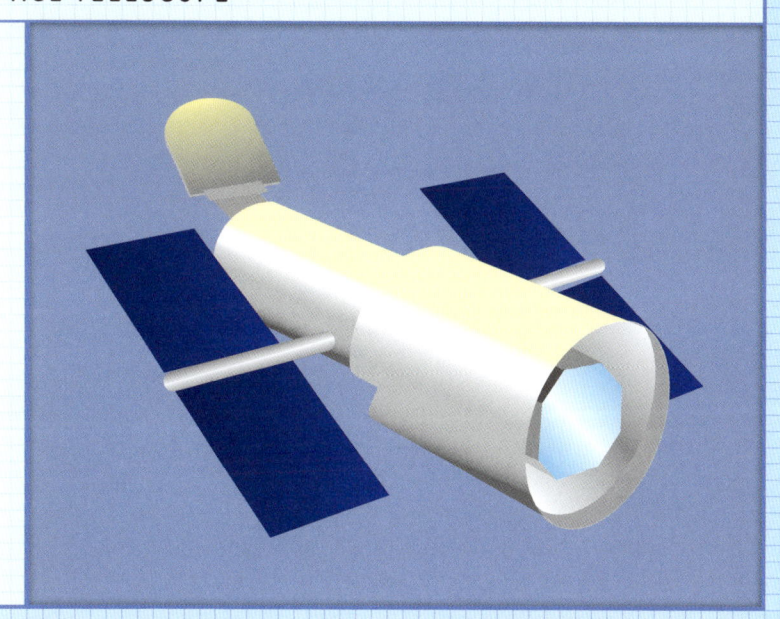

SUPER HOT

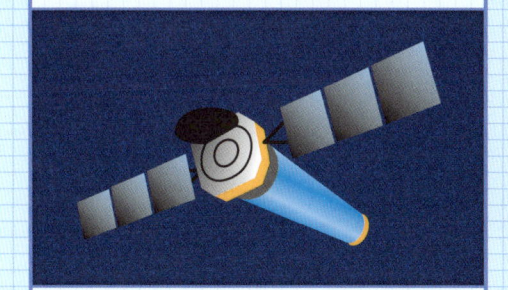

X-rays are some of the most high-energy light waves, released by extremely hot objects in space. The Chandra X-ray Observatory has helped astronomers to see exploding stars, galaxy clusters and matter swirling into black holes.

SUN WATCH

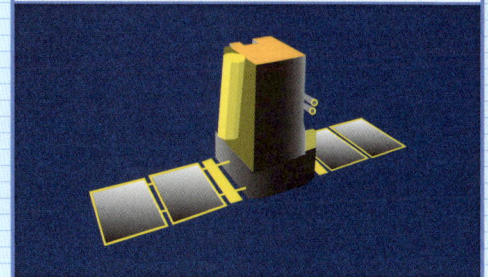

ESA's Solar and Heliospheric Observatory (SOHO) has spent more than 25 years staring at the Sun. Its spectacular pictures have helped scientists investigate our nearest star inside out, and predict solar storms.

IN DEMAND

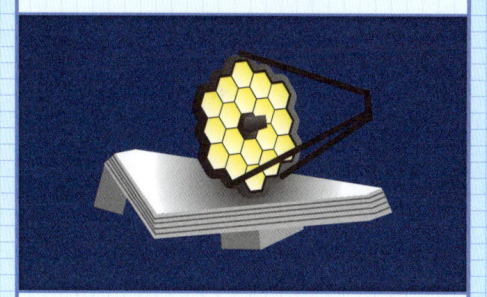

The Webb Space Telescope is the world's most powerful. Scientists from around the world compete for time with it, though only around one in nine proposals is successful. Read about its extraordinary powers on page 144.

LIFE IN SPACE

FROZEN, AIRLESS, AND TEEMING WITH COSMIC **RADIATION**, SPACE IS A DEADLY ENVIRONMENT FOR ALMOST ALL LIVING THINGS. HOWEVER, TECHNOLOGY HAS HELPED HUNDREDS OF HUMANS (AND A WIDE RANGE OF OTHER CREATURES) TO SPEND TIME IN NEAR-EARTH SPACE, SOME INVITED, SOME NOT.

ALL ABOUT

Robotic space probes have ferried an amazing assortment of instruments across the solar system, beaming back treasure troves of data and even hauling back samples of rock. However, nothing beats the insight that comes from exploring a place in person.

Just a few years after the first satellites were launched into orbit, living things began spending time in space too. However, these top pilots weren't the first astronauts and cosmonauts (the name for an astronaut from the Russian-speaking world). The first earthlings in space were fruit flies, passengers on a rocket that soared just over 60 miles above Earth's surface. Back on the ground, scientists studied the flies carefully and found that they had not been harmed by cosmic radiation. For the next 14 years, all kinds of other animals were sent into space to check that space travel would be safe for humans, before the first human spaceflight in 1961.

Ten years later, the world's first space station, Salyut 1 (USSR), was launched—a base for humans to live and carry out scientific research in space. Since then, 12 space stations have been launched into Low Earth Orbit. The ISS (see page 60) is the largest and longest lasting. Human visitors have been joined by a host of other creatures involved in scientific research, from frogs and fish to wasps, spiders, and ants. Today, mice are the main mammals making the trip and have even been successfully bred in space.

EXPLORATION TIMELINE

1947	Fruit flies launched aboard a V2 rocket become the first animals in space.
1957	A dog named Laika becomes the first animal in orbit, aboard Sputnik 2.
1960	Dogs named Strelka and Belka became the first animals returned safely to Earth from orbit, aboard Sputnik 5.
1961	Yuri Gagarin is the first human in space, aboard Vostok 1.
1968	Zond 5 carries living things around the Moon for the first time, including tortoises, flies, mealworms, plants, and bacteria.
1968	Frank Borman, Jim Lovell, and Bill Anders are the first humans to fly around the Moon, aboard Apollo 8.
1969	Neil Armstrong is the first human to walk on the Moon's surface, on the Apollo 11 mission.

ARE WE THERE YET?

- A human officially becomes an astronaut when they cross the Kármán line, an imaginary boundary 60 miles above Earth's surface.
- A car traveling at 60 mph would take an hour to get there. Today's crewed missions take just 2 to 3 minutes!

HELPING HUMANS

Space missions involving animals have helped scientists find out more about the effects of space travel on living things, and how to make it as safe as possible for human astronauts.

★ COULD LIFE ALREADY EXIST ELSEWHERE IN OUR SOLAR SYSTEM? JOIN THE HUNT ON PAGE 98 ★

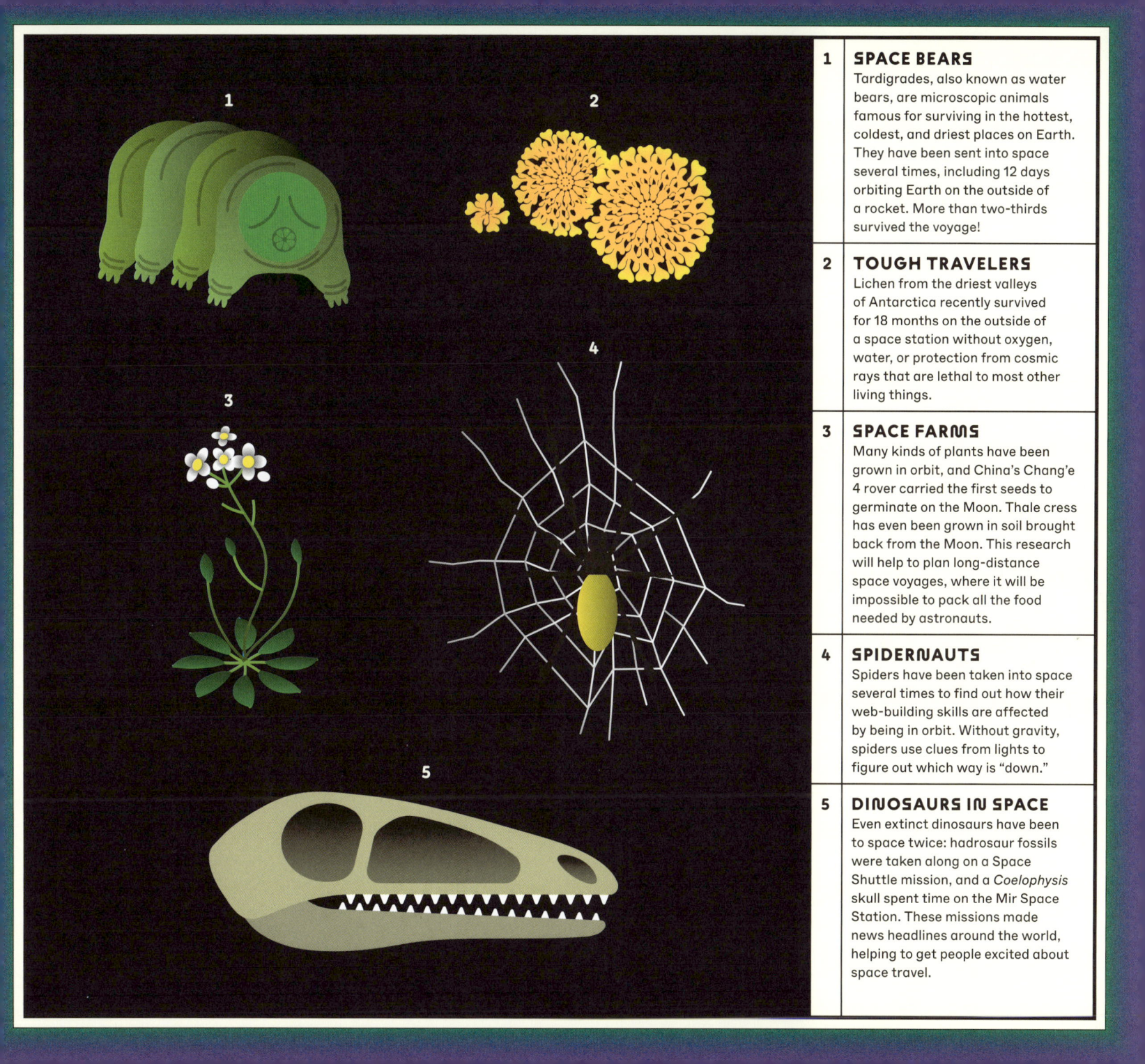

#	
1	**SPACE BEARS** Tardigrades, also known as water bears, are microscopic animals famous for surviving in the hottest, coldest, and driest places on Earth. They have been sent into space several times, including 12 days orbiting Earth on the outside of a rocket. More than two-thirds survived the voyage!
2	**TOUGH TRAVELERS** Lichen from the driest valleys of Antarctica recently survived for 18 months on the outside of a space station without oxygen, water, or protection from cosmic rays that are lethal to most other living things.
3	**SPACE FARMS** Many kinds of plants have been grown in orbit, and China's Chang'e 4 rover carried the first seeds to germinate on the Moon. Thale cress has even been grown in soil brought back from the Moon. This research will help to plan long-distance space voyages, where it will be impossible to pack all the food needed by astronauts.
4	**SPIDERNAUTS** Spiders have been taken into space several times to find out how their web-building skills are affected by being in orbit. Without gravity, spiders use clues from lights to figure out which way is "down."
5	**DINOSAURS IN SPACE** Even extinct dinosaurs have been to space twice: hadrosaur fossils were taken along on a Space Shuttle mission, and a *Coelophysis* skull spent time on the Mir Space Station. These missions made news headlines around the world, helping to get people excited about space travel.

THE INTERNATIONAL SPACE STATION

THE INTERNATIONAL SPACE STATION (ISS) IS THE LARGEST SPACECRAFT EVER BUILT. IT HAS BEEN A BASE IN SPACE FOR HUNDREDS OF ASTRONAUTS FROM MORE THAN 20 NATIONS.

Look up at dawn or dusk, and you may spot a tiny light speeding across the sky, higher than any airplane and faster than any planet. The ISS orbits Earth 250 miles above our heads, completing a lap of the globe every 90 minutes. At times, the glint of sunlight reflected from its giant solar arrays makes it the sky's third brightest object.

For a quarter of a century, the ISS has been humans' main base in space, hosting up to seven permanent crew at a time. It is not the first space station, nor the only one orbiting right now, but it is celebrated as an example of what international teamwork can achieve. The ISS was assembled by five space agencies (NASA, Roscosmos, ESA, JAXA, and CSA). Astronauts and cosmonauts representing more than 20 countries have visited. Privately funded missions sometimes dock too, carrying paying visitors or commercial modules.

The ISS was built with the help of 36 Space Shuttle flights (NASA). When this program finished in 2011, Soyuz spacecraft (Roscosmos) became the main way to get to the ISS. Since 2020, astronauts have also made the journey in commercial spacecraft. Supplies and scientific equipment are hauled up separately on uncrewed cargo craft, which also carry waste away to burn up in Earth's atmosphere.

Astronauts and cosmonauts typically live on the ISS for six months, carrying out scientific experiments on behalf of teams on Earth. They also carry out repairs and updates—such as installing more powerful roll-out solar arrays. Astronauts are part of research themselves, helping us understand the effects of spending time in space. These findings will help plan missions to the Moon and Mars.

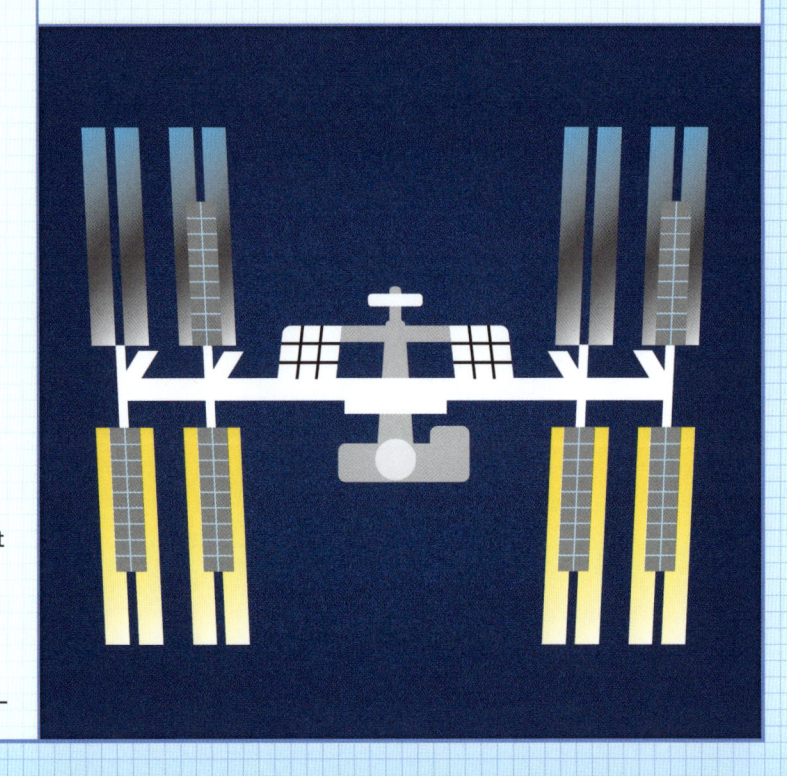

KEY FACTS

- Crew: Up to seven permanent crew.
- Construction began: 1998.
- Continuous occupation began: November 2000.
- Fully operational: May 2009.
- Visiting astronauts: More than 280.
- **Orbital period**: 90 to 93 min.
- Orbital speed: 17,000 mi/h.
- Orbital height: Around 250 miles.
- Total length of pressurized modules: 220 feet.
- Total length: 357 feet.
- Wingspan of original solar arrays: 240 feet.
- Mass: More than 924,000 lbs.

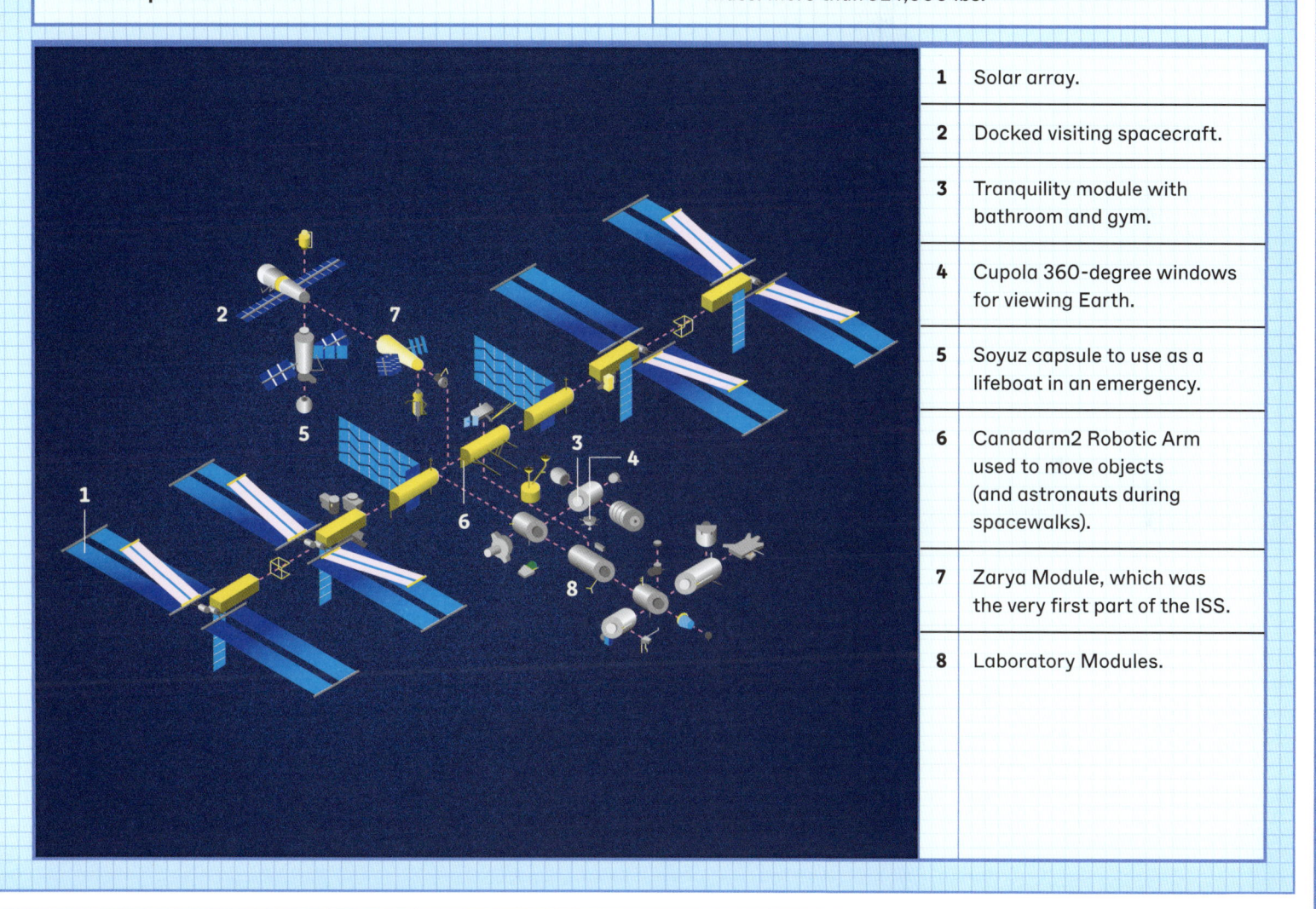

1	Solar array.
2	Docked visiting spacecraft.
3	Tranquility module with bathroom and gym.
4	Cupola 360-degree windows for viewing Earth.
5	Soyuz capsule to use as a lifeboat in an emergency.
6	Canadarm2 Robotic Arm used to move objects (and astronauts during spacewalks).
7	Zarya Module, which was the very first part of the ISS.
8	Laboratory Modules.

SPACE DEBRIS

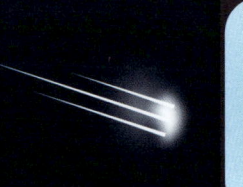

OVER THE LAST 65 YEARS, HUMANS HAVE MADE NEAR-EARTH SPACE EVEN MORE DANGEROUS. MILLIONS OF PIECES OF SPACE JUNK FROM OLD MISSIONS AND ACCIDENTAL COLLISIONS NOW ORBIT OUR PLANET. TRAVELING AT HIGH SPEED, THEY CAN POSE A MAJOR HAZARD FOR NEW MISSIONS.

ALL ABOUT

Like the surface of our planet, near-Earth space is littered with human-made objects that are no longer being used. Space debris includes: large objects, such as expired satellites and burned-out rocket stages; medium-sized objects, from telescope lens covers to shrapnel created in explosions; and tens of millions of tiny objects, such as flecks of paint chipped off spacecraft.

At supersonic speeds, even a fleck of paint can be very dangerous. A particle just 0.5 in wide orbiting at 22,000 mi/h collides with the same energy as a car crashing at 25 mph. In 2016, a piece of space debris just an eighth of an inch wide punched a 15-in hole in ESA's Sentinel 2 satellite.

With luck, spacecraft can survive these small strikes. But a collision with a larger piece of debris is game over. For this reason, pieces of space debris measuring more than 4 in are tracked using ground-based telescopes, radar, and sensors in space. More than 35,000 have been recorded so far. If a major collision is predicted, rocket boosters can be used to nudge an orbiting space station or satellite into a safer orbit.

Every year, hundreds more satellites and microsatellites are launched. Space junk is not just a problem for these satellites. Spacecraft and crewed missions must pass through near-Earth space on their way to other destinations. To try and protect near-Earth space for the future, all the major space agencies have issued guidelines to reduce or even eliminate space junk.

Newer satellites are being designed with sustainability in mind, but more active measures will be needed to remove older objects from orbit. It will be difficult and expensive to clean up space, but it's important if space travel is to continue in the future.

EXPLORATION TIMELINE

1957 A spent stage of the rocket that launched Sputnik 1 into orbit is the first piece of space debris.

1961 Part of a Thor-Ablestar launch vehicle explodes in space, creating more than 200 fragments large enough to track.

1985 The Solwind P78-1 satellite is destroyed in a test of an anti-satellite missile, creating a cloud of thousands of pieces of debris.

2007 FengYun-1C weather satellite is destroyed on purpose, adding more than 2,300 trackable fragments into orbit.

2009 Two satellites—Iridium-33 and Kosmos2251—accidentally collide for the first time.

2016 A piece of space debris punches a 15-in hole in the solar panel of the Sentinel 2 satellite.

2023 ESA completes first assisted reentry of a dead satellite.

KEY FACTS

- More than 14,000 tons of material currently orbits Earth, including around 3,000 inactive satellites.
- More than 35,000 pieces of orbital debris larger than 4 in are being tracked.
- ESA estimates that there are more than 130 million pieces of orbital debris smaller than 4 in.

SUSTAINABLE SPACE

New satellites are designed with sustainability in mind—such as tying lens caps to cameras, and building in fuel and procedures for deorbiting. New ideas are being tested to collect and de-orbit older objects. These include giant nets, harpoons, and even laser beams that heat tiny pieces of debris so much they evaporate!

FIND OUT WHY SO MANY SATELLITES HAVE BEEN PUT INTO ORBIT ON PAGE 54

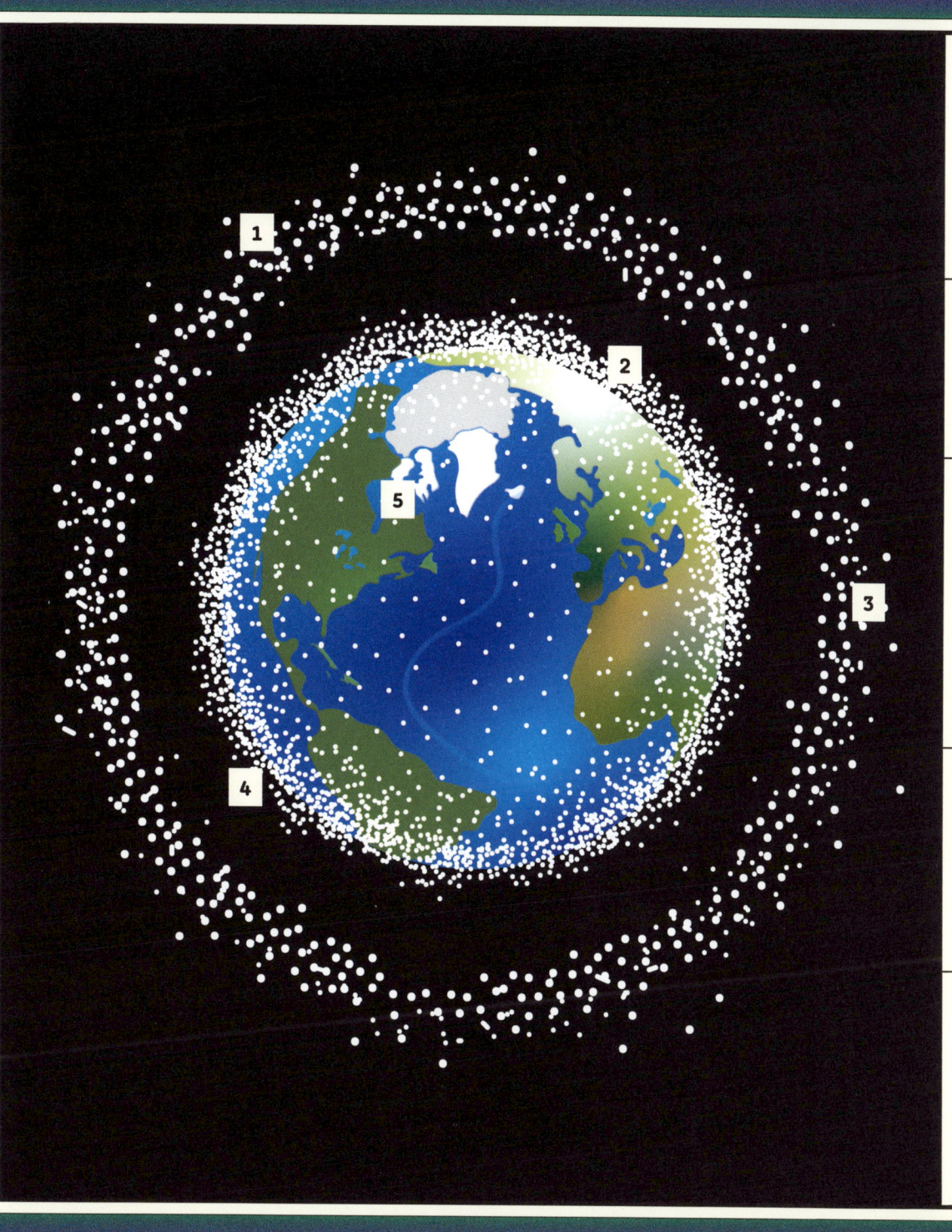

#		
1	**LITTER HIGHWAY**	More than half of all space debris is less than 1,200 miles from Earth's surface. Objects less than 370 miles high will slow and fall out of orbit within a few years. Above this, it can take hundreds or even thousands of years for objects to de-orbit naturally.
2	**HIGH SPEED**	Objects in Low Earth Orbit are moving at more than 4 mi/s relative to the ground—much faster than bullets fired from a gun. At this speed, even small objects can do huge damage.
3	**SPACE CRASH**	The consequences of a big collision in orbit were first seen in 2009, when a working communications satellite called Iridium-33 collided with a dead military communications satellite called Kosmos 2251 480 miles above Earth. The crash produced more than 2,000 pieces of space debris bigger than a tennis ball, and thousands of smaller pieces.
4	**DODGING DEBRIS**	As it's home to humans, the ISS has strong shields that protect it from debris up to 0.5 in across. When tracking systems warn that a large piece of debris will come less than a few miles of the ISS, small rockets are used to nudge the space station out of its path.
5	**SHOOTING SATELLITES**	Old satellites and rocket parts fall back to Earth around once a week. While most are burned up and destroyed as they fall through Earth's atmosphere, larger items and tougher components sometimes reach Earth's surface.

REUSABLE SPACECRAFT

ROCKETS AND SPACECRAFT ARE VERY EXPENSIVE TO BUILD AND LAUNCH, ESPECIALLY WHEN CARRYING HUMANS INTO SPACE. JUST 10 YEARS AFTER THE FIRST HUMAN SPACEFLIGHT, ENGINEERS BEGAN DESIGNING REUSABLE SPACECRAFT.

The Space Shuttle System was the world's first reusable space vehicle. Five shuttles were built—each the size of a small airliner—and they carried more than 800 astronauts on 135 missions between 1981 and 2011.

The Space Shuttle System launched vertically like a rocket. Two solid fuel boosters on each side of the external tank provided the main thrust for liftoff. After 2 minutes, the boosters were jettisoned above the ocean. After parachuting down into the ocean, they could be recovered, refurbished, and reused. After spending time in orbit, the orbiter's wings allowed it to glide back down through Earth's atmosphere and land on a long runway at around 250 mi/h, using a parachute to brake.

The Space Shuttle System flew for 30 years, shuttling astronauts, parts, and supplies to and from orbit, building the ISS, launching probes such as Galileo, and deploying the Hubble Space Telescope.

SPACE SHUTTLE SYSTEM

1. Reusable boosters.

2. External fuel tank. This tank was empty after 8.5 minutes, and burned up as it fell back to Earth.

3. Orbiter with two main engines and 44 smaller thrusters. The main engines were used at launch, fed with propellants from the external tank. The smaller thrusters moved the orbiter around in space.

4. Crew cabin for up to 10 astronauts.

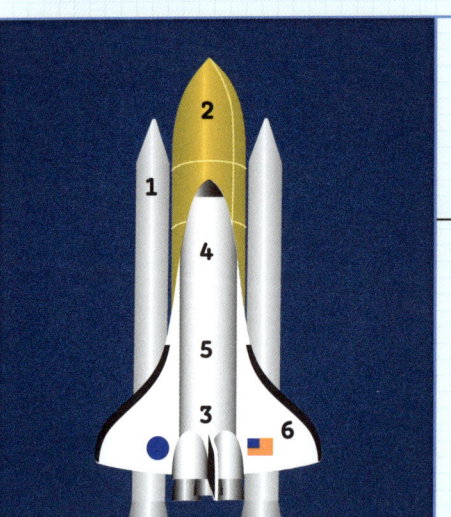

5. Payload bay could carry huge cargoes, and was equipped with a remote manipulator system—a large robot arm for picking up cargo and moving it around in space.

6. 24,000 ceramic tiles protected the shuttle from extreme temperatures caused by friction with the atmosphere on reentry. The tiles were fragile and had to be replaced after each flight, if found to be damaged.

SPACEPLANES

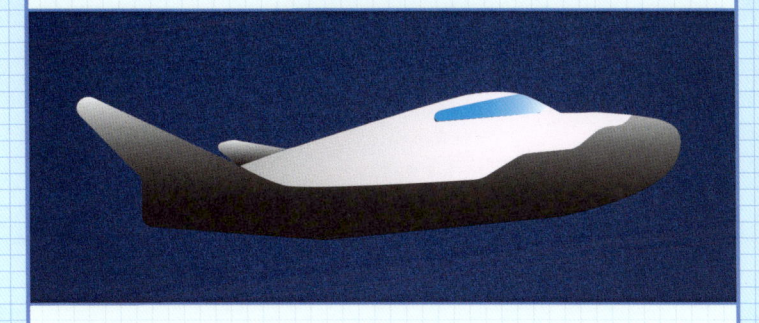

The Dream Chaser (Sierra Space) is a reusable spaceplane that will carry cargo to the ISS. It will be launched into space using a rocket, and its winglets will let it land on a runway when it returns to Earth.

SPACE RIDER

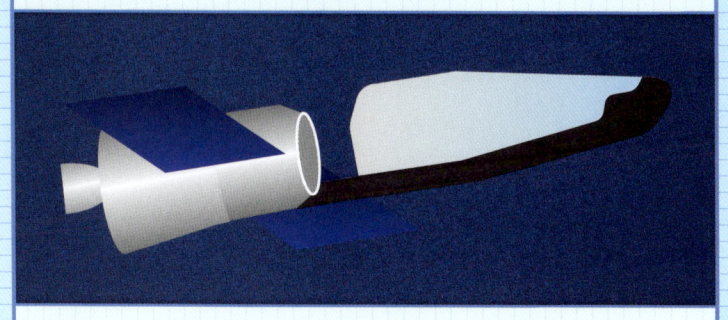

ESA is developing its own reusable space laboratory. After carrying experiments into space and orbiting for around two months, Space Rider will land back on Earth with the help of a parafoil (controllable gliding parachute), ready to be refurbished for the next mission.

REUSABLE ROCKETS

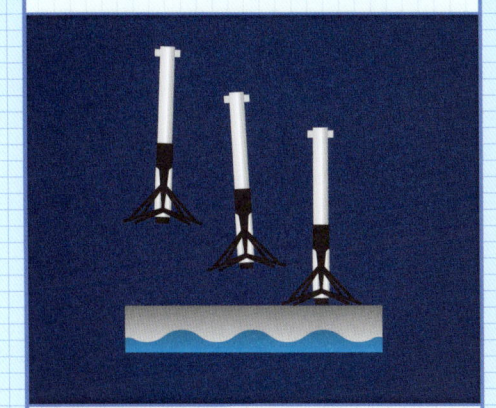

In 2024, fully reusable rockets got a step closer when a Falcon 9 booster (SpaceX) maneuverd itself back to the launchpad to be successfully caught by a pair of mechanical arms.

REUSABLE CAPSULES

The SpaceX Dragon spacecraft was the first private spacecraft to transport humans to the ISS. Six parachutes help it to land safely in the ocean after reentering Earth's atmosphere.

STARLINER

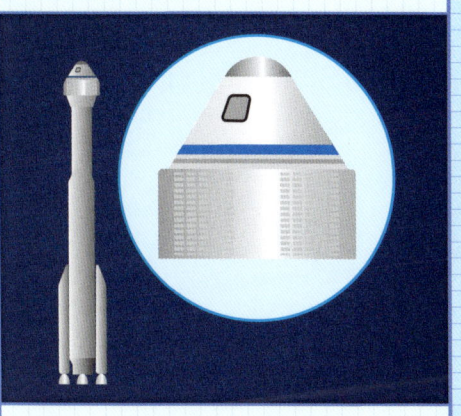

Boeing's CST-100 Starliner is designed to transport astronauts to and from the ISS. Its crew capsule can be reused up to 10 times.

METEORS & METEORITES

CATEGORY	AGE	
METEOROID	FROM 200 MILLION TO 4.6 BILLION YEARS	EXTRATERRESTRIAL ROCKS ARE OFTEN SPOTTED HURTLING THROUGH EARTH'S ATMOSPHERE, AND CAN EVEN BE FOUND ON OUR PLANET ITSELF.

ALL ABOUT

Meteors—better known as "shooting stars"—are thin trails of light that appear suddenly in the night sky and disappear just as quickly. These glowing trails are caused by pieces of rock or dust from outer space plunging through Earth's atmosphere. When these **meteoroids** collide with the atmosphere, both air and rock are heated to tremendous temperatures. Very hot objects glow, and meteors can sometimes be seen from more than 60 miles away. They also emit radio waves, helping scientists to track them.

The smallest meteoroids are grains of dust dislodged from comets as their orbits bring them near to the Sun (see page 124). Their dust trails continue to orbit the Sun. Earth's own path around the Sun takes it in and out of comet dust trails all the time, causing meteor showers in the night sky.

Most meteoroids are destroyed by their journey through the atmosphere. However, medium-sized rocks make it all the way to the ground, where they become known as meteorites. More than 50,000 have been found so far. The largest is the Hoba West meteorite in Namibia, a lump of iron and nickel 9 feet across.

The largest meteorites punch through Earth's atmosphere as if it wasn't there. They are still traveling so fast when they hit the ground that they crater Earth's surface, often destroying themselves in the process.

Meteorite strikes large enough to leave a crater are very rare, but scientists do keep a careful eye on the skies, using computers to track Near-Earth Objects and to predict any close approaches to Earth.

KEY FACTS

- Around 48 tons of meteorites land on Earth daily.
- Meteoroids are traveling around 45,000 mi/h when they enter our planet's atmosphere.
- It takes a meteor 10 to 15 seconds to reach the ground.

TEMPERATURE

3,272 °F (traveling through Earth's atmosphere)

NAMED AFTER

Meteor showers are usually named after a constellation or star that is behind them in the sky. Meteorites are named after the place they are found.

WHAT IS IT MADE OF?

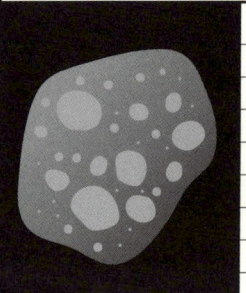

- Meteorites have a black glassy coating, known as a fusion crust.
- Most are stony, with crystals of metallic, silicate, and sulfide minerals, and are rich in nonmetals such as oxygen.
- Iron-rich meteorites like Hoba West are rarer. They are mainly iron, with some nickel and cobalt.

MICROMETEORITES

The tiniest micrometeorites are no bigger than the period at the end of this sentence and are easily mistaken for dust. However, they are often magnetic, and under a microscope it's possible to see their glassy shells.

★ FIND OUT WHAT EARLY CULTURES THOUGHT OF METEORS ON PAGE 32 ★

#		
1	**METEOR SHOWERS**	It's possible to predict when large meteor showers will happen, because we know when Earth's orbit will take it through a stream of particles left behind by a comet. Every August, for example, Earth passes through a stream of meteoroids left behind by comet 109P/Swift-Tuttle, causing the Perseid meteor shower.
2	**FEROCIOUS FIREBALL**	Rarely, a large meteor appears as a huge fireball in the sky and may explode before it hits the ground. In 2013, a tennis court–sized asteroid formed a fireball over Russia then exploded. The shock wave shattered more than 3,600 windows and injured 1,600 people.
3	**LUNAR METEORITES**	Most meteorites found on Earth are chunks of asteroids (see page 86). A few meteorites from the surface of Mars and the Moon have also been found, each one thrown out into space by an earlier meteorite impact.
4	**IRON METEORITES**	Some meteorites are very high in iron and nickel. They are easy to tell apart from Earth rocks, as they are very heavy for their size, magnetic, and often covered in smooth dents formed by swirling, superheated air. They help us understand what the cores of our solar system's rocky planets might be like.
5	**ROCKS ON ICE**	It's easiest to spot meteorites that land on glaciers and ice sheets. Their burned black surface shows up against the white background. Special meteorite-hunting missions in Antarctica have discovered more than 45,000 space rocks so far.

OUR SOLAR SYSTEM

EARTH IS JUST ONE OBJECT AMONG BILLIONS THAT ORBIT OUR NEAREST STAR, THE SUN.

A handful of these objects are planets too, many with orbiting satellites of their own. However, these planets and their moons are vastly outnumbered by smaller objects orbiting the Sun—from rocky asteroids and icy comets, to dwarf planets locked away by the Sun's gravity in places where its light is barely visible.

Many of these objects lie millions of miles from their nearest neighbor. However, they are not simply lonely worlds separated by empty space, but parts of a constantly changing system.

Each solar system object—from the largest planet to the smallest dust grain—interacts with other objects. Giant planets tear moons apart, creating the rings that circle their spherical surfaces. Asteroids collide with planets, delivering new materials, carving out craters, and sending new meteoroids spinning into space. Comets create dust trails that later light up our skies as "shooting stars."

By figuring out the details linking distant objects, astronomers are helping to explain how our solar system formed and how it will continue to change in the future.

MERCURY

CATEGORY	AGE
PLANET	4.5 BILLION YEARS

SMALL BUT SPEEDY, MERCURY'S MYSTERIOUS FEATURES SEEM TO INCLUDE A GIANT METAL CORE. THIS COSMIC PINBALL OF A PLANET HURTLES ROUND THE SUN, COMPLETING FOUR LAPS IN THE TIME IT TAKES EARTH TO ORBIT ONCE.

ALL ABOUT

From Mercury's surface, the Sun looms almost three times larger than it does in Earth's sky. Scorching surface temperatures are made more extreme by Mercury's slow spin through space, stretching each solar day into a six-month ordeal. On the day side of the planet, the ground becomes hot enough to melt lead. But this heat does not stick around for long.

Because Mercury is only slightly larger than Earth's Moon, its gravity is too weak to hold a blanket of gases in its grip. Without an atmosphere, heat is quickly lost to space once the Sun sets, and temperatures plummet by as much as 1,112°F.

No atmosphere also means no safety blanket to slow meteors on a crash course with the planet, and no moving air to reshape the surface. As a result, Mercury is still covered in craters from meteorite impacts dating back billions of years.

Many of these bowls and basins are filled with lava, once flowing freely across the surface, now frozen into solid rock. There are no volcanic eruptions on Mercury today, but there are clues that the planet's humongous metallic core may still be partly molten. Just as on Earth, electric currents generated in a swirling molten metal core seem to the be most likely explanation for Mercury's magnetic field.

KEY FACTS

- A day lasts 59 Earth days.
- A year lasts 88 Earth days.
- No natural satellites.
- Light from the Sun reaches Mercury in 3.2 min.
- Around 18 Mercurys would fit inside Earth.

TEMPERATURE

☼ 806°F
❄ -292°F

NAMED AFTER

Named by the Ancient Romans after their speedy messenger god, Mercury.

WHAT IS IT MADE OF?

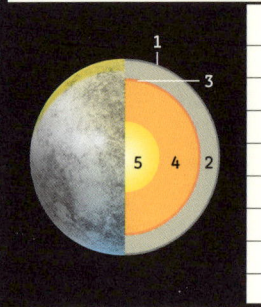

1. Wispy exosphere (outermost and thinnest layer of atmosphere) of atoms knocked off the ground by the solar wind.
2. Thin crust, rich in silicon.
3. Thin mantle.
4. Huge outer core, made of molten metal.
5. Huge inner core, made of solid metals.

PAST, PRESENT, FUTURE

Mercury's gravity is twice as strong as the Moon's, telling us that the planet must have an enormous metallic core for its size. One theory is that Mercury was once much bigger, losing huge chunks of crust and mantle to space in an enormous collision.

★ A MOLTEN CORE ALSO CREATES A MAGNETIC FIELD AROUND EARTH (PAGE 29) ★

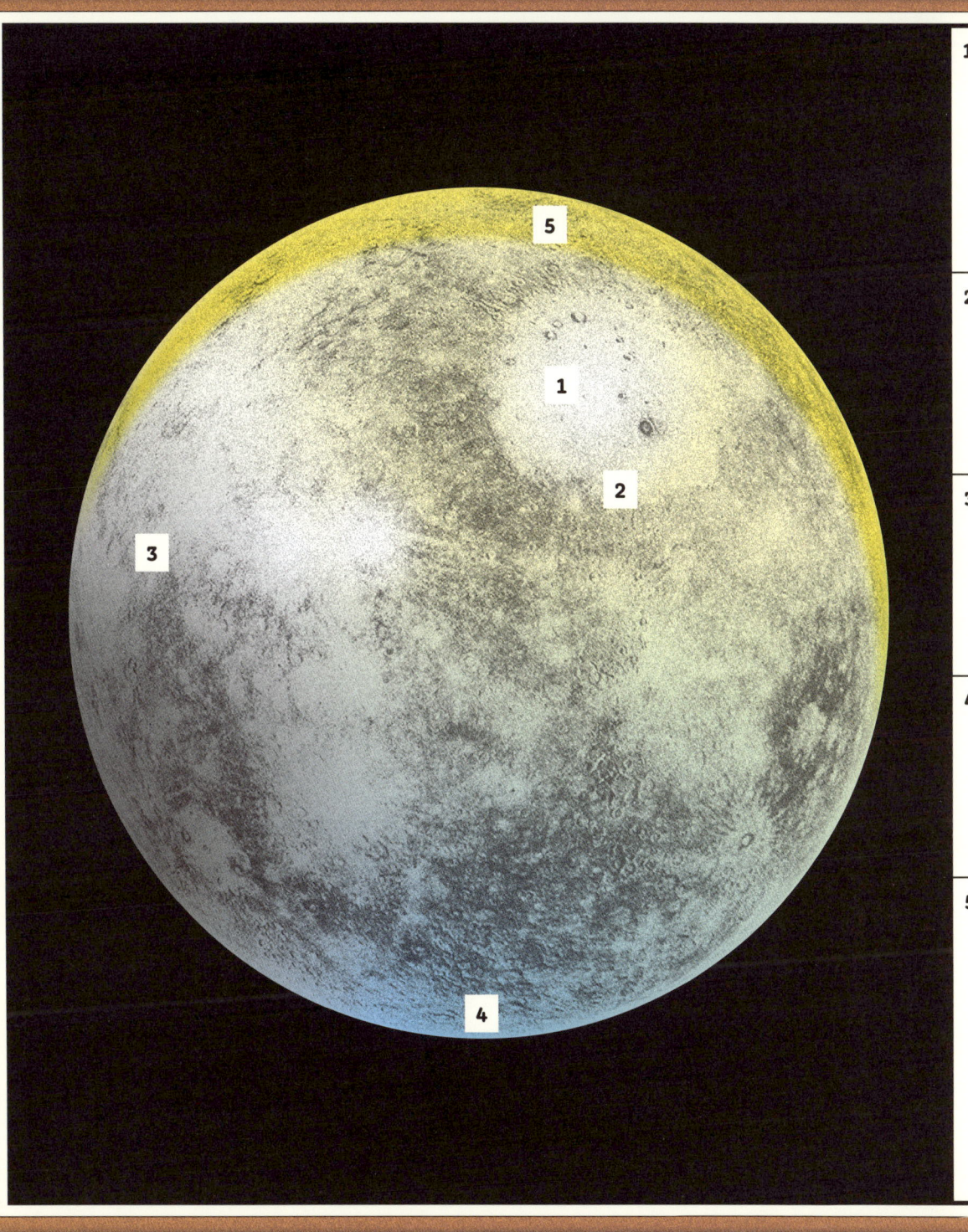

#	
1	**GIANT CRATER** At almost 1,000 miles across, the Caloris Basin is one of the largest meteorite craters in the solar system. The impact—around 3.8 billion years ago—was so powerful that earthquakes traveled all the way around Mercury and shattered the surface on the opposite side.
2	**TOWERING CLIFFS** Stronger gravity on Mercury means that rubble from meteorite impacts isn't thrown as far as it is on the Moon. Instead, the debris piles up around the rims of its craters. The walls of the Caloris Basin are more than 1 mile high.
3	**SHRIVELLED APPLE** Mercury's insides shrank as the planet cooled, causing the crust to crumple and crack, like the skin of a dried-up apple. Long ridges and cliffs crisscross the surface, including Great Valley, which is larger than Earth's Grand Canyon.
4	**ICY BOTTOM** Mercury is barely tilted at all on its axis, which means its poles are never angled toward the Sun. This also means that sunlight never reaches the bottom of deep craters at the poles, where signs of frozen water have been detected.
5	**DOUBLE SUNRISE** With a slower rotation than Earth, Mercury only spins three times on its axis for every two trips around the Sun. This creates some bizarre effects (at least, to us), including two sunrises at the start of each Mercury day!

ROBOTIC LANDERS

LANDERS ARE SPACECRAFT DESIGNED TO TOUCH DOWN ON THE SURFACE OF PLANETS, MOONS, AND OTHER SPACE OBJECTS. MOST ARE ROBOTIC, MEANING THEY WORK AUTONOMOUSLY, RATHER THAN BEING CONTROLLED FROM EARTH.

Venera 7 (USSR) was the first spacecraft to successfully land on another planet. It touched down on Venus in 1970, sending back data for 23 minutes before it was destroyed by the extreme conditions. The data it did manage to send back showed a temperature of 887°F and a crushing atmospheric pressure 92 times greater than the air pressure at Earth's surface!

Every lander must be designed for the particular conditions it will encounter. Venera missions 3, 4, 5, and 6 tried to land on Venus, but were destroyed by high pressures and temperatures before they could reach the ground. This helped engineers to improve the design for Venera 7. After Venera 7's success, another seven Venera probes landed on Venus, as well as two Pioneer Venus probes (NASA) and two Vega probes (USSR).

Landers can do things that orbiting probes cannot, including examining rock and soil samples, detecting seismic vibrations, photographing landscapes, and "sniffing" the atmosphere at the surface. The information collected by landers has revolutionized our understanding of the planets, moons, comets, and asteroids of our solar system.

VENERA 7

1. Spherical lander probe, in a sealed titanium shell with no seams or holes.
2. Weight: 1,080 lbs.
3. Around 37 miles above the ground, a hatch was blown in the titanium shell using explosives, and a small parachute was deployed for a speedy descent through Venus's thick atmosphere.
4. Tools inside included a thermometer for measuring temperatures, a barometer for measuring pressure, and a radio antenna to transmit data back to Earth.
5. The rest of the spacecraft acted as a "bus" that carried the lander probe to Venus.

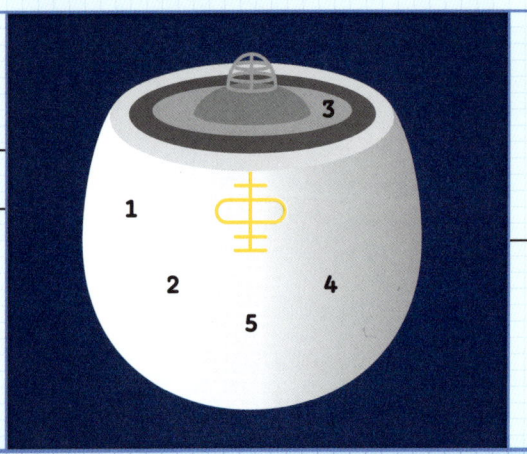

LUNAR LANDERS

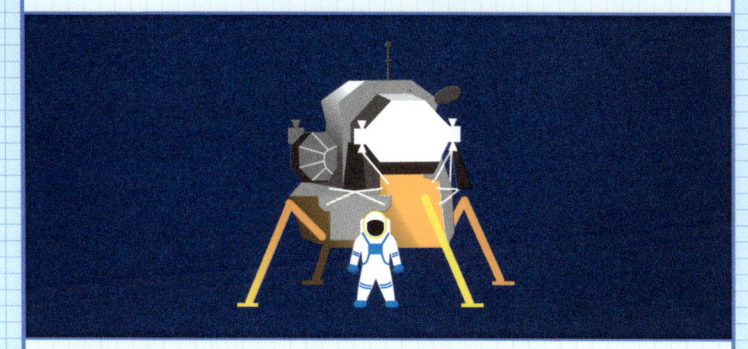

Landing on the Moon poses completely different challenges to landing on Venus. The lack of atmosphere means parachutes cannot be used to slow a lander down as it falls to the surface. Rockets must be used instead. More than 25 landers have successfully touched down on the Moon's surface. Six of these were crewed Eagle landers.

MARS LANDERS

More than 10 robotic landers have successfully touched down on Mars. Mars InSight (NASA) carried instruments to detect marsquakes, to help scientists study the deep interior of the planet. Most famous, though, are the Mars missions that have deployed robotic rovers and even a tiny helicopter (see page 85).

LANDING ON OTHER MOONS

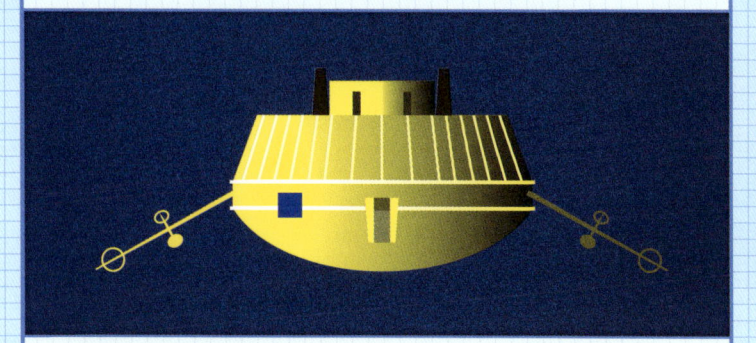

In 2005, Cassini's Huygens probe landed on the surface of Saturn's moon Titan (see page 104). It was the first spacecraft to land on a surface in the outer solar system, and the most distant lander deployed so far. It sent back pictures of the icy, pebble-strewn "sand" on the surface.

CRASH LANDINGS

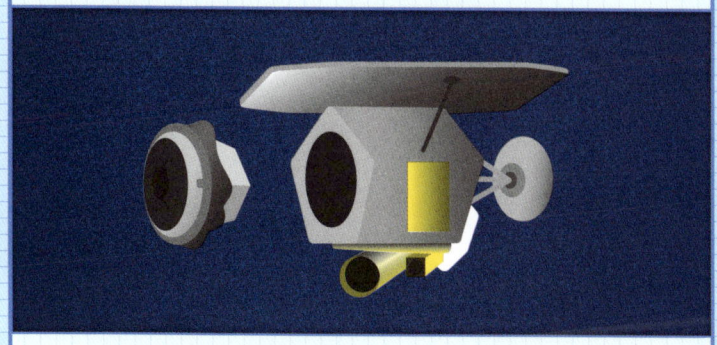

Impactors are objects designed to crash into the surface of a space object, rather than landing gently. They are used to study gas planets without a hard surface to land on. The space probe Deep Impact (NASA) released a small impactor which slammed into the comet Tempel 1 (see page 124).

EXPLORING MERCURY

MERCURY'S SMALL SIZE AND ITS POSITION NEAREST THE SUN MAKE IT INCREDIBLY HARD TO VISIT, OR EVEN PEER AT FROM A DISTANCE. THIS EXPLAINS WHY IT IS CURRENTLY THE LEAST EXPLORED PLANET IN THE SOLAR SYSTEM.

ALL ABOUT

Imagine you're at one end of a football pitch, watching a friend run around the goalposts at the other end. It would be impossible to look at your friend without seeing the goal too. For space scientists, the friend is Mercury and the goal is the Sun. Peering at the solar system's innermost planet necessarily means staring directly at a star.

By day, the Sun's brightness drowns out the tiny pinprick of light reflected from Mercury's surface. By night, both the Sun and Mercury are hidden on the other side of Earth. The only chance to glimpse Mercury with your eyes (or through a telescope) comes just before sunrise or just after sunset, when the Sun is below the horizon and its dazzling light appears dimmed.

Mercury's proximity to the Sun makes it difficult to send space probes to orbit the planet too. As spacecraft approach Mercury, the Sun's enormously strong gravity speeds them up, just when they should be slowing down to be captured by Mercury's gravity. Carrying enough fuel to brake is impossible. Instead, orbiters must take a long and complicated route, flying past Earth, Venus, and Mercury multiple times and using the gravity of these planets to slow the spacecraft a little each time. It's why missions to Mercury and Jupiter take around the same time, even though Mercury is typically ten times closer.

EXPLORATION TIMELINE

Anc.	Discovered and named in ancient times (visible with the naked eye at dawn and sunset).
1631	First viewed through a telescope by Galileo Galilei and Thomas Harriot.
1974	Mariner 10 is the first flyby probe to visit Mercury.
2011	MESSENGER becomes Mercury's first orbital probe, mapping the entire planet between 2011 and 2015.
2015	MESSENGER crashes into Mercury at the end of its mission.
2018	BepiColombo launches and begins its journey to Mercury.

ARE WE THERE YET?

- Mariner 10 took just 147 days to reach Mercury on its flyby.
- MESSENGER and BepiColombo took the seven-year scenic route, using flybys of other planets to ensure they approached Mercury slowly enough to enter its orbit.

HELPING HUMANS

About 13 times every century, Mercury passes between Earth and the Sun. Watching the planet cross the Sun's disc has helped scientists learn how to detect planets orbiting distant stars.

Tracking Mercury's path around the Sun also helped to prove Einstein's ideas about gravity (see page 30).

★ IN FIVE BILLION YEARS, MERCURY FACES A FIERY FATE (PAGE 149) ★

#	
1	**MARINER 10** Mariner 10 (NASA) was the first spacecraft sent to Mercury, flying by three times and sending back thousands of pictures of its cratered surface.
2	**MESSENGER** Thirty years passed before a probe was sent to orbit Mercury. MESSENGER (NASA) completed more than 4,000 orbits over four years, gathering enough information to map the entire surface. MESSENGER also discovered that deep craters at Mercury's north pole appear to contain water ice.
3	**HIDDEN TAIL** Micrometeorites and solar "tornadoes" are constantly knocking atoms off Mercury's surface. MESSENGER captured images of a wispy "tail" of atoms being pushed away from the planet by the solar wind. The tail is around 15 million miles long, and always points away from the Sun.
4	**BEPICOLOMBO** The latest mission to explore Mercury is BepiColombo. The spacecraft is made up of two orbiting observatories—ESA's Mercury Planetary Orbiter (MPO) and JAXA's Mercury Magnetospheric Orbiter (MMO)—to help scientists understand how the planet's history has shaped its unusual features.
5	**CREATIVE CRATERS** Craters on Mercury are named after famous artists, musicians, and writers, such as the Brontë sisters (pictured). Cliffs and steep slopes are named after ships used in important scientific expeditions.

VENUS

CATEGORY	AGE
PLANET	4.5 BILLION YEARS

EARTH'S SISTER PLANET IS AN EVIL TWIN—WITH EXTREME GLOBAL WARMING, TENS OF THOUSANDS OF VOLCANOES AND AN ATMOSPHERE THAT CRUSHES VISITORS.

ALL ABOUT

Venus's size, gravity, and internal structure are very similar to Earth's. Once upon a time, Venus even had a watery ocean on its surface. Today that ocean is long gone, boiled away as Venus orbits the Sun too close for comfort.

The evaporating water filled Venus's skies with clouds, trapping some of the Sun's heat. A similar greenhouse effect keeps Earth warm. However, Venus's volcanoes turned global heating into global incineration. Eruptions flooded the surface with superheated lava and released vast amounts of carbon dioxide—an even more potent greenhouse gas.

Today, Venus's atmosphere is almost pure carbon dioxide, and, day or night, the surface is hot enough to cook a pizza in 90 seconds. Not that anyone has tried. The weight of the thick atmosphere presses down on the surface with 92 times more force than Earth's air—enough to crush all but the strongest submersibles. Even breezes hit with the force of breaking waves.

There is nowhere to hide from the heat, which is carried to every part of the planet by winds. Even cooler clouds high in the atmosphere offer little comfort. Sulfur dioxide gas released by volcanoes dissolves in each cloud droplet, creating the same strong acid found in car batteries. At least these acid raindrops evaporate before they ever reach the ground.

Venus has no moons, but in 2002 astronomers spotted 2002 VE68, an asteroid that has followed Venus around the Sun for at least 7,000 years. After an illustrator misspelled the name on a poster, calling it "Zoozve," the quasi-moon became internet famous. In 2024, the International Astronomical Union officially renamed it Zoozve to match the spelling mistake!

KEY FACTS

- A day lasts 243 Earth days.
- A year lasts 225 Earth days.
- No natural satellites, but one quasi-moon.
- Light from the Sun reaches Venus in 6 min.
- Around 1.5 million Venus-sized planets would fit inside the Sun.

TEMPERATURE

867°F

NAMED AFTER

The Roman goddess of love and beauty. Most surface features on Venus are named after famous or mythical women, or female first names.

WHAT IS IT MADE OF?

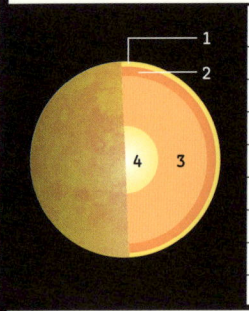

1. Atmosphere of mainly carbon dioxide with a little nitrogen, and sulfuric acid clouds.
2. Thin rocky crust, mainly basalt.
3. Thick rocky mantle.
4. Solid iron-rich core.

PAST, PRESENT, FUTURE

Venus spins backward compared to other planets in our solar system, meaning the Sun rises in the west. The slow speed of Venus's spin is a clue that its direction may have been reversed by a huge collision in the past.

★ DISCOVER VENUS'S ULTIMATE FATE ON PAGE 149 ★

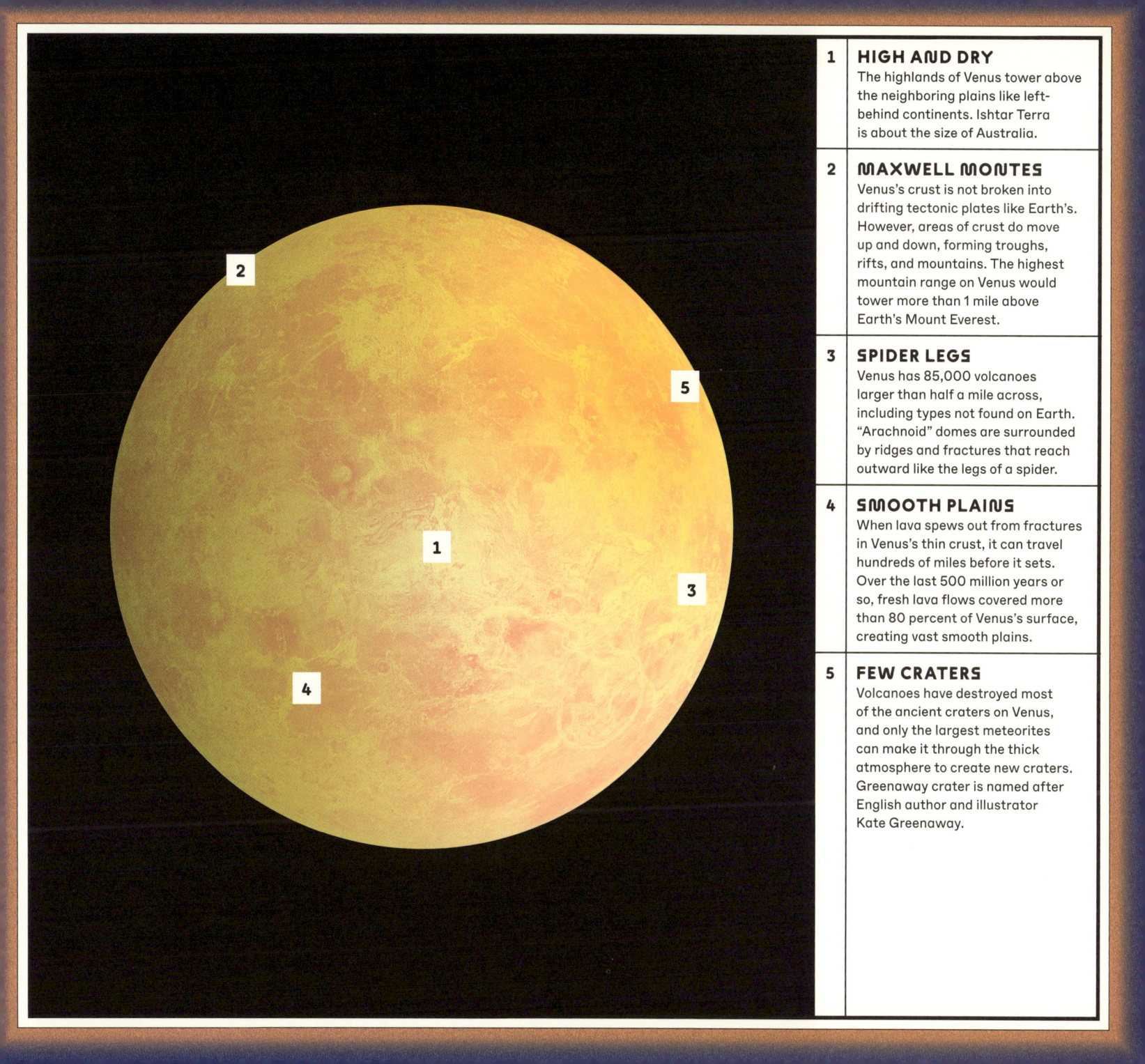

1	**HIGH AND DRY** The highlands of Venus tower above the neighboring plains like left-behind continents. Ishtar Terra is about the size of Australia.
2	**MAXWELL MONTES** Venus's crust is not broken into drifting tectonic plates like Earth's. However, areas of crust do move up and down, forming troughs, rifts, and mountains. The highest mountain range on Venus would tower more than 1 mile above Earth's Mount Everest.
3	**SPIDER LEGS** Venus has 85,000 volcanoes larger than half a mile across, including types not found on Earth. "Arachnoid" domes are surrounded by ridges and fractures that reach outward like the legs of a spider.
4	**SMOOTH PLAINS** When lava spews out from fractures in Venus's thin crust, it can travel hundreds of miles before it sets. Over the last 500 million years or so, fresh lava flows covered more than 80 percent of Venus's surface, creating vast smooth plains.
5	**FEW CRATERS** Volcanoes have destroyed most of the ancient craters on Venus, and only the largest meteorites can make it through the thick atmosphere to create new craters. Greenaway crater is named after English author and illustrator Kate Greenaway.

EXPLORING VENUS

MANY SPACE PROBES HAVE VISITED VENUS, BUT THOSE THAT DARED TO PLUNGE INTO ITS CRUSHING, ACIDIC ATMOSPHERE OR LAND ON ITS SCORCHING SURFACE HAVE SURVIVED JUST A FEW HOURS.

ALL ABOUT

Just like Mercury, looking toward Venus also means staring at the Sun. For this reason it's only possible to glimpse Venus from Earth's surface in the early morning or early evening, when the Sun is below the horizon. Venus's thick clouds reflect most of the sunlight that reaches the planet, making it the brightest object in the night sky after the Moon.

However, this thick blanket of clouds makes it difficult to discover much about Venus using Earth-based telescopes. To find out what lay beneath the clouds, we had to wait until we could send space probes to visit the planet.

Using radar—a system for detecting the presence, distance, direction and speed of objects, by sending out pulses of radio waves and detecting the signals that bounce back—orbiters such as Magellan (NASA) have collected enough information to allow scientists to map the entire surface of Venus. Thermal sensors carried by probes such as Venus Express (ESA) have helped to identify minerals on the surface and have spotted active volcanoes. These instruments helped scientists figure out what the landscape would look like. However, getting an actual photograph of the surface has been far harder.

The first probes dropped into Venus's atmosphere were immediately crushed or roasted. So far, only four landers have survived long enough to send back pictures of Venus's surface. All we have is a few 40-year-old snapshots of broken rocks in a desolate sulfur-tinged gloom. This has not deterred space agencies from planning new missions, and there are plenty of questions left to answer.

EXPLORATION TIMELINE

Anc.	Discovered and named in ancient times (visible with the naked eye just before sunrise and just after sunset).
1610	First viewed through a telescope by Galileo Galilei.
1962	Mariner 2 is the first flyby probe to visit Venus.
1966	Venera 3 is the first probe to crash-land on Venus.
1967	Venera 4 is the first probe to send back data from Venus's atmosphere.
1970	Venera 7 becomes the first probe to make a controlled landing on Venus (and the first to land on any planet).
1975	Venera 9 and 10 are the first probes to go into orbit around Venus.
1990	Magellan enters orbit around Venus.
2006	Venus Express arrives at Venus.

ARE WE THERE YET?

- When Venus passes between Earth and the Sun, it is only 100 times farther away than the Moon.
- The flyby probe Mariner 2 took 110 days to reach Venus. Orbiters have to make a longer, slower trip: Venus Express took 153 days.

HELPING HUMANS

In 1610, Galileo Galilei noticed that Venus has phases like the Moon. This was proof that other objects in our solar system orbit the Sun. In the 1700s, tracking Venus as it passed in front of the Sun (known as a transit) helped astronomers calculate the distance between Earth and the Sun.

★ IS ALIEN LIFE HIDING IN VENUS'S HIGHEST CLOUDS? SEE THE EVIDENCE ON PAGE 79 ★

#		
1	**CLOUD TOPS**	Most of the water that was once in Venus's atmosphere has been destroyed by intense sunlight, but there are still watery clouds at the very top, 28 to 40 miles above the ground. Some astrobiologists think that the brown streaks in these clouds may be a sign of microbial life.
2	**VENERA PROBES**	During the Space Race (a historical competition between nations including the USA and USSR to achieve milestones in space exploration), the USSR launched 28 probes to Venus. Venera 9 was the first to send back photographs of the surface. Venera 13 sent the first color pictures and sound recording from another planet, and even "tasted" the soil.
3	**FLYING VISIT**	Mariner 2 (NASA) was the first probe to visit Venus and was the first successful flyby of any planet. Even from 22,000 miles away, the probe's instruments could tell that below the cloud cover, the surface is horribly hot.
4	**WEIRD WEATHER**	Venus Express (ESA) spent almost eight years orbiting Venus, spotting a giant double hurricane at the planet's south pole. It also spotted flashes that could be lightning, or meteors being incinerated by the thick atmosphere.
5	**FIVE-YEAR DELAY**	In 2010, JAXA's Akatsuki probe missed the stop on its approach to Venus. In a brilliant example of clever problem-solving, engineers managed to reroute the spacecraft around the Sun to enter Venus's orbit five years later.

MARS

CATEGORY	AGE	
PLANET	4.5 BILLION YEARS	A SMALL PLANET WITH BIG FEATURES, MARS BOASTS THE LARGEST VOLCANOES AND CANYONS IN THE SOLAR SYSTEM, AND DUST STORMS VISIBLE FROM EARTH.

ALL ABOUT

Today Mars is a dry and cool planet, but its surface is littered with evidence of an exciting past. Many Martian landscapes look eerily like Earth's, with river valleys, lake beds, and flood plains. These dried-up features may have been carved by liquid water, which flowed across the surface of Mars billions of years ago.

The water may be gone, but winds whip up dust storms the height of skyscrapers, which take weeks to die down. The fast-moving dust carves rocks into strange shapes, and causes the edges of craters and canyons to collapse in landslides.

Mars's crust is not split into huge, moving plates like Earth's crust, so lava can ooze out of the same spot for a billion years or more, gradually forming gigantic volcanoes. As parts of the crust bulged upward due to superheated magma below, nearby land was stretched beyond breaking point, and collapsed to form breathtaking canyons.

Mars's small size means its molten insides cooled far more quickly than Earth's. Today its core is almost certainly solid, and the days of vast lava flows are over. But marsquakes are still detected, suggesting that volcanism on Mars has not ended completely. Nor has Mars's watery past. As well as ice caps at the poles, glaciers still flow on the planet, hidden underneath layers of rock and dust. From time to time, salty liquid water may even trickle down valley walls.

KEY FACTS

- A day lasts 24 hr, 37 min.
- A year lasts 687 Earth days.
- Two orbiting moons, Phobos and Deimos.
- Light from the Sun reaches Mars in 13 min.
- More than six Mars-sized planets would fit inside Earth.

TEMPERATURE

☼ 77°F
❆ -193°F

NAMED AFTER

The Roman god of war, as its red color was compared to blood. Phobos and Deimos were named after the horses pulling his mythical chariot.

WHAT IS IT MADE OF?

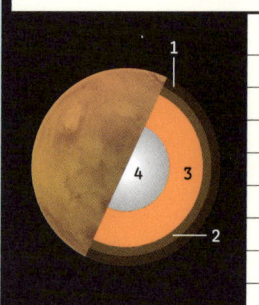

1. Thin atmosphere of mainly carbon dioxide, with some nitrogen and argon.
2. Thin crust, made of iron, magnesium, aluminum, calcium, and potassium.
3. Rocky mantle, rich in silicates.
4. Small dense core, made of iron, nickel, and sulfur.

PAST, PRESENT, FUTURE

The tiny moon Phobos is falling toward Mars, getting 0.8 in closer every year. In 50 million years or so it will crash into Mars and break apart, perhaps giving Mars dusty rings to match its dusty surface.

* FIND OUT WHY SUPERGIANT STAR ANTARES IS OFTEN MISTAKEN FOR MARS ON PAGE 153 *

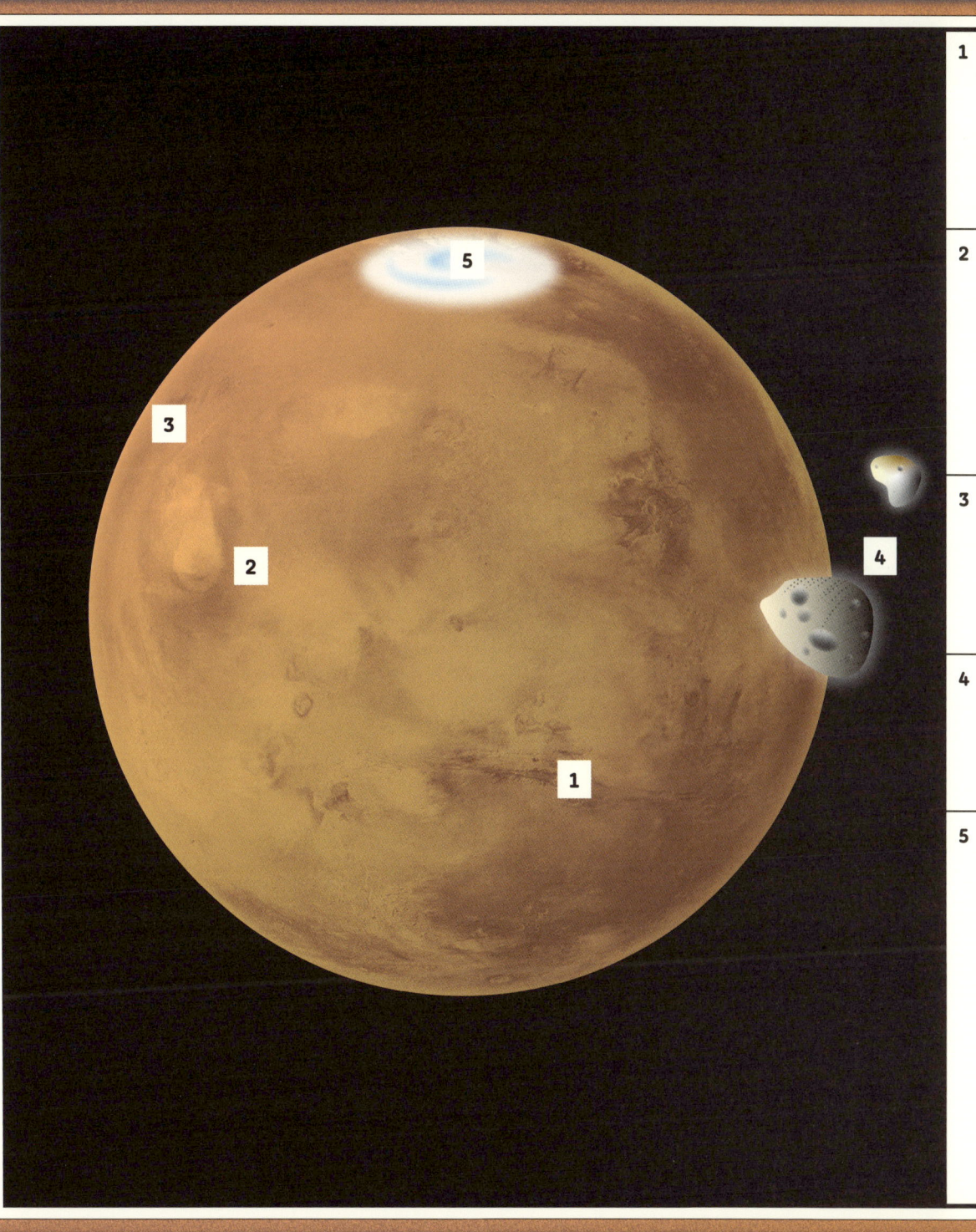

#	
1	**VALLES MARINERIS** The solar system's largest canyon is visible through a telescope from Earth. It's nicknamed Mars's Grand Canyon, but Valles Marineris is more than 10 times longer, 10 times wider, and nearly 5 times deeper than Earth's largest valley!
2	**OLYMPUS MONS** Mars also boasts the largest volcano in the solar system. Its base measures a whopping 372 miles across, meaning that the volcano covers an area bigger than the United Kingdom. To reach the peak you'd have to climb more than 2.5 times the height of Mount Everest.
3	**RUST COLORED** Mars's rusty-red color really does come from rust, formed when iron in Mars's rocks and soil reacted with oxygen to form iron oxide. It even makes the planet look like a reddish star in Earth's night sky.
4	**TWIN MOONS** Mars's tiny moons Phobos and Deimos are probably asteroids that were captured by the planet's gravity. Close up, they look like wonky potatoes.
5	**POLAR CAPS** Thanks to its tilted axis, Mars has seasons. In Martian winters, a layer of frozen water and carbon dioxide covers the pole pointing away from the Sun. By summer this ice cap shrinks as the carbon dioxide and some of the water evaporate to form thin clouds.

EXPLORING MARS

MARS IS ONE OF THE BEST-EXPLORED OBJECTS IN THE SOLAR SYSTEM. ROBOTS ROAM ITS SURFACE, SPACECRAFT STARE DOWN FROM ITS SKIES, AND A HELICOPTER HAS EVEN HOVERED OVER THE RED PLANET.

ALL ABOUT

The first maps of Mars were made in the late 1800s, by people who peered through telescopes and marveled at the features coming into focus. Some of these astronomers imagined they saw watery seas, crisscrossing canals, or entire alien civilizations.

Space probes were first sent to Mars in the 1960s. The photos they beamed back showed no trace of alien cities, but did raise all sorts of new questions. Most intriguing were features that looked like gullies carved by water. Was there water on Mars? And if so, could there be life?

Over the last 50 years, more spacecraft have been sent to Mars than any other planet in the solar system, from orbiters and landers to robot rovers (see page 85). We now have better maps of Mars's surface than of Earth's ocean floors. The data collected has proved that there is still water on Mars—and lots of it. But just like the first mission, each fact found raises a hundred more questions.

Some of these could be answered by returning samples of Martian rocks and soil to Earth, but the ultimate goal is to send humans to investigate Mars and its mysteries in person. The number-one question is the same one we were asking 50 years ago: is there (or has there ever been) life on Mars?

EXPLORATION TIMELINE

Anc.	Discovered and named in ancient times (visible with the naked eye).
1610	First viewed through a telescope by Galileo Galilei.
1877	Moons first discovered by Asaph Hall.
1962	Mariner 4 is Mars's first flyby probe.
1971	Mariner 9 becomes Mars's first orbital probe.
1971	Mars 2 is the first probe to crash-land on Mars.
1971	Mars 3 carries out the first controlled landing on Mars, but only transmits data for a few seconds.
1976	Viking 1 carries out a controlled landing on Mars.
1997	Sojourner, delivered by the Mars Pathfinder spacecraft, is the first robotic rover to explore Mars.
2021	Ingenuity Mars Helicopter, delivered by Mars 2020, is the first robotic drone to explore Mars.

ARE WE THERE YET?

- A car speeding at 60 mph would take around 70 years to get to Mars at its closest point to Earth.
- Viking 1 took 11 months to reach Mars.
- Today, spacecraft can make the journey in six to nine months.

HELPING HUMANS

Back in 1672, astronomers were able to calculate the distance between Earth and the Sun by peering at Mars from Europe and South America at the same time—a method known as triangulation (see page 178). This taught us that the solar system was much bigger than people thought at the time.

★ WHERE THERE IS WATER, THERE MAY BE LIFE (PAGE 98) ★

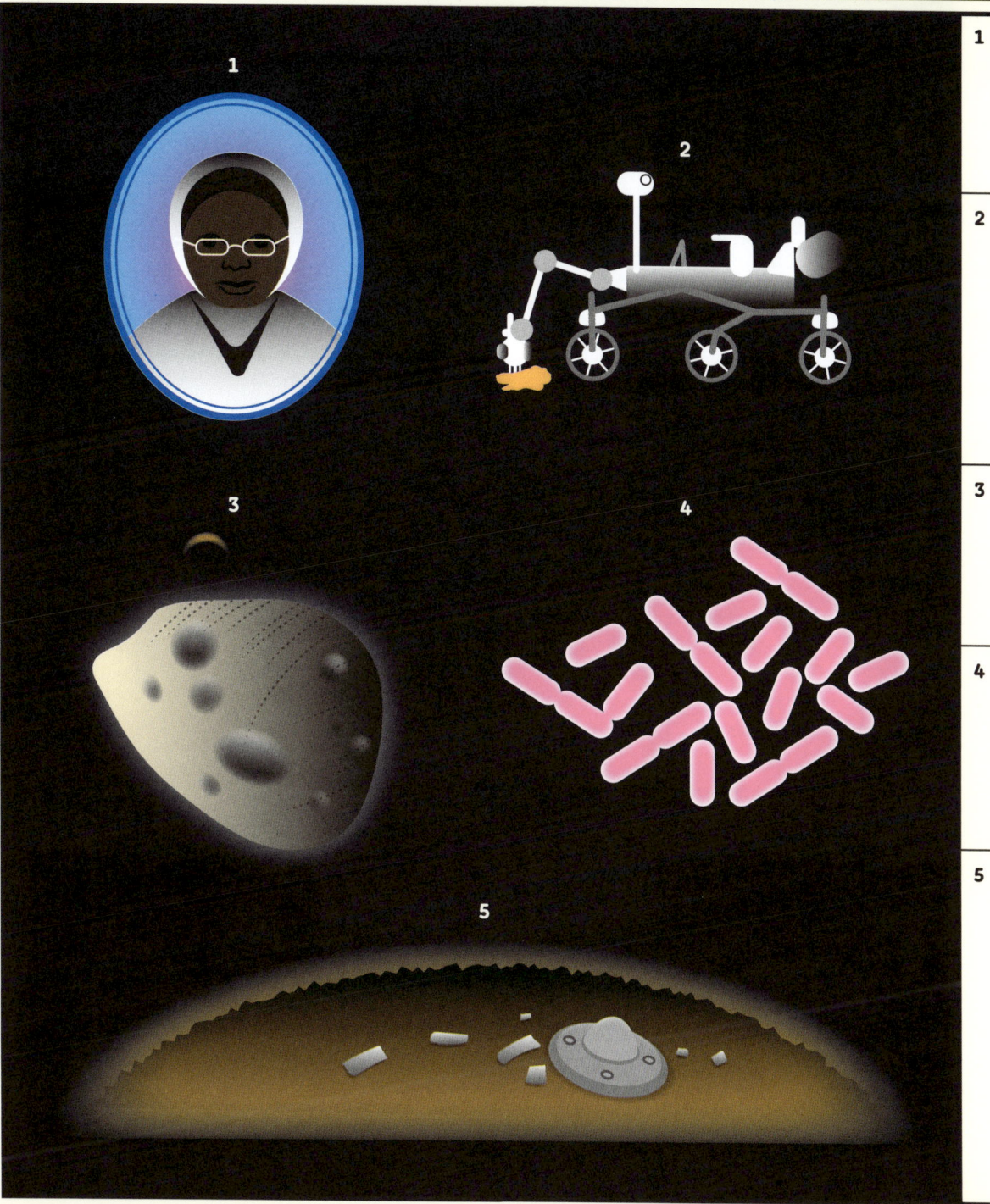

#	
1	**HISTORIC HERO** The first robot rover on Mars was called Sojourner, after Sojourner Truth, a hero of the Civil Rights movement. The name was suggested by a 12-year-old girl who won a competition.
2	**ROCK STAR** More than 300 meteorites found on Earth are thought to be from Mars. These bits of solid lava are fascinating, but geologists could discover even more by studying fresh samples of Martian rock. Perseverance rover (see page 85) has started a collection in preparation for a future mission to return the rocks to Earth.
3	**GROOVY MOON** The first close-up pictures of Mars's moons were taken by Mariner 9 (NASA). Both have some hefty craters, but Phobos also has mysterious grooves and pits that haven't yet been explained.
4	**TINY ALIENS?** If there were once aliens on Mars, they were most likely to be microbes—the smallest, simplest life-forms. Some of the samples Perseverance collected from the bottom of a dried-up lake could include tiny fossils.
5	**SPACE JUNK** So many missions to Mars means that space junk is piling up on (and around) the planet. More than 7.75 tons of debris is strewn across the surface, including jettisoned parts, defunct rovers, crashed spacecraft, and a drill bit dropped by Perseverance.

ROBOTIC ROVERS

ROBOT ROVERS ARE DESIGNED TO TRAVEL ACROSS THE SURFACE OF A PLANET OR MOON, EXPLORING A WIDE AREA IN DETAIL. REMOTE CONTROL FROM EARTH MEANS SCIENTISTS CAN SELECT WHICH FEATURES TO INVESTIGATE.

Aliens landing on Mars would find a planet populated by robots, including six rovers that have explored the surface. Sojourner (NASA) was the first rover to be successfully deployed on Mars, in 1997. It was an important test of the technologies needed to not only land on another planet but to navigate across the surface.

In 2004, the rovers Spirit and Opportunity (NASA) landed in different areas of Mars. Spirit traveled almost 5 miles across the surface before getting stuck in deep sand. Opportunity roamed more than 12 miles, but also stopped working when its solar panels became covered in dust. These rovers examined rocks and minerals and proved that liquid water once existed on Mars's surface.

While Sojourner was just 26 in long, more recent Mars rovers have been much larger. The car-sized Curiosity rover (NASA) landed in Mars's Gale Crater in 2012. A laboratory on wheels, it carries scientific instruments from six countries. It has discovered methane in Mars's atmosphere, and organic compounds in the soil.

In 2021, Curiosity was joined by Perseverance rover (NASA), which has been searching for signs of ancient life on Mars, and collecting rock and soil samples in the hope they will one day be returned to Earth for study. Perseverance was the first rover to send back sound recordings from Mars. China has also landed a rover on Mars.

LUNAR ROVERS

The Lunokhod lunar rovers (USSR) were the first robotic rovers to explore a distant object. These remote-controlled vehicles carried cameras across the Moon's surface, and sampled the lunar soil.

MOON BUGGY

Several other rovers have explored the Moon's surface, including NASA's Lunar Rover Vehicles (driven by astronauts) and China's Yutu rovers. The Yutu-2 rover (CNSA) was the first to touch down on the far side of the Moon.

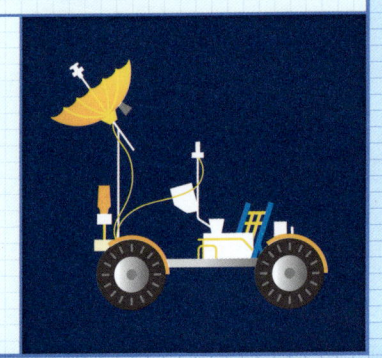

PERSEVERANCE ROVER AND THE INGENUITY MARS HELICOPTER

Landing locations for rovers are carefully chosen to meet scientific goals and ensure the rover can travel across the terrain. Perseverance landed in a crater that was an ancient lake—the kind of place where fossils are found on Earth.

Radio signals take between 4 and 24 minutes to make a round trip from Earth to Mars and back, so rovers can't be driven in real-time. Instead, the information collected by the rover's cameras and lasers are used to update a 3D model of the landscape. Rover drivers use this to plan the path for the next drive, avoiding obstacles and traps such as sinking sand and sharp rocks. The rover is also programmed to problem-solve if it gets into a tricky situation.

Instructions are sent via the Deep Space Network—a network of antennas in Spain, the USA, and Australia, used to send messages to spacecraft in outer space.

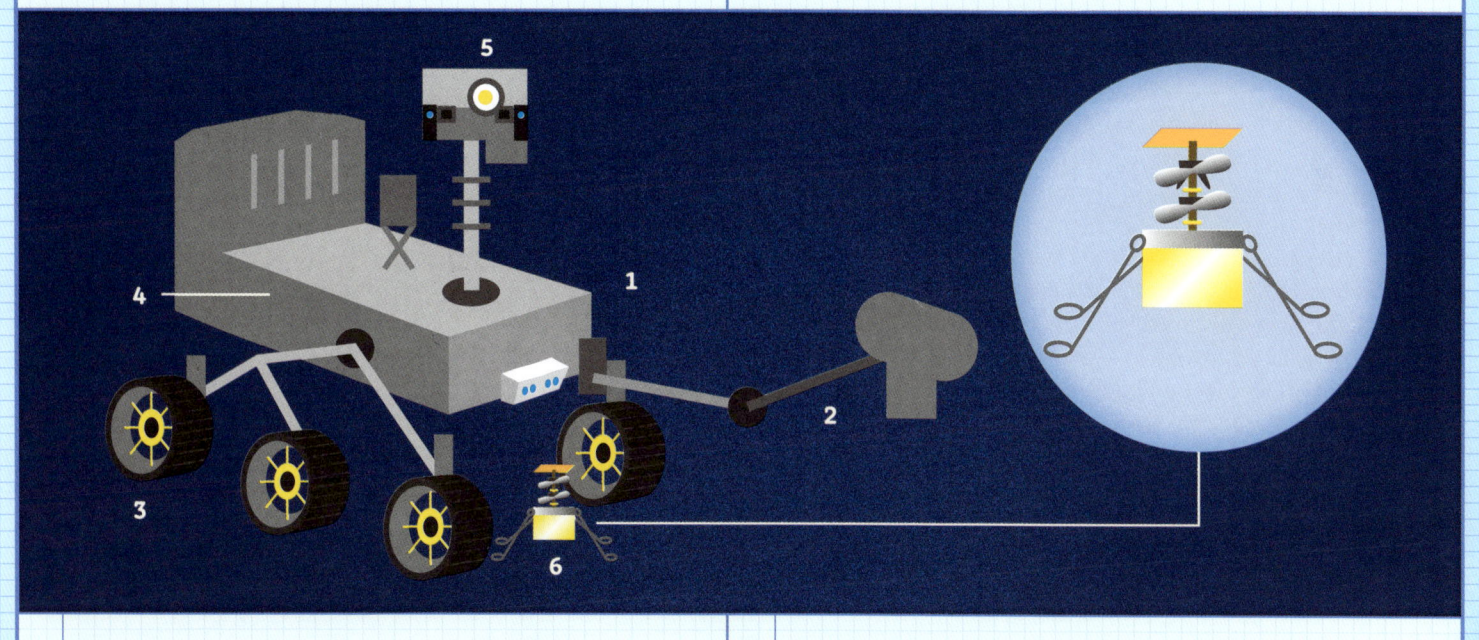

1	Perseverance's top speed is 500 feet per hour.
2	Robot arm has a drill for taking rock samples, science instruments, and a camera for close-up pictures.
3	Front and back wheels can turn a full 360° for tight turns.
4	Two computer "brains" protected inside body.
5	Mast holds five cameras high above the ground, for a "human-eye" view.
6	As part of the Mars 2020 mission (NASA), Perseverance rover lowered the Ingenuity Mars Helicopter (only 20 in high) to the surface. Over three years it completed 72 flights above the surface, and is the first aircraft to achieve powered and controlled flight on another planet.

CERES & THE ASTEROID BELT

CATEGORY	AGE
DWARF PLANET	4.5 BILLION YEARS

IMAGINE THE ASTEROID BELT AS A BOX OF CEREAL STREWN AROUND THE SUN, WITH **CERES** BY FAR THE LARGEST LUMP — BIG ENOUGH FOR A PROMOTION FROM ASTEROID TO DWARF PLANET.

ALL ABOUT

Ceres was discovered by accident, through a telescope aimed at the stars. At first it was thought to be a comet, but astronomers soon began spotting other small objects in the "gap" between Mars and Jupiter. Scientists named these asteroids, and within 100 years, a million more asteroids had been spotted in what is now known as the asteroid belt. However, in a twist of fate, Ceres is no longer counted as an asteroid!

The asteroids of the asteroid belt are thought to be leftover rubble from a planet that began to form in the early days of the solar system, but never quite made it—perhaps because Jupiter's giant gravity gobbled up too much of the raw material.

Ceres is the largest object in the asteroid belt—and was considered large enough to be classified as a dwarf planet when this category was created in 2006. Ceres is less than a third of the size of Earth's Moon, but has a familiar rounded shape, and a planetlike structure with a core, mantle, and crust. There are even clues that it once had a liquid ocean, and that salty water still lurks just beneath the surface.

The asteroid belt contains asteroids of every other size imaginable, from mountain-sized boulders to specks of dust. At around the width of the United Kingdom, asteroid 4 Vesta is the second-biggest object in the belt.

Asteroids are found elsewhere in the solar system too, including the tarry Trojans that trail Jupiter and the icy Centaurs that orbit the Sun between Jupiter and Neptune.

CERES FACTS

- A day lasts 9 hr.
- A year lasts 4.6 Earth years.
- No natural satellites.
- Light from the Sun reaches Ceres in 22 min.
- Ceres would fit inside Earth more than 2,500 times.

CERES TEMPERATURE

☀ -27°F
❄ -135°F

NAMED AFTER

Ceres is named after the Roman goddess of harvests. Asteroids are numbered in order of discovery; Ceres's official name is 1 Ceres.

WHAT IS CERES MADE OF?

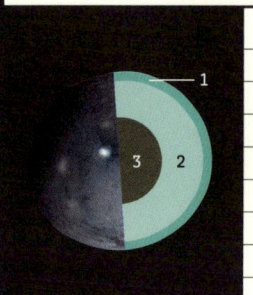

1. Thin, dusty crust, rich in carbon and clay minerals that hold water.
2. Layer of water ice, perhaps with a thin layer of briny liquid water beneath the crust.
3. Rocky inner core.

PAST, PRESENT, FUTURE

Most asteroids are not large enough to be rounded like Ceres and 4 Vesta. Their wonky shapes are the result of collisions that have fractured or shattered asteroids into ever-smaller fragments over 4.5 billion years. In some cases, the rubble collected back together to form loose lumps far less dense than planets.

✶ OTHER DWARF PLANETS LIE IN THE OUTER SOLAR SYSTEM, FAR BEYOND NEPTUNE (PAGE 116) ✶

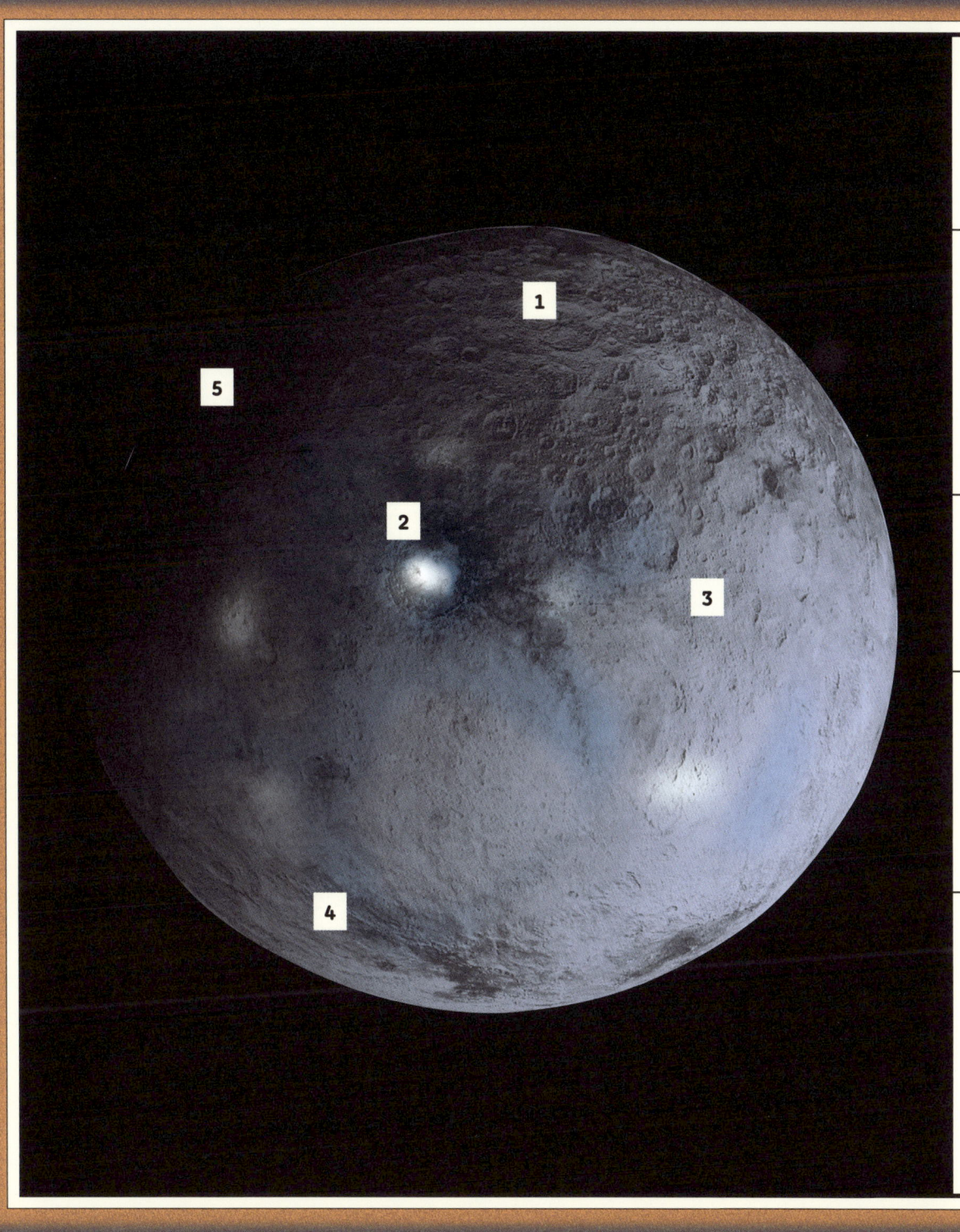

#		
1	**CRATER COVERED**	Like other bodies in the asteroid belt, Ceres is covered in craters—but not as many as you might expect after 4.5 billion years of collisions! Something must have reformed its surface in the not-so-distant past.
2	**BRIGHT SPOTS**	There are 300 bright spots, known as faculae, that sparkle against Ceres's otherwise dull and dark surface. Each spot is made of sodium carbonate, left behind when salty water bubbled up to the surface and instantly evaporated into space. The 57-mile Occator Crater has many of these bright, briny deposits on its floor.
3	**ICE VOLCANOES**	In places, freezing salty water mixed with mud has oozed out from the mantle more slowly, forming cryovolcano domes. The ice volcano Ahuna Mons towers 3 miles above Ceres's surface.
4	**WATERY WORLD**	Solid and liquid water makes up about half of Ceres's weight, making the dwarf planet an interesting place to hunt for alien life. Dawn (NASA) found traces of complex carbon-based chemicals. On Earth, these are only made by living things.
5	**CARBON RICH**	Asteroids are not very colorful, but their brightness is a clue to what they are made of. As a carbonaceous or C-type asteroid, Ceres contains a lot of carbon and most of its surface is almost coal-black.

EXPLORING ASTEROIDS

ASTEROIDS ARE NEITHER BIG ENOUGH NOR BRIGHT ENOUGH TO LEARN LOTS ABOUT THROUGH TELESCOPES. HOWEVER, MULTIPLE MISSIONS HAVE CHASED THEM AROUND THE SOLAR SYSTEM FOR A CLOSE ENCOUNTER.

ALL ABOUT

Measurements made with telescopes can tell us certain things about asteroids, such as the speed at which they spin. But confirming the size and shape of asteroids had to wait until spacecraft could be sent to take a closer look.

Since the early 1990s, probes have photographed asteroids, landed on their surfaces, and returned samples to Earth. One mission even changed the course of an asteroid's orbit!

The first probes to travel through the asteroid belt were on their way to the outer solar system. These trips confirmed that spacecraft are unlikely to crash into an asteroid by mistake. Though there are millions of asteroids in the main asteroid belt, they are spread across a vast area of space.

Another big surprise was that many asteroids have satellites of their own. The tiny moonlet Dactyl was first to be spotted, in fuzzy photographs of 243 Ida taken by the Galileo probe. We still don't know how such small objects can capture space rocks with their weak gravity and hold on to them.

Some asteroids, such as 90 Antiope, even turned out to be made of multiple rocks orbiting one another. These double or triple systems can be spotted with telescopes. One of them was chosen as a target for NASA's DART mission, to test a technique for altering the path of an asteroid (see page 90) to defend our planet from asteroid impacts in the future.

Meteorite strikes large enough to leave a crater are very rare, and asteroid impacts of the kind that wiped out the dinosaurs are far rarer still, impacting Earth just once every 30 million years on average. However, scientists keep a careful eye, using computers to track Near-Earth Objects and predict any close approaches.

EXPLORATION TIMELINE

1801	Giuseppe Piazzi discovers Ceres using a telescope.
1991	Galileo probe flies by 951 Gaspra and takes the first close-up photo of an asteroid.
2000	NEAR Shoemaker becomes the first probe to orbit an asteroid, 433 Eros.
2001	NEAR Shoemaker carries out the first controlled landing on an asteroid, 433 Eros.
2005	Hayabusa probe collects a sample of dust from the surface of 25143 Itokawa.
2010	Hayabusa returns its dust sample to Earth.

ARE WE THERE YET?

- Voyager 1 took 81 days to reach the asteroid belt, zooming through on its way to the outer solar system.
- Dawn took nearly four years to navigate from Earth to 4 Vesta. After leaving 4 Vesta, the probe took another two and a half years to reach Ceres.

HELPING HUMANS

By returning samples from near-Earth asteroids, JAXA's Hayabusa probes and NASA's OSIRIS-REx spacecraft let scientists look at building blocks from the very beginning of our solar system. Understanding what asteroids are made of also helps us predict how they will respond to impacts or explosions.

FIND OUT HOW SUPERCOMPUTERS HELP TO TRACK ASTEROIDS ON PAGE 206

#	
1	**DOUBLE MISSION** NASA's Dawn mission was the first to orbit two different objects in space: the massive asteroid 4 Vesta and the dwarf planet 1 Ceres. To do this, it used super high-tech ion engines, an idea first seen in science-fiction stories!
2	**MEGA MOUNTAIN** When Ceres was named a dwarf planet, 4 Vesta became the most massive asteroid in the solar system. Its once-molten surface is home to the solar system's second-tallest mountain—a peak twice the height of Mount Everest.
3	**NEAR-EARTH PATH** Near-Earth asteroids follow paths around the Sun that occasionally cross Earth's own orbit. Any that may pass perilously close to our planet are closely monitored and their future paths are carefully plotted so we aren't taken by surprise like the dinosaurs.
4	**MINING ASTEROIDS** M-type asteroids contain lots of metal, including precious metals such as platinum. Even a small M-type asteroid contains more nickel and iron than humans use in a year. It will probably always be too hard and expensive to bring asteroid-mined metals back to Earth, but they could one day be used for building structures and solar panels in space.
5	**ASTEROID HUNTERS** Anyone can be an asteroid hunter. Unlike other space objects, an asteroid's name is chosen by the person who discovered it. The asteroid 101955 Bennu was named by a nine-year-old boy, after the Ancient Egyptian god of rebirth.

DEFLECTING AN ASTEROID

NASA'S DART MISSION WAS THE FIRST ATTEMPT TO ALTER AN ASTEROID'S PATH THROUGH SPACE, AND WAS A HUGE SUCCESS.

Asteroids with orbits that cross Earth's own path around the Sun are carefully tracked, using powerful supercomputers and artificial intelligence (see page 206). Their future paths are calculated so that we aren't taken by surprise. More than 35,000 near-Earth asteroids have been spotted, but only around 2,400 have been flagged as Potentially Hazardous Asteroids (PHAs). Space scientists are also working on plans for preventing any future collisions. A tiny change in the speed or path of a PHA, made far enough in advance, would see it sail safely past Earth. In 2022, NASA's DART mission was the first test of a plan to alter an asteroid's path through space. It was a huge success.

PHAS

PHAs are asteroids that are projected to pass within 4.6 million miles of Earth, with a diameter of 459 feet or more, large enough to punch through Earth's atmosphere without slowing down. This does not mean that PHAs will impact Earth, just that we should watch them carefully.

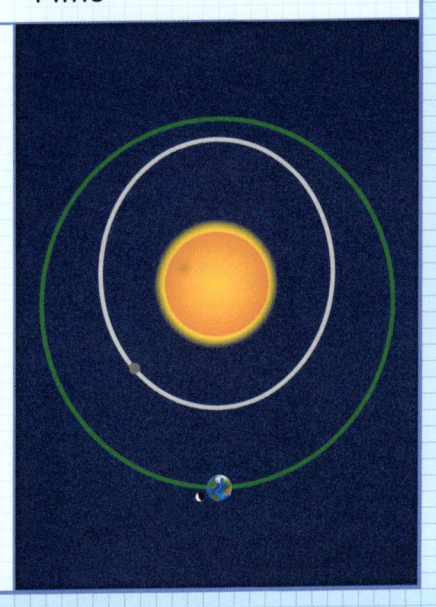

PREVENTING COLLISIONS

PHAs can't just be blasted out of space with explosives, like in a movie. This would create hundreds of smaller asteroids, on a crash course with Earth. Instead, plans focus on ways to drag, push, or nudge an asteroid off course, perhaps using giant lasers.

THE DART MISSION

The Double Asteroid Redirection Test (DART) was launched by NASA in 2021. It was a small, box-shaped spacecraft, with an ion engine powered by two large, roll-out solar panels.

Rather than burning fuel like a rocket, the ion engine released a flow of charged particles (ions), creating a gentle push. DART also carried a camera, to take pictures of the asteroid as it approached. This helped the on-board computer navigate precisely once it got close.

The small spacecraft intentionally collided with the moon of a near-Earth asteroid, 65803 Didymos. Didymos was chosen because it is a double asteroid system. Astronomers knew it would be much easier to detect changes in the moonlet's orbit around Didymos than to spot a tiny change in the asteroid's orbit around the Sun.

The aftermath of the collision was watched closely by telescopes 6 million miles away on Earth, as well as space telescopes. A tiny satellite called LICIACube (ASI) provided a "close-up" view from tens of miles away.

These observations confirmed that the moonlet's orbit around Didymos had been dramatically changed by the collision. Crashing a spacecraft into an asteroid really can change the asteroid's path through space.

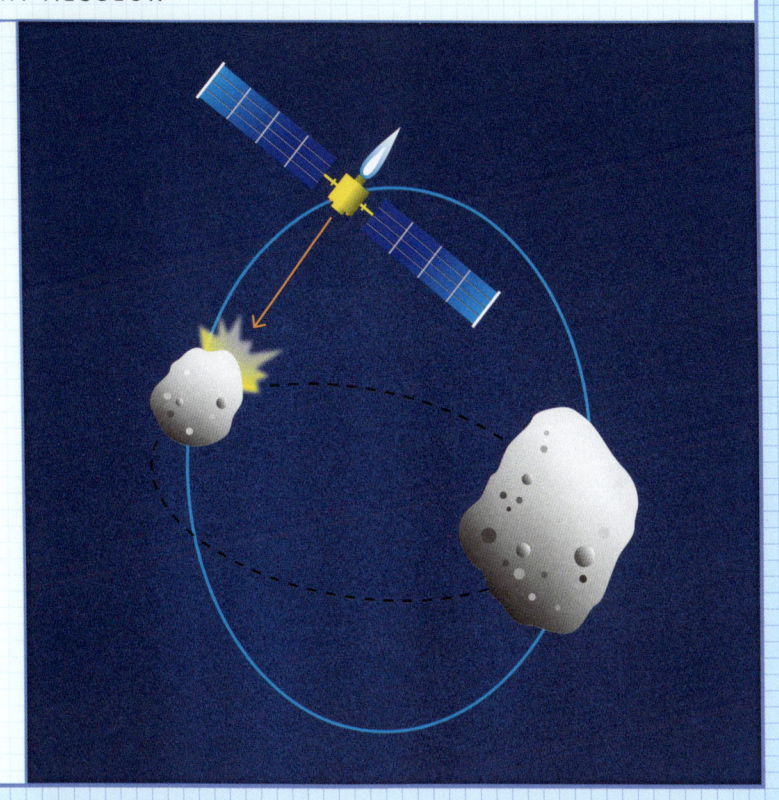

THE HERA MISSION

The follow-up Hera mission (ESA) will visit Didymos several years after the collision, to take detailed measurements of the effect of the collision. Made up of three spacecraft, Hera will help to confirm how large and how fast future impacts would need to be to deflect asteroids of different sizes.

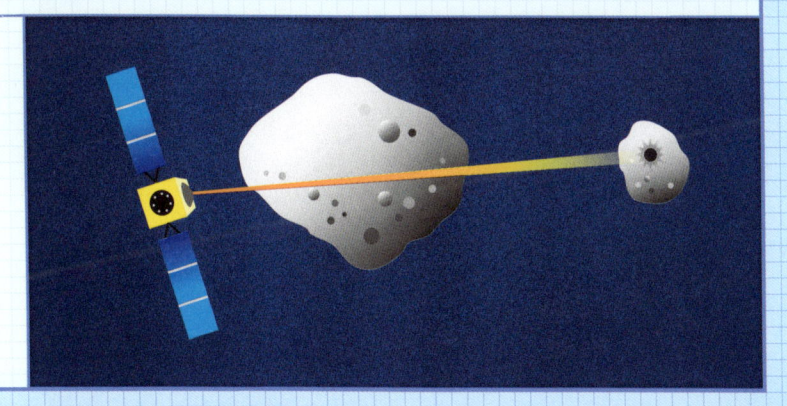

JUPITER

CATEGORY	AGE	
PLANET	4.59 BILLION YEARS	OUR SOLAR SYSTEM'S LARGEST PLANET IS A SECRETIVE WORLD, HIDDEN BENEATH COLORFUL CLOUDS AND SUPERSIZED STORMS THAT SWIRL AROUND THE SURFACE.

ALL ABOUT

Ruler of all Roman gods, Jupiter is a good name for a planet that swept up most of the material left behind after the Sun formed. Even if the solar system's other seven planets were smooshed together, Jupiter would still outweigh them by two and half times.

This gas giant is far less dense than rocky planets like Earth, though. Like a star that didn't get big enough to ignite, it's mainly made of hydrogen and helium. The colorful surface that we see through telescopes is not solid, but the top of a thick layer of clouds. They include bright, reflective water ice clouds, but also clouds formed from ammonium hydrosulfide, a chemical with a strong rotten egg smell. This is mixed with smog, giving Jupiter its red and brown colors.

The cloud layer is 1,800 miles deep in places, getting denser the deeper you go. Like Earth's clouds, the clouds on Jupiter don't all extend to the same height. Some pop out above others, creating a cloudscape that casts shadows on the surface, similar to the shadows cast by hills and mountains on Earth.

Jupiter's enormous gravitational pull squeezes its atmosphere, causing it to heat up and become thick and soupy. Near the core, the atmosphere is liquid. There is so much pressure here that hydrogen begins to behave like a metal, conducting electricity and creating Jupiter's intense magnetic field.

The journey to Jupiter's center ends at its fuzzy core, which, at 43,232 °F, is hotter than the surface of the Sun.

KEY FACTS

- A day lasts 9.92 hr.
- A year lasts 11.86 Earth years.
- At least 95 moons.
- Light from the Sun takes 43 minutes to reach Jupiter.
- Around 1,000 Jupiters would fit inside the Sun.

TEMPERATURE

-166 °F

NAMED AFTER

The Roman god of the sky and thunder, and ruler of all the Roman gods.

WHAT IS IT MADE OF?

1. Thick gassy atmosphere.
2. Liquid hydrogen and helium layer.
3. Metallic hydrogen layer.
4. Small "fuzzy" core that does not seem to be solid.

PAST, PRESENT, FUTURE

Without a solid surface to disrupt its spiraling winds, storms on Jupiter last far longer than storms on Earth. One of these storms, called the Great Red Spot, was first glimpsed in 1665 by Giovanni Cassini. It has been tracked closely for more than 100 years as it changes in size and shape, but never stops raging.

★ EXPLORE HYDROGEN AND HELIUM, THE MAIN INGREDIENTS OF THE UNIVERSE, ON PAGE 156 ★

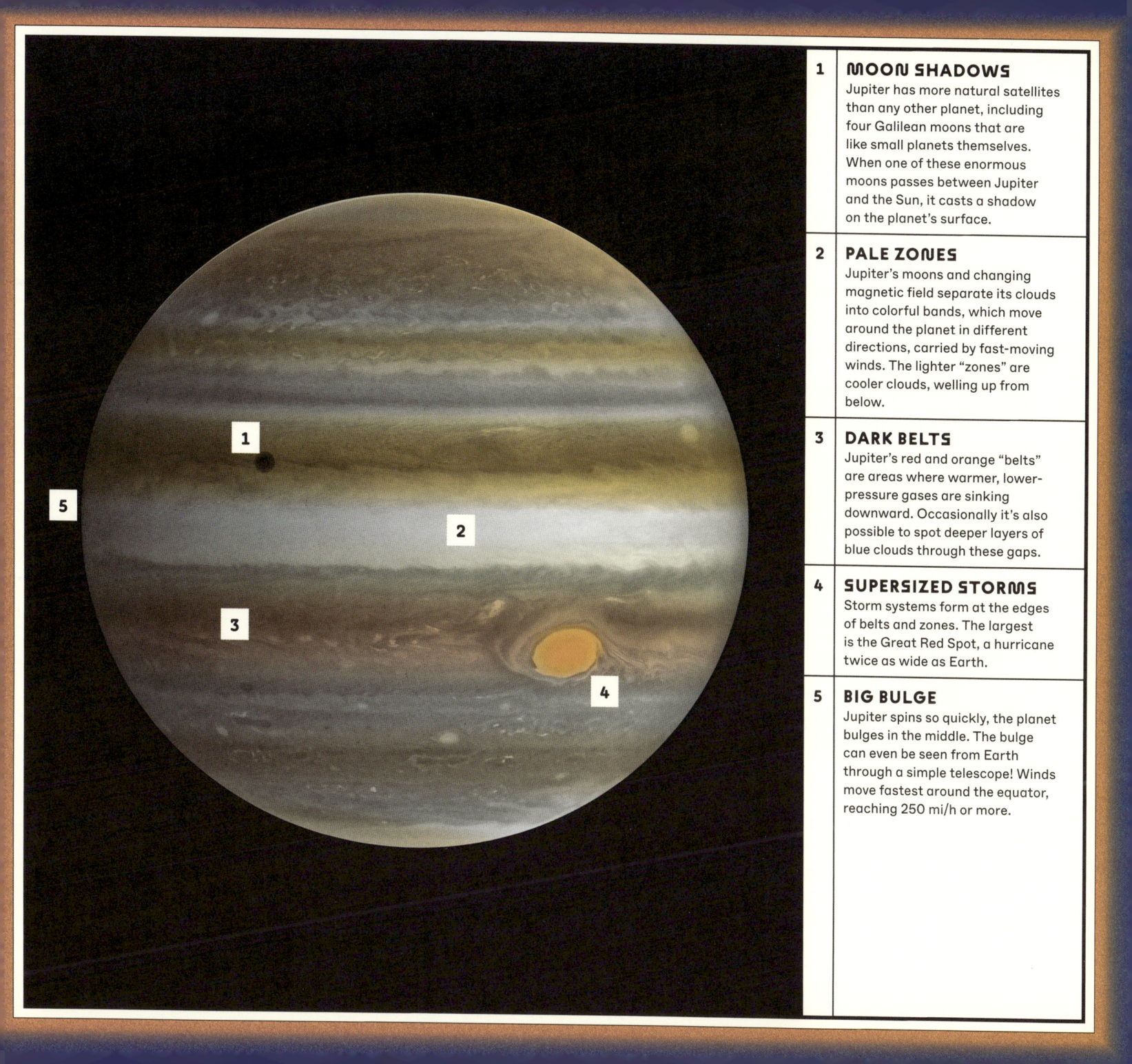

#	
1	**MOON SHADOWS** Jupiter has more natural satellites than any other planet, including four Galilean moons that are like small planets themselves. When one of these enormous moons passes between Jupiter and the Sun, it casts a shadow on the planet's surface.
2	**PALE ZONES** Jupiter's moons and changing magnetic field separate its clouds into colorful bands, which move around the planet in different directions, carried by fast-moving winds. The lighter "zones" are cooler clouds, welling up from below.
3	**DARK BELTS** Jupiter's red and orange "belts" are areas where warmer, lower-pressure gases are sinking downward. Occasionally it's also possible to spot deeper layers of blue clouds through these gaps.
4	**SUPERSIZED STORMS** Storm systems form at the edges of belts and zones. The largest is the Great Red Spot, a hurricane twice as wide as Earth.
5	**BIG BULGE** Jupiter spins so quickly, the planet bulges in the middle. The bulge can even be seen from Earth through a simple telescope! Winds move fastest around the equator, reaching 250 mi/h or more.

JUPITER'S MOONS

CATEGORY	AGE
SATELLITES (PLANETARY)	4.5 BILLION YEARS

JUPITER IS ORBITED BY SO MANY NATURAL SATELLITES THAT IT COULD BE MISTAKEN FOR A MINI SOLAR SYSTEM ITSELF. ITS FOUR LARGEST "GALILEAN" MOONS ARE AS UNIQUE AND INTERESTING AS ANY PLANET.

ALL ABOUT

Jupiter has at least 95 moons. Most seem to be rocky asteroids captured by the planet's enormous gravity, but four are so large they were spotted from simple telescopes over 400 years ago.

These are known as the Galilean moons, named after Galileo Galilei, who first observed them through a telescope in 1610. German astronomer Simon Marius named these moons Ganymede, Callisto, Io, and Europa. All four are large enough to have shaped themselves into spheres, meaning they would count as planets if they weren't already orbiting Jupiter. Each of them also has a planetlike structure with a core, mantle, and crust.

Three of the Galilean moons have frozen surfaces. They include both water ice and solid forms of methane and carbon dioxide. More excitingly, at least two moons are thought to have vast watery oceans below their surfaces. This makes them good places to hunt for alien life.

The Galilean moons all keep the same face toward Jupiter as they orbit. However, Ganymede, Europa, and Io are strongly affected by each other's gravity. This causes the tides that drive volcanoes on Io and fracture Europa's icy surface. The gravitational tug-of-war has also locked these moons in a perfectly synchronized orbital pattern, with Io making four orbits and Europa making two orbits for every orbit of Ganymede.

Jupiter has several small inner moons that may have been part of larger moons ripped apart by the planet's gravity. Meteorite strikes have sent dust and rubble flying from their surfaces, forming three faint rings around Jupiter. No one suspected the rings were there until the space probe Voyager 1 (NASA) flew past Jupiter in 1979.

ORBITAL PERIODS

- Ganymede: 7.2 days.
- Callisto: 16.7 days.
- Io: 1.8 days.
- Europa: 3.6 days.

TEMPERATURES

- Ganymede: -247°F
- Callisto: -256°F
- Io: -274°F
- Europa: -247°F

NAMED AFTER

Characters closely connected to the god Jupiter (Zeus) in Roman and Greek mythology.

WHAT IS GANYMEDE MADE OF?

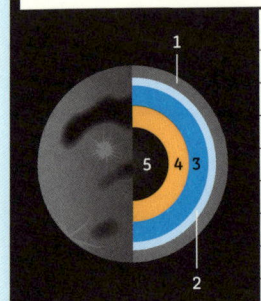

1. Icy crust.
2. Deep liquid water ocean
3. Thick layer of ice on the seafloor.
4. Rocky mantle.
5. Iron-rich core.

PAST, PRESENT, FUTURE

Before the Galilean moons were spotted, the only planetary satellite people knew about was Earth's Moon. The discovery that other planets could have moons helped to change ancient views about the universe, proving that not every object orbited either Earth or the Sun.

★ COULD THE GALILEAN MOONS HARBOUR LIFE? JOIN THE SEARCH ON PAGE 98 ★

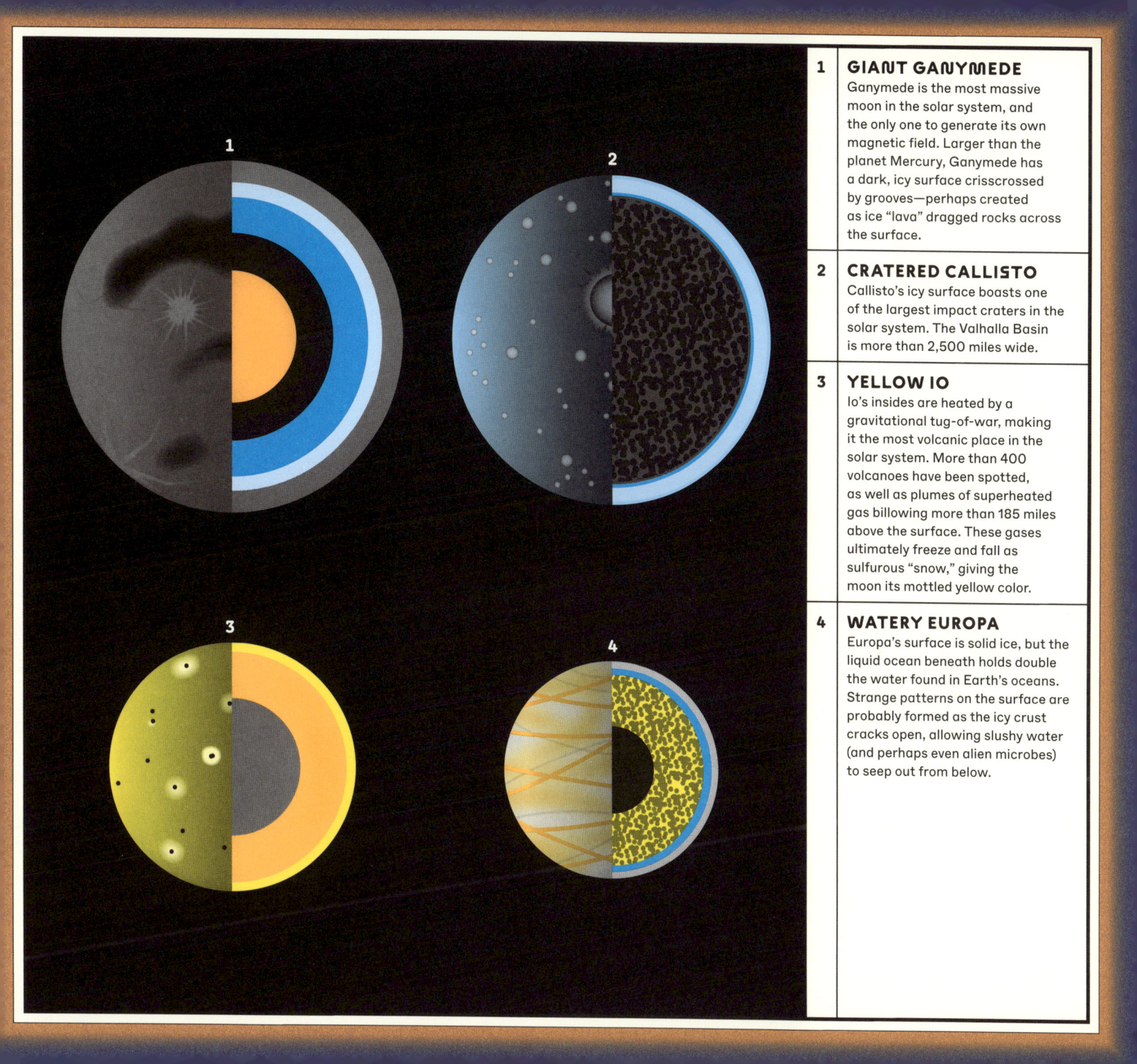

#		
1	**GIANT GANYMEDE**	Ganymede is the most massive moon in the solar system, and the only one to generate its own magnetic field. Larger than the planet Mercury, Ganymede has a dark, icy surface crisscrossed by grooves—perhaps created as ice "lava" dragged rocks across the surface.
2	**CRATERED CALLISTO**	Callisto's icy surface boasts one of the largest impact craters in the solar system. The Valhalla Basin is more than 2,500 miles wide.
3	**YELLOW IO**	Io's insides are heated by a gravitational tug-of-war, making it the most volcanic place in the solar system. More than 400 volcanoes have been spotted, as well as plumes of superheated gas billowing more than 185 miles above the surface. These gases ultimately freeze and fall as sulfurous "snow," giving the moon its mottled yellow color.
4	**WATERY EUROPA**	Europa's surface is solid ice, but the liquid ocean beneath holds double the water found in Earth's oceans. Strange patterns on the surface are probably formed as the icy crust cracks open, allowing slushy water (and perhaps even alien microbes) to seep out from below.

EXPLORING JUPITER

THE VOYAGER PROBES REVEALED THAT JUPITER'S FOUR LARGEST MOONS ARE EQUALLY EXCITING DESTINATIONS. SINCE THEN, SEVERAL SPACECRAFT HAVE MADE THE LONG JOURNEY, AND MORE ARE ON THEIR WAY.

ALL ABOUT

Pioneer 10 and 11 (NASA) were the first spacecraft to fly by Jupiter, on their way out of the solar system. Based on the blurry pictures these probes beamed back, scientists expected the Galilean moons to be fairly boring places. So they were shocked when, eight years later, the Voyager probes (NASA) revealed four fascinating worlds, with features ranging from vast volcanoes to hidden oceans.

NASA's Galileo mission was launched ten years later, to get a really good look. Named after the astronomer who first gazed at the planet through a telescope, the Galileo spacecraft orbited Jupiter for seven years. It even dropped a probe into Jupiter's swirling clouds.

Ulysses (NASA and ESA) and Cassini (NASA, ESA, and ASI) flew past Jupiter on their way to other destinations, but it was 2016 before another dedicated mission arrived at Jupiter. Juno (NASA) used its high-tech instruments to study storm clusters and lightning in Jupiter's clouds, and figure out Jupiter's fuzzy core. Then it set off on the ultimate solar system tour of the Galilean moons, detecting organic compounds on Ganymede, lava lakes on Io, and signs that Europa's icy shell moves around on the ocean beneath.

Future missions will focus even more closely on these fascinating moons. ESA's Jupiter Icy Moons Explorer (JUICE) launched in 2023 and will be closely followed by NASA's Europa Clipper. When they arrive in the 2030s, all eyes will once again be on this most extraordinary solar system neighborhood.

EXPLORATION TIMELINE

Anc.	Discovered and named in ancient times (visible with the naked eye).
1610	First viewed through a telescope by Galileo Galilei.
1972	First probe to fly by Jupiter.
1989	Galileo orbiter enters Jupiter's orbit.
1995	Juno becomes Jupiter's first polar orbiter.
2016	JUICE probe launched on its eight-year journey to Jupiter.
2034	JUICE will become the first probe to orbit one of Jupiter's moons, Ganymede.

ARE WE THERE YET?

- It would take almost 700 years to travel to Jupiter in a car at 60 mph.
- Juno took almost five years to reach Jupiter.
- In order to slow down enough to get into orbit around one of Jupiter's moons, JUICE is taking a scenic eight-year route.

HELPING HUMANS

Soon after they were discovered in the 1600s, Jupiter's moons were being used as a natural clock, helping sailors to figure out how far they had traveled east or west. This helped to avoid shipwrecks and led to much better maps of the world.

★ CATCH UP WITH THE VOYAGER PROBES ON PAGE 107 ★

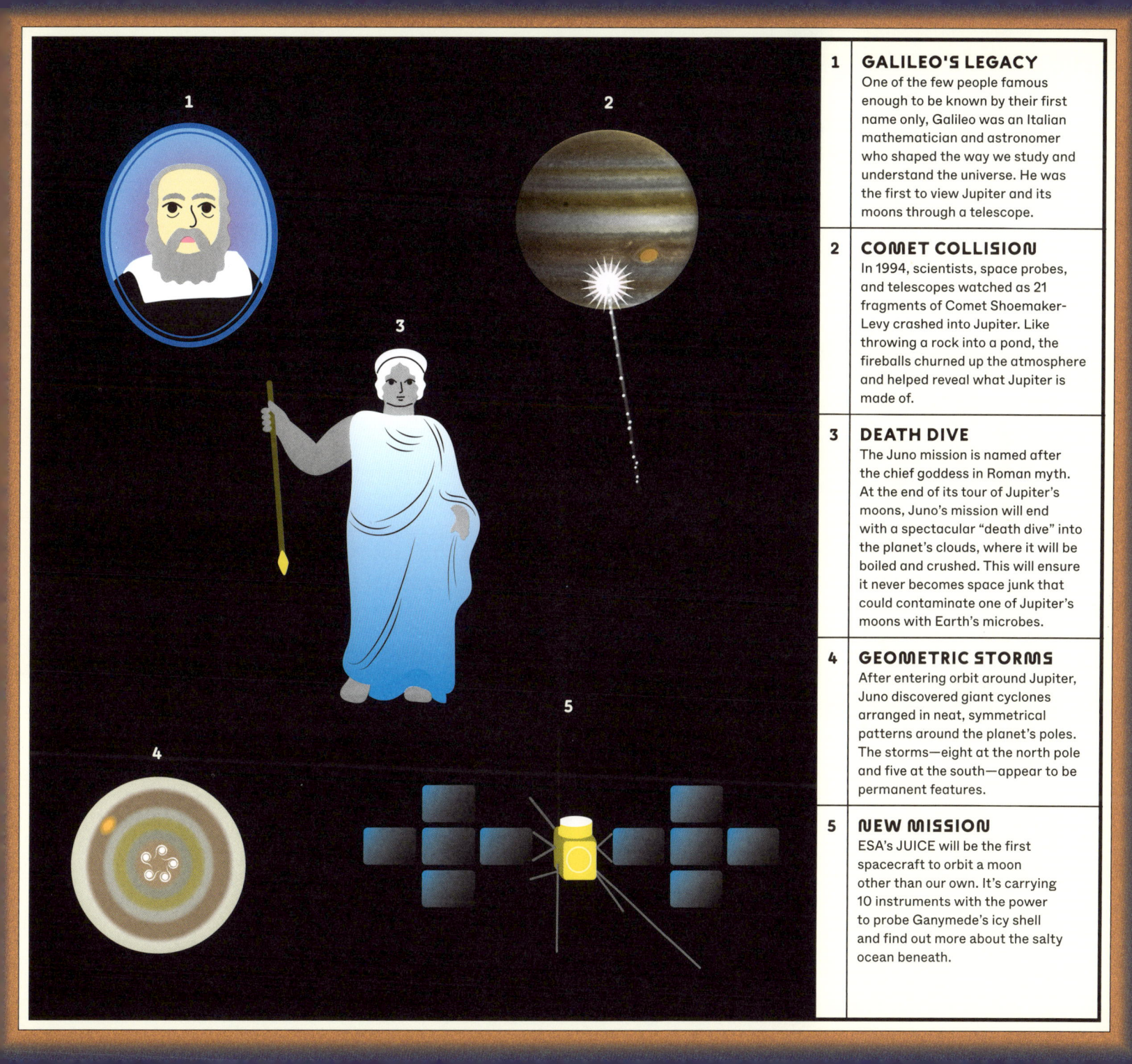

1	**GALILEO'S LEGACY**	One of the few people famous enough to be known by their first name only, Galileo was an Italian mathematician and astronomer who shaped the way we study and understand the universe. He was the first to view Jupiter and its moons through a telescope.
2	**COMET COLLISION**	In 1994, scientists, space probes, and telescopes watched as 21 fragments of Comet Shoemaker-Levy crashed into Jupiter. Like throwing a rock into a pond, the fireballs churned up the atmosphere and helped reveal what Jupiter is made of.
3	**DEATH DIVE**	The Juno mission is named after the chief goddess in Roman myth. At the end of its tour of Jupiter's moons, Juno's mission will end with a spectacular "death dive" into the planet's clouds, where it will be boiled and crushed. This will ensure it never becomes space junk that could contaminate one of Jupiter's moons with Earth's microbes.
4	**GEOMETRIC STORMS**	After entering orbit around Jupiter, Juno discovered giant cyclones arranged in neat, symmetrical patterns around the planet's poles. The storms—eight at the north pole and five at the south—appear to be permanent features.
5	**NEW MISSION**	ESA's JUICE will be the first spacecraft to orbit a moon other than our own. It's carrying 10 instruments with the power to probe Ganymede's icy shell and find out more about the salty ocean beneath.

LIFE IN OUR SOLAR SYSTEM

WATER IS SO IMPORTANT FOR LIFE ON EARTH THAT IT GUIDES THE SEARCH FOR LIFE ELSEWHERE IN THE SOLAR SYSTEM.

Scientists have good models of how the solar system formed, but the hardest thing to explain is life on Earth. Did it only start here, or did it once exist elsewhere in the solar system? Could it have been brought here by meteorites from other solar systems? Finding life or even fossils in other places would help us begin to answer these questions.

To focus their search, scientists start with water. Earth is said to be a "Goldilocks" planet, because it's not too hot or too cold for liquid water to exist on the surface. Venus and Mars also lie in the habitable "Goldilocks zone" around the Sun. But planets and moons can also be heated from within, so this doesn't rule out places in the outer solar system being habitable.

To figure out what alien life in our solar system might look like, astrobiologists study extremophiles on Earth. These are creatures, such as tardigrades, sea monkeys, and tubeworms, that survive and thrive in extremely cold, hot, dark, dry, high-pressure, acidic, or low-oxygen habitats—conditions often found elsewhere in our solar system.

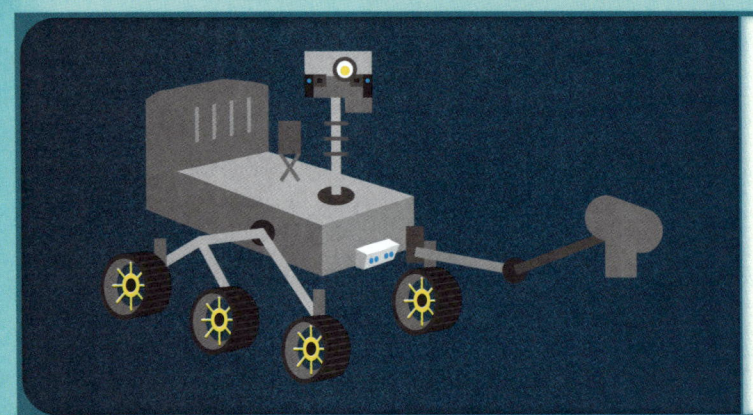

Mars has always inspired theories about aliens, including author Percival Lowell's claim in 1895 that strange marks on Mars were canals dug by Martians. Multiple probes, landers, and rovers have found no alien civilizations, but the search for life on Mars continues. There is plenty of evidence that liquid water once flowed across the surface of Mars, and that billions of years ago it had a thicker, warmer atmosphere. Perseverance rover has been collecting rocks on the bed of an ancient lake on Mars, in the hope they can one day be returned to Earth and examined.

Although Venus is in our solar system's Goldilocks zone, runaway global warming means no liquid water exists on its surface. However, droplets of water do exist in clouds high above the surface, where temperatures are just 86 to 158 °F and the air pressure is similar to Earth's. Mysterious dark streaks in the cloud tops may even be microbes, with sulfur coats to protect them from dangerous UV radiation.

Jupiter's moon Europa is completely covered in water. Although the surface is frozen, the ocean is probably liquid lower down, where it is warmed by Europa's core. There may be deep ocean vents, which on Earth are surrounded by living things that don't rely on the Sun's light or heat.

Although the giant planets don't have solid surfaces, their largest moons are exciting candidates in the hunt for alien life. Saturn's moon Titan has a dense, cloudy nitrogen atmosphere like Earth's, and oceans of liquid methane and ethane, warmed by the planet's core.

On Saturn's moon Enceladus, the Cassini probe flew through giant jets of water vapor spurting into space. Not only did they contain organic substances, they suggest that a huge water ocean under the surface is heated by tidal forces in the moon's rocky core.

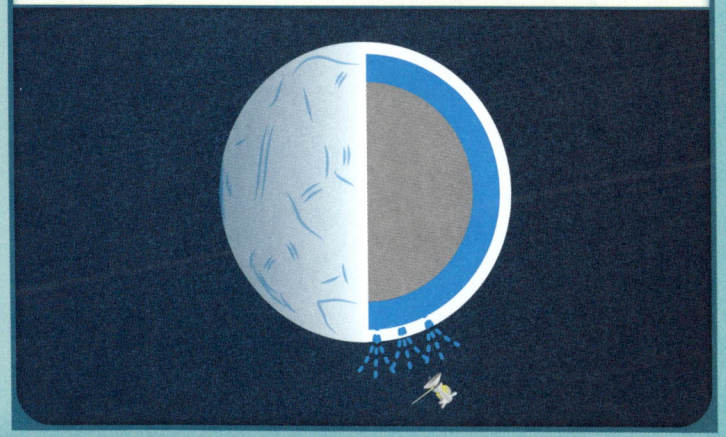

SATURN

CATEGORY	AGE
PLANET	4.59 BILLION YEARS

DESPITE BEING ALMOST TWICE AS FAR FROM THE SUN AS JUPITER, THIS GAS PLANET'S SPECTACULAR RINGS REFLECT SO MUCH SUNLIGHT, THEIR SPARKLE CAN BE SEE FROM EARTH THROUGH THE SIMPLEST TELESCOPES.

ALL ABOUT

Saturn is so distant that the sunlight reaching this planet is a hundred times weaker than the sunlight reaching Earth. However, it's enough to warm the upper layers of Saturn's atmosphere and cause seasonal changes in the weather.

And what weird weather. The fastest winds in the solar system race around Saturn's bulging equator, carrying clouds at up to 1,118 mi/h. Every few decades, raging storms rise through the yellow haze, becoming visible as white spots.

Beneath the clouds, things get stranger still. Like Jupiter, Saturn is not a solid planet but a giant ball of gas and liquid that becomes denser the deeper you go. In the deepest layers, liquid helium can no longer stay mixed with hydrogen and rains out toward the core. Scientists think this helium rain could help to explain Saturn's strange, lopsided magnetic field.

Saturn's most famous feature lies outside the planet. Each of its spectacular rings is a band of glittering, icy fragments orbiting the planet like a procession of tiny moons. Close up you would not see a solid surface, but billions of particles spaced a few feet apart. Some of these ice cubes are the size of houses or even mountains. Others are specks. Together they reflect so much sunlight that all but one ring can be seen through optical telescopes on Earth.

KEY FACTS

- A day lasts 10.66 hr.
- A year lasts 29.46 Earth years.
- More than 145 moons.
- Light from the Sun takes 80 min to reach Saturn.
- Earth could fit inside Saturn around 760 times.

TEMPERATURE

-220°F (at cloud tops)

NAMED AFTER

The Roman god of farming and money (and Jupiter's father).

WHAT IS IT MADE OF?

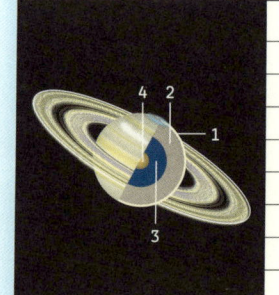

1. Thin gas atmosphere.
2. Outer layer of liquid hydrogen and helium.
3. Liquid metallic hydrogen and helium.
4. Possible rocky and icy core.

PAST, PRESENT, FUTURE

Saturn's ring particles are so "clean" and shiny, that some scientists think they may only be a few hundred million years old—very young in solar system terms. They could be fragments of an icy moon that was ripped apart by the planet's enormous gravitational force.

★ DISCOVER SOME OF SATURN'S MANY MOONS ON PAGE 102 ★

#		
1	**CLOUD BANDS**	Saturn's cloudy layer has separated into bands like Jupiter's, though the yellow, brown, and gray stripes are much harder to see.
2	**MEGASTORMS**	Every 20 to 30 years, a huge storm rages across the surface of Saturn, churning up its clouds and causing ammonia "mushballs" to hail down into deeper layers of the atmosphere. The storms look like giant versions of Earth's hurricanes, but are caused by heat from deep within the planet, rather than heat from the Sun.
3	**GLITTERING RINGS**	Imagine a sheet of paper 300 feet wide and you can get a sense of the dimensions of Saturn's rings, each one thousands of miles across but no higher than a two-story house. This makes the rings almost impossible to see when they are side-on to Earth.
4	**SHEPHERD MOONS**	Particles in the inner rings orbit much more quickly than those in the outer rings. The gaps between rings are caused by some of Saturn's smallest moonlets, which sweep up most of the ring particles in their orbit.
5	**LIGHT SHOWS**	Saturn's strong magnetic field (578 times as powerful as Earth's) acts like a giant **particle accelerator**, giving stray particles a huge energy boost. As the energetic particles spiral down and collide with the top layers of Saturn's atmosphere, they cause glowing aurorae at the poles.

SATURN'S MOONS

CATEGORY	AGE
SATELLITES (PLANETARY)	4.1 TO 4.4 BILLION YEARS

SATURN HAS MORE MOONS THAN ANY OTHER OBJECT IN THE SOLAR SYSTEM, THOUGH MANY HAVE BEEN HARD TO SPOT ALONGSIDE THE PLANET'S DAZZLING RINGS.

ALL ABOUT

Orbiting among and far beyond Saturn's glittering rings, Saturn's many moons have been historically hard to count. Planet-sized Titan was discovered in 1655, relatively easy to spot as the second-largest moon in the solar system. But it was 16 years before astronomers began adding to the list.

After 350 years, the invention of space telescopes, and several visits from spacecraft, more than 80 moons had been named. Then suddenly in 2023, astronomers announced the discovery of 63 more, spotted through a telescope mounted on top of a Hawaiian volcano. It proved that even the best-known corners of the solar system are still full of surprises.

Only Saturn's "major" moons—Titan, Rhea, Iapetus, Dione, Tethys, Enceladus, and Mimas—look and behave like regular moons. Many of the rest are tiny, wonky lumps of ice, tumbling chaotically around the planet. Others are small asteroids, captured in Saturn's orbit.

Titan is the only moon with a proper atmosphere, and the only place in the solar system (except Earth) with liquid oceans on its surface. Mimas and Tethys have old and heavily cratered surfaces. Bright patches on Dione and Rhea suggest ancient highlands peppered with active cryovolcanoes, while Iapetus has two faces, one snowy white and the other dark as coal. Two of Saturn's larger moons share their path around Saturn with a pair of smaller moons, known as Trojan moons. One of them is Calypso, the most reflective object in the solar system thanks to fresh ice collected on its surface.

With more than 140 smaller moons, each following their own rules, there are still plenty of surprises in store.

TITAN FACTS

- Titan is around 50 percent wider than Earth's Moon and wider even than Mercury.
- Titan takes 15 days and 22 hr to orbit Saturn.
- Titan is more than three times farther from Saturn than the Moon is from Earth.

TITAN TEMPERATURE

-292°F

NAMED AFTER

Saturn's moons are named after giants from different myths around the world.

WHAT IS TITAN MADE OF?

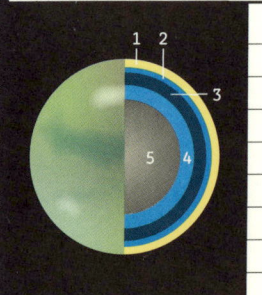

1 Dense, hazy atmosphere, mainly nitrogen, with some methane.
2 Outer crust of water ice, coated with organic molecules from the atmosphere.
3 Underground ocean of salty liquid water.
4 Shell of high-pressure water ice.
5 Rocky, silicate core.

PAST, PRESENT, FUTURE

In around five billion years, our Sun will expand to become a **red giant**. Objects in the outer solar system will receive much more light and warmth, perhaps giving life a chance to evolve on the watery moons of Jupiter and Saturn.

★ FIND OUT WHY TITAN AND ENCELADUS ARE TANTALIZING PLACES TO LOOK FOR ALIEN LIFE ON PAGE 98 ★

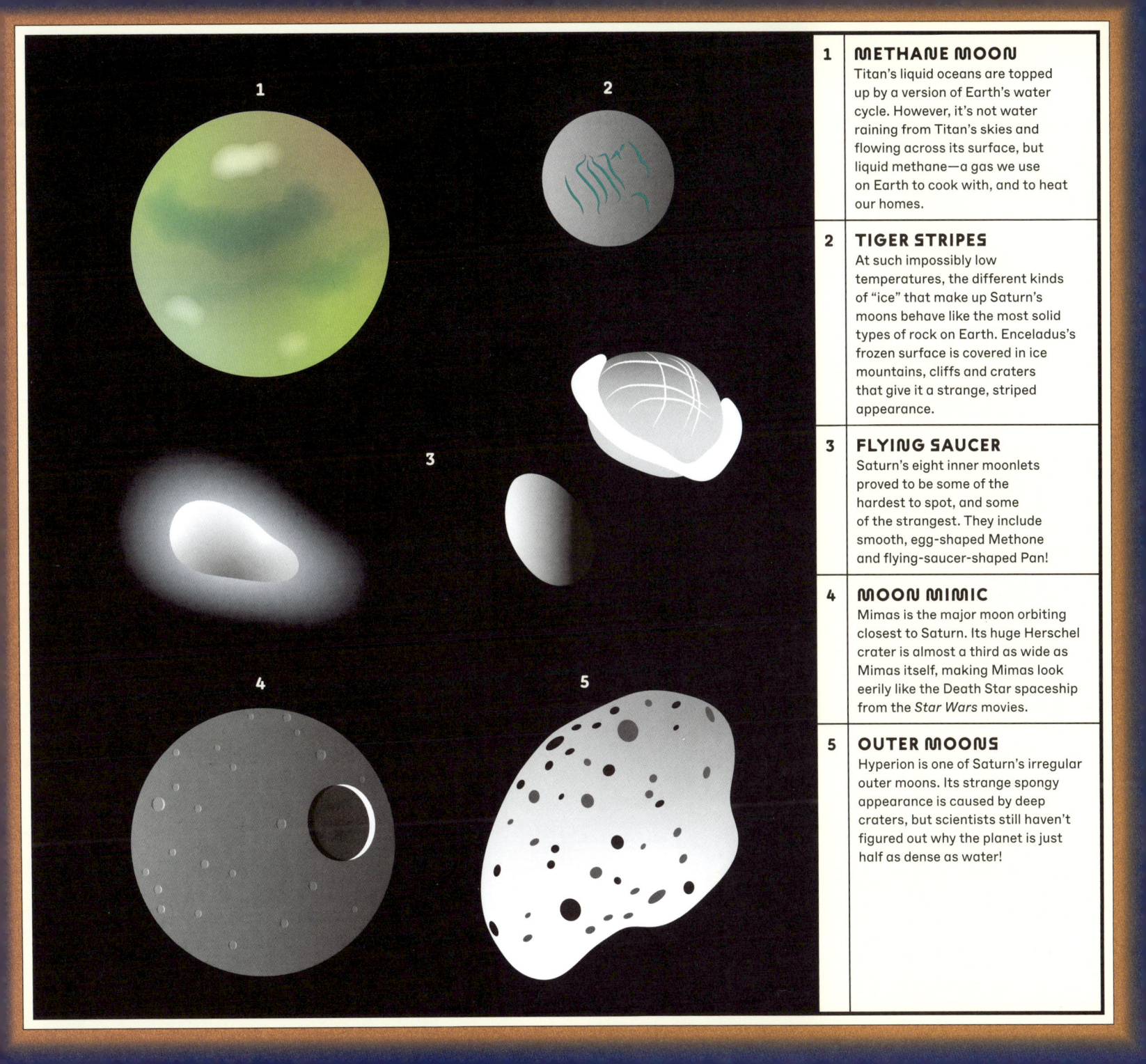

#	
1	**METHANE MOON** Titan's liquid oceans are topped up by a version of Earth's water cycle. However, it's not water raining from Titan's skies and flowing across its surface, but liquid methane—a gas we use on Earth to cook with, and to heat our homes.
2	**TIGER STRIPES** At such impossibly low temperatures, the different kinds of "ice" that make up Saturn's moons behave like the most solid types of rock on Earth. Enceladus's frozen surface is covered in ice mountains, cliffs and craters that give it a strange, striped appearance.
3	**FLYING SAUCER** Saturn's eight inner moonlets proved to be some of the hardest to spot, and some of the strangest. They include smooth, egg-shaped Methone and flying-saucer-shaped Pan!
4	**MOON MIMIC** Mimas is the major moon orbiting closest to Saturn. Its huge Herschel crater is almost a third as wide as Mimas itself, making Mimas look eerily like the Death Star spaceship from the *Star Wars* movies.
5	**OUTER MOONS** Hyperion is one of Saturn's irregular outer moons. Its strange spongy appearance is caused by deep craters, but scientists still haven't figured out why the planet is just half as dense as water!

EXPLORING SATURN

JUST FOUR SPACECRAFT HAVE MADE THE LONG TRIP TO SATURN. THEY INCLUDE THE CASSINI-HUYGENS PROBE, ONE OF THE MOST SUCCESSFUL AND GROUNDBREAKING SPACE MISSIONS EVER.

ALL ABOUT

Saturn is the most distant planet visible from Earth without a telescope. For about 10 months of the year, it appears as a wandering "star" in the night sky. With a simple telescope, you can even see the rings if Saturn happens to be at the right angle and they are tilted toward us. Galileo Galilei was the first to see this, and joked that they looked like ears!

Pioneer 11 (NASA) and both Voyager probes visited Saturn on their way to the very edges of the solar system, but it was NASA and ESA's Cassini-Huygens probe that revealed what Saturn was really like.

One of the largest, heaviest and most complicated probes ever built, Cassini orbited Saturn for 13 years, swooping through gaps in the rings and peering at 19 of its most interesting moons. It built a picture of a planet, moons, and rings more active and exciting than anyone had imagined.

Most amazing of all were Saturn's moons. After spotting jets of water vapor spraying from Enceladus, Cassini flew through them and detected simple organic molecules—the basic building blocks of life here on Earth.

The ultimate target, however, was Saturn's largest moon Titan. Seven months into the mission, the Huygens probe parachuted through Titan's thick, hazy atmosphere, landing on its surface. It had become the first spacecraft ever to land on an object in the outer solar system.

EXPLORATION TIMELINE

Anc.	Discovered in ancient times (visible with the naked eye for about 10 months of each year).
1610	Galileo Galilei views Saturn through a telescope.
1655	Christiaan Huygens discovers first moon of Saturn: Titan.
1979	Pioneer 11 is Saturn's first flyby probe.
2004	Cassini becomes the first probe to orbit Saturn.
2005	The smaller Huygens probe is dropped by Cassini and lands on Titan.
2017	Cassini plunges into Saturn's atmosphere, sending back data during five orbits and becoming Saturn's first atmospheric probe.

ARE WE THERE YET?

- Pioneer 11 reached Saturn in six and a half years.
- Voyager 1 took just three years and two months.
- Cassini-Huygens took six years and seven months, taking a more complicated route past Venus, Earth, and Jupiter in order to be captured by Saturn's gravity.

HELPING HUMANS

Watching collisions in Saturn's rings helps scientists figure out how our solar system formed. Meanwhile, the organic molecules, such as hydrocarbons, discovered on Titan and Enceladus could reveal how life on Earth got started.

★ FIND OUT MORE ABOUT GALILEO GALILEI'S DISCOVERIES ON PAGE 97 ★

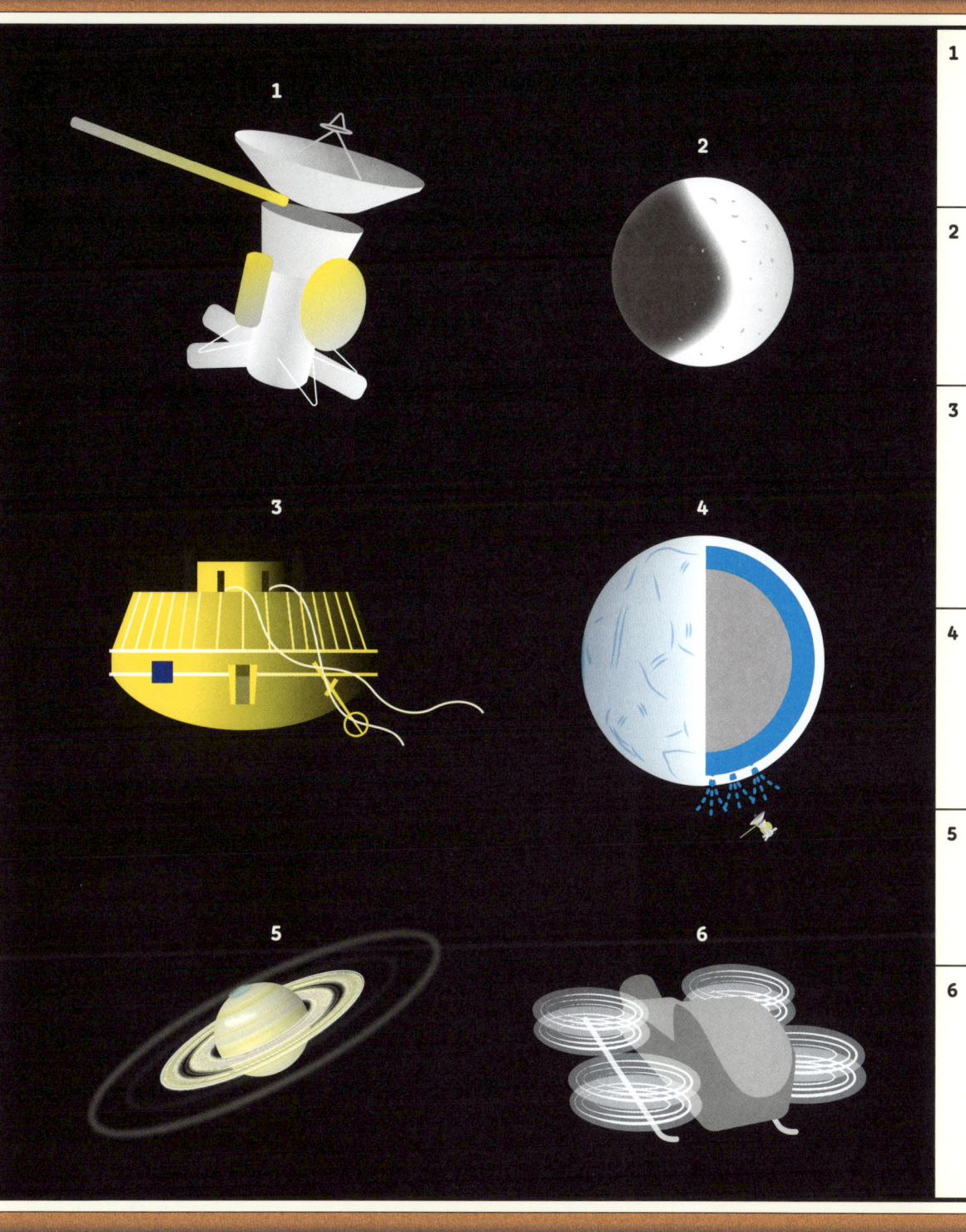

1	**LEGENDARY MISSION**	Most of our knowledge of Saturn was gathered by the Cassini-Huygens mission. Its journey ended with a death dive into Saturn's atmosphere, to stop its moons from ever becoming contaminated.
2	**NEW VIEWS**	Saturn's two-toned moon Iapetus was discovered by Italian astronomer Giovanni Cassini in the 1600s. About 350 years later, the Cassini probe revealed one snow-white side, and one as dark as coal.
3	**MOON LANDING**	Before Cassini-Huygens, Titan's surface had been hidden by its hazy orange atmosphere. Scientists didn't even know if Titan had solid ground. Huygens sent back photos of a rocky, sandy surface that looks like Mars—only every boulder and pebble was rock-hard ice.
4	**WATER JETS**	Cassini swooped so close to Enceladus, it was just 19 miles from the moon's icy crust. It even flew through jets of water spraying from cracks in the crust, proving that the planet's underground ocean must be heated from the inside.
5	**HOT RINGS**	Cassini revealed that each of Saturn's seven main rings is made up of thousands of thinner rings, packed with particles that constantly clump and collide.
6	**DRAGONFLY**	NASA has designed a drone to study Titan in amazing detail. With eight rotors, Dragonfly will be able to fly through Titan's thick atmosphere in a way that would be impossible on other moons that don't have atmospheres to provide the necessary lift.

INTERPLANETARY PROBES

SCIENTISTS HAVE DISCOVERED A GREAT DEAL ABOUT THE SOLAR SYSTEM USING EARTH-BASED TELESCOPES, BUT TO TRULY UNDERSTAND THESE WORLDS, WE NEEDED TO GET CLOSER.

A total of more than 200 probes—uncrewed spacecraft sent on missions to explore space and report back—have explored our solar system. Every planet has been visited, as well as several moons, asteroids, comets, and the Sun itself. Interplanetary probes travel long distances, observing objects as they fly past. Orbiters allow themselves to be captured by a planet's or moon's gravity, going into orbit around it so they can collect detailed information over a longer period.

Probes have also been put into orbit around a dwarf planet, asteroids, and a comet. Some probes have released smaller atmospheric probes, impactors that crash into an object and landers that touch down gently on an object's surface.

As well as sending back spectacular images, probes have mapped the surfaces of planets and moons using radar, "sniffed" their atmospheres, detected substances on the ground, watched alien weather, and measured magnetic fields. At the same time, the technology used to design probes has improved—from the tiny, sphere-shaped Luna 1 (USSR), to the 6.5-ton, truck-sized Jupiter Icy Moons Explorer (ESA) currently on its way to explore Jupiter's moons.

EARLY PROBES

Early probes were small and simple compared to the rockets used to launch them into space. Luna 1 (USSR) was the first spacecraft to escape Earth's gravity and fly past the Moon. It was a ball with five antennas, and a range of instruments for measuring magnetic fields, radiation, and micrometeorites.

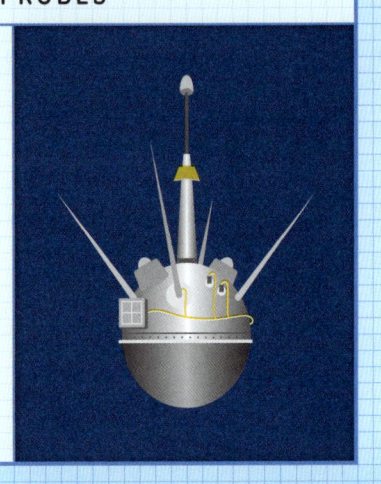

CASSINI PROBE

Although a probe's journey is preprogrammed, mission control also thinks on its feet to repurpose missions and equipment when needed. When the Cassini probe spotted unexpected jets of ice streaming from Saturn's moon Enceladus, its path was adjusted to let it swoop through a jet and collect samples.

NEW HORIZONS

NASA's New Horizons probe was the first to visit the distant dwarf planet Pluto and its moon Charon, before venturing deeper into the **Kuiper Belt** to observe even smaller objects (see page 118).

Launched in 2006 by an Atlas V rocket, New Horizons left Earth at a record launch speed of 35,800 mi/h. Even so, it took nine years to make its 3-billion-mile journey to Pluto, carrying out a flyby of Jupiter on the way.

The grand-piano-sized probe was packed with instruments to map Pluto's surface, "taste" its atmosphere, and take its temperature. After flying by Jupiter, the probe went into hibernation mode for the next seven years of the long journey, to conserve energy for the Pluto flyby.

Soon after New Horizons was launched, Pluto was downgraded from planet to dwarf planet (see page 26). However, New Horizon's amazing photographs of Pluto's blue skies, red snow, mountains, and glaciers made many think that this distant world still deserves planet status.

Pluto is so far away that radio signals traveling at the speed of light took four and a half hours to reach Earth. It took New Horizons 16 months to beam back all its data about Pluto.

New Horizon's nuclear power source will last until around 2040. It has been programmed for a new mission to collect data about the solar wind in the farthest reaches of the solar system.

BEYOND THE SOLAR SYSTEM

The Voyager probes are the only spacecraft to have beamed signals back from outside our solar system. After flying past the systems of Jupiter and Saturn, Voyager 1 crossed the heliopause—the outer edge of the area around the Sun where its magnetic field and solar wind are felt—in 2012, entering interstellar space beyond the reach of the solar wind. Voyager 2 followed in 2018, after making flybys of all four gas giants.

URANUS

CATEGORY	AGE
PLANET	4.59 BILLION YEARS

THIS ICE GIANT SAUNTERS AROUND THE SOLAR SYSTEM ON ITS SIDE. FROM A DISTANCE IT APPEARS SERENE BLUE-GREEN, BUT URANUS HAS SOME OF THE WILDEST WEATHER IN THE SOLAR SYSTEM.

ALL ABOUT

Although Uranus is smaller than Jupiter and Saturn, it is still a giant planet. Its core alone is the size of Earth. Lying twice as far from the Sun as Saturn, this ice giant takes an entire human lifetime to complete one orbit of our star.

The main "ices" that make up Uranus's mantle and atmosphere are water, methane, and ammonia. The methane soaks up most of the faint red, yellow, and orange sunlight that reaches the planet. The hazy upper atmosphere reflects mainly blue and green light.

Uranus is not alone in space, but orbited by multiple moons and 13 narrow rings. Rather than reflective ice, the rings are made up of charcoal-dark dust or boulders, so they don't sparkle like Saturn's rings. The rings also appear to circle the planet from top to bottom, thanks to the dramatic tilt of Uranus's axis.

Perhaps due to a huge collision in the past, Uranus has been knocked on to its side and "rolls" rather than spins around the Sun. This means extreme seasons, with each half of the planet experiencing decades of summer, followed by decades of dark winter. Even in the summer, though, Uranus remains bitterly cold. Its minimum temperature of -371.6°F is one of the coldest measured anywhere in the solar system.

Beneath the cloud tops, winds race around Uranus at up to 560 mi/h. Violent cyclones have been spotted, far less stable and harder to predict than the famous storms of Jupiter. Because a year on Uranus lasts so long, today's scientists are seeing each of its seasons for the first time. There are many mysteries left to solve, including why Uranus is colder than Neptune in places—despite being far closer to the Sun—and why temperatures on the planet are continuing to fall.

KEY FACTS

- A day lasts 17.24 hr.
- A year lasts 84 Earth years.
- At least 28 moons.
- Light from the Sun reaches Uranus in 2 hr, 40 min.
- Earth could fit inside Uranus 63 times.

TEMPERATURE

☼ -319°F
❄ -371°F

NAMED AFTER

The Ancient Greek god of the sky. However, its discoverer originally named it "George's Star" after the king of Great Britain and Ireland at the time.

WHAT IS IT MADE OF?

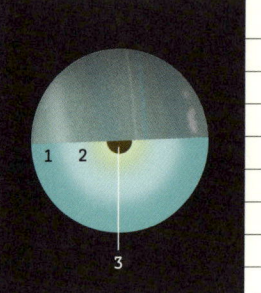

1. Thick, cloudy atmosphere, mainly hydrogen and helium, with a small amount of methane.
2. Dense, slushy mantle, made of different ices (water, methane, and ammonia).
3. Small rocky core.

PAST, PRESENT, FUTURE

Uranus's surface is far cooler than expected—it is as cold as Neptune, which lies much farther from the Sun. A catastrophic impact in the past could explain this, as it may have caused Uranus to cool down more quickly than the other planets in the solar system.

★ FIND OUT HOW SPACE SCIENTISTS OVERCAME TECHNICAL CHALLENGES TO EXPLORE URANUS ON PAGE 110 ★

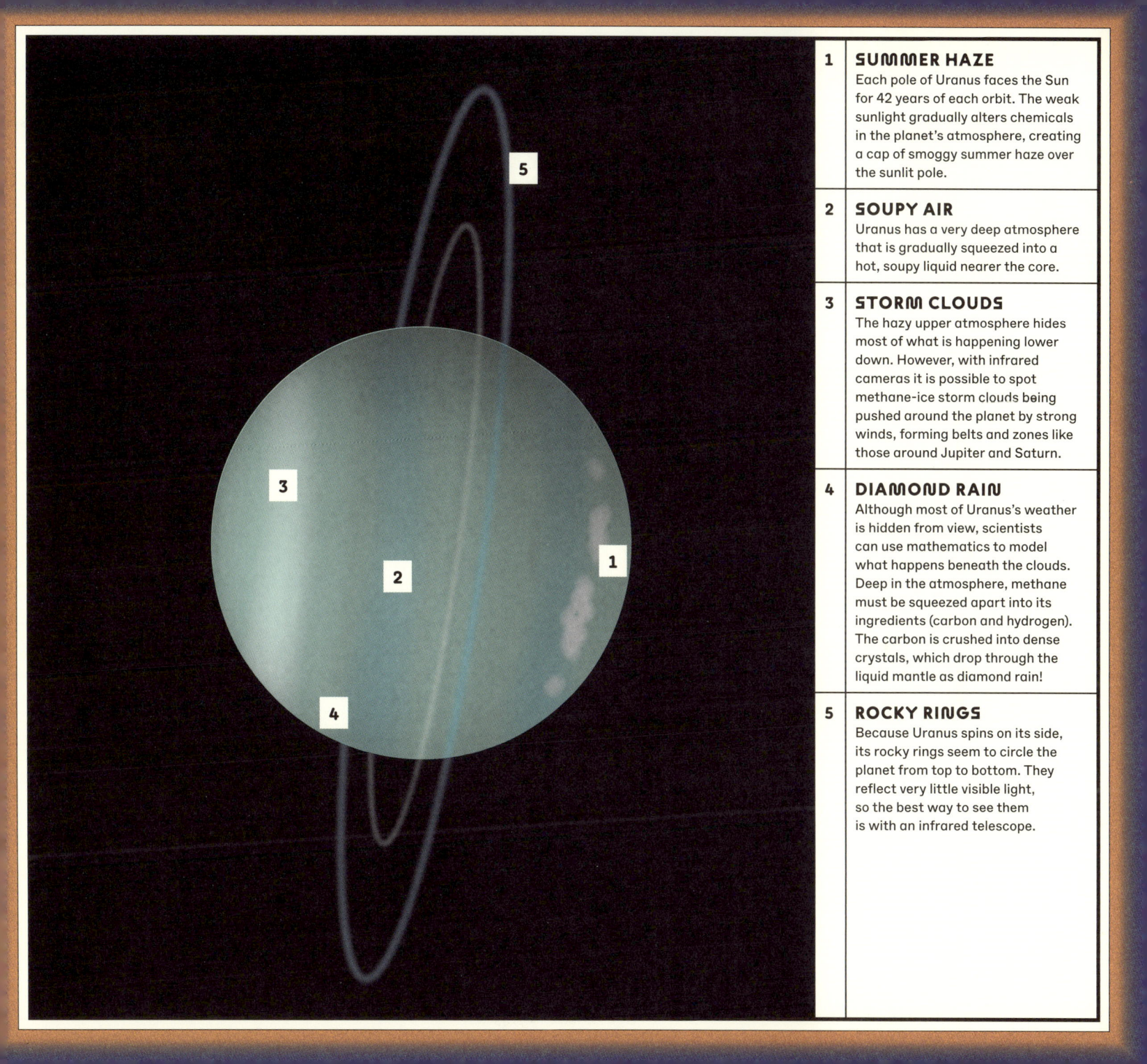

1	**SUMMER HAZE** Each pole of Uranus faces the Sun for 42 years of each orbit. The weak sunlight gradually alters chemicals in the planet's atmosphere, creating a cap of smoggy summer haze over the sunlit pole.
2	**SOUPY AIR** Uranus has a very deep atmosphere that is gradually squeezed into a hot, soupy liquid nearer the core.
3	**STORM CLOUDS** The hazy upper atmosphere hides most of what is happening lower down. However, with infrared cameras it is possible to spot methane-ice storm clouds being pushed around the planet by strong winds, forming belts and zones like those around Jupiter and Saturn.
4	**DIAMOND RAIN** Although most of Uranus's weather is hidden from view, scientists can use mathematics to model what happens beneath the clouds. Deep in the atmosphere, methane must be squeezed apart into its ingredients (carbon and hydrogen). The carbon is crushed into dense crystals, which drop through the liquid mantle as diamond rain!
5	**ROCKY RINGS** Because Uranus spins on its side, its rocky rings seem to circle the planet from top to bottom. They reflect very little visible light, so the best way to see them is with an infrared telescope.

EXPLORING URANUS

ONLY ONE SPACECRAFT HAS ZOOMED PAST THIS DISTANT PLANET SO FAR. IN JUST SIX HOURS, IT GATHERED MOST OF THE INFORMATION WE HAVE ABOUT THIS MYSTERIOUS ICE GIANT.

ALL ABOUT

Although it is sometimes possible to see Uranus in the night sky without a telescope, the planet is so faint and slow-moving that for many thousands of years it was mistaken for a star. British astronomer William Herschel, peering through a telescope in 1781, was the first to realize he was seeing a planet. This discovery doubled the size of the known solar system at the time.

Features of this distant planet were figured out slowly as telescopes became more powerful. The rings were discovered almost 200 years after Uranus, when scientists noticed that a star behind Uranus became dimmer as the rings passed in front of it.

When the space probe Voyager 2 (NASA) flew past Uranus on its way to Neptune, scientists were poised to learn as much as they could. The first close-up brought new moons into view and gave astronomers a proper look at the rings. Voyager 2 also snapped photos of some of Uranus's largest moons, capturing cragged surfaces, vast canyons, and steep cliffs.

The Hubble Space Telescope and Webb Space Telescope have also helped reveal some of Uranus's mysteries (and yet more moons) from almost 1.8 billion miles away. Recently, the New Horizons probe (NASA) peered back at the planet from the Kuiper Belt, allowing us to see both sides at the same time!

EXPLORATION TIMELINE

- **1781** — Uranus discovered by William Herschel with a telescope.
- **1787** — The first of Uranus's moons are discovered by William Herschel.
- **1986** — Voyager 2 becomes the first probe to fly past Uranus.
- **2005** — Two new rings and two new moons of Uranus are discovered in photographs taken by the Hubble Space Telescope.
- **2024** — Hubble and New Horizons peer at Uranus at the same time, from different directions.

ARE WE THERE YET?

- Uranus orbits 19 times farther from the Sun than Earth.
- A car traveling at 60 mph would take more than 3,250 years to travel this far.

HELPING HUMANS

Spotting moons of a planet allows scientists to "weigh" planets, by looking at how long each moon takes to travel around its orbit.

This is how scientists calculated that Uranus has a mass just 14.5 times that of Earth, despite taking up 63 times as much space.

★ FIND OUT WHAT NEW HORIZONS IS DOING IN THE KUIPER BELT ON PAGE 118 ★

1	**MANY MOONS** Uranus has five major moons—Miranda, Ariel, Umbriel, Titania, and Oberon—and a host of small outer moons and inner moonlets. Most are dark and dense rocky worlds. Some may have oceans of salty water beneath their icy surfaces.
2	**WHAT'S IN A NAME?** Many of Uranus's moons are named after characters from Shakespeare's plays, including Titania from *A Midsummer Night's Dream* (pictured). Her name is given to Uranus's largest moon, which is about half the size of Earth's moon.
3	**SUMMER SMOG** Powerful space telescopes are the main way that scientists find out more about Uranus at the moment. The Webb Space Telescope's infrared camera has revealed exciting features that were previously invisible, including a summer smog cap over the North Pole.
4	**COUNTING RINGS** Astronomers are still spotting new moons and rings around Uranus. The two features are closely connected. Dust and rubble knocked off moons by meteorites feeds the rings.

NEPTUNE

CATEGORY	AGE
PLANET	4.59 BILLION YEARS

THE OUTERMOST PLANET IN OUR SOLAR SYSTEM IS SO DIMLY LIT BY THE SUN THAT IT'S NEVER VISIBLE IN THE NIGHT SKY. YET SOMEHOW ITS LARGEST MOON TRITON IS GETTING WARMER.

ALL ABOUT

Like fellow ice giant Uranus, Neptune probably started off closer to the Sun. Around 600 million years after the solar system formed (long before breakfast on cosmic timescales) it was pushed out to the coldest, dimmest orbit of any major planet. Even dwarf planet Pluto sometimes passes closer to the Sun.

From this distance, the Sun is 900 times dimmer than it is on Earth. Neptune actually gives out more heat than it gets from the Sun, though nobody yet knows why. This inner heat source warms the atmosphere from below, causing supersonic winds that race around the planet.

Among Neptune's many moons, Triton stands out as special. For starters, it's 200 times as big as all of Neptune's other moons put together. It is bigger even than Pluto. It also orbits Neptune in the opposite direction to the planet's spin. This suggests that Triton was a dwarf planet from the nearby Kuiper Belt that strayed too close and got captured by Neptune's gravity.

Triton has one of the coldest surfaces in the solar system, with an ice cap of frozen nitrogen. If you released some of Earth's air on Triton, it would immediately freeze and fall to the ground as snow. However, the moon also seems to heat itself from within. Cryovolcanoes dot its surface, erupting with icy slush that slowly flattens craters and smooths the surface.

KEY FACTS

- A day lasts 16.11 hr.
- A year lasts for 164.8 Earth years.
- At least 16 moons.
- Light from the Sun takes 4 hr to reach Neptune.
- Earth would fit inside Neptune around 57 times.

TEMPERATURE

-353°F (at cloud tops)

NAMED AFTER

The Roman god of the sea. The moon Triton is named after the son of Poseidon, the Ancient Greek version of Neptune.

WHAT IS IT MADE OF?

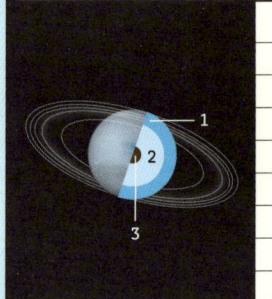

1. Thick, hazy atmosphere of mostly hydrogen and helium, with a little methane.
2. Huge mantle of hot, dense "ices" (water, methane, and ammonia).
3. Small rocky core.

PAST, PRESENT, FUTURE

Triton is closer to Neptune than our Moon is to Earth. One day, Neptune's gravitational force will tear the moon apart. The dust and rubble will probably form a new ring system around the planet.

★ FIND OUT HOW SCIENTISTS HAVE EXPLORED THIS LONELY PLANET ON PAGE 114 ★

1	**CLINGY PARENT** Some of Neptune's smaller moons orbit the planet at vast distances, but Neptune manages to keep hold of them because the Sun is too far away to compete.
2	**SUPERSONIC WINDS** Neptune's supersonic winds are some of the strongest in the solar system, raging around the planet at up to 1,300 mi/h. They carry clouds in belts and bands, though these are far harder to see than those on Saturn and Jupiter. In recent years, the wispy, white methane clouds that once streaked Neptune's surface have disappeared.
3	**DARK SPOTS** Mysterious dark spots have been spotted on Neptune's cloudy surface. Astronomers aren't yet sure if they are storms (like Jupiter's Great Red Spot), gaps in the clouds, or something more mysterious like dark patches of haze. On Earth, haze is created when sunlight strikes tiny particles of pollution in the air.
4	**THIN RINGS** Neptune has at least five thin and fragile rings, as well as partial rings called arcs that do not make a complete circle around the planet.
5	**LONG SUMMERS** Despite being so far from the Sun, Neptune does have seasons. The side of the planet tilted toward the Sun forms more clouds during a 40-year summer, becoming brighter.
6	**BULGING MIDDLE** Neptune spins so fast on its axis that its equator noticeably bulges. Deep inside the planet, liquid in the icy mantle swirls around, creating the planet's powerful magnetic field.

EXPLORING NEPTUNE

LIKE URANUS, NEPTUNE IS A LONELY PLANET THAT HAS ONLY BEEN VISITED BY ONE SPACE PROBE. UNTIL RECENTLY, MOST OF THE WORLD DIDN'T EVEN KNOW THE PLANET'S TRUE COLOR.

ALL ABOUT

Neptune was discovered because astronomers went exploring to find it. After tracking Uranus on its long journey around the solar system, they noticed a wobble in the orbit of this icy giant that could only be explained by the gravitational pull of a planet-sized object nearby.

They calculated the exact spot where that planet should be, pointed telescopes at it and, found Neptune. The first of its moons was discovered just 17 days later.

Even through a telescope, Neptune is so distant and dim that it looks like any other faint star in the sky. To get a proper look, scientists had to wait until Voyager 2 (NASA) passed the planet on its way out of the solar system.

The space probe got within 3,000 miles of Neptune's cloud surface, and sent back photos of three strange dark spots on the surface. It also spotted six new moonlets and confirmed Neptune's narrow rings really existed.

Since that visit, space scientists have had to rely on telescopes to keep exploring Neptune. Neptune's rings were detected by telescope, when stars appeared to blink on and off as the planet's rings passed in front. New moons and moonlets have been spotted by ground-based telescopes and by the Hubble Space Telescope. More recently, the Webb Space Telescope has beamed back spectacular **infrared** images of Neptune's rings.

For planetary scientists, the ultimate goal is a dedicated mission to Uranus and Neptune. Many proposals have been put forward, but they are always competing with other interesting targets in space. At the moment, only China's space agency, CNSA, is considering a trek to the ice giants.

EXPLORATION TIMELINE

1846	Neptune is discovered by William Lassell with a telescope.
1846	William Lassell discovers Neptune's largest moon, Triton.
1949	A second moon is discovered by Gerard Kuiper.
1984	Neptune's rings are detected for the first time.
1989	Voyager 2 becomes Neptune's first flyby probe, discovering several new moons and confirming that the planet has rings.

ARE WE THERE YET?

- After taking nine years to reach Uranus, it was another three years before Voyager 2 sped past Neptune.
- Neptune is a whopping 30 times farther from the Sun than Earth.
- A car traveling at 60 mph would take more than 5,000 years to travel this far.

HELPING HUMANS

Using NASA's Kepler telescope, astronomers were able to track Neptune's daily rotation, cloud movements, and changes in reflected sunlight.

As astronomers develop techniques to watch Neptune from a great distance, they also learn how to find out more about exoplanets in different solar systems.

★ FIND OUT WHICH ELEMENT IS NAMED AFTER NEPTUNE ON PAGE 157 ★

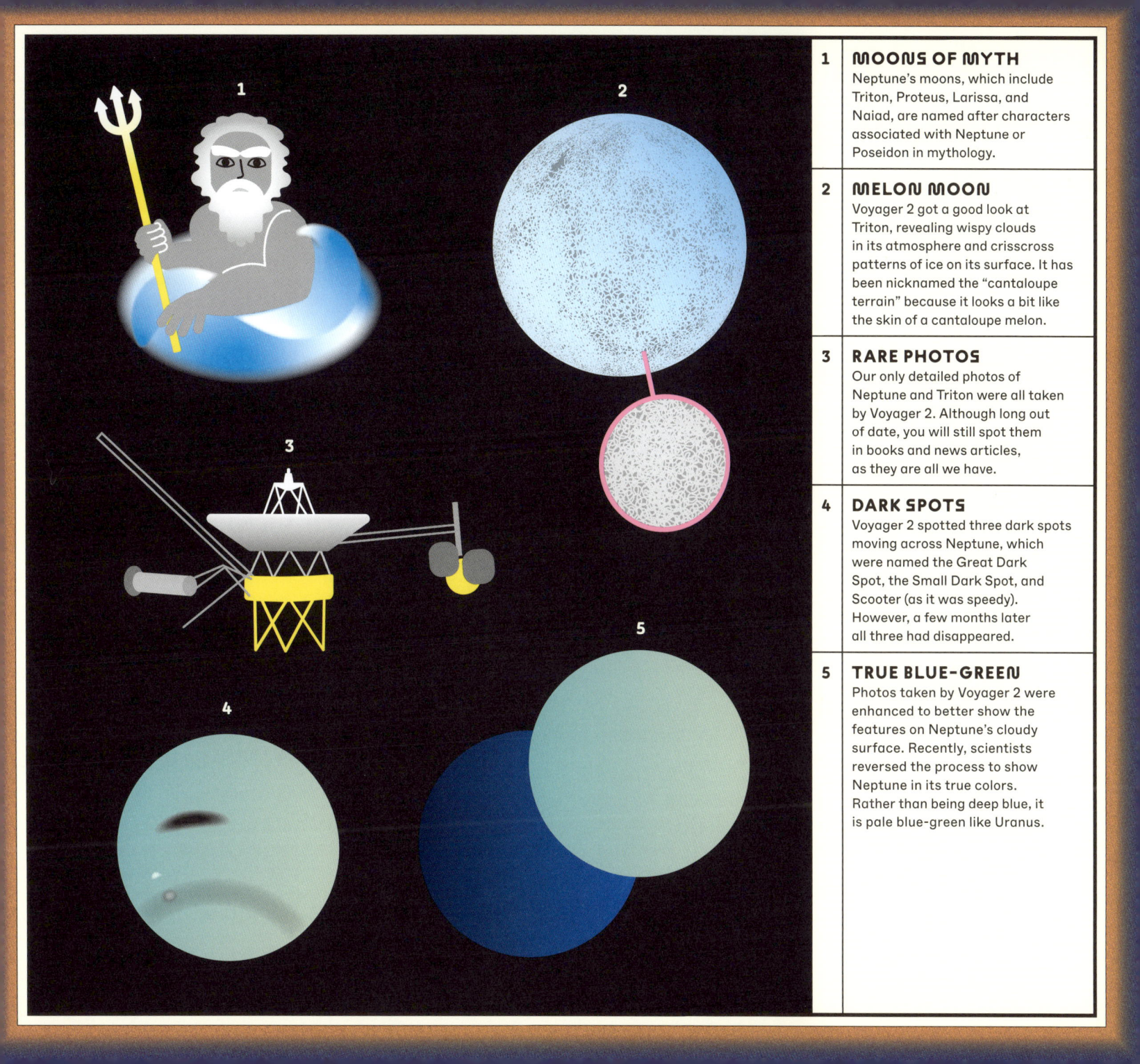

#		
1	**MOONS OF MYTH**	Neptune's moons, which include Triton, Proteus, Larissa, and Naiad, are named after characters associated with Neptune or Poseidon in mythology.
2	**MELON MOON**	Voyager 2 got a good look at Triton, revealing wispy clouds in its atmosphere and crisscross patterns of ice on its surface. It has been nicknamed the "cantaloupe terrain" because it looks a bit like the skin of a cantaloupe melon.
3	**RARE PHOTOS**	Our only detailed photos of Neptune and Triton were all taken by Voyager 2. Although long out of date, you will still spot them in books and news articles, as they are all we have.
4	**DARK SPOTS**	Voyager 2 spotted three dark spots moving across Neptune, which were named the Great Dark Spot, the Small Dark Spot, and Scooter (as it was speedy). However, a few months later all three had disappeared.
5	**TRUE BLUE-GREEN**	Photos taken by Voyager 2 were enhanced to better show the features on Neptune's cloudy surface. Recently, scientists reversed the process to show Neptune in its true colors. Rather than being deep blue, it is pale blue-green like Uranus.

PLUTO & THE KUIPER BELT

CATEGORY	AGE
DWARF PLANET/ PLUTOID	4.5 BILLION YEARS

DWARF PLANET PLUTO HOLDS A SPECIAL PLACE IN PEOPLE'S HEARTS AND IN OUR ASTRONOMICAL HISTORY— ESPECIALLY AFTER NEW HORIZONS PHOTOGRAPHED ITS SPECTACULAR SURFACE.

ALL ABOUT

Beyond Neptune's orbit lies an area of the solar system called the Kuiper Belt. Like the asteroid belt between Mars and Jupiter, it's a disc made up of billions of bits of rocky rubble, all orbiting the Sun at different speeds. The largest of these **Kuiper Belt Objects (KBOs)** is dwarf planet Pluto.

Unlike the gas and ice giants of the outer solar system, Pluto is a small, rocky world, covered in a thick layer of ices, including water ice that forms jagged mountains. Liquid water oceans may still exist below the surface. Pluto's long, elliptical orbit sometimes brings it closer to the Sun than Neptune. As the surface warms, some of the ice on the surface becomes a gas, forming a wispy atmosphere.

Five smaller objects have been spotted orbiting Pluto. The largest is Charon, so close in size to Pluto that they can be thought of as a double planet. From Pluto's surface, Charon would look eight times wider than our Moon does from Earth. Pluto's other moons are called Nix, Hydra, Kerberos, and Styx.

The distance from Neptune's orbit to the outer edge of the Kuiper Belt is roughly the same as the distance from Neptune to the Sun. In this vast area of space, astronomers have spotted more than 2,000 "Trans-Neptunian Objects," including many with similar characteristics to Pluto. So far, just three have been officially named as dwarf planets: Eris, Haumea, and Makemake.

KEY FACTS

- A day lasts 6.39 Earth days.
- A year lasts 248 Earth years.
- Five natural satellites.
- Light from the Sun takes 5.5 hr to reach Pluto.
- Pluto would fit inside Earth 170 times.

TEMPERATURE

☀ -400 °F
❄ -375 °F

NAMED AFTER

The Roman god of the underworld. Pluto's moons are named after other characters from the underworlds of mythology.

WHAT IS IT MADE OF?

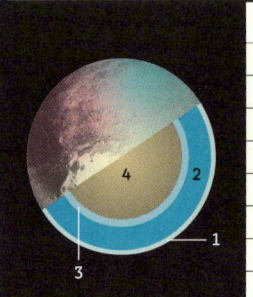

1 Thick nitrogen ice surface.
2 Mantle of water ice.
3 Possible thin layer of liquid water surrounding core.
4 Large rocky core.

PAST, PRESENT, FUTURE

For 76 years, Pluto was considered to be the ninth planet in our solar system. However, when Eris was discovered and turned out to be even more massive than Pluto, astronomers decided to create a new "dwarf planet" category. In 2006, Pluto lost its planet status.

★ FIND OUT MORE ABOUT ERIS ON PAGE 119 ★

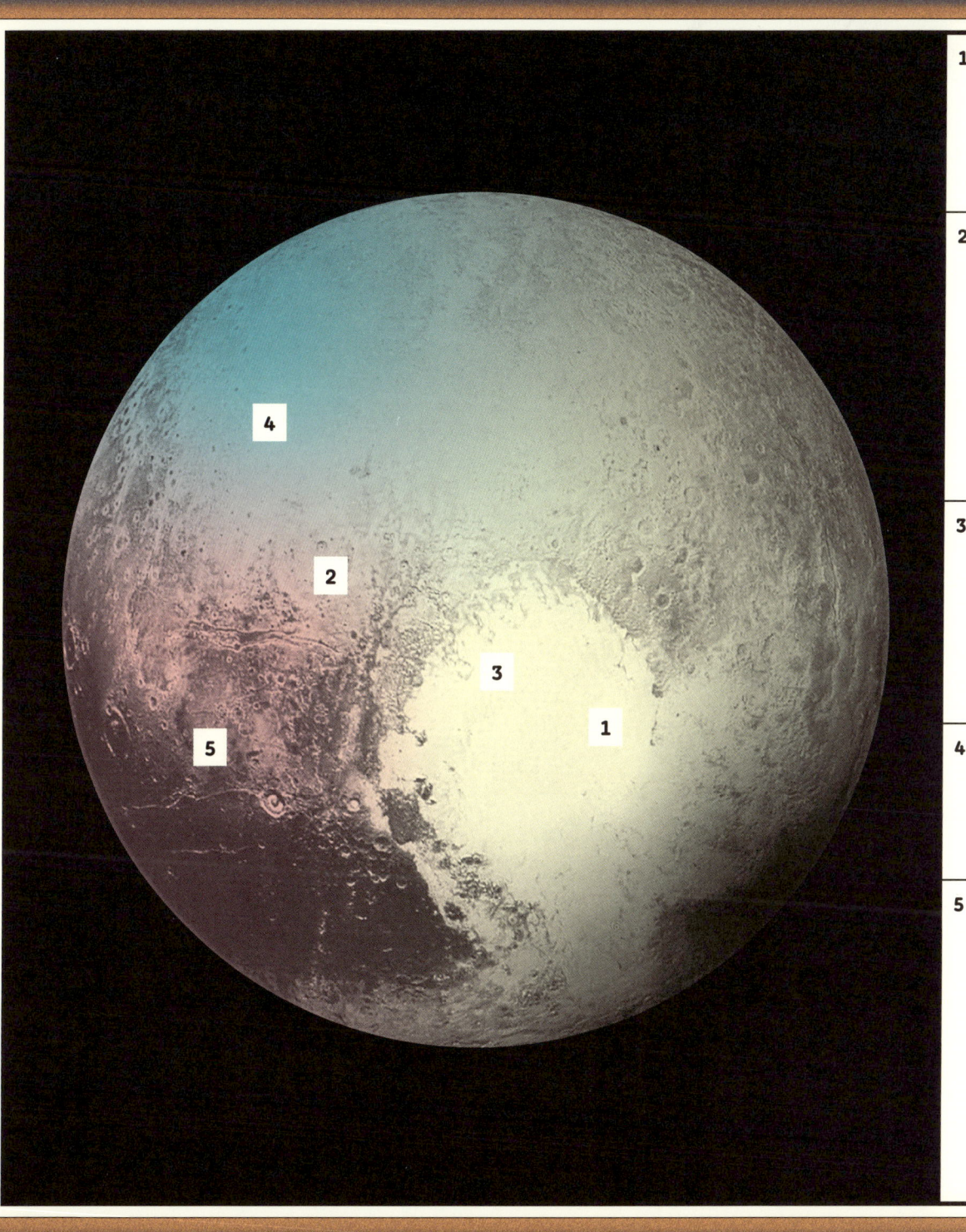

#	
1	**TOMBAUGH REGIO** This large, white, heart-shaped area of Pluto's surface is a huge glacier of nitrogen ice. It's named after the person who discovered Pluto when they were a young, beginner astronomer.
2	**BURNEY CRATER** Pluto's name was suggested by an 11-year-old British girl called Venetia Burney. Her grandfather passed the idea on to astronomers at the University of Oxford. In 2017, a crater on Pluto was named after Venetia! An instrument on the New Horizons space probe has also been named after her. It shows you are never too young to make your mark on the universe.
3	**WATER ROCK** In this area of Pluto's "heart," frozen water lies beneath the nitrogen ice sheet. In places, water ice mountains poke up through the nitrogen, towering up to 3.75 miles above the surface. At such low temperatures, the water ice is as tough as any rock on Earth.
4	**BLUE SKY** When Pluto is closest to the Sun, methane in its thin atmosphere begins to form smog. This smog scatters the blue part of sunlight, giving Pluto a hazy blue sky.
5	**RED SNOW** The bright red parts of Pluto's surface have puzzled scientists. They may come from chemicals that form in the "air" during the summer, then fall to the ground in winter, reacting with the icy surface.

EXPLORING THE KUIPER BELT

PLUTO AND CHARON ARE THE BEST-KNOWN OBJECTS IN THE KUIPER BELT, HAVING BEEN VISITED BY THE SPACE PROBE NEW HORIZONS. OTHER OBJECTS, SUCH AS THE DWARF PLANET ERIS, HAVE ONLY BEEN PHOTOGRAPHED FROM A GREAT DISTANCE BY TELESCOPES.

ALL ABOUT

Like the asteroid belt, the Kuiper Belt is made up of billions of lumps of rock leftover from the formation of the solar system, orbiting the Sun in a giant doughnut-shaped disc. However, the Kuiper doughnut is colder, darker, and much more distant. This makes it much harder to explore.

Pluto was the first object to be spotted in the Kuiper Belt and only because someone was looking for it. Scientists had predicted that a ninth planet must be out there, to explain the small wobbles in Neptune's orbit. More than 60 years later Eris was discovered, proving that Pluto was not a standalone planet, but one of a group of similar-sized objects.

Since then, more than 2,000 other Kuiper-Belt Objects (KBOs) have been spotted, and the total number is bound to be in the billions. We now know that the main belt (lying 30 to 50 times as far from the Sun as Earth) merges into a much larger area called the scattered disc, where Eris is found. Some scattered disc objects are a mind-blowing 1,000 times farther from the Sun than Earth.

New Horizons (NASA) was the first space probe sent to explore the Kuiper Belt, swooping very close to Pluto and its moons before heading to the smaller KBO, Arrokoth. New Horizons is still moving through the Kuiper Belt, and may get the chance to photograph another KBO before its mission ends.

EXPLORATION TIMELINE

1930	Pluto discovered by telescope by Clyde Tombaugh.
1951	Gerard Kuiper publishes a scientific paper predicting objects beyond Pluto.
1983	Pioneer 10 becomes the first space probe to enter the Kuiper Belt region.
1992	Second KBO, now named Albion, discovered by David Jewitt and Janet Luu.
2005	Dwarf planet Eris is discovered.
2006	New Horizons is launched.
2015	New Horizons reaches Pluto and photographs its surface.
2019	New Horizons flies past Arrokoth.

ARE WE THERE YET?

- New Horizons launched in 2006 and reached Pluto almost 10 years later, covering more than 3 billion miles.
- It would take a car on a motorway almost 5,500 years to travel that far.
- New Horizons is expected to exit the Kuiper Belt in 2028 or 2029.

HELPING HUMANS

While scientists search for new KBOs for New Horizons to visit, the spacecraft is busy helping out with other missions. Traveling so far from Earth, New Horizons can detect features of the universe that are usually hidden from us by the Sun's glare.

FIND OUT MORE ABOUT THE GROUNDBREAKING NEW HORIZONS MISSION ON PAGE 107

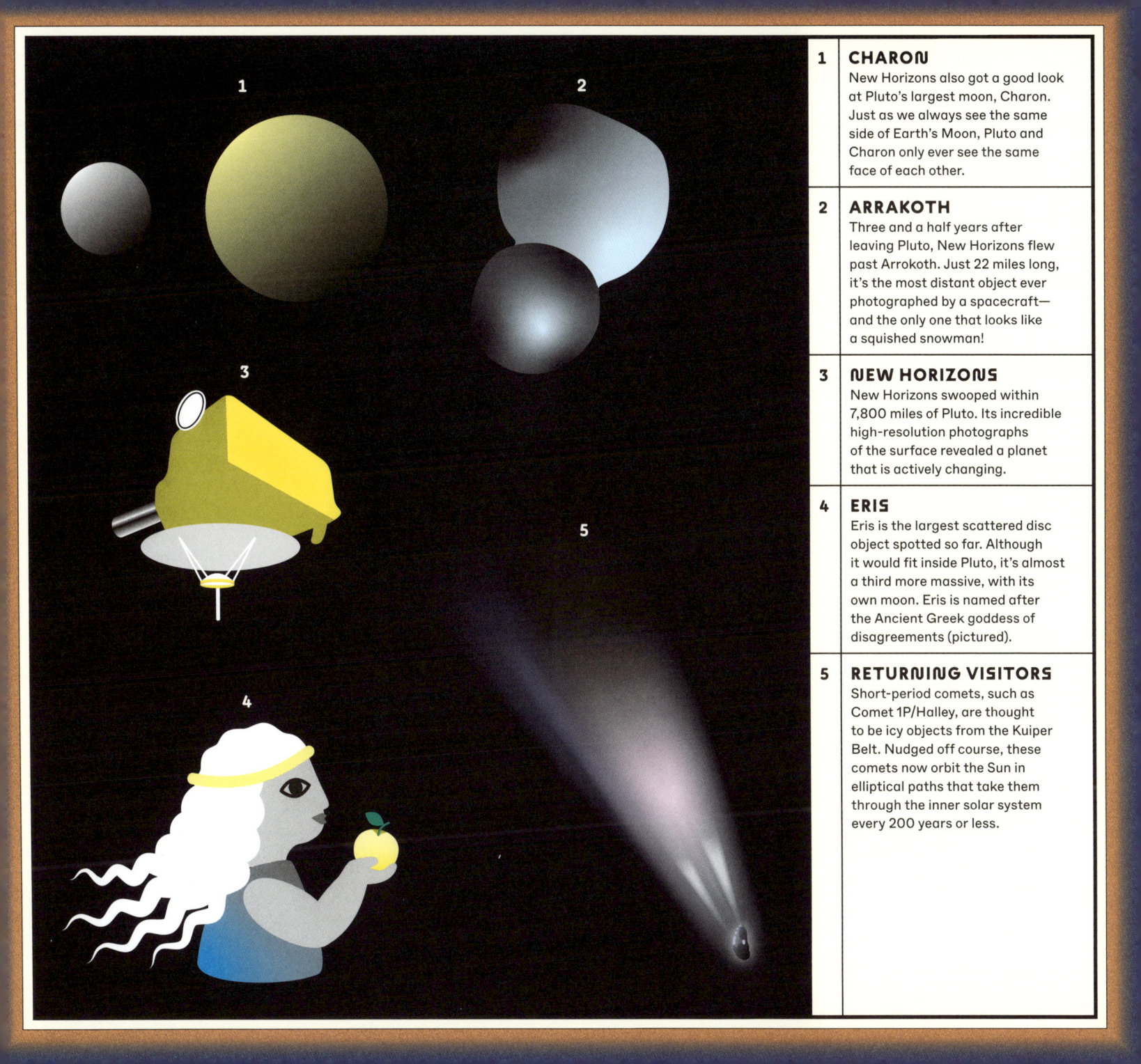

1	**CHARON**	New Horizons also got a good look at Pluto's largest moon, Charon. Just as we always see the same side of Earth's Moon, Pluto and Charon only ever see the same face of each other.
2	**ARRAKOTH**	Three and a half years after leaving Pluto, New Horizons flew past Arrokoth. Just 22 miles long, it's the most distant object ever photographed by a spacecraft— and the only one that looks like a squished snowman!
3	**NEW HORIZONS**	New Horizons swooped within 7,800 miles of Pluto. Its incredible high-resolution photographs of the surface revealed a planet that is actively changing.
4	**ERIS**	Eris is the largest scattered disc object spotted so far. Although it would fit inside Pluto, it's almost a third more massive, with its own moon. Eris is named after the Ancient Greek goddess of disagreements (pictured).
5	**RETURNING VISITORS**	Short-period comets, such as Comet 1P/Halley, are thought to be icy objects from the Kuiper Belt. Nudged off course, these comets now orbit the Sun in elliptical paths that take them through the inner solar system every 200 years or less.

THE OORT CLOUD

CATEGORY	AGE
SHELL OF ICY, COMET-LIKE OBJECTS	UNKNOWN

BEYOND THE KUIPER BELT LIES A PART OF OUR SOLAR SYSTEM KNOWN ONLY IN THEORY. THE OORT CLOUD IS THOUGHT TO BE THE RESERVOIR FROM WHICH COMETS COME HURTLING ACROSS THE SOLAR SYSTEM.

ALL ABOUT

Space scientists think that the solar system is surrounded by a vast cloud of small, icy objects, slowly orbiting the Sun in all kinds of different directions.

The scale of this Oort cloud is hard to imagine. Although trillions of objects lie within the cloud, they are so spread out in space that each one is many millions of miles from its nearest neighbors. The space probe Voyager 1 (NASA) was launched almost 50 years ago and is currently speeding through the area just beyond the Kuiper Belt—known as the scattered disc—at more than 37,000 mi/h. But even at this speed, it won't reach the beginning of the Oort cloud for 300 years. It will take another 30,000 years to pass all the way through.

Because it lies in cold, silent darkness, no one has seen the Oort cloud through a telescope of any kind. There is no sunlight to be reflected, and no heat to be detected. No one knows if these objects were originally formed in the solar system and gradually scattered outward, or if they once orbited other stars and were captured by the Sun's gravity.

But scientists think that we have close encounters with some Oort cloud objects, when something disturbs their slow orbit around the Sun, and they come hurtling through the inner solar system as comets. Investigating these long-period comets is our best way to try and understand the Oort cloud and its origins.

KEY FACTS

- The Oort cloud is up to 3.2 light-years thick.
- Oort cloud objects may have formed much closer to the Sun, before being scattered outward by the gravitational tug of large planets such as Jupiter.

TEMPERATURE

Around -449°F, just a few degrees above absolute zero.

NAMED AFTER

Dutch astronomer Jan Oort, one of the first people to predict that this cloud of objects exists. Also known as the Öpik–Oort cloud.

WHAT IS IT MADE OF?

Billions of icy comets, forming a thick spherical bubble or shell around the solar system. Each object may be a chunk left over from the formation of the planets, and made of the same stuff.

EPIC JOURNEY

Light from the Sun takes from 10 to 28 days to reach the inner Oort cloud, but at least a year to make it out the other side.

★ EXPLORE A PLANNED MISSION TO INTERCEPT A COMET FROM THE OORT CLOUD ON PAGE 124 ★

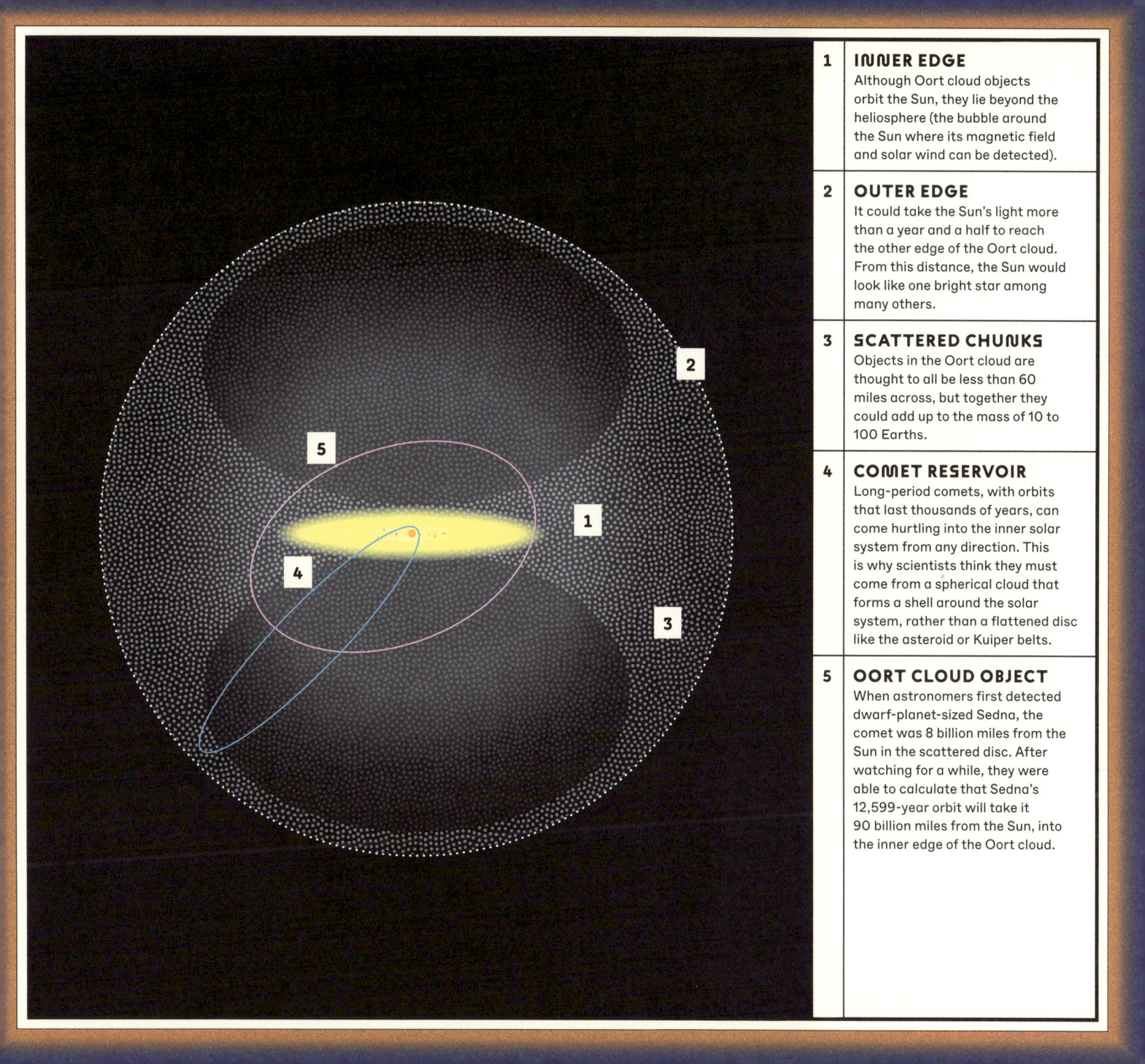

1	**INNER EDGE** Although Oort cloud objects orbit the Sun, they lie beyond the heliosphere (the bubble around the Sun where its magnetic field and solar wind can be detected).
2	**OUTER EDGE** It could take the Sun's light more than a year and a half to reach the other edge of the Oort cloud. From this distance, the Sun would look like one bright star among many others.
3	**SCATTERED CHUNKS** Objects in the Oort cloud are thought to all be less than 60 miles across, but together they could add up to the mass of 10 to 100 Earths.
4	**COMET RESERVOIR** Long-period comets, with orbits that last thousands of years, can come hurtling into the inner solar system from any direction. This is why scientists think they must come from a spherical cloud that forms a shell around the solar system, rather than a flattened disc like the asteroid or Kuiper belts.
5	**OORT CLOUD OBJECT** When astronomers first detected dwarf-planet-sized Sedna, the comet was 8 billion miles from the Sun in the scattered disc. After watching for a while, they were able to calculate that Sedna's 12,599-year orbit will take it 90 billion miles from the Sun, into the inner edge of the Oort cloud.

COMET 1P/HALLEY

CATEGORY	AGE	
SHORT-PERIOD COMET	AT LEAST 16,000 YEARS IN ITS CURRENT ORBIT	SHORT-PERIOD COMETS ORBIT THE SUN EVERY 200 YEARS OR LESS. HALLEY IS ONE OF THE MOST FAMOUS, BECOMING VISIBLE IN THE NIGHT SKY ROUGHLY EVERY 76 YEARS.

ALL ABOUT

Comet 1P/Halley was not the first comet spotted from Earth, but the one that helped astronomers figure out what comets are. In 1705, astronomer Edmond Halley figured out that historical documents describing comets crossing the sky in 1531, 1607, and 1682 were all talking about the same object—an object that must be in orbit around the Sun. He predicted that this object would return in 1758, and when this prediction came true the comet was named "Halley's comet" in his honor.

Halley's comet may have begun as a Kuiper Belt Object, an icy lump of rubble left over from the formation of the solar system. Something caused its orbital path to change, sending it zooming around the Sun in an oval path that crosses the inner solar system, taking it closer to the Sun than Venus.

As the comet travels from the deep freeze of the outer solar system toward our broiling star, a layer of its icy surface is vaporized. The energized dust and gas form a giant, spherical cloud around the nucleus, known as a coma. This temporary atmosphere is so huge, and reflects so much sunlight, that the comet appears to glow brightly.

As the dust and gas of the coma are bathed in solar radiation, they form tails that can grow millions of miles long. These tails shrink again as the comet moves back into the colder part of its orbit.

KEY FACTS

- Halley's comet spins on its axis once every 2.2 to 7.5 Earth days.
- It takes about 76 Earth years to orbit the Sun once.
- Comets are not as big as they look. Almost a billion comets the size of Halley would fit inside Earth.

TEMPERATURE

-94°F

NAMED AFTER

English astronomer Edmund Halley. The label 1P tells us that it was the first periodic comet to be discovered.

WHAT IS IT MADE OF?

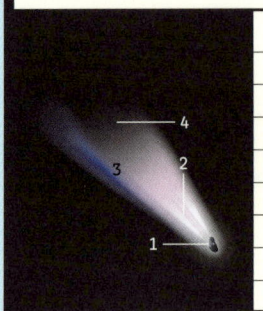

1. Nucleus made of frozen water and other ices, with a dark, dusty surface.
2. Glowing coma, formed by jets of gas and dust from the sunlit side.
3. Long, thin gas tail blown away from the Sun by solar wind.
4. Broad dust tail, curved along the path of the comet's orbit.

PAST, PRESENT, FUTURE

Large amounts of gas and dust from a comet's coma are lost to space. With each trip around the Sun, Halley loses 6.5 to 10 feet of its surface. After around 2,000 more orbits, it will disappear altogether.

★ FIND OUT MORE ABOUT THE FIRST SIGHTINGS OF HALLEY'S COMET ON PAGE 33 ★

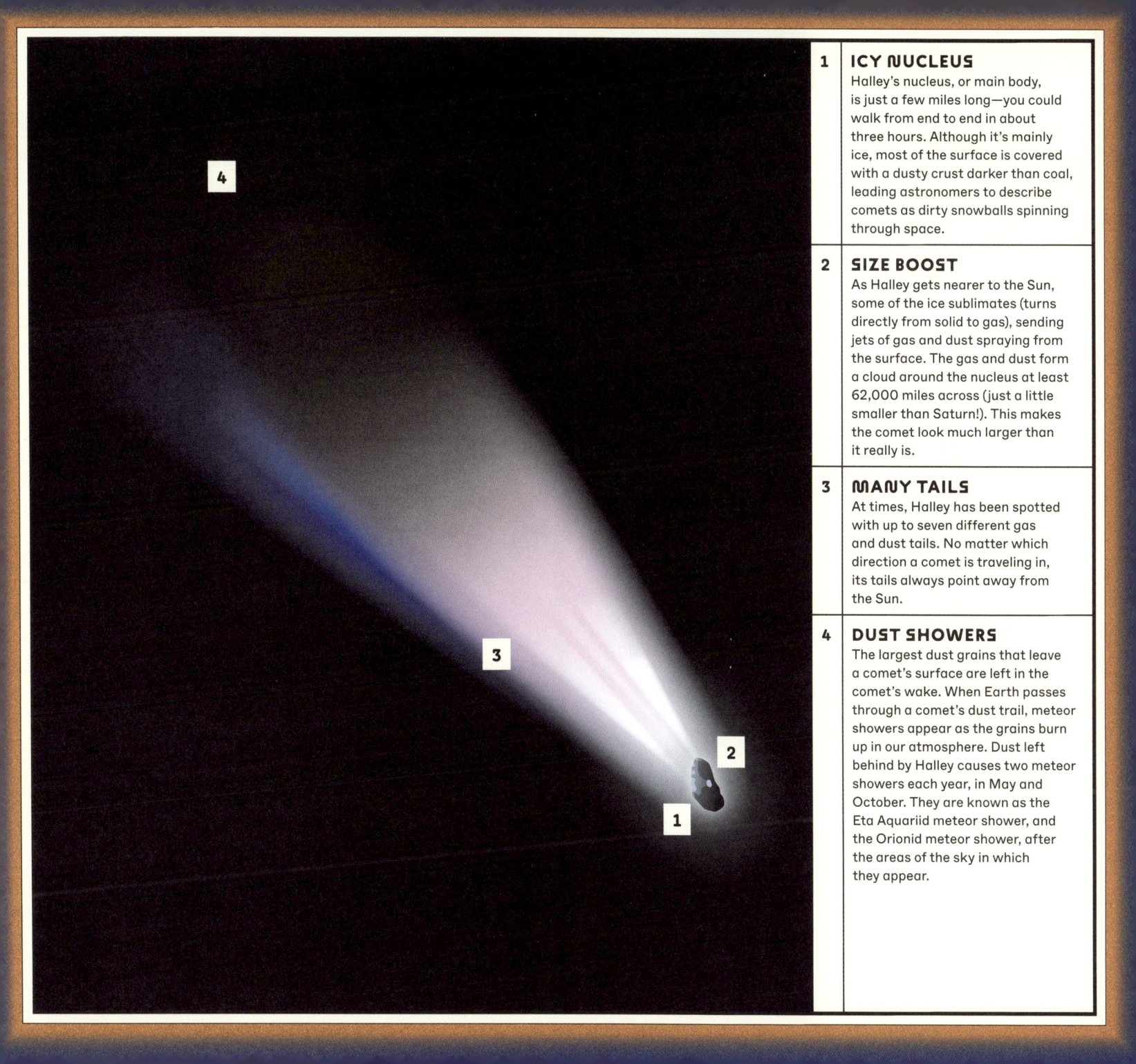

#		
1	**ICY NUCLEUS**	Halley's nucleus, or main body, is just a few miles long—you could walk from end to end in about three hours. Although it's mainly ice, most of the surface is covered with a dusty crust darker than coal, leading astronomers to describe comets as dirty snowballs spinning through space.
2	**SIZE BOOST**	As Halley gets nearer to the Sun, some of the ice sublimates (turns directly from solid to gas), sending jets of gas and dust spraying from the surface. The gas and dust form a cloud around the nucleus at least 62,000 miles across (just a little smaller than Saturn!). This makes the comet look much larger than it really is.
3	**MANY TAILS**	At times, Halley has been spotted with up to seven different gas and dust tails. No matter which direction a comet is traveling in, its tails always point away from the Sun.
4	**DUST SHOWERS**	The largest dust grains that leave a comet's surface are left in the comet's wake. When Earth passes through a comet's dust trail, meteor showers appear as the grains burn up in our atmosphere. Dust left behind by Halley causes two meteor showers each year, in May and October. They are known as the Eta Aquariid meteor shower, and the Orionid meteor shower, after the areas of the sky in which they appear.

EXPLORING COMETS

COMETS ARE FROZEN FRAGMENTS OF THE EARLY SOLAR SYSTEM. EXPLORING THEM CAN HELP US FIGURE OUT HOW OUR PLANET FORMED.

ALL ABOUT

When Halley's comet last passed Earth in 1986, several space probes were ready and waiting to fly past and collect data. ESA's Giotto mission got the closest, taking the first close-up picture of a comet from less than 370 miles away.

Halley won't be back until 2061, but many other comets have been explored in the meantime. As well as flybys, space probes have swooped through comet tails and coma, returned comet dust to Earth, crashed into a comet to confirm what lies beneath the crust, and even landed on the surface of a comet. The ESA probe Rosetta made history when it went into orbit around the small, duck-shaped Comet 67P. Rosetta beamed back thousands of images, and even dropped a small robot lander called Philae onto the icy surface. Visiting a comet like this was a huge technological feat. Comet 67P was only around 300 million miles from Earth at the time, but a much longer route was taken to ensure Rosetta arrived at exactly the right speed to be captured by its weak gravity.

So far, all the comets visited by spacecraft have been short-period comets, whose orbits around the Sun take less than 200 years. There is a good reason for this—we have figured out the orbits of these comets based on historical records, so we know exactly where to send a spacecraft to meet them.

The next goal is to visit a long-period comet from the Oort cloud. ESA is planning a mission called Comet Interceptor, which hopes to fly past a comet on its first trip past the Sun, allowing us to see close-up an object unchanged since the very beginning of the solar system. The challenge for comet hunters is to spot a long-period comet coming in time to plan a mission.

EXPLORATION TIMELINE

1860	Comet C/1860 M1 is the first comet to be discovered by telescope, and to have its orbit calculated (later visible to the naked eye).
1985	ICE flies through the tail of Comet 21P/Giacobini-Zinner.
2004	Stardust probe returns samples of dust collected from the coma of Comet 81P/Wild 2.
2004	Rosetta is launched.
2005	Deep Impact releases an impactor that crashes into Comet 9P/Tempel 1.
2014	Rosetta goes into orbit around Comet 67P/Churyumov-Gerasimenko.
2014	Rosetta's Philae lander touches down on Comet 67P/Churyumov-Gerasimenko.

ARE WE THERE YET?

- The Rosetta spacecraft took 10 years to reach Comet 67P/Churyumov-Gerasimenko, covering more than 4 billion miles during the journey.

HELPING HUMANS

When Earth was first formed, it was too hot to have liquid water. For a long time, scientists wondered if our oceans came from a comet that crashed into Earth and melted. However, missions to "taste" comets have proved that most of our water was probably delivered by asteroids.

★ FIND OUT HOW ONE ASTRONOMER DISCOVERED 18 COMETS USING BINOCULARS ON PAGE 25 ★

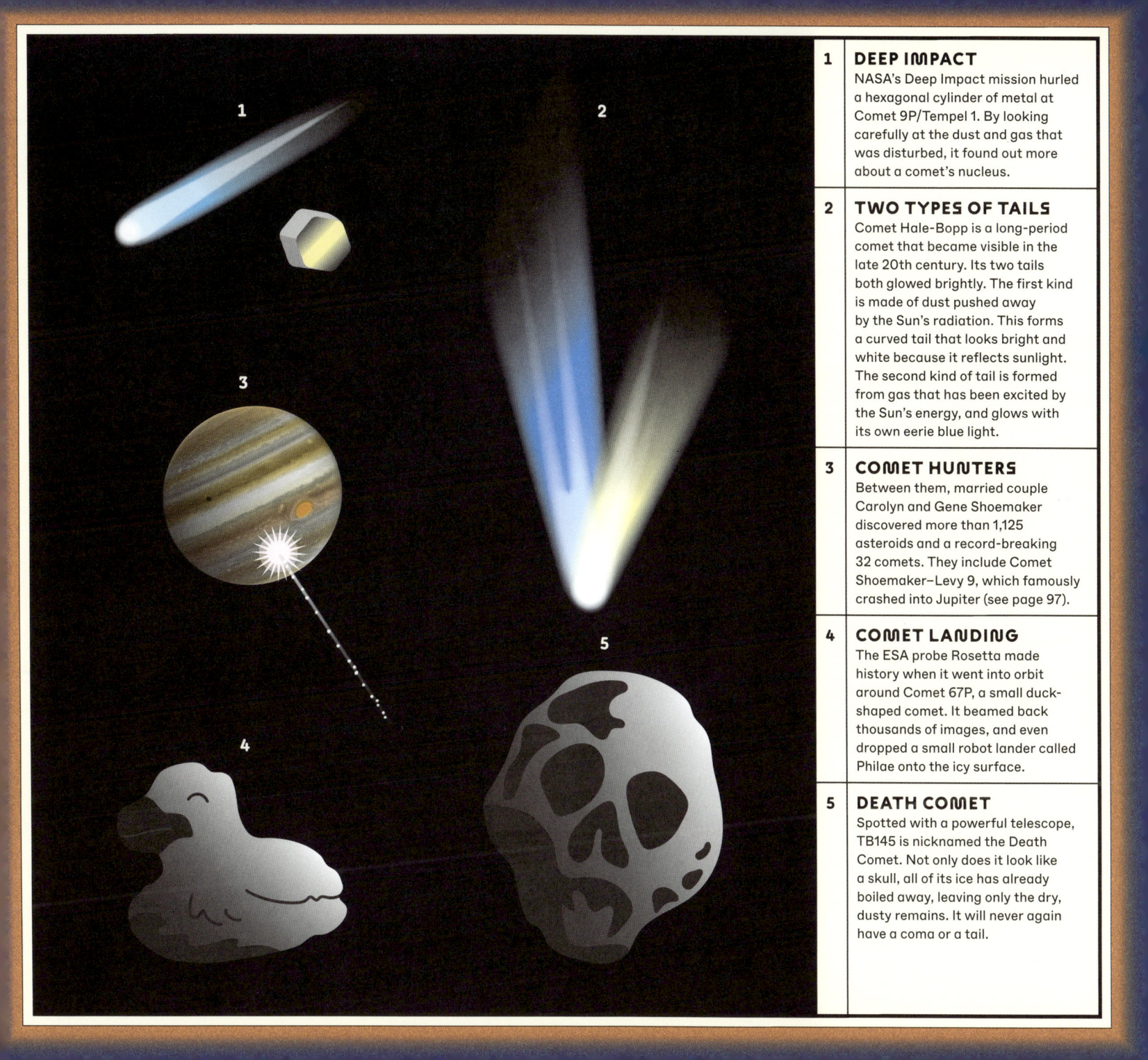

1	**DEEP IMPACT** NASA's Deep Impact mission hurled a hexagonal cylinder of metal at Comet 9P/Tempel 1. By looking carefully at the dust and gas that was disturbed, it found out more about a comet's nucleus.
2	**TWO TYPES OF TAILS** Comet Hale-Bopp is a long-period comet that became visible in the late 20th century. Its two tails both glowed brightly. The first kind is made of dust pushed away by the Sun's radiation. This forms a curved tail that looks bright and white because it reflects sunlight. The second kind of tail is formed from gas that has been excited by the Sun's energy, and glows with its own eerie blue light.
3	**COMET HUNTERS** Between them, married couple Carolyn and Gene Shoemaker discovered more than 1,125 asteroids and a record-breaking 32 comets. They include Comet Shoemaker–Levy 9, which famously crashed into Jupiter (see page 97).
4	**COMET LANDING** The ESA probe Rosetta made history when it went into orbit around Comet 67P, a small duck-shaped comet. It beamed back thousands of images, and even dropped a small robot lander called Philae onto the icy surface.
5	**DEATH COMET** Spotted with a powerful telescope, TB145 is nicknamed the Death Comet. Not only does it look like a skull, all of its ice has already boiled away, leaving only the dry, dusty remains. It will never again have a coma or a tail.

STARS

HUMANS HAVE BEEN STARGAZING FOR THOUSANDS OF YEARS, BUT JUST A CENTURY HAS PASSED SINCE SCIENTISTS WORKED OUT WHAT STARS ARE MADE OF AND WHY THEY SHINE.

Much of what we know comes from our experience of living near the Sun. This is the star we rely on for light, warmth, food—and life itself. It's also the most-studied star, with spacecraft now venturing into its superheated atmosphere. However, the Sun only gives us a snapshot of a middle-aged, medium-sized star, shining steadily with visible light. To truly understand stars, we've had to seek out the clues hidden from our eyes.

Stars emit many kinds of radiation that we can't see, as well as streams of fast-moving particles known as **stellar winds** and cosmic rays. Instruments and telescopes that detect these invisible signals have helped astronomers discover newborn **protostars**, tempestuous teenage stars, and long-dead stellar remnants, including **neutron stars** and black holes.

A star's life lasts millions or billions of years. By looking at stars of different ages, astrophysicists have pieced together the entire stellar life cycle—from a star's birth in vast **molecular clouds** to its dramatic death as a red giant or supernova.

Understanding stars is key to understanding not only the universe, but ourselves, for the stardust forged in and scattered by stars is the stuff of every other object that exists, from new stars and planets, to people.

THE SUN

CATEGORY	AGE
STAR	4.6 BILLION YEARS

FOR EARTHLINGS, THE SUN IS THE MOST IMPORTANT STAR OF ALL. THIS GIANT BALL OF GLOWING PLASMA POWERS OUR PLANET AND IS CLOSE ENOUGH TO BURN OUR SKIN.

ALL ABOUT

In cosmic terms, the Sun is nothing special—just one of 20 billion medium-sized stars in our galactic neighborhood. However, the Sun is so close to Earth that light leaving its surface reaches our planet in just eight minutes. This ring-side seat has helped scientists to discover how stars work.

Stars are far more massive than planets. Unlike planets, stars produce their own light—a consequence of being so massive. As Isaac Newton figured out, objects with more mass have more gravitational force (see page 30). The Sun's immense gravity creates temperatures and pressures far more extreme than any on Earth.

At the Sun's core, hydrogen fuel is squeezed by pressures a billion times greater than New York City's skyscrapers exert on the ground below, reaching a scorching 27 million°F. In these extreme conditions, hydrogen atoms are crushed together so violently they combine to form larger atoms of helium—something that would never happen naturally on a planet. This nuclear fusion releases vast amounts of energy.

The energy released at the core slowly makes its way outward. First it must move through the dense radiative zone, where matter is so tightly packed that energy can take hundreds of thousands of years to reach the top. Next is the turbulent convective zone, where vast bubbles of superheated plasma well upward like the bubbles in boiling soup. Finally the energy reaches the Sun's relatively cool surface—the photosphere—where it escapes into space as radiation. It's this escaping light energy that makes a star shine.

KEY FACTS

- The Sun spins on its axis once every 27 days, on average. It spins more quickly at the equator than the poles.
- The Sun contains the same amount of matter as 333,000 Earths, but takes up 1.3 million times as much space.

TEMPERATURE

9,932°F

NEAREST

Our nearest star's official name is Sol, the Latin word for the Sun. This is why "solar" is used to describe things to do with the Sun.

WHAT IS IT MADE OF?

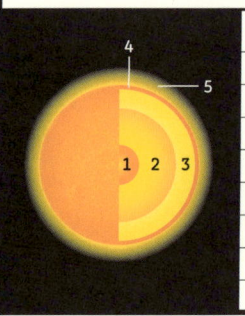

Like all stars, the Sun is mostly hydrogen and helium. On Earth, these elements are found as gases. The Sun is so hot that its hydrogen and helium exist as a dense, electrically charged type of gas known as plasma. This diagram shows the core (1), radiative zone (2), convective zone (3), photosphere (4), and **corona** (5).

PAST, PRESENT, FUTURE

Every second, the Sun fuses around 660 million tons of hydrogen into helium, releasing energy in the process. By learning about star life cycles, scientists have calculated that the Sun has enough hydrogen left to burn for another five billion years.

★ FIND OUT HOW THE SUN SHAPES LIFE ON EARTH ON PAGES 18 AND 132 ★

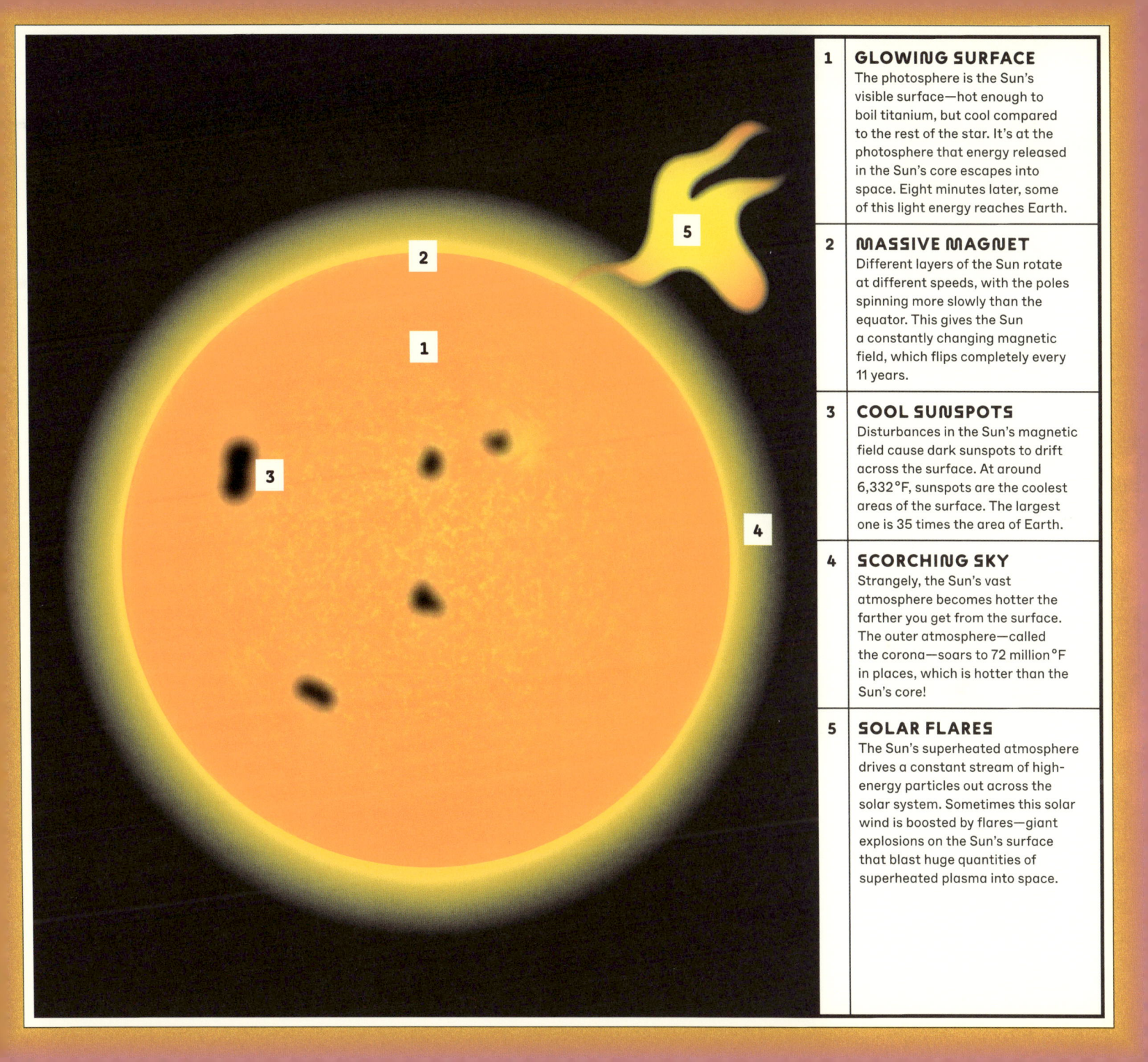

1	**GLOWING SURFACE**	The photosphere is the Sun's visible surface—hot enough to boil titanium, but cool compared to the rest of the star. It's at the photosphere that energy released in the Sun's core escapes into space. Eight minutes later, some of this light energy reaches Earth.
2	**MASSIVE MAGNET**	Different layers of the Sun rotate at different speeds, with the poles spinning more slowly than the equator. This gives the Sun a constantly changing magnetic field, which flips completely every 11 years.
3	**COOL SUNSPOTS**	Disturbances in the Sun's magnetic field cause dark sunspots to drift across the surface. At around 6,332°F, sunspots are the coolest areas of the surface. The largest one is 35 times the area of Earth.
4	**SCORCHING SKY**	Strangely, the Sun's vast atmosphere becomes hotter the farther you get from the surface. The outer atmosphere—called the corona—soars to 72 million°F in places, which is hotter than the Sun's core!
5	**SOLAR FLARES**	The Sun's superheated atmosphere drives a constant stream of high-energy particles out across the solar system. Sometimes this solar wind is boosted by flares—giant explosions on the Sun's surface that blast huge quantities of superheated plasma into space.

EXPLORING THE SUN

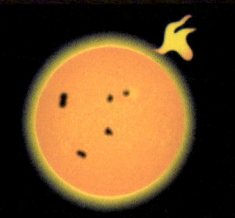

HOW DO YOU EXPLORE AN OBJECT THAT'S DANGEROUS TO LOOK AT AND DEADLY TO APPROACH? THIS IS THE CHALLENGE FACING SOLAR SCIENTISTS, WHO STUDY OUR NEAREST STAR.

ALL ABOUT

Although the Sun is the brightest object in the sky, it is one of the hardest to study. Looking directly at the Sun is incredibly dangerous. In the 1600s and 1700s, several famous scientists damaged their eyes trying to peer at sunspots.

From the 1800s, new technologies helped astronomers to study the Sun more safely. The invention of photography allowed astronomers to see details usually hidden by the Sun's glare. Spectroscopy—splitting sunlight into its different colors—helped scientists figure out what the Sun and other stars are made from.

However, even the world's most powerful ground-based telescopes can only squint at the Sun from 93 million miles away. The biggest leaps in understanding followed the invention of rockets, which allowed us to put instruments in space and see the Sun from outside Earth's protective atmosphere.

Since the 1950s, dozens of spacecraft have carried instruments closer and closer to our nearest star. They have helped scientists build a detailed model of what happens inside the Sun, and how its solar wind and magnetic field affect objects in our solar system. NASA's Solar Parker Probe has even flown into the Sun's corona, touching a star for the first time. A host of new missions are poised to uncover more of the Sun's secrets.

EXPLORATION TIMELINE

28 BCE	Ancient Chinese astronomers observe sunspots from Earth's surface.
800s	Arabic astronomers build the first modern observatory.
1800	William Herschel passes sunlight through a glass prism, splitting it into a rainbow of colors.
1845	Hippolyte Fizeau and Léon Foucault take the first detailed photograph of the Sun.
1960	Pioneer 5 becomes the first probe to orbit the Sun.
1962	Orbiting Solar Observatory (OSO 1) becomes the first space-based solar observatory.
2004	The Genesis space probe returns a sample of the solar wind to Earth.
2021	Parker Solar Probe becomes the first spacecraft to send back data from inside the Sun's atmosphere.

ARE WE THERE YET?

- On average the Sun is 93 million miles from Earth. A car traveling at 60 mph would take about 170 years to travel this distance.
- Particles of the solar wind slam into Earth's atmosphere around three days after leaving the Sun's atmosphere.

HELPING HUMANS

Huge eruptions on the Sun's surface cause surges in the solar wind. When they reach Earth, these solar storms can disrupt radio signals, short-circuit satellites, and even cause whales to lose their way. Solar observatories outside Earth's atmosphere help give advance warning of this bad "space weather."

★ FIND OUT HOW SPECTROSCOPY WORKS ON PAGE 138 ★

1	**STELLAR BARCODES**	In 1925, British-American astronomer Cecilia Payne-Gaposchkin used spectroscopy to discover that the Sun (and other stars) are mainly made from hydrogen and helium. This changed our understanding of the universe.
2	**TIME TO SHINE**	The Sun's corona is a million times fainter than its fiery surface. A total solar eclipse (see page 19) is an important chance for telescopes to photograph the corona, without the glare of the surface getting in the way.
3	**EYE ON THE GROUND**	Hawaii's Inouye Solar Telescope is the most powerful ground-based solar telescope. Its detailed pictures of the Sun's surface reveal the patterns of boiling gas that cover the Sun. Each of these "cells" is around double the size of the United Kingdom, with bright, hot plasma welling up at the center, before moving to the darker edges where it cools and sinks again. These images help scientists understand the Sun's magnetic field and solar storms.
4	**EYE IN THE SKY**	Positioned 1 million miles from Earth, ESA/NASA's Solar and Heliospheric Observatory (SOHO) has been staring at the Sun for more than 25 years. It has helped us understand the Sun from the inside out, viewing short-term solar storms and the 11-year cycle of changes in its magnetic field.
5	**TOUCHING THE SUN**	NASA's Parker Solar Probe made history in 2024 when it got within 3.8 million miles of the Sun's surface—seven times closer than any other spacecraft.

THE SUN-EARTH SYSTEM

A BETTER UNDERSTANDING OF OUR NEAREST STAR HAS ALSO HELPED SCIENTISTS EXPLAIN CONDITIONS ON EARTH, AND WHY THEY HAVE CHANGED OVER TIME.

The Earth receives about a half of one-billionth of the energy streaming across the solar system from the Sun, but this is the main energy source for most processes on our planet.

The Sun's energy drives the water cycle and causes winds and ocean currents. In turn, these shape weather patterns and climate. They are the reason that rain falls, glaciers form, rivers flow, and lakes don't dry up. Rain and wind also play a huge role in the rock cycle, as mountains and coasts are eroded, and sediments are carried to where they will eventually form new types of rock.

Through photosynthesis (see page 19), the Sun's energy is also the ultimate source of energy in most food chains. This drives cycles of carbon and other nutrients, as living things grow, decay, and are recycled into new life.

THE GREENHOUSE EFFECT

Some of the gases in Earth's atmosphere trap energy from the Sun, stopping it from escaping back into space. Without this natural "greenhouse effect," Earth's climate would be too cold for living things.

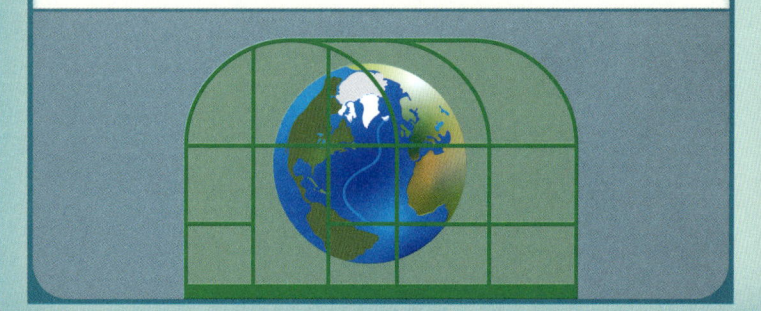

CLIMATE CHANGE

Since humans began burning fossil fuels, we have released lots of extra greenhouse gases into the atmosphere. This has increased the natural greenhouse effect, leading to a rise in the average global temperature. Global warming is having a big effect on local weather patterns, because heat is what drives Earth's water cycle and winds.

THE WATER CYCLE

Every day, Earth's surface is warmed by the Sun, cooling again by night. This regular heating and cooling causes winds to blow and drives the water cycle. Every second, around 13 million tons of water are lifted from the oceans into the air, eventually falling back down to land and sea.

SPACE WEATHER

The Sun doesn't release energy steadily like a lightbulb. Gigantic explosions on its surface, called solar flares, often fling extra plasma into space. When these solar storms collide with Earth they create colorful aurorae, and may also disrupt radio signals, fry electricity grids, short-circuit GPS and communication satellites, and confuse migrating animals, such as whales.

HARVESTING THE SUN'S ENERGY

Humans have always found ways to use the Sun's energy, from drying food to warming homes, or using windmills to grind wheat. When we burn fossil fuels such as oil, as well as biofuels or wood, we release solar energy captured by plants. The Sun's energy is the indirect source of wind and hydropower, and the direct source of solar power.

SEASONS

The seasons are explained by the tilt of Earth's axis. One hemisphere tilts away from the Sun for half the year and toward the Sun for the other half. This gives shorter and colder days in winter and longer and warmer days in summer.

TOUCHING THE SUN

HOW DO YOU SEND SCIENTIFIC INSTRUMENTS INTO A SCORCHING STAR WITHOUT DESTROYING THEM? THIS WAS THE CHALLENGE MET BY SOLAR PARKER PROBE, ONE OF THE MOST REMARKABLE SPACE MISSIONS OF ALL TIME.

In 2021, NASA's Parker Solar Probe (PSP) became the first spacecraft to fly into the Sun's corona. By the end of its seven-year mission, it had swooped within 4 million miles of the Sun's visible surface, collecting data to help answer the most puzzling questions about our nearest star.

To make this possible, PSP was designed to survive brutal conditions. Temperatures in the corona reach more than 1.8 million °F, heated by flares of energy from the star's surface.

The spacecraft was also sandpapered by tiny grains of space dust smashing into the speeding probe at up to 6,700 mi/h.

These were problems worth solving. The data collected by PSP and its companion Solar Orbiter (ESA) will help us understand how energy flows away from stars, and help forecast space weather. This will protect life and technology on—and off—Earth. Most excitingly, these discoveries will raise questions we haven't yet thought of.

FALLING WITH STYLE

To approach the Sun in a controlled way, PSP had to gradually reduce its sideways speed, using Venus's gravity to help it brake. With each orbit, PSP's sideways motion slowed and the Sun pulled the probe a little closer.

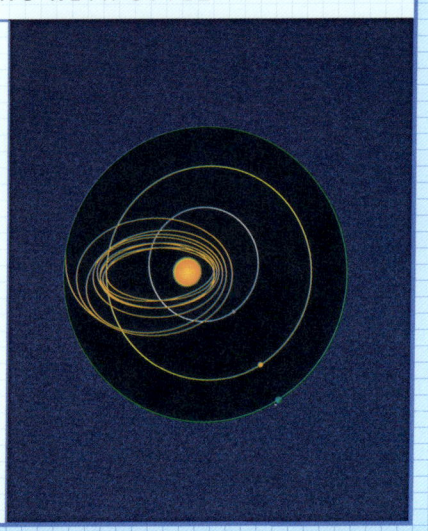

SOLAR ORBITER

ESA's Solar Orbiter is packed with high-tech scientific instruments for taking close-up photos of the Sun, including the first-ever images of the Sun's poles. It will help to link changes in the Sun's surface to the changes PSP measures in the corona.

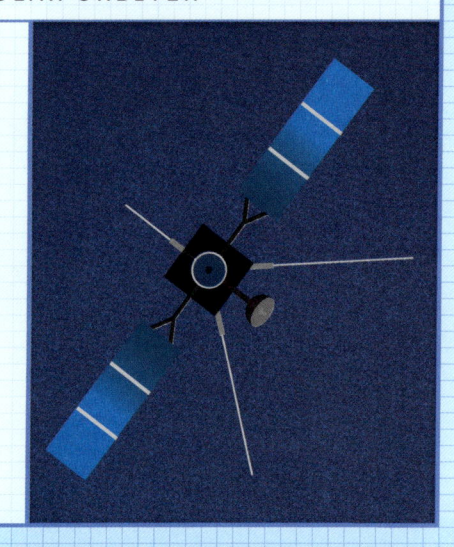

PARKER SOLAR PROBE

1. PSP's 4.5-in thermal shield can withstand temperatures of nearly 3,002°F. Although particles in the corona reach temperatures far hotter than this, they are very spread out so only transfer their heat slowly. As PSP zooms through the corona, the cone-shaped shield is heated to around 2,732°F, but the instruments behind the shield don't get any warmer than 86°F.

2. Radio antennas allow instructions to be sent to PSP, and data to be beamed back to Earth.

3. Two solar panels provide power for the instruments and to send signals back to Earth.

4. PSP is packed with instruments to "sniff" the solar wind, and measure its magnetic fields. A long arm holds them away from the Sun. The instruments were tested by pointing old IMAX film projectors at them to mimic the Sun's heat and light.

5. Accelerating to speeds of 435,000 mi/h as it swooped into the corona, PSP is the fastest human-made object ever. It is quick enough to travel from London, United Kingdom, to Sydney, Australia, in 87 seconds.

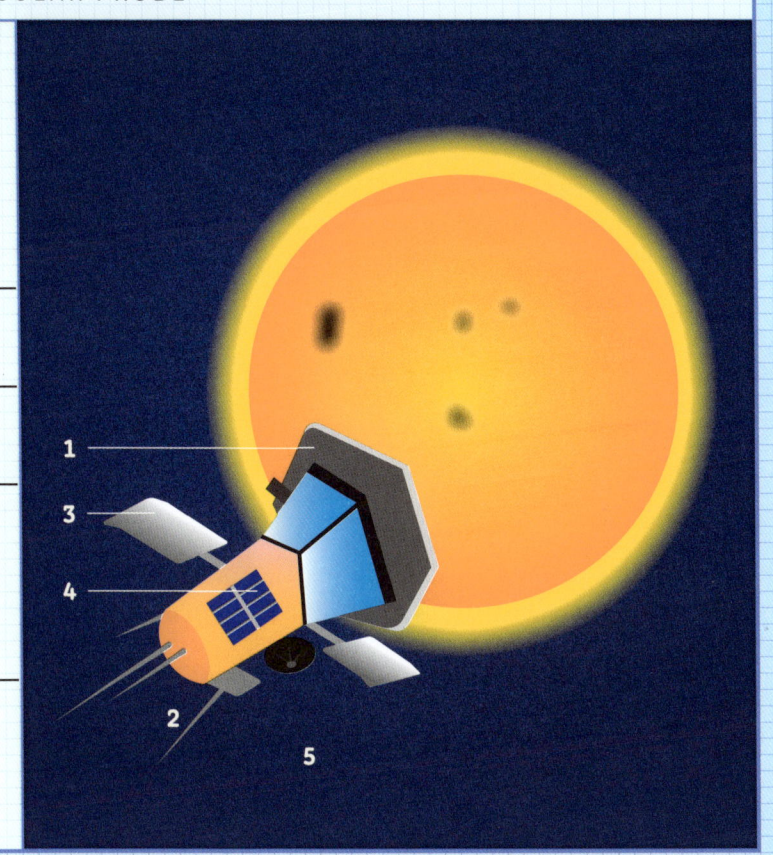

STAR SOUNDS

As PSP zooms through the corona, it detects disturbances in the solar wind. Back on Earth, these ripples have been converted to sound waves, allowing scientists to listen to the solar wind! You can listen to the reconstructed sound on NASA's website. It really is otherworldly, seeming to howl and whistle, with occasional high-pitched chirps.

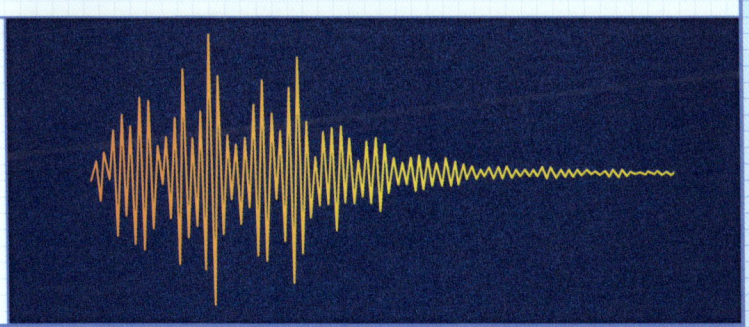

EXPLORING OTHER STARS

TELESCOPES BROUGHT FAINTER STARS INTO VIEW, BUT THE REAL GAME CHANGER WAS THE INVENTION OF TECHNOLOGY TO DETECT TYPES OF STARLIGHT—AND STARS—THAT ARE INVISIBLE TO OUR EYES.

ALL ABOUT

Ancient astronomers were the first to record differences between stars, and we still describe a star's brightness in the night sky using a system developed thousands of years ago. The brightest are said to have an apparent magnitude of 1. Magnitude-6 stars—100 times dimmer—are the faintest visible by eye (see page 22).

By collecting more light, telescopes allow astronomers to detect far fainter stars—especially when coupled with cameras much more sensitive than our eyes. However, a star may look faint simply because it is far away. A huge leap came with the invention of spectroscopy in the 1800s. By splitting starlight into its different colors, spectroscopes allow astronomers to precisely measure a star's ingredients and temperature, allowing them to figure out its true brightness. This is known as a star's **absolute magnitude**.

In the 1900s, scientists discovered that the energy radiating from stars goes far beyond the visible light our eyes can detect. Modern astronomy relies on instruments that can detect radio waves, infrared and ultraviolet radiation, X-rays and gamma rays, as well as high-energy particles known as cosmic rays. Since the 1950s, space rockets have taken these instruments high above Earth's atmosphere for a much better view, and high-speed computers have helped to analyze mind-boggling amounts of data.

We may have been stargazing for thousands of years, but it's the technology of the last 100 years that has allowed astrophysicists to deduce the entire life cycle of stars—from their beginnings in mysterious dark clouds, to their spectacular deaths when they run out of fuel.

EXPLORATION TIMELINE

Anc.	Astronomical observatories date back at least 12,000 years.
1610	Galileo Galilei uses telescope to view stars.
1800	William Herschel detects infrared radiation.
1850	A star other than the Sun (Vega) is photographed.
1911	Victor Hess detects high-energy particles from space.
1932	Karl G. Jansky detects radio waves from space.
1946	A rocket launched above Earth's atmosphere measures the Sun's ultraviolet spectrum.
1949	X-rays from the Sun are detected by rockets launched above Earth's atmosphere.
1968	First Orbiting Astronomical Observatory launched.
2012	Voyager 1 space probe leaves our solar system and enters interstellar space.

ARE WE THERE YET?

- Proxima Centauri is the nearest star to Earth after the Sun. Its light takes 4.2 years to reach Earth. Even the fastest-ever spacecraft would take more than 7,000 years to make the journey.
- Earendel is the most distant star detected so far. Its light takes 12.9 billion years to reach Earth.

OUR PLACE IN SPACE

Studying stars has helped humans to answer some of our biggest questions about life on Earth. We now understand that both our planet and its living things are formed from stardust—atoms forged inside stars and scattered across space as those stars died.

★ FIND OUT HOW OPTICAL TELESCOPES TRANSFORMED STARGAZING ON PAGE 24 ★

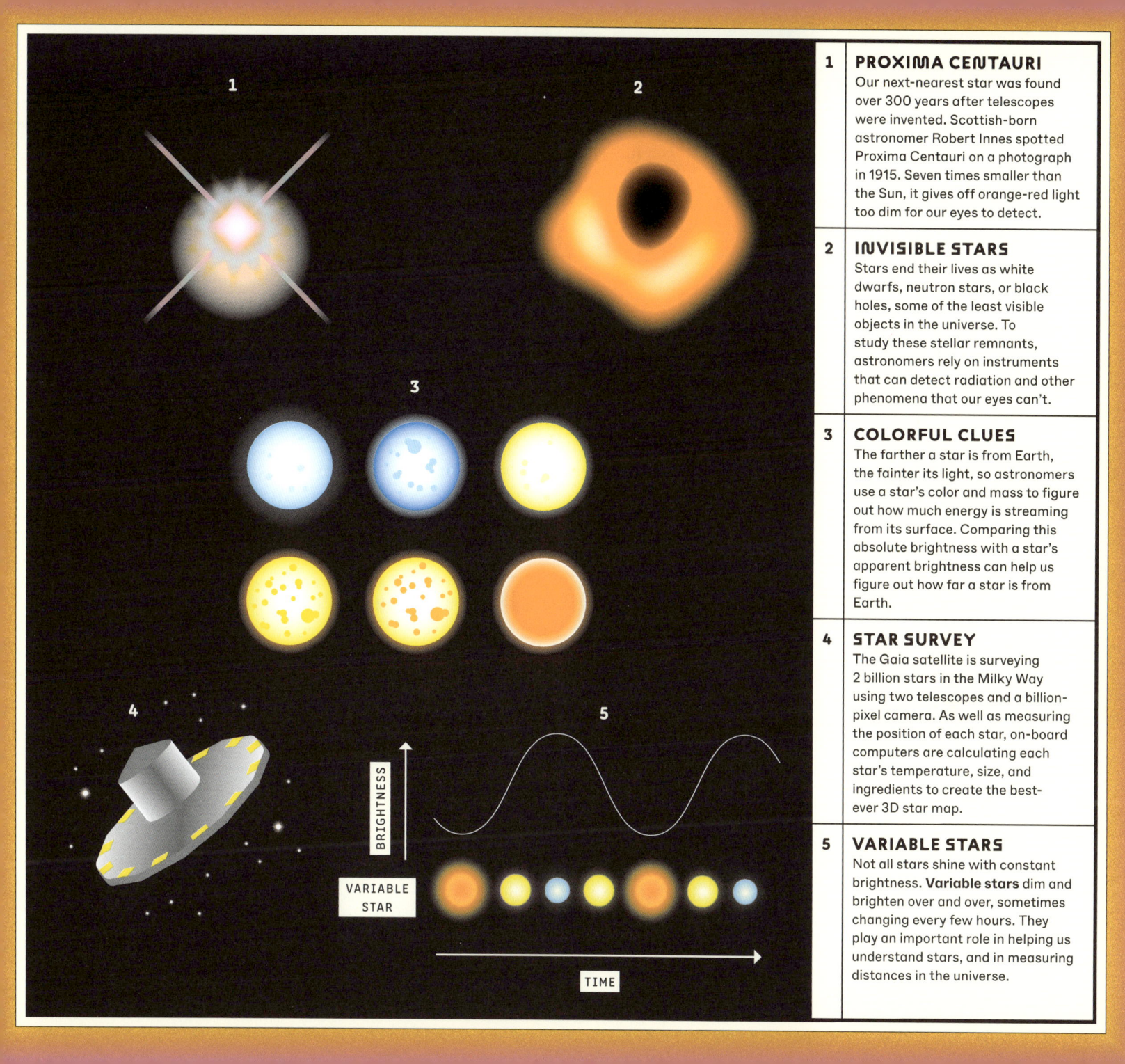

1	**PROXIMA CENTAURI** Our next-nearest star was found over 300 years after telescopes were invented. Scottish-born astronomer Robert Innes spotted Proxima Centauri on a photograph in 1915. Seven times smaller than the Sun, it gives off orange-red light too dim for our eyes to detect.
2	**INVISIBLE STARS** Stars end their lives as white dwarfs, neutron stars, or black holes, some of the least visible objects in the universe. To study these stellar remnants, astronomers rely on instruments that can detect radiation and other phenomena that our eyes can't.
3	**COLORFUL CLUES** The farther a star is from Earth, the fainter its light, so astronomers use a star's color and mass to figure out how much energy is streaming from its surface. Comparing this absolute brightness with a star's apparent brightness can help us figure out how far a star is from Earth.
4	**STAR SURVEY** The Gaia satellite is surveying 2 billion stars in the Milky Way using two telescopes and a billion-pixel camera. As well as measuring the position of each star, on-board computers are calculating each star's temperature, size, and ingredients to create the best-ever 3D star map.
5	**VARIABLE STARS** Not all stars shine with constant brightness. **Variable stars** dim and brighten over and over, sometimes changing every few hours. They play an important role in helping us understand stars, and in measuring distances in the universe.

LIGHT

OBJECTS IN THE UNIVERSE RADIATE MANY DIFFERENT TYPES OF ELECTROMAGNETIC RADIATION, BETTER KNOWN AS LIGHT. THE VISIBLE LIGHT WE CAN SEE WITH OUR EYES IS JUST A SMALL PART OF THE ELECTROMAGNETIC SPECTRUM.

Light is energy that can travel vast distances across empty space. For most of history, humans only knew about the visible light that can be detected by our eyes. In the late 1600s, Isaac Newton used a prism to split sunlight, showing it is actually a mixture of many different colors.

Our eyes have evolved to be sensitive to visible light, because that is the main type of light that passes through Earth's atmosphere, and bounces off objects that we need to see. Most other wavelengths are blocked by the atmosphere.

During the 1800s, scientists discovered invisible types of electromagnetic radiation, and realized they are all part of the same "rainbow," or spectrum of electromagnetic radiation. In the 1900s, astronomers learned to detect radio waves, infrared light, ultraviolet light, X-rays, and gamma rays streaming toward Earth from space. They understood that there is a hidden universe out there, radiating light at wavelengths we can't see with our eyes.

ELECTROMAGNETIC WAVES

Light energy can be thought of as waves, rippling through space. Like ripples in water, the waves have peaks and troughs. The distance between two peaks is known as the wavelength. A long wavelength means peaks occur infrequently. Radio waves have the lowest frequency of all, with up to hundreds of miles between peaks. This means they don't carry very much energy. Short wavelengths mean peaks arrive with a high frequency. As a result, high-frequency waves carry more energy.

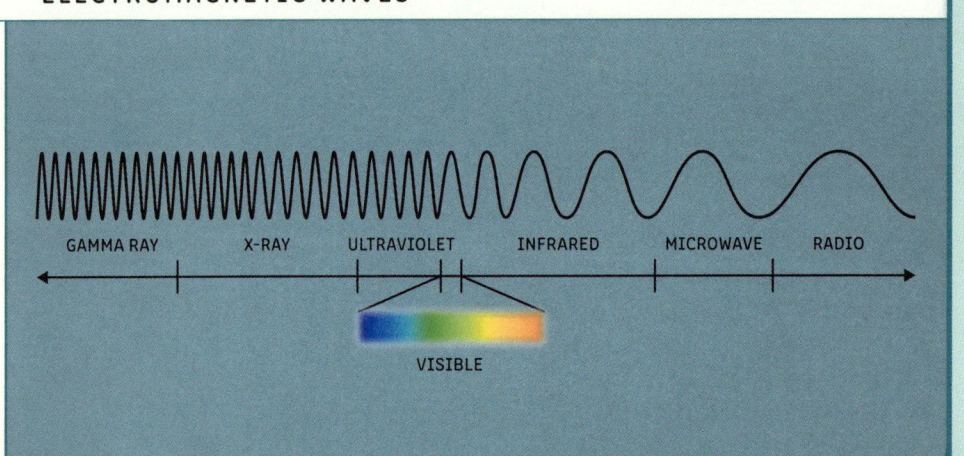

GAMMA RAY — X-RAY — ULTRAVIOLET — INFRARED — MICROWAVE — RADIO

VISIBLE

SPLITTING LIGHT

In the 1800s, William Herschel found that light at the red end of the spectrum warmed a thermometer more than light at the blue end. But the "empty" area beyond the spectrum's red end was warmest of all! He had discovered "invisible" infrared light. The following year, ultraviolet light was discovered at the blue end of the spectrum.

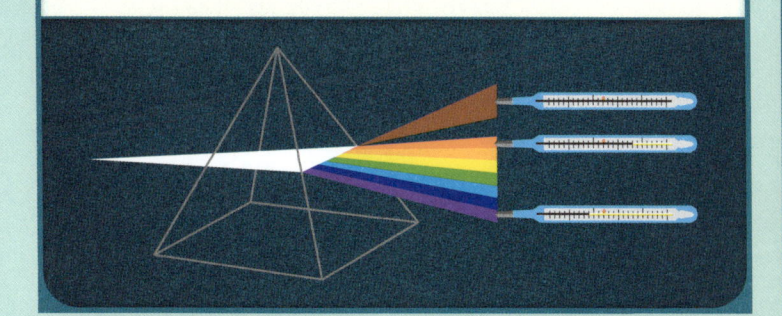

TAKING STELLAR TEMPERATURES

Spectrums tell us about the temperature of objects in space, because the types of light emitted by objects changes with their temperature. Cool clouds of cosmic dust mainly emit low-energy radio waves. Slightly warmer planets radiate infrared light. Hot stars radiate higher-energy visible light and UV as well. Only the hottest objects emit light at the X-ray and gamma ray end of the spectrum.

SPECTROSCOPY

Splitting light into a spectrum shows the mixture of different wavelengths coming from a source. This information can tell us a lot about the source itself. In the 1800s, chemists learned that every chemical emits a unique mix of light when heated—known as an emission spectrum. In the 1900s, astronomers learned to use spectroscopy to identify these chemical "fingerprints" in the light from stars and other distant objects, telling us what they are made from.

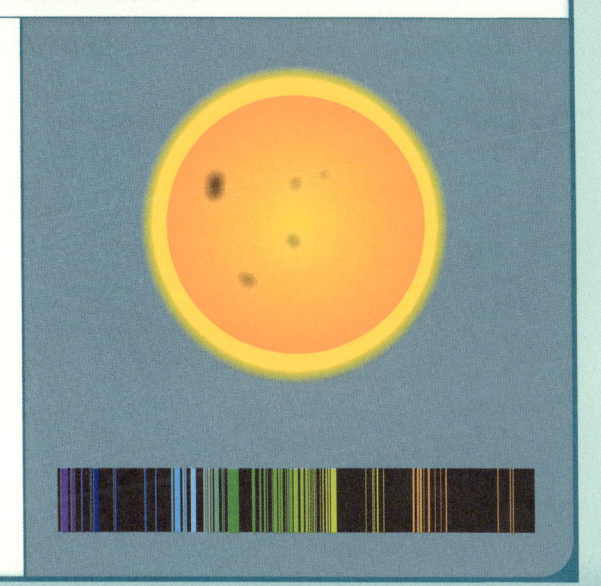

THE SPEED OF LIGHT

Light is the fastest thing in the universe, zooming across space at almost 186,000 miles per second. In the 1860s, James Clerk Maxwell used math to prove that the speed of light never changes. Knowing this "constant" has been very important in measuring and understanding things in the universe that do change.

The speed of light is known as c, after *celeritas*, a Latin word for speed. It is familiar from Einstein's most famous equation.

$$E = mc^2$$

STELLAR NURSERIES

CATEGORY	AGE
MOLECULAR CLOUDS	10 TO 30 MILLION YEARS

STRANGE THOUGH IT SEEMS, SCORCHING STARS ARE BORN INSIDE A GALAXY'S COLDEST, DARKEST CLOUDS. BABY STARS GROW BY GOBBLING THIS SURROUNDING GAS AND DUST, SLOWLY DESTROYING THEIR NEBULOUS NURSERIES.

ALL ABOUT

The "empty" space between stars is speckled with drifting gas and dust. In most places, these atoms are so spread out as to be trillions of times thinner than Earth's air. But sometimes interstellar gas and dust gather more closely, forming vast molecular clouds.

Although cosmic dust is just a small part of these clouds, it is dense enough to block the light from surrounding stars, making molecular clouds the coldest, darkest spots in the universe. This lack of heat and light is what allows new stars to take shape. Various things disturb the gas and dust inside molecular clouds, including shock waves from nearby supernovae. With very little heat energy to force atoms and molecules apart, denser clumps begin to form inside the cloud.

These clumps eventually collapse under their own gravity. Matter swirls toward the center of a clump, which flattens into a spinning disc. As the molecules are squeezed more closely together, they bump into each other more often. This friction causes them to heat up, like air squeezed in a bicycle pump, but on a cosmic scale.

Baby stars (known as protostars) grow at the very center of these discs, becoming hotter and more massive as they pull in yet more gas and dust from the surrounding cloud. As the pressure and temperature builds, the cloud acts like a blanket, stopping all the heat from escaping. Even so, it will be millions of years before the core of the protostar becomes hot and dense enough for the star to ignite.

KEY FACTS

- Molecular clouds range from 1 to 300 light-years across.
- The largest clouds contain enough matter to form several million Suns.
- Like clouds on Earth, they are continually being disturbed and can form any shape.

TEMPERATURE

As cold as -441°F.

NEAREST

The Taurus Molecular Cloud is one of the nearest star-forming regions. It lies 430 light-years from Earth.

WHAT IS IT MADE OF?

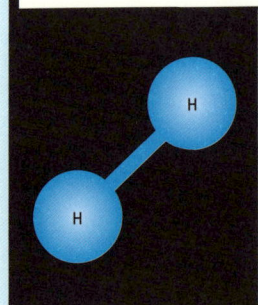

- The main component of molecular clouds is hydrogen, in the form of H_2 molecules.
- They also contain hundreds of other molecules, including water, carbon monoxide, and even larger carbon-based molecules such as sugar.
- About 1 percent of each cloud is cosmic dust.

OUR PLACE IN SPACE

Star nurseries are some of the most beautiful objects to peer at through a telescope. They have helped scientists figure out how stars form, giving us a glimpse of what the Sun's neighborhood would have looked like five billion years ago.

★ FIND OUT MORE ABOUT A SUPERNOVA EXPLOSION ON PAGE 154 ★

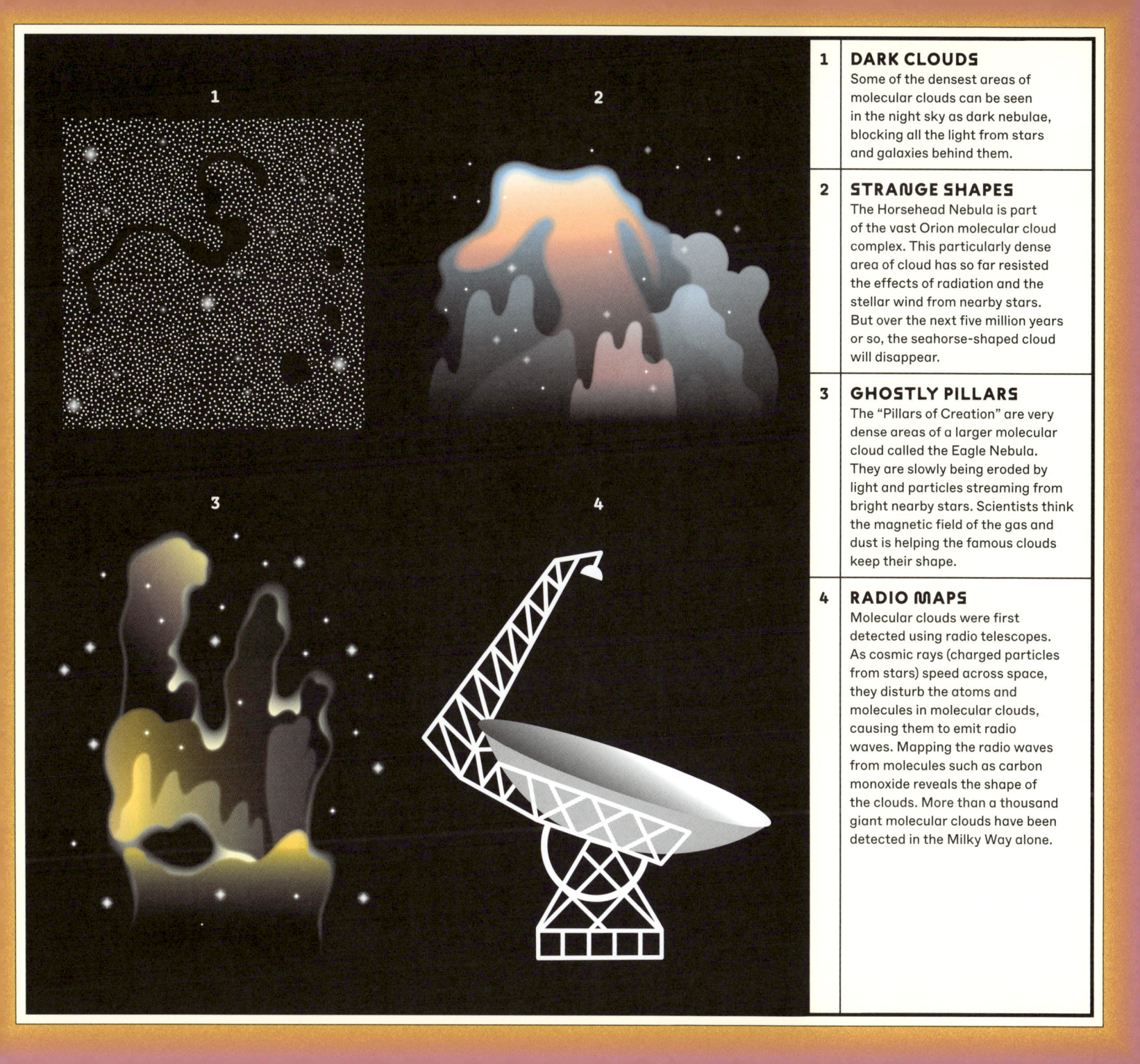

1	**DARK CLOUDS** Some of the densest areas of molecular clouds can be seen in the night sky as dark nebulae, blocking all the light from stars and galaxies behind them.
2	**STRANGE SHAPES** The Horsehead Nebula is part of the vast Orion molecular cloud complex. This particularly dense area of cloud has so far resisted the effects of radiation and the stellar wind from nearby stars. But over the next five million years or so, the seahorse-shaped cloud will disappear.
3	**GHOSTLY PILLARS** The "Pillars of Creation" are very dense areas of a larger molecular cloud called the Eagle Nebula. They are slowly being eroded by light and particles streaming from bright nearby stars. Scientists think the magnetic field of the gas and dust is helping the famous clouds keep their shape.
4	**RADIO MAPS** Molecular clouds were first detected using radio telescopes. As cosmic rays (charged particles from stars) speed across space, they disturb the atoms and molecules in molecular clouds, causing them to emit radio waves. Mapping the radio waves from molecules such as carbon monoxide reveals the shape of the clouds. More than a thousand giant molecular clouds have been detected in the Milky Way alone.

EXPLORING YOUNG STARS

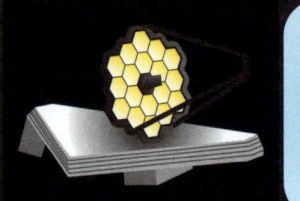

FOR THE FIRST FEW MILLION YEARS OF THEIR LIVES, STARS LIE HIDDEN INSIDE THEIR DENSE CLOUD NURSERIES. THEIR EFFECTS ON THIS SURROUNDING GAS AND DUST ARE THE ONLY CLUES TO THE TRANSFORMATION HAPPENING INSIDE.

ALL ABOUT

Protostars are born inside a dense disc of gas and dust. They feed on this for millions of years, gradually gathering mass until their core pressure and temperature is high enough for fusion to begin.

Long before it properly ignites, a young star glows because it is hot. However, the surrounding gas and dust block our view of this first faint light. This is why astrophysicists still know less about the beginning of a star's life than the end. Powerful infrared telescopes, such as the Webb Space Telescope, can now detect the faint infrared radiation (heat) that makes its way through the dust, revealing the different stages that young stars go through as they splutter into life.

Young stars are very active, pulling in material, ejecting fast-moving jets of gas from their poles and creating spectacular glowing nebulae. The sudden heating of material falling into the star can cause bright flares of high-energy radiation, too. Young stars take different paths to adulthood, depending on their mass. Stars destined to be around the size of our Sun spend their teenage years as T Tauri stars, varying in brightness as they begin to shine. More massive stars become brighter more quickly, when still surrounded by dust clouds or dense discs of debris. They spend their teenage years as Herbig Ae/Be stars.

Only when a star has found the right balance does it become stable and begin to shine, as a fully-fledged adult or "main-sequence" star. Debris left in the disc begins to gather into planets. The surrounding clouds are cleared by a steady stellar wind, and the new star becomes visible to light-detecting telescopes. In our galaxy, a new star reaches this stage three to four times every Earth year.

EXPLORATION TIMELINE

1800s	Herbig-Haro objects first observed.
1852	The first T Tauri star is spotted.
1940s	George Herbig and Guillermo Haro recognize Herbig-Haro objects as a special type of emission nebula.
1945	T Tauri stars are recognized as pre-main-sequence stars.
1960	Herbig Ae/Be stars are first defined.
1995	Astronomers announce they have detected a brown dwarf star, Teide 1, in the Pleiades star cluster.
2001	Pictures taken by the Hubble Space Telescope provide first direct evidence of protoplanetary discs around young stars.
2024	The Webb Space Telescope is used to identify more than 1,000 potential **young stellar objects** in a star-forming region of the Small Magellanic Cloud.

ARE WE THERE YET?

- The nearest young stellar objects are in the Taurus and Ophiuchus molecular clouds, around 400 light-years from Earth.

OUR PLACE IN SPACE

Studying the early lives of low-mass stars helps astrophysicists figure out how our own Sun and its planets formed almost five billion years ago.

Young stellar objects also help us better understand the chemistry of the entire universe, and how galaxies change over time.

★ NEW STARS RARELY FORM ON THEIR OWN. FIND OUT ABOUT MULTIPLE STAR SYSTEMS ON PAGE 162 ★

#	
1	**T TAURI STARS** Stars around the size of our Sun may take up to 100 million years to gather enough mass for hydrogen fusion to begin. During this time, they are known as T Tauri stars.
2	**COSMIC LIGHTSABER** As protostars gather mass, jets of superheated gas erupt from their poles. The fast-moving gas collides with the surrounding gas and dust, creating a long, thin, double-sided glowing nebula called a Herbig-Haro object. The shape of shock waves rippling through the nebula help astronomers trace the history of the star.
3	**HERBIG AE/BE STARS** These teenage stars are 2 to 8 times the mass of our Sun. The swirling discs of debris and dust around them are often brighter than those of T Tauri stars, providing lots of clues about what is happening inside.
4	**FUTURE PLANETS** Planets form in the discs of debris left behind once a star has ignited. The ALMA telescope captured an image of the debris disc around HL Tauri, a young star 480 light-years from Earth. The gaps in the disc could be where new planets are forming, gathering up the leftover gas and dust in their path.
5	**FAILED STARS** Not every protostar gobbles up enough mass to ignite. Objects that gather less than 0.08 of the Sun's mass become brown dwarfs— would-be stars that glow very faintly until they cool completely. Because they are thousands of degrees cooler than active stars, brown dwarfs are very hard to spot.

INFRARED ASTRONOMY

WE ARE ALL FAMILIAR WITH LIGHT AT INFRARED WAVELENGTHS. IT'S THE PART OF SUNLIGHT THAT WARMS OUR SKIN ON A SUNNY DAY. BUT THE SUN IS FAR FROM THE ONLY SOURCE OF INFRARED LIGHT REACHING EARTH.

Every object emits electromagnetic radiation (light) of some kind. Objects far cooler than stars—such as planets, brown dwarfs, and clouds of cosmic dust—glow with low-energy infrared light, rather than visible light. This means they can only be detected using infrared telescopes.

However, these cool objects aren't the only things worth looking at with an infrared telescope. Starlight includes some infrared light too, and, unlike visible light, this infrared light can make its way through clouds of dust in space without being scattered. To an infrared telescope, it's as if the dust doesn't exist. It can see young stars forming inside a molecular cloud, or peer through the dusty disc of the Milky Way to reveal objects previously hidden from view. Infrared telescopes also have the power to detect much older "redshifted" light than optical telescopes can (see box below).

Infrared astronomy began in the 1800s, when British astronomer William Herschel discovered infrared radiation in sunlight. Today, the Webb Space Telescope (NASA, CSA, and ESA) is the world's most powerful infrared telescope.

COSMOLOGICAL REDSHIFT

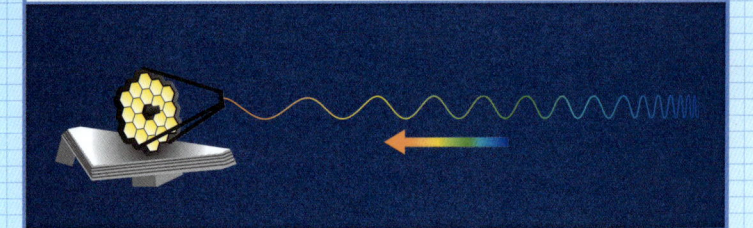

As light travels through an expanding universe (see page 190), its waves stretch and shift toward the red end of the spectrum. By the time the once-visible light from most distant galaxies arrives at Earth, it has become infrared light, and can only be detected by infrared telescopes.

FALSE COLORS

We can't see infrared light with our eyes, so computers are used to convert telescope data into pictures. This means choosing false colors to represent the light at different wavelengths. Colorful images of nebulae often combine visible and invisible wavelengths into one spectacular image.

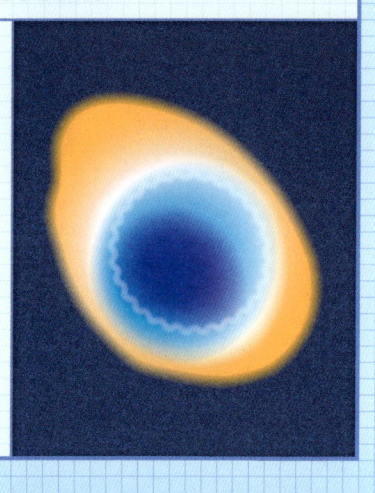

WEBB SPACE TELESCOPE

1. The Webb Space Telescope's four infrared detectors work like digital cameras, but use materials that respond to infrared rather than visible light.

2. To remain sensitive, infrared detectors must be kept very cool. The Webb Space Telescope's tennis-court-sized heat shield protects it from radiated heat.

3. A 21.6-foot, gold-plated mirror reflects infrared light toward the detectors.

4. The mirror's enormous surface area helps it gather six times more light than the Hubble Space Telescope's mirror.

5. To fit in a rocket cargo bay, the Webb Space Telescope had to be folded up for launch, then unfolded and assembled in space. In total, 20,000 people worked on this groundbreaking project.

6. The Webb Space Telescope is not orbiting Earth, like Hubble. Instead it orbits the Sun, at a point known as the second Lagrange Point (L2), 994,000 miles from Earth. At this special point, the combined gravity of Earth and Sun hold the telescope in line with Earth. This ensures that the Webb Space Telescope's heat shield not only protects it from the Sun, but from heat and reflected light from Earth and the Moon, too.

7. The Webb Space Telescope's mirror has a total light-collecting area of more than 270 square feet, compared to the Hubble Space Telescope's 48.5 square feet. Here, both mirrors are shown next to a human adult for scale.

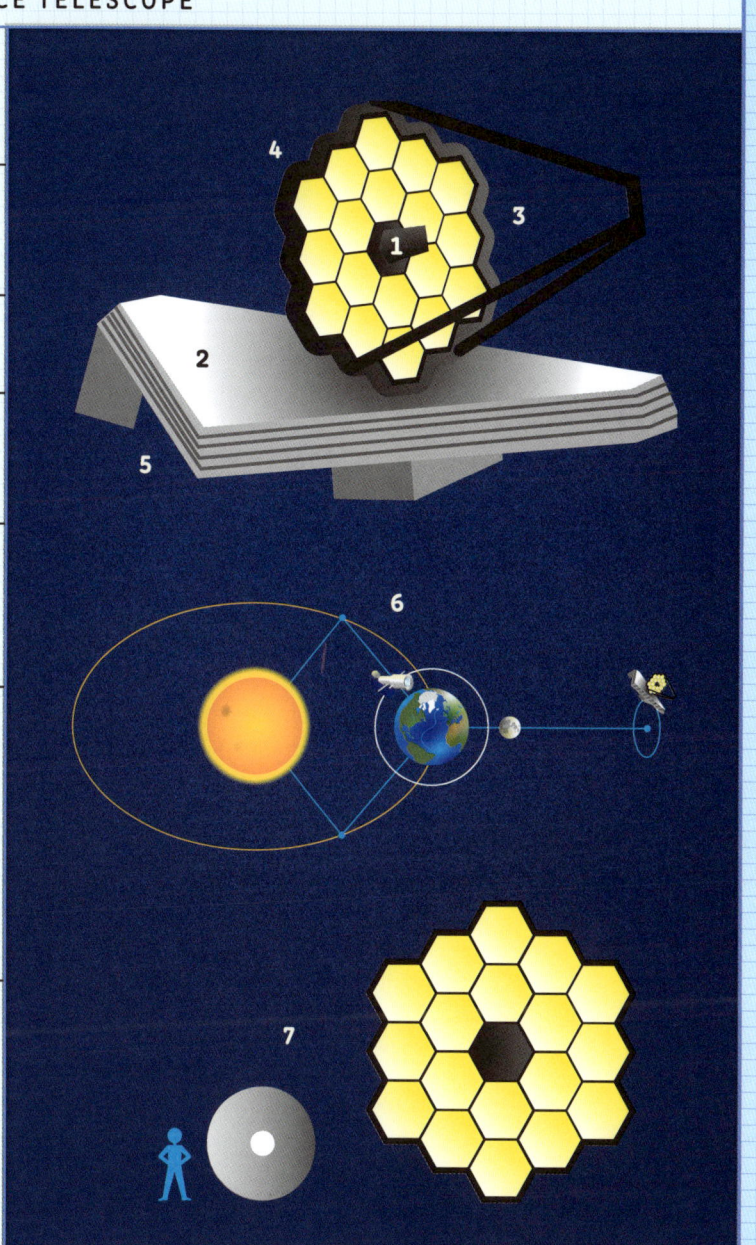

MAIN-SEQUENCE STARS

CATEGORY	AGE
MAIN-SEQUENCE STAR	MILLIONS TO BILLIONS OF YEARS

MOST STARS IN THE UNIVERSE ARE CURRENTLY **MAIN-SEQUENCE STARS**, BURNING STEADILY WITH RED, ORANGE, YELLOW, WHITE, OR BLUE LIGHT.

ALL ABOUT

Once a star has ignited and is steadily burning hydrogen to helium, it's known as a main-sequence star.

This is the longest stage of a star's life, lasting millions or billions of years. Most stars in the universe are currently main-sequence stars, but they are not all the same. A glance at a starry sky reveals big differences in color and brightness. The name comes from a famous graph called the Hertzsprung-Russell diagram, which plots stars by brightness and temperature. Most stars in the sky lie on the "main sequence"—a line running from hot, bright stars on the top left to cool, dim stars on the bottom right.

In the 1800s, scientists realized that these differences are not to do with a star's age or ingredients, but how much hydrogen fuel it started with. The most massive main-sequence stars are the biggest, hottest, and brightest. Stars ten times as massive as our Sun, for example, are more than a thousand times as luminous. Although these massive stars start with more fuel, they burn through it very quickly. Some spend just 10 million years on the main sequence, making them extremely rare.

Stars with less mass burn more faintly, so their fuel lasts billions or even trillions of years. Around 8 percent of stars are medium-sized, like our Sun, shining steadily with yellowish light. They stay on the main sequence for around 10 billion years.

More than three-quarters of main-sequence stars are tiny red dwarfs, just a tenth of our Sun's mass. Their reddish light is so dim, none are visible by eye from Earth. They may burn for a thousand times longer than our Sun, but even a red dwarf can't stay on the main sequence forever. Just as a star's mass affects how it lives, mass also shapes how a star dies.

KEY FACTS

- A typical main-sequence star spins once every 15 days, but hotter stars spin faster than cooler stars.
- Main-sequence stars range from a tenth to a hundred times the mass of our Sun.

TEMPERATURE

From 3,632°F to more than 90,032°F.

NEAREST

Our Sun is the nearest main-sequence star to Earth. Alpha Centauri is the next nearest visible without a telescope.

A BALANCING ACT

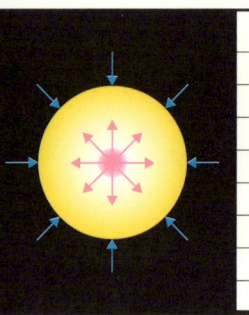

In a main-sequence star, energy released by nuclear fusion at the core creates outward pressure that balances the crushing pressure of the inward gravitational force. This keeps main-sequence stars stable in size, surface temperature, color, and brightness.

OUR PLACE IN SPACE

Our Sun is about halfway through its time on the main sequence. This means its energy output is very steady, keeping conditions on our planet stable enough for life.

★ EXPLORE THE HERTZSPRUNG-RUSSELL DIAGRAM ON PAGE 214 ★

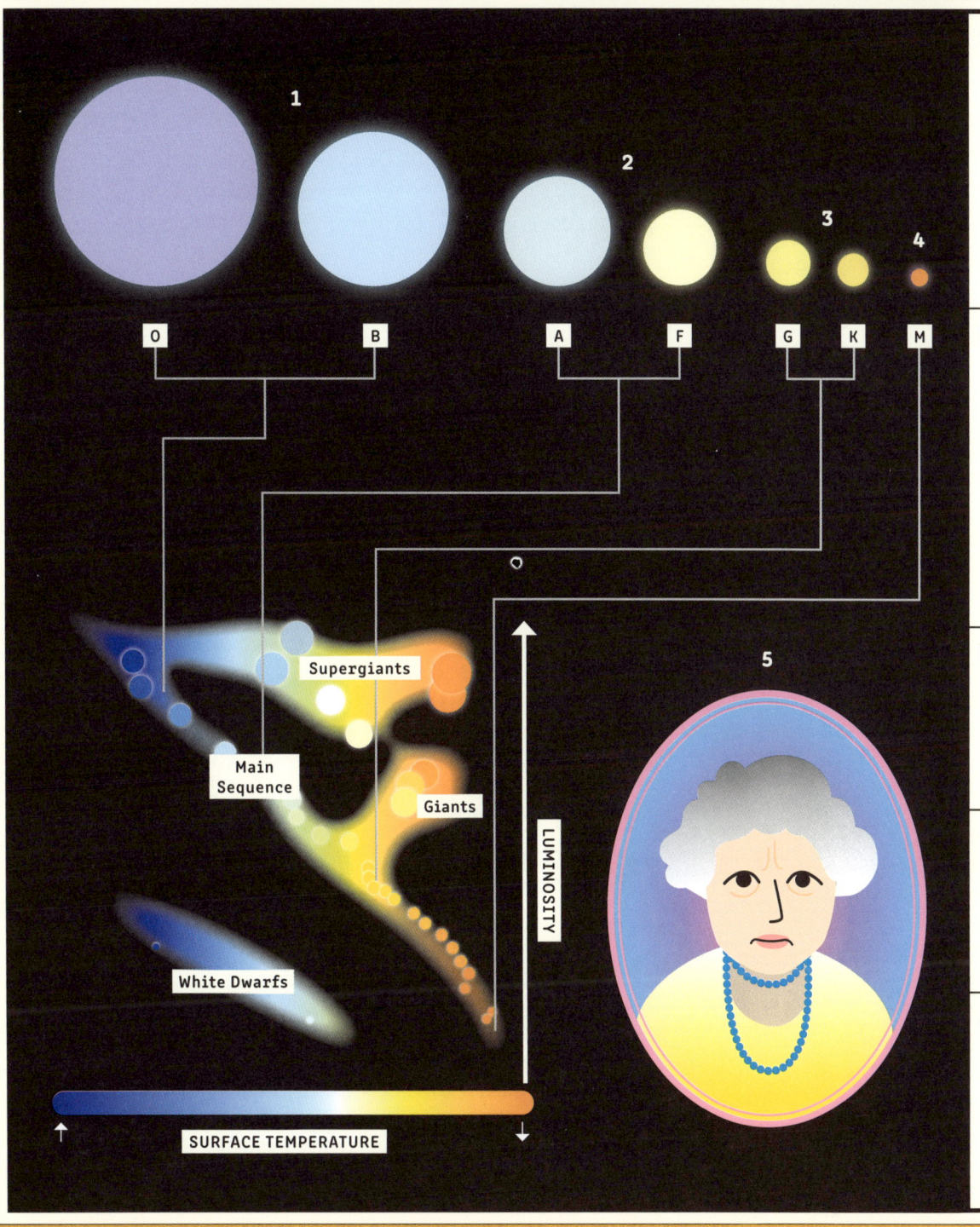

#		
1	**HOT BLUE STARS**	The three bright stars on Orion's belt are O-type stars, the most massive and rarest main-sequence stars of all. Surface temperatures of 90,032°F and higher mean they shine with intense blue-violet light. Blue-white B-type stars are cooler (with surface temperatures of 18,032 to 54,032°F) but still shine some 20,000 times more brightly than our Sun.
2	**WHITE STARS**	A typical A-type star is three times the mass of our Sun, with a surface temperature from 13,352°F to about 18,032°F. Sirius is in this group, shining with white light 40 times as luminous as the Sun. F-type stars such as Polaris are slightly more massive than our Sun, but reach a higher surface temperature of up to 12,812°F, burning through their fuel twice as quickly.
3	**SUN-LIKE STARS**	Our Sun is a G-type star, burning yellow-white thanks to a surface temperature of around 9,932°F. Yellow-orange K-class stars are about 80 percent of the Sun's mass, but will shine for five times as long.
4	**RED DWARF STARS**	Red-orange M-type stars are the most common stars. Cooler than the Sun, with a surface temperature of 3,632°F to 6,332°F, these red dwarfs burn for around 100 billion years with dim orange-red light.
5	**STELLAR CAREER**	Annie Jump Cannon created the Harvard system that astronomers still use to classify stars by color and surface temperature. In the late 1800s, Annie classified more than 350,000 stars, more than anyone else in the history of astronomy.

RED GIANTS

CATEGORY	AGE
AGEING STAR	THIS STAGE LASTS FOR ABOUT A BILLION YEARS

AS STARS RUN OUT OF HYDROGEN FUEL, THE BALANCE OF FORCES INSIDE THE STAR SHIFTS, WITH DRAMATIC RESULTS. LOW-MASS STARS LIKE OUR SUN BECOME BIGGER, BRIGHTER, AND REDDER.

ALL ABOUT

Stars up to about eight times the mass of our Sun stay on the main sequence for billions of years, fusing hydrogen to helium. During this time, the energy released by fusion creates an outward force that perfectly balances the crushing inward force of the star's gravity. The star's size, temperature, color, and brightness stay steady. But eventually, the hydrogen begins to run out.

Dying stars do not cool and dim slowly, like dying fires. For a star, cooling down means collapse. As hydrogen fusion slows, gravity begins to win the battle, squeezing the helium core and making it denser. This raises the temperature of the core, like squeezing the air in a bicycle pump causes it to get hotter.

This extra heat ignites fusion in a thin layer of hydrogen around the core, releasing more energy. The outer layers of the star absorb this energy and expand, puffing the star up to hundreds of times its original size, and stopping it from collapsing due to gravity. The star becomes brighter. However, the energy reaching the surface is spread across a much larger area, making the star's surface cooler than before, so the escaping light is redder.

Over hundreds of millions of years, the helium core of this red giant continues to shrink due to gravity, and its temperature continues to rise. Eventually, the helium core becomes hot enough for helium atoms themselves to fuse, creating carbon and some oxygen too.

KEY FACTS

- Red giants were once main-sequence stars half to eight times the Sun's mass.
- Red giants are 200 to 1,000 times wider than the Sun.
- A red giant's core spins around ten times faster than its surface layers.

TEMPERATURE

☀ 5,792 °F
❄ 3,992 °F

NEAREST

Gacrux is Earth's nearest red giant star. Its name is short for Gamma Crucis, the third-brightest star in the Southern Cross constellation.

WHAT IS IT MADE OF?

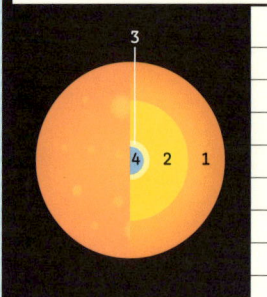

1. Cool, red photosphere.
2. Hugely expanded envelope of low-density hydrogen gas.
3. Hydrogen and helium fusion happens in shells around the core.
4. Small, dead core made of helium.

OUR PLACE IN SPACE

All red giant stars reach the same peak brightness. Using the powerful Hubble Space Telescope (see page 57) astronomers can compare red giants in the Milky Way and other galaxies, and use the difference in apparent brightness to figure out how far away those galaxies are.

★ FIND OUT WHY SOME STARS BECOME RED SUPERGIANTS RATHER THAN RED GIANTS ON PAGE 152 ★

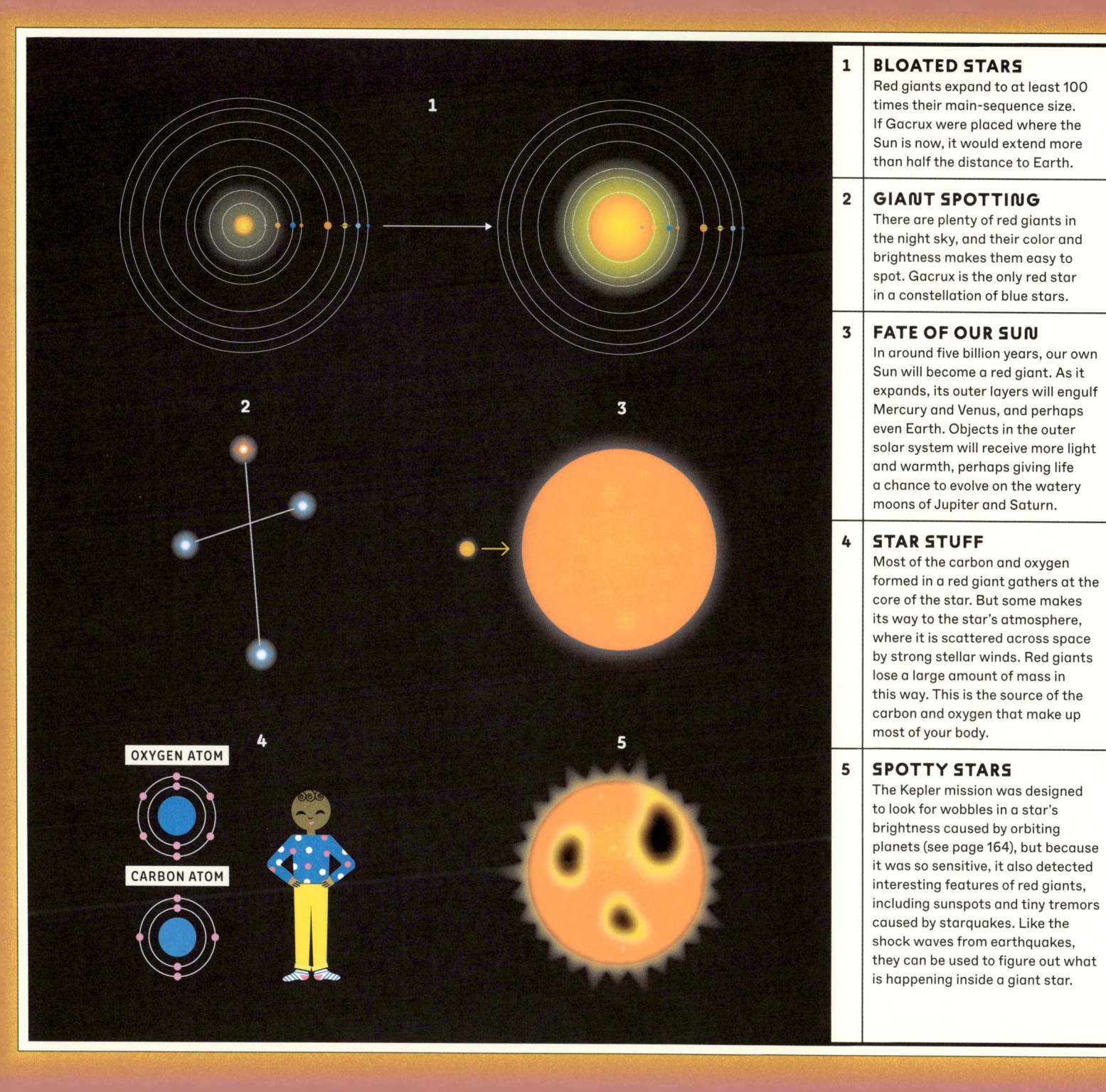

1	**BLOATED STARS**	Red giants expand to at least 100 times their main-sequence size. If Gacrux were placed where the Sun is now, it would extend more than half the distance to Earth.
2	**GIANT SPOTTING**	There are plenty of red giants in the night sky, and their color and brightness makes them easy to spot. Gacrux is the only red star in a constellation of blue stars.
3	**FATE OF OUR SUN**	In around five billion years, our own Sun will become a red giant. As it expands, its outer layers will engulf Mercury and Venus, and perhaps even Earth. Objects in the outer solar system will receive more light and warmth, perhaps giving life a chance to evolve on the watery moons of Jupiter and Saturn.
4	**STAR STUFF**	Most of the carbon and oxygen formed in a red giant gathers at the core of the star. But some makes its way to the star's atmosphere, where it is scattered across space by strong stellar winds. Red giants lose a large amount of mass in this way. This is the source of the carbon and oxygen that make up most of your body.
5	**SPOTTY STARS**	The Kepler mission was designed to look for wobbles in a star's brightness caused by orbiting planets (see page 164), but because it was so sensitive, it also detected interesting features of red giants, including sunspots and tiny tremors caused by starquakes. Like the shock waves from earthquakes, they can be used to figure out what is happening inside a giant star.

WHITE DWARF STARS

CATEGORY	AGE
STELLAR REMNANT	BILLIONS OF YEARS

AS THEY RUN OUT OF FUEL, LOW-MASS STARS LIKE OUR SUN FACE A SLOW BUT BEAUTIFUL ENDGAME, SHEDDING THEIR OUTER LAYERS TO CREATE SPECTACULAR NEBULAE AS THEY TRANSFORM FROM RED GIANTS INTO WHITE DWARFS.

ALL ABOUT

As Sun-like stars reach the end of their lives, they swell into red giants and begin to shed their outer layers (see page 148). Eventually, a red giant runs out of helium fuel that can be fused into heavier elements.

Without energy being released by fusion, there is nothing pushing outward from the core of the star. Gravity wins the battle it has been fighting for billions of years, and the core collapses in on itself. A star the size of our Sun is suddenly squeezed into a ball the size of Earth! This superdense stellar remnant is known as a white dwarf. Meanwhile the outer layers of the dead star escape into space.

White dwarf stars are very common. More than 95 percent of all stars are small or medium-sized, so will become white dwarfs when they die—including our own Sun.

When they first form, white dwarfs are some of the hottest objects in the universe, glowing with the energy left over from their earlier life and the heat generated by squeezing so much matter into such a small space.

For a short time, the white dwarf's intense light energizes this surrounding shell of ejected gas and dust, causing it to glow brightly. This glowing cloud is known as a planetary nebula. It includes elements forged inside the star, and chemicals that formed as this stardust was scattered across space.

Planetary nebulae only glow for a few tens of thousands of years, but their story does not end there. Their gas and dust drift through space until it one day becomes the raw material for new stars.

KEY FACTS

- A typical white dwarf star is roughly as wide as Earth, but contains up to 1.44 times as much material as our Sun.
- Planetary nebulae glow for tens of thousands of years.
- White dwarfs glow for billions of years as they cool.

TEMPERATURE

Up to 450,032 °F when newly formed.

NEAREST

Sirius B is Earth's nearest white dwarf star, 8.6 light-years from Earth.

WHAT IS IT MADE OF?

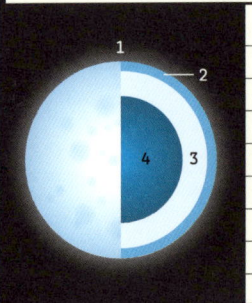

1. Outer layers have escaped into space, forming a glowing planetary nebula.
2. Thin shell of leftover hydrogen.
3. Thin shell of helium, created by the star in its main-sequence stage.
4. Large core of carbon and oxygen, created by the star in its red giant stage.

OUR PLACE IN SPACE

Studying white dwarfs helps astronomers understand the end point for most stars, and how matter behaves at extreme temperatures and pressures.

FIND OUT HOW SOME WHITE DWARFS TURN INTO SUPERNOVA ON PAGE 154

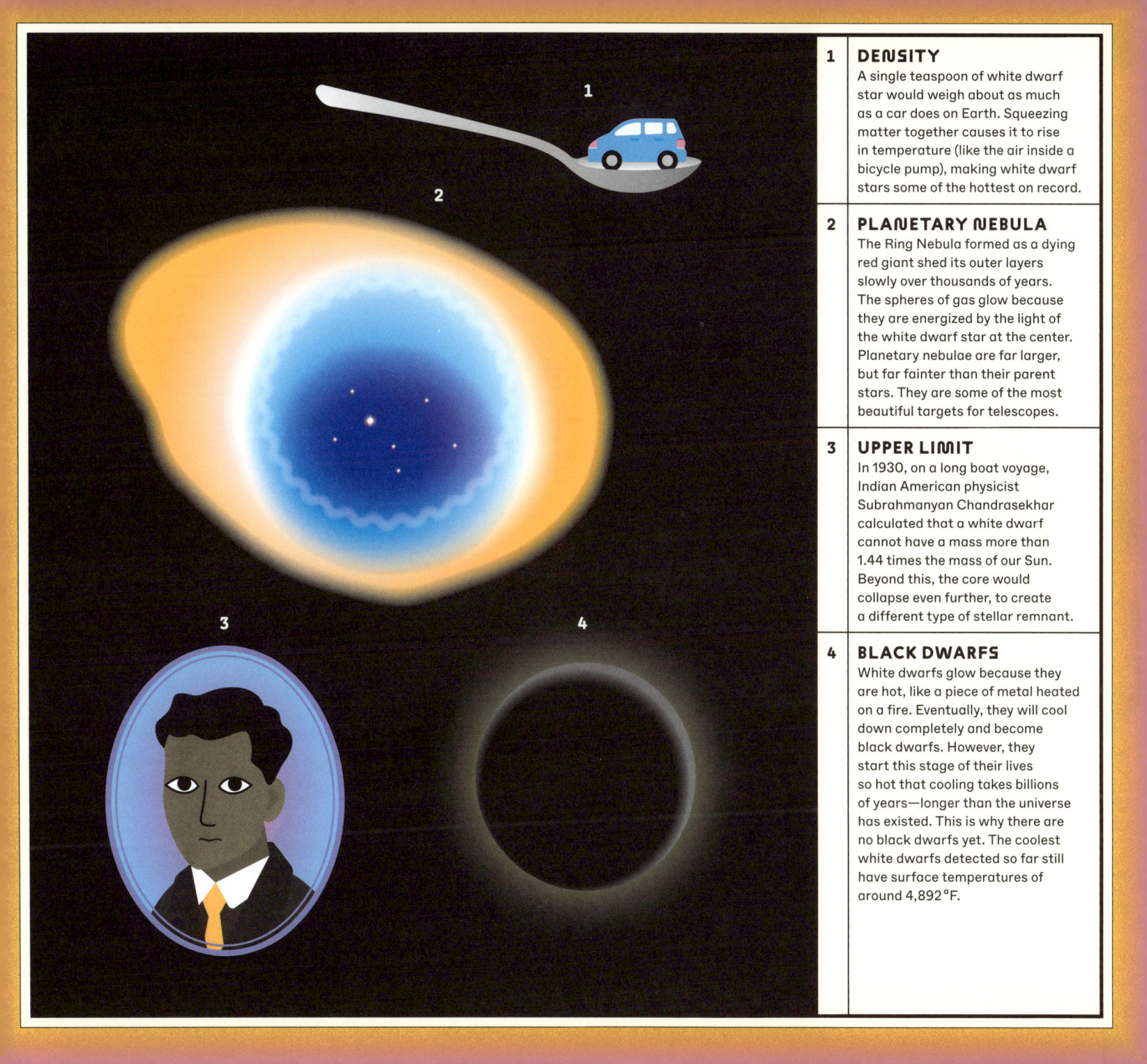

#	Topic	Description
1	**DENSITY**	A single teaspoon of white dwarf star would weigh about as much as a car does on Earth. Squeezing matter together causes it to rise in temperature (like the air inside a bicycle pump), making white dwarf stars some of the hottest on record.
2	**PLANETARY NEBULA**	The Ring Nebula formed as a dying red giant shed its outer layers slowly over thousands of years. The spheres of gas glow because they are energized by the light of the white dwarf star at the center. Planetary nebulae are far larger, but far fainter than their parent stars. They are some of the most beautiful targets for telescopes.
3	**UPPER LIMIT**	In 1930, on a long boat voyage, Indian American physicist Subrahmanyan Chandrasekhar calculated that a white dwarf cannot have a mass more than 1.44 times the mass of our Sun. Beyond this, the core would collapse even further, to create a different type of stellar remnant.
4	**BLACK DWARFS**	White dwarfs glow because they are hot, like a piece of metal heated on a fire. Eventually, they will cool down completely and become black dwarfs. However, they start this stage of their lives so hot that cooling takes billions of years—longer than the universe has existed. This is why there are no black dwarfs yet. The coolest white dwarfs detected so far still have surface temperatures of around 4,892°F.

RED SUPERGIANTS

CATEGORY	AGE	
AGEING STARS	THIS STAGE LASTS FROM 3 MILLION TO 100 MILLION YEARS	AS THE MOST MASSIVE STARS BEGIN TO RUN OUT OF FUEL, THEY BECOME RED **SUPERGIANTS**. THESE BRIGHT BUT COOL STARS ARE THE FIRST STAGE OF A JOURNEY THAT ENDS IN A SUPERNOVA EXPLOSION.

ALL ABOUT

Massive stars live their main-sequence lives like smaller stars do: fusing hydrogen into helium at their cores. However, stars more than eight times the mass of our Sun burn through their fuel far more quickly. As they age, they swell into red supergiants—ten times wider than red giants, and a thousand times wider than our Sun.

A red supergiant's enormous mass means its core pressure and temperature become more extreme. After fusing helium atoms into carbon, the star continues to burn heavier elements, creating atoms of oxygen, neon, magnesium, silicon, and iron. Convection carries some of these newly created elements into the star's vast atmosphere, where powerful stellar winds scatter them across space.

With each new type of fusion, additional energy is released. But by the time this energy makes it to the surface of a supergiant, it is spread over a vast area. As a result, the average surface temperature of a red supergiant is cooler than the surface of our Sun. Red supergiant stars shine very brightly, but with orange-red light.

Most red supergiants are variable stars. Their brightness changes as the star burns through each new fuel, converting mass to energy and finding a new balance to stop the core from collapsing. However, each adjustment lasts a shorter and shorter time. When a red supergiant begins fusing silicon into iron, it has just a day or so left to live.

KEY FACTS

- Red supergiants contain 8 to 40 times as much matter as the Sun.
- They expand up to 1,500 times the diameter of the Sun.
- They spin very slowly. Betelgeuse rotates once every 30 Earth-years.

TEMPERATURE

5,792°F to 7,592°F

NEAREST

Betelgeuse is our nearest red supergiant, lying around 700 light-years from Earth.

WHAT IS IT MADE OF?

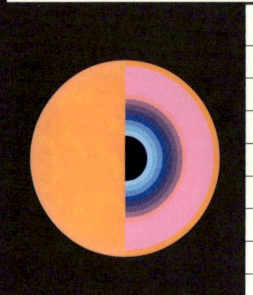

Toward the very end of its life, a red supergiant is layered like an onion. Each layer is made up of different elements forged inside the star, with an iron core. Fusion takes place between each layer, releasing the energy that stops the star from collapsing.

OUR PLACE IN SPACE

Studying the life and death of supergiant stars helps us understand where elements heavier than hydrogen and helium come from. For a complete list of these building blocks of the universe and their origins, see page 156.

★ THE NEXT STAGE FOR A SUPERGIANT IS A SUPERNOVA EXPLOSION (PAGE 154) ★

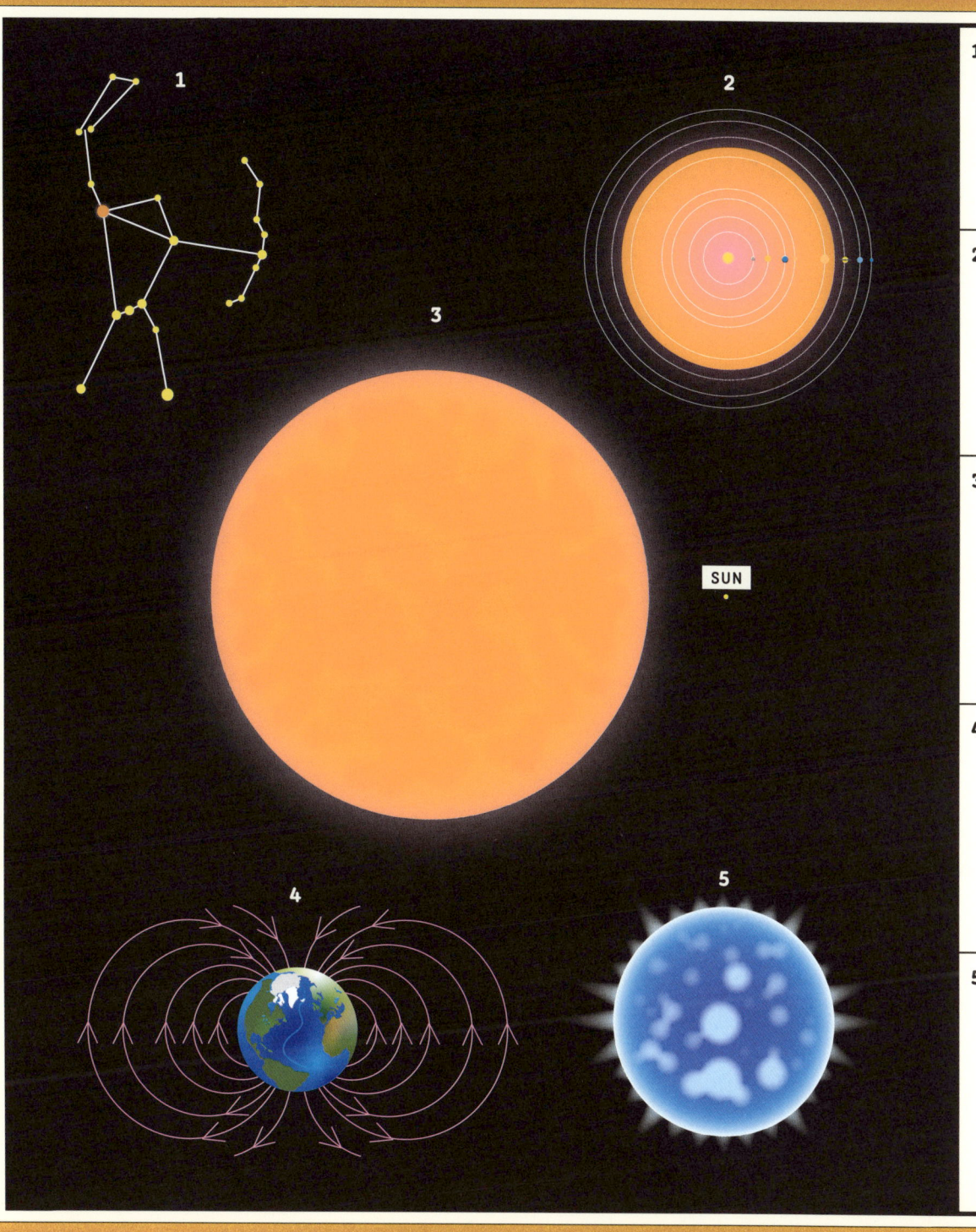

#		
1	**BETELGEUSE**	Red supergiants are some of the brightest stars in our night sky. As a result, many were named by ancient astronomers. Betelgeuse (named after the Arabic for "giant's shoulder") is part of the constellation Orion.
2	**ANTARES**	Antares looks so red in the night sky, it is often mistaken for the planet Mars. It is even named after Ares, the Greek version of the Roman god, Mars. Antares is so big it would easily reach the orbit of Mars or even Jupiter if it were placed where the Sun is now.
3	**RED HYPERGIANT**	VY Canis Majoris is one of the Milky Way's most colossal stars. Around 17 times the mass of our Sun, it has puffed up to at least 1,500 times the width. It is as luminous as 270,000 Suns combined, meaning it can be seen with a small telescope from 4,000 light-years away.
4	**HEAVY ELEMENTS**	The iron making up Earth's core—and the iron in your body—was created by fusion inside a red supergiant star. Extremely heavy elements such as bismuth are also formed in these stars over thousands of years by a different process, then blown out across space by strong stellar winds.
5	**BLUE SUPERGIANTS**	Blue supergiants may form when two stars fall toward each other and merge (see page 162) or when a red supergiant contracts before going supernova. These hottest, brightest stars in the universe include Rigel, a star at least 60,000 times brighter than our Sun.

SUPERNOVAE

CATEGORY	AGE
STELLAR REMNANT	FADES IN DAYS, WEEKS, OR MONTHS

IT'S DIFFICULT TO SPOT A FLEETING SUPERNOVA, BUT THE GLOWING CLOUDS THEY LEAVE BEHIND REVEAL THE CHAOS CAUSED WHEN MASSIVE STARS EXPLODE AT THE END OF THEIR LIVES.

ALL ABOUT

When fusion in a supergiant star finally stops, there is nothing left to resist the crushing inward force of gravity. In less than a second, the star's core collapses, heating up to a billion degrees in the process. The result is a powerful supernova explosion, flinging the outer layers of the star out across space many times faster than the speed of sound.

Just a small fraction of this energy is released in the form of visible light, but it's enough to be seen throughout the galaxy and beyond. In 1054, astronomers in ancient China and Japan spotted a bright "guest star" that we now know was a supernova. The light from this explosion had traveled across space for 6,500 years before reaching Earth, but was still so bright it could be seen in the daytime.

As the initial flash of light from a supernova travels away from the explosion, it lights up rings of gas shed by the star as it died. This light pulse is followed by shock waves, which travel more slowly than light but have the power to push out gas and dust from the star's outer layers at speeds of up to 45 million mi/h.

In turn, this fast-moving material bulldozes the interstellar gas and dust around the star, squeezing, heating, and sweeping it outward. A giant, glowing nebula forms around the dead star. This expanding shell continues to change and glow brightly for hundreds or thousands of years. The nebula formed by the 1054 supernova was first spotted through a telescope in 1731. Now known as the Crab Nebula, it is still glowing brightly today. After 1,000 years of cooling, the hottest areas are still 18,032 to 27,032°F, meaning the nebula as a whole releases 100,000 times more energy than the Sun.

KEY FACTS

- A supernova explosion happens in the Milky Way roughly once a decade.
- The collapsed core of the dead star becomes a neutron star, pulsar (see page 158), or black hole (see page 160).

TEMPERATURE

Up to 1.8 billion °F at the moment a star goes supernova.

NEAREST

The nearest supernova in recent years was 2023ixf. It exploded 21 million light-years away, in the Pinwheel Galaxy.

WHAT IS IT MADE OF?

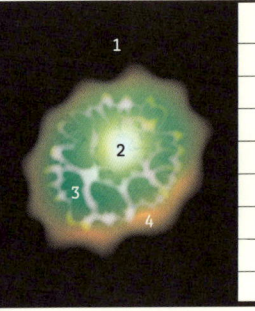

1. The Crab Nebula (vast cloud of glowing gas and dust formed by a supernova).
2. Tiny, bright pulsar at center (collapsed core of the former star).
3. Shock waves push shells of gas and dust outward in all directions.
4. Hydrogen carved into wispy filaments by the pulsar's powerful stellar wind.

OUR PLACE IN SPACE

In astronomy, light is information, so bright supernova explosions give astronomers the chance to find out more about the life and death of stars. They are also used as standard candles to help figure out the scale of the universe (see page 179).

★ MOST OF A SUPERNOVA'S ENERGY IS RELEASED AS HIGH-ENERGY PARTICLES CALLED NEUTRINOS (PAGE 185) ★

#	
1	**ELEMENT FACTORIES** Supernova explosions are the main source of most elements heavier than oxygen—including some of the key ingredients of your body. These elements form in just seconds in the extreme conditions produced by a supernova. The explosion also spreads the elements across the galaxy, where they mingle with the existing interstellar gas and dust.
2	**STRING OF PEARLS** In 1987, a blue supergiant star in a nearby galaxy exploded with the power of 100 million Suns—the brightest and nearest supernova to Earth in 400 years. The remnant of SN1987A is one of the most-studied space objects ever, and the Webb Space Telescope is now revealing new details.
3	**GAMMA RAY BURSTS** To spot distant supernovas, astronomers look for the short bursts of very high-energy radiation produced by billion-degree temperatures at the moment a star goes supernova. These gamma ray bursts appear in the sky around once a day, lasting anything from a fraction of a second to 20 minutes. Other telescopes can then be pointed in the right direction.
4	**SPACE HEIST** A different type of supernova explosion can happen when a white dwarf star steals enough matter from another star to become unstable. As nuclear fusion reignites inside this incredibly dense star, a vast amount of energy is released in an instant, blowing the star apart in a supernova up to five billion times as bright as our Sun.

MATTER

AS WELL AS ASKING WHAT IS OUT THERE, ASTRONOMERS ASK WHAT THINGS ARE MADE OF. THE MIND-BOGGLING ANSWER IS THAT EVERYTHING IN THE UNIVERSE IS MADE OF JUST OVER 90 BASIC INGREDIENTS.

Matter is the name for anything in the universe that takes up space, from the smallest particles to the most massive stars.

In the 1900s, astronomers learned to use spectroscopy to find out what stars and other objects in space are made from (see page 138). It turned out to be the same matter that things on Earth are made from: the chemical elements.

Each element is a different type of atom. More than 100 different types of elements—or atoms—have been discovered so far. The most abundant elements in the universe are hydrogen and helium. They have the simplest atoms, and formed in the first few minutes after the **Big Bang**.

Hydrogen and helium are the building blocks for other types of atoms, but creating new elements is not easy. Most are made by nuclear fusion, at the extreme pressures and temperatures found deep inside stars, or when atoms are flung out across the universe as stars die.

A few "superheavy" elements require even more extreme conditions. They are created when neutron stars collide, or matter swirls toward black holes. Once created, atoms are scattered across the universe by stellar winds and dying stars. This stardust goes on to form new stars, and is also the source of every atom in your body.

Because elements heavier than hydrogen and helium are only formed as stars live and die, newer stars contain more of them (because they formed from the ashes of older stars). This is one way that spectroscopy can help reveal the age of stars and galaxies.

THE BUILDING BLOCKS OF MATTER

Atoms are made of even smaller particles, called **protons**, **neutrons**, and **electrons**. Each atom is a bit like a tiny version of our solar system: most of the matter in an atom is concentrated at the very center. Protons and neutrons are found here, in the nucleus. Tiny electrons can be thought of like the planets, speeding around this dense nucleus.

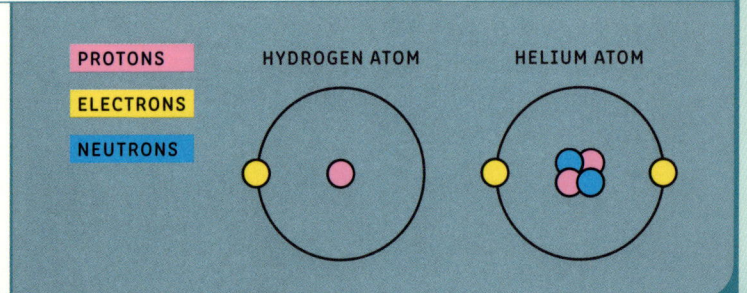

PROTONS
ELECTRONS
NEUTRONS

HYDROGEN ATOM

HELIUM ATOM

THE ORIGIN OF THE ELEMENTS

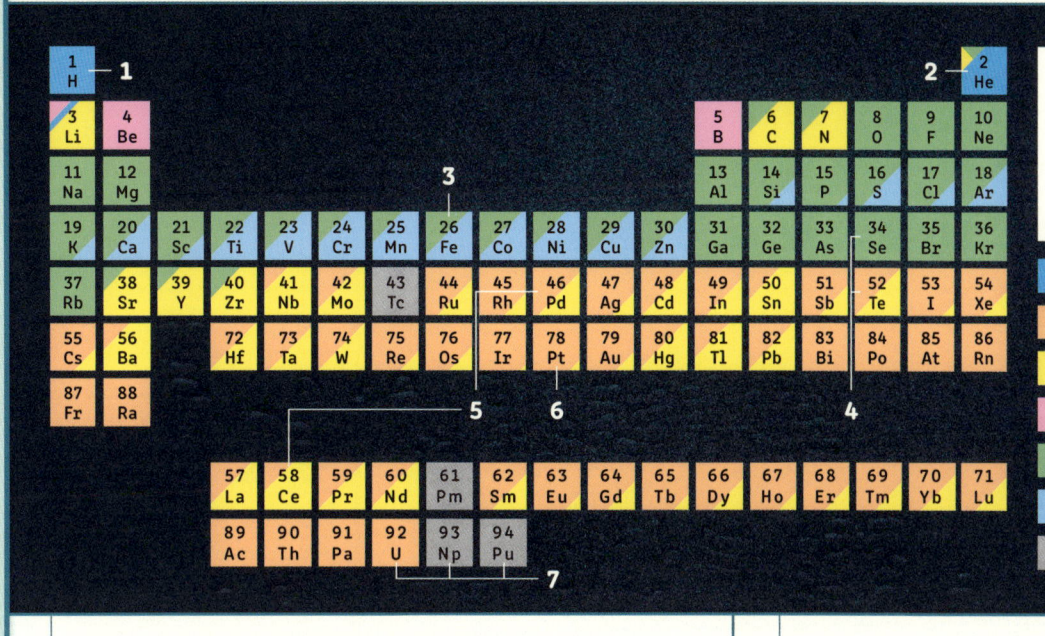

The periodic table is a famous chart that lists all the known elements, grouping them by the features of their atoms. This periodic table has been shaded to show where in the universe each element was formed.

- BIG BANG FUSION
- MERGING NEUTRON STARS
- DYING LOW-MASS STARS
- COSMIC RAY FISSION
- EXPLODING MASSIVE STARS
- EXPLODING WHITE DWARFS
- RADIOACTIVE DECAY OR SYNTHETIC

1 Hydrogen (H) was the main element formed in the minutes after the Big Bang (see page 194), and it is the main fuel for nuclear fusion in stars. It is still by far the most abundant element in the universe.	**5** Cerium (Ce) and palladium (Pd) are named after the giant asteroids Ceres and Pallas.
2 Most of the helium (He) atoms in the universe were formed shortly after the Big Bang. Helium atoms are also created in main-sequence stars, as hydrogen atoms are fused together, releasing energy in the process. Helium is named after the Greek word for the Sun, *Helios*.	**6** Superheavy elements such as platinum (Pt) are made during the most violent events in the universe, such as when super-dense neutron stars collide.
	7 Uranium (U), neptunium (Np), and plutonium (Pu) are named after the planets Uranus and Neptune, and dwarf planet Pluto (which had planet status at the time). They are the heaviest naturally occurring elements found on Earth.
3 Once a star begins running out of hydrogen fuel, it begins fusing helium, creating elements all the way up to iron (Fe).	
4 Selenium (Se) is named after the Greek word for the Moon, *Selene*, while tellurium (Te) is named after the Latin word for Earth, *terra*.	**8** Atoms of heavier elements (this includes elements 95–118, not pictured) have been created artificially on Earth using giant particle accelerators. Several have been named after scientists, such as Einsteinium and Copernicium.

NEUTRON STARS & PULSARS

CATEGORY	AGE
STELLAR REMNANT	UP TO 200 MILLION YEARS

IMAGINE SQUISHING 500,000 EARTHS TO THE SIZE OF A SMALL CITY AND YOU START TO GET A SENSE OF WHY NEUTRON STARS ARE SOME OF THE STRANGEST SPACE OBJECTS OF ALL.

ALL ABOUT

Neutron stars form when giant stars die in a supernova explosion. As the star's outer layers are hurled across space, the core collapses. The leftover material is crushed into a small, hot, and unimaginably dense ball just 12 to 16 miles across—a thousand times smaller than a white dwarf (see page 150).

A neutron star's extreme gravity means that its surface is almost perfectly smooth. If starquakes do shatter the crust, the mountains that form are no more than a tiny fraction of an inch high. Neutron stars don't produce energy from fusion at their cores, but glow because they are incredibly hot.

Although neutron stars were predicted using math in the 1930s, scientists thought they would be too small and dim to detect. However, everything changed with the chance discovery of pulsars in the 1960s.

Pulsars are rapidly spinning neutron stars with a magnetic field trillions of times stronger than Earth's. Intense beams of radio waves and other radiation escape from the star's North and South Poles. As the star spins, these beams sweep across space like the beams from a lighthouse, so the star seems to blink on and off when seen from Earth.

Since the discovery of pulsars in the 1960s, thousands of neutron stars have been found scattered throughout our galaxy, and some have even been spotted outside the Milky Way. They form alone or in pairs, which may eventually collide. Collisions between neutron stars are the most violent events in the universe, sending gravitational waves rippling out through the fabric of space itself.

KEY FACTS

- Neutron stars spin up to 716 times a second.
- They pack the mass of 1 to 2.5 Suns into a ball just 12 miles across. This is like crushing 500,000 aircraft carriers into a tennis ball.

TEMPERATURE

Hundreds of billions °F when first formed.

NEAREST

The nearest neutron star spotted so far lies around 400 light-years from Earth, in the constellation Corona Australis.

WHAT IS A PULSAR MADE OF?

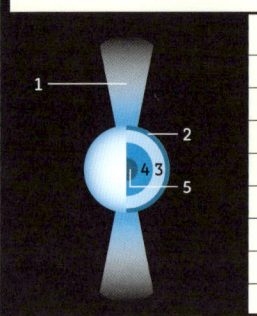

1 Beams of radiation sweep across space as the star spins.
2 Very thin atmosphere of hydrogen, helium, and carbon.
3 Crust, containing ions and electrons.
4 Outer core, made up of a soupy mix of **subatomic** particles, rich in neutrons.
5 Ultradense inner core.

OUR PLACE IN SPACE

Their regular spin, measured by pulses of light, means pulsars can be used like clocks. They have helped physicists to discover an exoplanet (see page 164), test Albert Einstein's theory of general relativity (see page 198), measure distances in the universe, and detect gravitational waves (see page 200).

★ FIND OUT WHICH ELEMENTS ARE CREATED DURING NEUTRON STAR COLLISIONS ON PAGE 155 ★

#	
1	**PULSATING STARS** Jocelyn Bell Burnell was scanning space for radio waves from **quasars** (see page 182), when she spotted a strange radio signal blinking on and off every 1.3 seconds. She had discovered the first "pulsating radio star," or pulsar.
2	**EXTREME DENSITY** On Earth, a single tablespoon of neutron star would weigh 1.1 gigatons (1 billion tons).
3	**COSMIC WHIRLPOOLS** Neutron stars that are not pulsars can be detected if they are part of a **binary system**, and actively pulling gas and dust from a nearby star. As the stolen material swirls toward the neutron star, it forms a large, glowing **accretion disc**.
4	**MAKING GOLD** Collisions between neutron stars create conditions where the heaviest atoms, such as gold, silver, platinum, and uranium, form. Scientists think neutron star collisions may also create as-yet-unknown superheavy elements.
5	**MAGNETARS** Rare neutron stars known as magnetars are the most magnetic objects in the universe. Their magnetic fields are 1,000 times more powerful than that of a typical neutron star, and could distort the atoms in your body from 620 miles away! Only around 30 magnetars have been spotted so far. The telltale sign is a flash of high-energy X-rays and gamma rays released when the ultrastrong magnetic field causes starquakes in a magnetar's solid crust. In the blink of an eye, one magnetar starquake released as much energy as our Sun has given out in the last 100,000 years.

BLACK HOLES

CATEGORY	AGE
STELLAR REMNANT	UNKNOWN

BLACK HOLES ARE DARK STARS SO DENSE THAT EVEN LIGHT CANNOT ESCAPE THEIR GRAVITY. MOST BLACK HOLES FORM WHEN THE CORE OF A MASSIVE STAR COLLAPSES.

ALL ABOUT

Stellar-mass black holes form when stars at least 20 times the Sun's mass die in a supernova explosion. While the star's outer layers are ejected, the core collapses. Unlike in a neutron star, the mass of this collapsing core is too great for any source of internal pressure to hold it up. It continues collapsing into an infinitely dense object known as a singularity.

It is impossible to see or even imagine a singularity, but they can be described and explored using mathematics. A singularity has a gravitational force so extraordinary that even light can't escape if it strays too close. This creates a "black hole" in space where no matter or light of any kind can possibly leave to reach our eyes or telescopes.

Black holes formed by collapsing stars are also known as collapsars. It's estimated that there are 100 million in our Milky Way galaxy alone. Most of what we know about them is based on theory rather than observation. However, astronomers have learned to detect black holes by looking out for their effects on other objects. They might spot a wobble in the orbit of a star that can't be explained in any other way. They might spot light from a distant galaxy being bent around other objects by a black hole's extraordinary gravity. Or best of all, they might spot a glowing disc of material that is being pulled into a black hole from a nearby star. These bright accretion discs can help astronomers calculate the properties of the black hole itself.

A different type of black hole is found at the center of most galaxies. These supermassive black holes contain up to a billion times the mass of our Sun. Scientists aren't yet sure if they formed from collapsing clouds of gas, or the merger of thousands of smaller black holes.

KEY FACTS

- Black holes spin faster than any other object in space—at more than 90 percent of the speed of light.
- Stellar-mass black holes contain from 3 to 100 times the mass of our Sun.
- The diameter of the event horizon depends on the black hole's mass.

TEMPERATURE

Almost absolute zero (coldest temp possible, at -459.67°F).

NEAREST

The closest stellar-mass black hole detected so far is Gaia-BH1, around 1,560 light-years from Earth.

WHAT IS IT MADE OF?

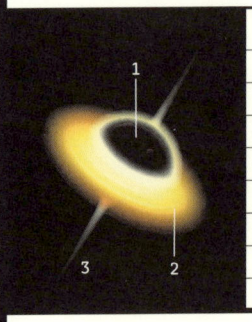

1 It's impossible to see the singularity at a black hole's center. Its outer edge—the event horizon—is the distance from the singularity at which nothing can escape.
2 A black hole may have a glowing accretion disc of matter being pulled in.
3 Some black holes fire out huge jets of particles at close to the speed of light.

OUR PLACE IN SPACE

Around 50 stellar-mass black holes have been detected in the Milky Way so far. They are helping astronomers understand the supermassive black holes thought to lie at the center of almost every galaxy (see page 182).

★ WHAT MAKES SUPERMASSIVE BLACK HOLES DIFFERENT? FIND OUT ON PAGE 182 ★

#		
1	**GRAVITY WELL**	Einstein's general theory of relativity (see page 198) helps us understand how black holes work. The enormous mass of a singularity warps the fabric of the universe so much that nothing can escape the "gravity well."
2	**TEARING STARS APART**	Accretion discs form when gas and dust fall toward a massive object such as a black hole, releasing energy as they swirl in. The glowing disc is visible up until the moment it crosses the event horizon. Sometimes an entire star becomes teardrop-shaped, as a black hole's gravity rips it apart.
3	**HAWKING RADIATION**	Theoretical physicist Stephen Hawking changed our understanding of black holes, predicting that they glow faintly as radiation leaks from the very edges. Over time, black holes must shrink as they evaporate. So far, this has been impossible to observe. The most massive black holes are predicted to last for 10^{100} (a googol)—10 followed by 100 zeros—years before they disappear.
4	**LURKING GIANT**	At 33 times the mass of our Sun, Gaia-BH3 is the most massive stellar-mass black hole detected in the Milky Way. Its name shows that it was the third black hole detected by the Gaia space observatory (pictured).

MULTIPLE STAR SYSTEMS

CATEGORY	AGE	
BINARY AND MULTIPLE STARS	UP TO 13.53 BILLION YEARS	LONELY STARS LIKE OUR SUN ARE NOT THE NORM. MOST STARS ARE FOUND IN PAIRS (OR LARGER GROUPS), ORBITING ONE ANOTHER IN A LONG GRAVITATIONAL DANCE.

ALL ABOUT

In the night sky, stars such as Sirius (the Dog Star) and Polaris (the North Pole Star) look like single points of light. However, telescopes have revealed that these famous stars—and likely more than 80 percent of all stars—are part of stellar systems: two or more stars so close together that they are linked by gravity.

Stars of any type can be companions. Sirius is a main-sequence star accompanied by a faint white dwarf. Polaris is a triple system: a yellow supergiant, a smaller Sun-sized star just 1.7 billion miles apart, and a tiny dwarf star orbiting farther out.

Even stars that appear to be alone often turn out to be orbiting a hidden companion, such as a neutron star or black hole. They are detected by spotting wobbles in the light of the visible star as it's tugged in different directions. Small wobbles might mean a planet, but larger ones can only be explained by a companion star. Another clue is the sudden brightening of light from a system, as one star steals material from its companion, creating a spectacular, glowing accretion disc.

As astronomers use more powerful telescopes to peer at younger stars (see page 142), they are spotting so many binary systems that they are beginning to suspect all Sun-like stars are born in pairs. This would mean that single stars like our Sun exist for one of two reasons—either the system broke apart, or the companions merged in a dramatic collision. Our Sun's hypothetical twin has even been given a name—Nemesis. It may have been this star that shifted the path of the asteroid that wiped out the dinosaurs.

KEY FACTS

- Stars in binary or multiple systems are distinguished using capital letters. For example, Alpha Centauri A (also known as Rigil Kentaurus) is the brightest star in the Alpha Centauri system. Alpha Centauri B is the second brightest.

NEAREST

Our closest star, Proxima Centauri, is part of a triple star system. The three stars of the Alpha Centauri system lie between 4.25 and 4.4 light-years from Earth.

GRAVITATIONAL DANCE

Stars in a binary system are bound to each other by gravity. They each orbit their common center of mass, a point somewhere between the stars. The position of this point depends on the mass of each star in the system lying closest to the more massive of the two stars (shown as a white dot in this picture).

OUR PLACE IN SPACE

Binary systems have played a starring role in helping astronomers calculate the mass of stars—especially rare stars. By observing how far apart two stars are, and how quickly they orbit one another, small wobbles in the light from each star can be used to calculate the mass of each one.

★ EXPLORE HOW ASTRONOMERS DETECT PLANETS ORBITING DISTANT STARS ON PAGE 164 ★

#		
1	**BINARY STARS**	A pair of stars orbiting one another is known as a binary system. If you stood on a planet in certain binary systems, you would see two suns in the sky.
2	**LIGHT SHOW**	Interactions between companion stars can create spectacular nebulae. At the center of the Southern Crab Nebula, a red giant is shedding its outer layers. Some of the material is being drawn into, and then ejected by, a companion white dwarf star—creating the glowing crab-shaped cloud.
3	**MULTIPLE STARS**	Star systems may also capture nearby stars. In the unusual six-star system TYC 7037-89-1, three pairs of binary stars orbit one another in a complex gravitational dance. Systems with up to seven stars have been spotted.
4	**X-RAY BINARIES**	These involve a normal star paired with a neutron star or black hole. As material from the normal star falls into the super-dense companion it can heat to over 1.8 million °F, releasing bursts of high-energy X-rays. Cygnus X-1—the first black hole to be discovered—was spotted by detecting these energy bursts.
5	**COSMIC COLLISIONS**	As one star in a system loses mass, it may fall toward its companion, ending in a violent collision. This is rare, but is thought to have caused V838 Monocerotis to suddenly become 600,000 times brighter than the Sun in 2002. Scattered light from the outburst lit up vast clouds of dust around the star, creating a spectacular nebula that lasted for more than two years.

EXPLORING EXOPLANETS

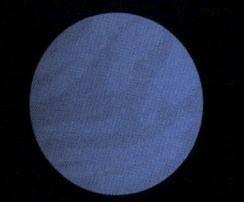

IT'S THOUGHT THAT MOST STARS HAVE AT LEAST ONE PLANET, MEANING A TRILLION EXOPLANETS IN THE MILKY WAY ALONE. IT'S ALREADY CLEAR THAT THEY DON'T FOLLOW THE SAME RULES AS PLANETS IN OUR SOLAR SYSTEM.

ALL ABOUT

In a universe of 200 billion trillion stars, there are bound to be at least as many exoplanets. However, planets outside our own solar system are notoriously hard to spot. Planets don't produce their own light like stars do. The faint light reflected from an exoplanet's surface is easily drowned out by the dazzling light from its parent star.

Because of this, most exoplanets are found not by looking for the planet itself, but by spotting the effect it has on a nearby star. Astronomers look out for the slight dimming of a star's light as an object passes in front of it. If the dimming happens over and over again in a regular way, that object might just be an orbiting planet. Two dedicated NASA space telescopes—Kepler and the Transiting Exoplanet Survey Satellite (TESS)—have discovered thousands of exoplanets using this transit method.

Once potential exoplanets are spotted, they can be scrutinized using more powerful ground and space-based telescopes. Astronomers have learned to use the smallest of clues to measure a planet's size, orbital path, temperature, and even the substances in its atmosphere. From there, it's possible to predict conditions on the surface. These often prove to be far stranger than any found in our own solar system, from skies that rain molten glass or iron, to a bright pink planet, a lava planet, a planet as puffy as marshmallow, and a planet made entirely of diamond.

Scientists are particularly interested in planets orbiting in the **habitable zone** of their stars. These planets may be the right temperature for liquid water to exist on their surface, giving them the potential to support the type of life found on Earth.

EXPLORATION TIMELINE

1992	The first two exoplanets (Poltergeist and Phobetor) are spotted orbiting a pulsar.
1995	51 Pegasi is the first exoplanet spotted orbiting a main-sequence star.
1999	An exoplanet is discovered using the transit method for the first time. First multi-planet system discovered.
2001	First exoplanet discovered in a star's habitable zone.
2001	First measurement of an exoplanet's atmosphere.
2007	First map of an exoplanet's surface.
2009	Kepler mission launches.
2018	Transiting Exoplanet Survey Satellite (TESS) launches.
2019	CHaracterising ExOPlanet Satellite (CHEOPS) launches.

ARE WE THERE YET?

- The closest known exoplanet is Proxima Centauri b, which lies 4.2 light-years from Earth. A car traveling at 60 mph would take 10.8 million years to drive that far.
- The farthest exoplanet detected is SWEEPS-11, which lies almost 28,000 light-years from Earth.

HELPING HUMANS

Before we could see exoplanets, all the "rules" for planet formation were based on the small sample of planets in our own solar system. Studying exoplanets helps us to understand those rules better—realizing, for example, that planets can move from their original position, and even swap places.

★ EXOPLANETS ARE A FOCUS OF THE SEARCH FOR LIFE OUTSIDE OUR SOLAR SYSTEM (PAGE 166) ★

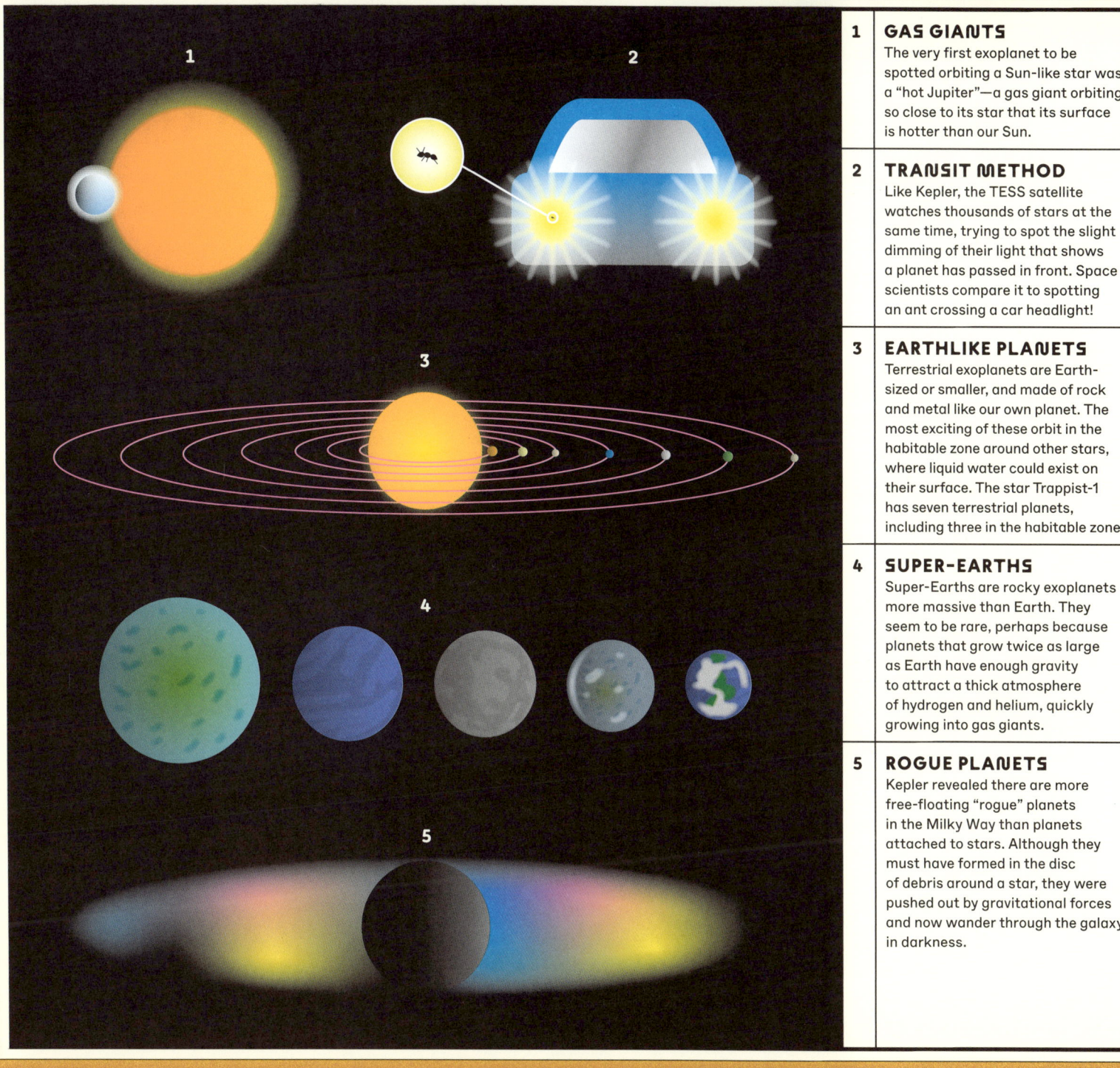

1	**GAS GIANTS**	The very first exoplanet to be spotted orbiting a Sun-like star was a "hot Jupiter"—a gas giant orbiting so close to its star that its surface is hotter than our Sun.
2	**TRANSIT METHOD**	Like Kepler, the TESS satellite watches thousands of stars at the same time, trying to spot the slight dimming of their light that shows a planet has passed in front. Space scientists compare it to spotting an ant crossing a car headlight!
3	**EARTHLIKE PLANETS**	Terrestrial exoplanets are Earth-sized or smaller, and made of rock and metal like our own planet. The most exciting of these orbit in the habitable zone around other stars, where liquid water could exist on their surface. The star Trappist-1 has seven terrestrial planets, including three in the habitable zone!
4	**SUPER-EARTHS**	Super-Earths are rocky exoplanets more massive than Earth. They seem to be rare, perhaps because planets that grow twice as large as Earth have enough gravity to attract a thick atmosphere of hydrogen and helium, quickly growing into gas giants.
5	**ROGUE PLANETS**	Kepler revealed there are more free-floating "rogue" planets in the Milky Way than planets attached to stars. Although they must have formed in the disc of debris around a star, they were pushed out by gravitational forces and now wander through the galaxy in darkness.

LIFE OUTSIDE OUR SOLAR SYSTEM

CALCULATIONS PREDICT THAT THOUSANDS OF ALIEN CIVILIZATIONS MAY BE TRYING TO GET IN TOUCH WITH US RIGHT NOW. SO WHY HAVEN'T WE HEARD FROM THEM?

Many astrophysicists have no doubt that aliens are out there. It is too unlikely that in such a vast universe, life only exists on Earth. The question is how many planets are home to aliens with the technology to contact Earth?

Radio seems the most likely method for long-distance alien communication. As early as the 1920s, radio telescopes have been used to scan for radio signals from intelligent life. The Allen Telescope Array was the first designed especially for this purpose. No alien signals have been detected yet, but perhaps this is not surprising. Radio signals could be sent at thousands of different frequencies, from anywhere in the universe. The chances of a radio telescope being set to the right frequency and pointed at the right part of the sky at the right time are low.

Pointing telescopes directly at exoplanets could help. Just as with the search for life in our solar system, the most exciting exoplanets from an alien-seeking viewpoint are those that might have liquid water on their surface: Earth-sized planets in the habitable zone of their star.

In 1974, astronomers sent their own radio message toward some of the oldest stars in the Milky Way. The hope is that these ancient stars may be orbited by ancient planets with advanced alien civilizations. Traveling at the speed of light, the signal will take 25,000 years to arrive (and another 25,000 years for any response to reach Earth!).

DRAKE EQUATION

The Drake equation captures all the different considerations in one formula to estimate the number of advanced alien civilizations in the Milky Way. It has been used to predict that anything between zero and a million alien civilizations are trying to make contact right now.

To use the equation, just plug in estimates for the rate at which stars form in our galaxy (R_*), the fraction of stars that have planets (f_p), the number of planets in the habitable zones of their stars (n_e), the fraction of these planets on which life is likely to develop (f_l), the fraction of those planets on which this life has had enough time to become intelligent (f_i), the proportion of these where the intelligent life has time to invent radio communication (f_c), and the average time that advanced civilizations survive before going extinct (L).

$$N = R_* \cdot f_p \cdot n_e \cdot f_l \cdot f_i \cdot f_c \cdot L$$

THE GOLDEN RECORD

Each of the Voyager probes (see page 107) carries messages etched on a gold disc—pictures, music, and sounds from Earth, plus greetings in 55 languages—in case they are intercepted in their journey across interstellar space.

HABITABLE WORLDS OBSERVATORY

NASA is planning a space telescope to search for habitable planets beyond our solar system. The Habitable Worlds Observatory would be able to image planets directly, to spot markers of life in their atmospheres such as carbon dioxide, methane, and water vapor. Doing this for just 25 exoplanets should statistically be enough to tell us if life in the universe is common or rare.

HELLO, NEIGHBOR

Nearby star systems are popular targets for radio scans, because it's more likely signals sent by nearby aliens would have had time to reach Earth. Excitingly, an Earth-sized exoplanet has been spotted orbiting Proxima Centauri, the nearest star to the Sun!

ALIEN STORIES

Despite the fact we have no direct evidence they exist, aliens have captured human imagination for hundreds of years, appearing in thousands of stories and films. Around a fifth of people in the United Kingdom believe Earth has already been visited by aliens, and a third of Americans point to UFO sightings as proof that aliens exist.

GALAXIES

JUST OVER A CENTURY AGO, MOST PEOPLE BELIEVED THE UNIVERSE WAS MADE UP OF ONLY THE STARS VISIBLE FROM EARTH AND A FEW FUZZY CLOUDS KNOWN AS NEBULAE, SURROUNDED BY EMPTY SPACE.

All these objects appeared to be a similar size through telescopes, and there was no way of knowing how far they were from Earth. In the 1920s, bigger and better telescopes revealed that some of the nebulae weren't just glowing clouds of dust and gas, but were star systems or "island universes" far outside our own. The universe had just become far bigger than anyone expected.

Stars are not evenly spread through the universe, but collected in groups called galaxies. A galaxy is a vast system of stars, gas, and dust, held together by its own gravity. Small galaxies hold a few million stars, while the largest have several trillion. Astronomers use individual stars to figure out how old and distant galaxies are. Most interesting—and mysterious—of all stars are the supermassive black holes thought to lie at the center of every galaxy.

Our own star, the Sun, is part of a spiral-shaped galaxy called the Milky Way. We will only ever have a side-on view of our own galaxy. But by looking at other spiral galaxies, astronomers have been able to figure out what the Milky Way looks like, and where we sit within it.

Like stars, galaxies also gather in groups and clusters. Interactions between the galaxies in a cluster are common, creating galaxies with peculiar shapes and extreme activity. Astronomers are learning how to reconstruct the violent interactions of the past, to reveal how galaxies have been shaped by collisions and mergers.

THE MILKY WAY

CATEGORY	AGE
GALAXY	13 BILLION YEARS

OUR SOLAR SYSTEM IS PART OF THE MILKY WAY, A SPIRAL GALAXY OF 200 BILLION STARS, AT LEAST AS MANY PLANETS, AND VAST CLOUDS OF INTERSTELLAR GAS AND DUST.

ALL ABOUT

This view of the Milky Way galaxy—with its glowing central bar hugged by spiraling arms—is one we'd never get from Earth. From our planet, orbiting a medium-sized star in one of the minor arms, 26,000 light-years from the center, we can only stare at our home galaxy sideways on.

Our view of the galactic bulge is blocked by dense dust, and the glow of billions of stars. They include stellar objects of every stage, age, and size, from newly formed protostars, to steadily shining main-sequence stars, and from red giants and white dwarfs to stellar-mass black holes.

Most of these stars are found in the flattened disc, along the long arms that give the galaxy its shape. This disc measures at least 100,000 light-years across, with a thickness of just 1,000 to 2,000 light-years. Millions more stars are found in globular clusters, glittering spheres of tightly packed stars orbiting in the outer "halo" of the galaxy.

The bar-shaped central bulge itself is home to around 10 billion stars. They are so closely packed that it would be like placing a million stars between the Sun and our next closest star, Proxima Centauri. At the very center of this bulge lies a supermassive black hole, known as Sagittarius A*.

Every star, planet system, and speck of gas and dust in the Milky Way orbits the center of this galaxy. Along with its neighboring stars, our Sun orbits at around 515,000 mi/h, completing one "galactic year" every 225 million Earth years. The last time the Sun was in its current position, it was dinosaurs enjoying the view.

KEY FACTS

- The Milky Way has a total mass of around 1.50 trillion Suns.
- It has two major arms, two minor arms, and many smaller arms.

NAMED AFTER

The Milky Way is named after the bright band of stars that sweeps across Earth's sky like a trail of spilled milk. The arms are named after the constellations we see in the sky when we look toward them: Sagittarius, Perseus, Norma, and Scutum-Centaurus.

COSMIC STRUCTURES

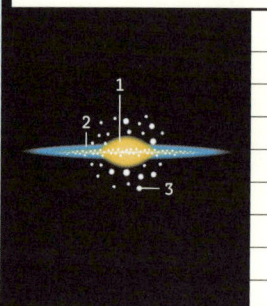

1. Side-on, the disc of the Milky Way looks like a pancake with a central bulge.
2. Stars in the disc, including our Sun, orbit the center on the same plane as the disc.
3. Stars in globular clusters orbit much farther from the center, and on all planes.

PAST, PRESENT, FUTURE

The Milky Way began as a collapsing cloud of gas and dust. The first stars that formed in this cloud are the ancient stars that orbit in globular clusters today. Its halo and galactic disc formed later, the galaxy growing as it gobbled up smaller galaxies.

* VIOLENT COLLISIONS WITH OTHER GALAXIES HAVE SHAPED THE MILKY WAY (PAGE 186) *

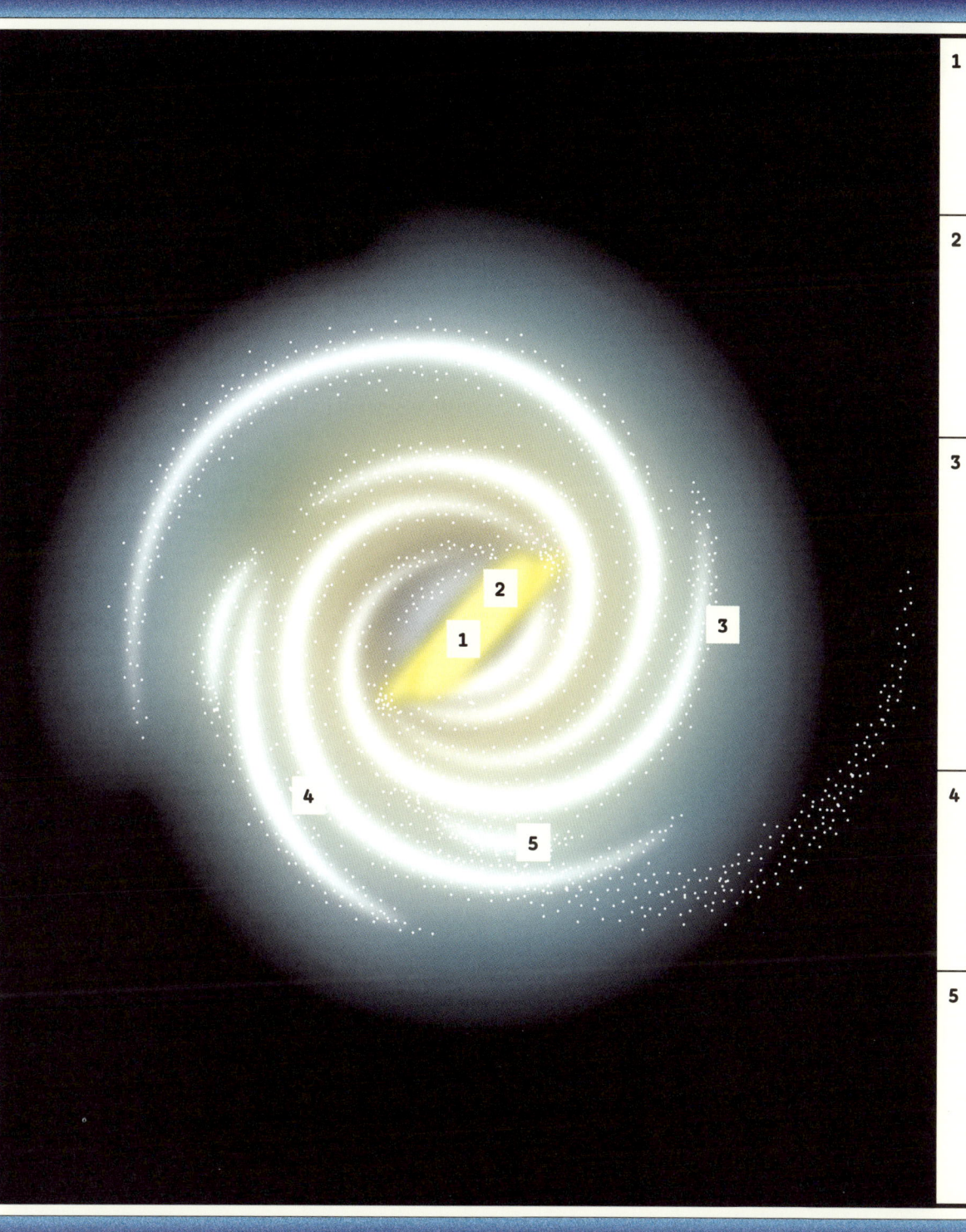

1	**GALACTIC BULGE**	Most of the 10 billion stars within the galaxy's peanut-shaped central bulge are ancient red giants, and they orbit the center of the galaxy more quickly than stars found farther out.
2	**BLACK HOLE**	At the center of the Milky Way is a powerful source of radio waves, thought to be a supermassive black hole. It is known as Sagittarius A*. Although small compared to the rest of the galaxy, it is around 15 million miles across, with the mass of around 4 million Suns.
3	**GALACTIC DISC**	The flattened disc contains billions of bright, young stars and vast quantities of interstellar dust and gas. Dust is only a small fraction of the interstellar medium—the matter and radiation that drifts in the space between stars—but these tiny micron-sized grains of carbon and silicate soak up and scatter light energy from the rest of the galaxy. This gives the galaxy its cloudy, milky look and blocks the view of optical telescopes.
4	**SPIRAL ARMS**	The stars, gas, and dust of the disc are most concentrated in its spiraling arms, named after constellations. This is where most star formation is currently happening, and where most of the galaxy's light is emitted.
5	**YOU ARE HERE**	Our solar system lies around halfway between the center and edge of the disc, on the inner edge of the Orion-Cygnus Arm.

EXPLORING OUR GALAXY

MAPPING THE MILKY WAY IS LIKE TRYING TO SURVEY A FOREST WHILE CLINGING TO A SINGLE TREE. HOWEVER, NEW TOOLS AND TELESCOPES ARE GATHERING SO MUCH DATA THAT DISCOVERIES ARE COMING THICK AND FAST.

ALL ABOUT

Figuring out what our galaxy looks like has been one of the toughest challenges for astronomers. We'll never be able to step outside our galaxy to photograph it (we'd need to be 36,000 light-years away to get the whole galaxy in the shot). Instead, astronomers must compare what they see around us with what they know about other galaxies.

The biggest clue is the hazy, star-speckled band of light we see when we look toward the galaxy's center on a very dark night. This concentration of light in a narrow band suggests we are looking toward the center of a flat disc. If we were in an elliptical galaxy (see page 176), we'd expect to see the same intensity of light and number of stars in all directions.

Figuring out how these stars are arranged means mapping as many as possible. ESA's Hipparcos mission, begun in 1989, charted the position of over 100,000 stars. ESA's Gaia satellite took over in 2013, measuring the position, distance, speed, direction, and age of over 2 billion Milky Way stars, lying up to a hundred times farther away than those spotted by Hipparcos.

This data has revealed the Milky Way is a spiral galaxy, with a bar-shaped galactic center. The number of arms continues to be questioned, but current models assume two major arms, two minor arms, and several smaller ones.

Gaia's data is leading to new insights on our galaxy's history and future, assisted by infrared telescopes that can peer through the dust to see individual stars in the chaotic galactic center. This "galactic archaeology" promises to solve many puzzles. For example, a past collision with another galaxy could explain why the Milky Way's disc is not completely flat. This warped shape means the Milky Way rotates with a wobble, like a spinning top.

EXPLORATION TIMELINE

1610	Using an optical telescope, Galileo spots clusters of stars within the cloudy band known as the Milky Way.
1750s	Scientists speculate that the Milky Way is a disc and that nebulae are separate, distant galaxies.
1785	William Herschel draws a map of the Milky Way, discovering it is disc-shaped.
1923	Edwin Hubble proves there are other galaxies beyond the Milky Way.
1932	Radio waves are detected from the center of the Milky Way.
1974	Astronomers discover a black hole at the center of the Milky Way.
2005	Spitzer Space Telescope confirms shape of the Milky Way.
2022	Radio telescope takes first photo of the shadow of supermassive black hole Sagittarius A*.

ARE WE THERE YET?

- Earth lies around 26,000 light-years from the center of the Milky Way.
- Our fastest spacecraft (Solar Parker Probe, speeding at 430,000 mi/h) would take around 40 million years to travel that far.

HELPING HUMANS

Measuring the motion of the globular star clusters that orbit our galaxy has helped scientists to calculate the mass of the Milky Way more accurately, at 1.5 trillion Suns. Around 90 percent of this mass is mysterious dark matter—invisible to any instrument invented so far (see page 202).

ARTIFICIAL INTELLIGENCE HELPS ANALYZE VAST QUANTITIES OF DATA FROM MISSIONS LIKE GAIA (PAGE 206)

#	
1	**STAR CLUSTERS** Some of the oldest stars in the Milky Way are gathered in 150 to 200 ball-shaped clusters, which orbit the center in a giant sphere outside the main disc and bulge. Each cluster contains hundreds of thousands of ancient stars that formed around 12.5 billion years ago, long before the galaxy's disc and spiral arms.
2	**DUST SCREEN** Infrared and radio telescopes can peer through the dense dust of the Milky Way to resolve details of the center. A source of powerful radio waves is thought to be a supermassive black hole, known as Sagittarius A*. Using a planet-sized radio telescope, astronomers managed to photograph the shadow of this black hole in 2022.
3	**DOUBLE BUBBLE** NASA's Fermi Space Telescope has detected two giant bubbles of superheated gas sitting above and below the center of the Milky Way's disc. They may have been ejected from the galaxy during a more active past.
4	**STAR STREAMS** Because Gaia can track the movement of individual stars, it reveals structures made up of stars following the same path around the galaxy. It uncovered two ancient star streams—Shakti and Shiva—named after the Hindu deities (pictured). Their movement helps us reconstruct the history of the galaxy.
5	**JAN OORT** Dutch astronomer Jan Oort was the first to realize the stars of the Milky Way are all rotating around the galactic center. The Oort Cloud (see page 120) was named after him.

RADIO TELESCOPES

RADIO ASTRONOMY IS THE STUDY OF THE NATURAL RADIO WAVES EMITTED BY OBJECTS IN SPACE. IT IS USED TO DETECT THE HOTTEST, MOST VIOLENT EVENTS IN THE UNIVERSE AS WELL AS THE COLD, DARK GAS BETWEEN GALAXIES.

While only very hot objects emit visible light, everything in the universe—from stars and galaxies to individual molecules of gas—emits radio waves, the lowest-energy form of light.

Radio signals from space were first detected in the 1930s. Radio telescopes were quickly built to explore all kinds of new objects, from supernova remnants (see page 154) and spinning neutron stars (see page 158) to the glowing matter swirling toward supermassive black holes at the center of distant "radio" galaxies (see page 182).

Radio telescopes also revealed the coldest, darkest objects in the universe. These include dense interstellar gas and dust clouds (see page 140), and the dim afterglow of the Big Bang (see page 192).

Radio telescopes work day or night, whatever the weather, because radio waves are not scattered by Earth's air or blocked by clouds. They can even peer through dense clouds of gas and dust in space, to objects near the center of the Milky Way that are invisible to other kinds of telescopes.

RADIO WAVES

Radio waves are a type of electromagnetic radiation (light) invisible to our eyes. They have a much longer wavelength than visible light, ranging from a fraction of an inch to hundreds of miles. The radio waves with the shortest wavelengths are known as microwaves.

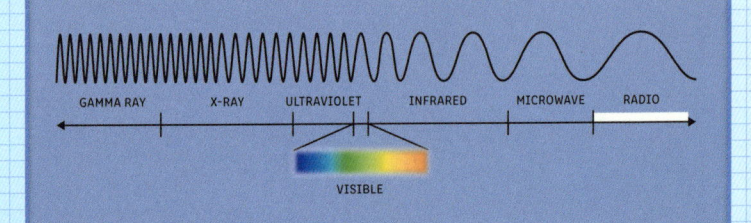

RADIO ARRAYS

The Square Kilometre Array Observatory (SKAO)—the world's largest telescope—actually links hundreds of antennas in different locations. This giant array will then act as one giant telescope, to gather radio waves from very faint and distant objects.

FIVE-HUNDRED-METRE APERTURE SPHERICAL TELESCOPE (FAST)

FAST is the world's largest single-dish radio telescope. The giant dish was built in a natural dip in a mountainous area of China.

To achieve the same level of detail as optical telescopes, radio telescopes have to be huge. The giant 1,640-foot dish gathers radio waves from space, and directs them toward a receiver, suspended from the six towers around the edge.

Supercomputers are used to process the signals that are collected, converting the data into images of the sky that we can see with our eyes. These are colored to convey different information, such as temperature, substances, or density.

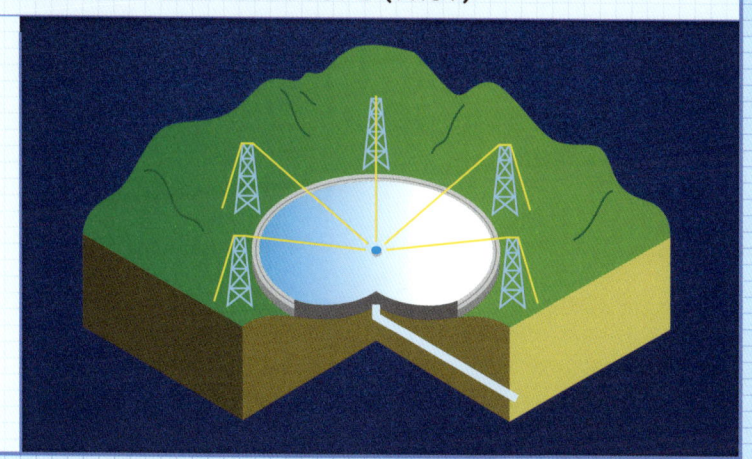

SAY CHEESE!

In 2017, the first-ever picture of a black hole was taken by the Event Horizon Telescope, an array of eight radio telescopes dotted around Earth's surface. The image shows the "shadow" of the supermassive black hole M87* at the center of the M87 galaxy, silhouetted by glowing matter swirling into the black hole.

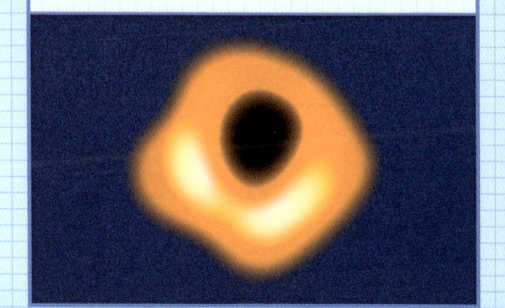

MYSTERIOUS BURSTS

Since 2007, radio telescopes have detected rapid bursts of radio waves from unknown sources in deep space. These happen anywhere in the sky, several times every day. Each fast radio burst lasts a fraction of a second and releases as much energy as the Sun does in a year. There are many different theories about their source, from erupting magnetars to alien spaceships!

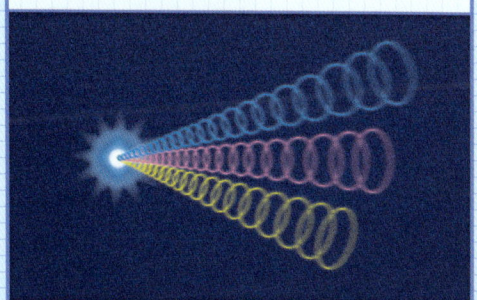

RADIO SIGNALS

Earth's atmosphere reflects some of the longest radio waves back into space, but overall huge radio telescopes on the ground can take better pictures than small radio telescopes in space, so there have been very few space-based radio telescopes. Meanwhile, we use the reflection of long-wave radio waves to bounce our own radio signals around the planet!

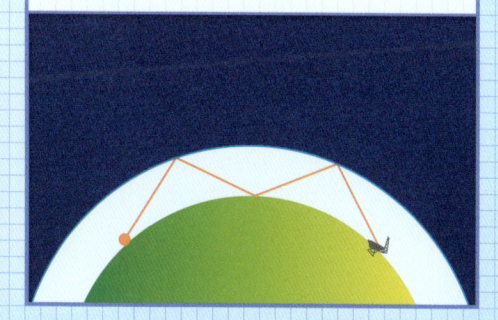

EXTERNAL GALAXIES

CATEGORY	AGE	
GALAXY	BETWEEN 500 MILLION AND 13.6 BILLION YEARS	GALAXIES COME IN MANY DIFFERENT SHAPES AND SIZES. THEY AREN'T SCATTERED EVENLY OR RANDOMLY ACROSS THE UNIVERSE, BUT ARE GATHERED BY GRAVITY INTO GROUPS, CLUSTERS, AND SUPERCLUSTERS.

ALL ABOUT

The Milky Way is just one galaxy among hundreds of billions in the universe. Seen from Earth, galaxies vary hugely in size and shape—from small faint smudges, to giant glowing pinwheels. Astronomers group them into three main types, based on their structure: spiral, elliptical, and irregular. Within each of these categories there are many subgroups.

Most galaxies began forming around the same time, shortly after the universe began. They have evolved in different ways, but the way they look to us through telescopes also depends on their distance from Earth. Light from more distant galaxies takes longer to reach us, so we see these galaxies how they were billions of years ago. When we gaze at our nearest galaxies, we see them as they were just 25,000 years ago.

The average distance between galaxies is around 10 million light-years. But galaxies don't drift through space untethered. Rather like stars, they are found bunched together in groups, clusters, and superclusters. Our Local Group of about 50 galaxies includes two spiral galaxies (Andromeda and the Milky Way), around 30 irregular galaxies, and some elliptical galaxies.

The Local Group is part of the larger Virgo cluster of at least 1,200 galaxies. Clusters like this are the largest structures in the universe held together by their own gravity. The deepest images of the universe reveal superclusters formed from hundreds or thousands of smaller groups and clusters. Our Virgo cluster lies at the center of a supercluster 110 million light-years across, containing the mass of 1.2 quadrillion Suns. Superclusters are not held together by their own gravity, but arranged in great sheets or filaments around mysterious, vast, empty voids in space.

KEY FACTS

- Size ranges from dwarf galaxies 100 light-years across to giant radio galaxies more than 16 million light-years across.
- M87 is the most massive known galaxy, with the mass of 6 trillion Suns.
- The smallest have the mass of just 100,000 Suns.

NAMED AFTER

Galaxies are named after their appearance (such as the Whirlpool Galaxy and the Cartwheel Galaxy), the constellation they are seen in (such as Andromeda) or their number in an astronomical catalog (such as M87).

COSMIC STRUCTURES

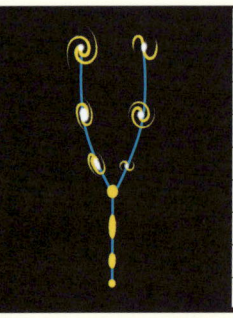

Galaxies can be grouped by their shape and structure. The systems used are often based on Edwin Hubble's original "tuning fork" classification, so-called because of this fork-shaped diagram. In addition to the details seen with optical telescopes, all galaxies have an invisible halo of gas and dark matter.

PAST, PRESENT, FUTURE

Most galaxies are between 10 billion and 13.6 billion years old. One of the oldest seen so far is JADES-GS-z14-0, which began forming around 300 million years after the Big Bang. The youngest seen so far is I Zwicky 18, thought to have formed around 500 million years ago.

★ EXPLORE THE COSMIC WEB STRUCTURE OF THE UNIVERSE ON PAGE 196 ★

#		
1	**SPIRAL GALAXIES**	The discs of these beautiful galaxies include two or more arms of stars, curving around a bright central bulge. Lots of new stars are forming in the arms, so the disc glows with their blue light. The older stars at the center are redder.
2	**BARRED SPIRALS**	There are lots of different types of spiral galaxies, including the barred spiral shape of our own Milky Way. The arms unwind from the ends of a bar of stars at the center.
3	**RED AND DEAD**	Round or oval elliptical galaxies are symmetrical, with a bright center but very little gas or dust and few newly forming stars. Their reddish light comes from older stars, especially red giants.
4	**ARMLESS SPIRALS**	Lenticular galaxies are like a cross between elliptical and spiral galaxies, with a central bulge and disc but no spiraling arms. They have lots of older stars, and very little new star formation.
5	**IRREGULAR GALAXIES**	Most galaxies have an irregular shape, with no symmetry or bright center. They usually glow with blue light, which is a sign of young new stars. Astronomers think they could be the results of other types of galaxies interacting, colliding, and merging, disturbing their shape and triggering star formation.
6	**PECULIAR GALAXIES**	These have distorted and unusual shapes, caused by collisions, mergers, and other galaxy–galaxy interactions (see page 186).

MEASURING & MAPPING THE UNIVERSE

TO OUR EYES, PLANETS, STARS, AND GALAXIES ALL APPEAR TO LIE THE SAME DISTANCE AWAY, AS IF THEY ARE EMBEDDED IN A SHELL AROUND EARTH. CALCULATING THEIR TRUE DISTANCES TOOK THOUSANDS OF YEARS OF INGENUITY.

Measuring distances is one of the trickiest challenges in astronomy. Ancient astronomers developed a triangulation method called parallax, which involves viewing a distant object from two different places. The position of the object appears to shift, but this is just an optical illusion. You can see it by holding up a finger in front of your face and closing one eye at a time. Your finger appears to move, because each eye is seeing it from a slightly different angle.

Measuring these angles, and the distance of the "baseline" between your eyes, gives you one side and two angles of a triangle. You can now use simple math to calculate the length of the other sides.

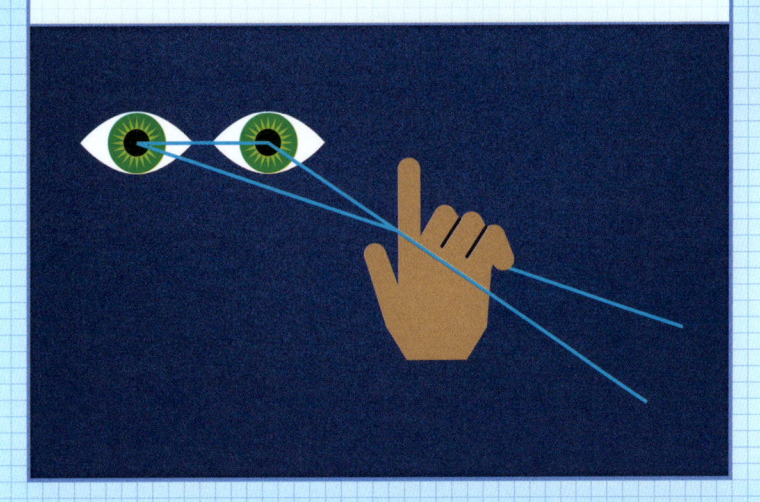

STELLAR PARALLAX

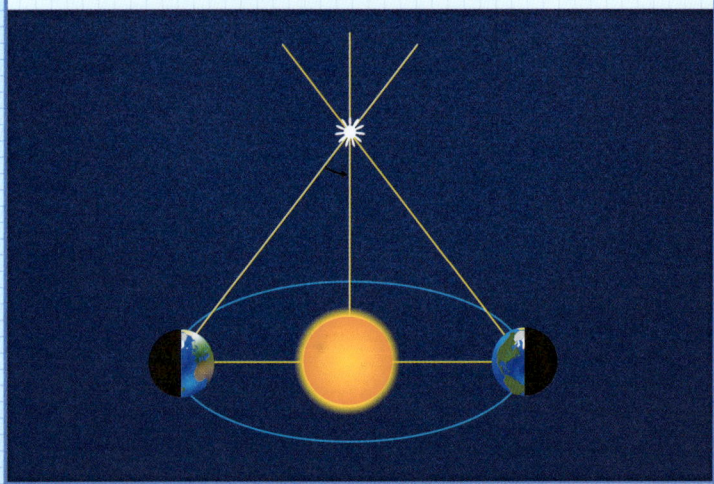

At first parallax was used to estimate the distance to the Moon and Sun, by viewing them from different places on Earth's surface. To measure the much greater distance to other stars, however, the baseline needs to be much, much longer. Astronomers realized that if they made one measurement and then waited six months, Earth would have moved to the other side of the Sun, creating a baseline 186 million miles long! This is known as stellar parallax. However, it was 1838 before telescopes were good enough to measure angles precisely enough to calculate the distance to a star.

PARALLAX IN PRACTICE

Today, stellar parallax measurements are taken by powerful radio telescopes on the ground, and by satellites high above Earth's atmosphere, such as Gaia. To measure the distance to a star, Gaia looks at it from opposite sides of the Sun, and measures how it seems to move compared to more distant stars in the background.

Space probes offer a chance to take parallax measurements with even longer baselines. The record is held by New Horizons (NASA), currently exploring the Kuiper Belt. From this distance, New Horizons has a very different view of the sky than the one from Earth. Because we know exactly how far away New Horizons is, we can use it for very accurate parallax measurements.

REDSHIFT

The color of distant galaxies holds clues to their distance from Earth. Since 1842, scientists have known that any waves given out by a moving object get squashed together or stretched out, depending on whether the object is moving toward or away from you. This is called the Doppler effect.

Starlight from other galaxies is redder than the light from stars of the Milky Way, telling us that the light waves have been stretched—and that the galaxies must be moving away from us. Edwin Hubble noticed that redshift increases with distance from Earth. This told him the universe is expanding.

Today, redshift data collected by space telescopes, and projects such as the Sloan Digital Sky Survey, is used to create detailed, 3D maps of the farthest reaches of the observable universe.

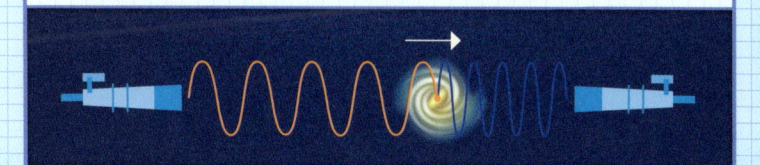

STANDARD CANDLES

More distant stars look fainter, but stars can also look faint because they are cool, old, or small. To use brightness as a measure of distance, astronomers needed to know the absolute magnitude of a star—the amount of energy it was sending into space.

American astronomer Henrietta Swan Leavitt was the first to solve this problem, using variable stars called Cepheids. These stars vary in brightness in a very regular way, going from bright, to dim, then bright again like clockwork. The timing of this depends on the absolute magnitude of the star. If two Cepheid stars share the same timing, any difference in their apparent brightness must be down to distance alone. An asteroid and a crater on the Moon have been named after Leavitt, to honor her and other deaf astronomers.

Several years later, Leavitt's breakthrough allowed Edwin Hubble to measure the distance to 12 Cepheid stars in the Andromeda nebula. He discovered that they are so distant, Andromeda must be a separate galaxy (see page 180). Since then, astronomers have discovered other objects of fixed absolute magnitude, such as supernova explosions and red giant stars, which can be used to measure vast distances in space.

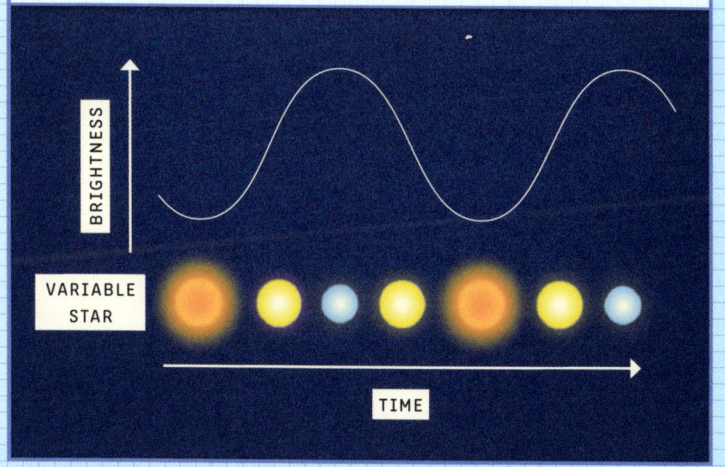

EXPLORING OTHER GALAXIES

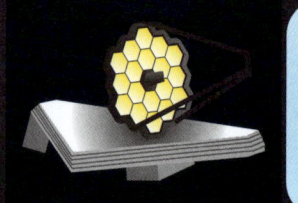

WE'VE ONLY KNOWN THERE ARE GALAXIES OUTSIDE OUR MILKY WAY FOR JUST OVER 100 YEARS. TODAY, THESE EXTERNAL GALAXIES ARE A KEY FOCUS OF ASTRONOMY, HELPING US UNLOCK THE SECRETS OF THE UNIVERSE.

ALL ABOUT

External galaxies lie much farther away from us than any of the stars of the Milky Way. The glare of our galaxy's billions of stars makes it hard to see farther into the darkness beyond. Even so, three of the nearest galaxies can be seen without a telescope. By the early 1900s, many astronomers were suggesting that these fuzzy patches of light could be separate galaxies. Others thought differently, and a fierce debate raged.

In the 1920s, Edwin Hubble solved the puzzle. First he used a powerful telescope to spot individual variable stars in the Andromeda nebula. Then he calculated the distance to some of these Cepheid stars (see page 179), proving Andromeda is located far outside the Milky Way.

This discovery instantly changed our understanding of the universe. Knowledge about other galaxies grew slowly at first, but accelerated in the 1950s, with the invention of telescopes to detect different kinds of light, and rockets to put these instruments in space for a much better view.

One of the most interesting findings was that galaxies don't just differ in shape and structure. Some are much more active, with centers 100 times brighter than the light from all their stars combined. This was the first clue that all but the smallest galaxies have a massive black hole at their heart, actively gobbling up stars, dust, and other matter. Understanding these black holes and their accretion discs has changed the way we understand the properties of galaxies, and how they affect one another.

EXPLORATION TIMELINE

964	Persian astronomer al-Sufi creates first record of two galaxies visible by eye.
1612	Simon Marius observes Andromeda with a telescope.
1750s	Thomas Wright and Immanuel Kant speculate that certain nebulae are separate galaxies.
1758	Charles Messier begins his famous list of astronomical objects, including 40 that turn out to be galaxies.
1923	Edwin Hubble proves there are external galaxies.
1936	Edwin Hubble classifies galaxies by shape.
1939	First radio galaxy (Cygnus A) discovered.
1978	Dark matter is deduced by Vera Rubin and team.
1995	First Hubble Deep Field survey captures over 3,000 galaxies in a single image.
2022	First Webb Space Telescope Deep Field survey captures over 25,000 galaxies in a single image.

ARE WE THERE YET?

- Earth lies around 25,000 light-years from our nearest external galaxy, the Canis Major Dwarf Galaxy. Our fastest spacecraft (Solar Parker Probe) would take around 40 million years to travel that far.

HELPING HUMANS

Studying galaxies helped astronomers discover we can only see around 5 percent of the matter in the universe. We know that huge quantities of invisible dark matter is out there because it affects the speed at which stars orbit the centers of spiral and elliptical galaxies.

* FIND OUT HOW GALAXIES INTERACT ON PAGE 186 *

#	
1	**CHARLES MESSIER** While French astronomer Charles Messier was hunting for comets, he made a list of 103 "fuzzy bodies" to rule out. Today we know that 40 of these are galaxies. They are still named with the letter M and the number he gave them.
2	**NEAR NEIGHBORS** The Large and Small Magellanic Clouds are two of our nearest external galaxies. They orbit the Milky Way. These small, irregular galaxies include lots of hot blue stars, star clusters, and gas clouds.
3	**ANDROMEDA** Andromeda (M31) is our closest large galaxy, 2.5 million light-years from Earth. From Earth, it looks around six times the size of the Moon in the night sky.
4	**EDWIN HUBBLE** When American astronomer Edwin Hubble proved that Andromeda is a separate galaxy, he forever changed the way we understand the universe. He was the first to accurately calculate the distance to external galaxies, and to classify them by shape. The Hubble Space Telescope (see page 57) is named after him.
5	**MONSTER GALAXY** M87 is the most massive galaxy spotted so far, with the mass of 6 trillion Suns. Most of a galaxy's mass does not come from its stars, planets, gas, and dust, but from the invisible and mysterious dark matter that surrounds these visible objects (see pages 202 and 204).

SUPERMASSIVE BLACK HOLES

CATEGORY	AGE
ACTIVE GALACTIC NUCLEI	UP TO 10 MILLION YEARS (QUASARS)

CERTAIN "ACTIVE GALAXIES" RELEASE FAR MORE ENERGY THAN CAN BE EXPLAINED BY THEIR STARS ALONE. THE EXTRA GLOW COMES FROM SUPERHEATED MATTER SWIRLING INTO A SUPERMASSIVE BLACK HOLE AT THE GALAXY'S CENTER.

ALL ABOUT

Like their smaller cousins, supermassive black holes are invisible because nothing—including light—can escape their gravity. They can't be seen through telescopes, so it was other clues that first alerted astronomers to the supermassive black holes lurking at the center of most galaxies.

The first radio telescopes revealed that certain "active galaxies" are a powerful source of radio waves, releasing far more energy than a normal galaxy. Over time, astronomers discovered that this extra energy comes from a small, bright core and includes high-energy radiation such as X-rays, suggesting this core is extremely hot.

A second clue came from observations in our own galaxy. Astronomers noticed that stars orbiting close to the center of the Milky Way reach extreme speeds of up to 5,000 mi/s. This can only be explained if they are orbiting a massive object. Astronomers tracked one of these stars, which reddened briefly during its orbit. This confirmed the light was being stretched by the mind-boggling gravity of a supermassive black hole.

Astrophysicists now think that all active galaxies contain supermassive black holes, busy gobbling up nearby stars, planets, gas, and dust. As this material falls toward the black hole, it forms a cosmic whirlpool, speeding up as it gets closer to the event horizon. Friction heats the disc to tens of millions of degrees, making the disc glow brightly with the energy of billions of stars. It's these glowing accretion discs that allow us to see the "shadow" of a black hole.

The most energetic active galaxies are known as quasars (or quasi-stellar radio sources), which dim once the supermassive black hole finishes gobbling up the material around it.

KEY FACTS

- Sagittarius A* has the mass of more than 4 million Suns.
- M87* is more than 1,000 times as massive, around 6.5 billion Suns.
- Sagittarius A*'s event horizon is about 12 billion miles from the singularity at its center.

NEAREST

Our nearest supermassive black hole is the one at the center of our own galaxy, Sagittarius A*, around 27,000 light-years from Earth. Our nearest quasar, Markarian 231, is around 600 million light-years away.

COSMIC STRUCTURES

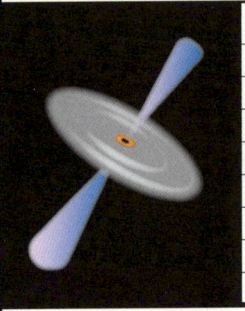

As supermassive black holes feed, the disc of matter that is falling into the black hole heats up and radiates energy. Powerful jets of hot gas are expelled from the poles at close to the speed of light. If the jets happen to be pointing toward Earth, the galaxy looks extra bright and is known as a blazar.

PAST, PRESENT, FUTURE

Understanding quasars helps to explain why galaxies seem to use up their star-forming gas and dust at different rates. Their enormous energy warms the interstellar gas in the galaxy, so it is less likely to clump together and form new stars.

COMPARE SMALLER-SCALE STELLAR-MASS BLACK HOLES ON PAGE 160

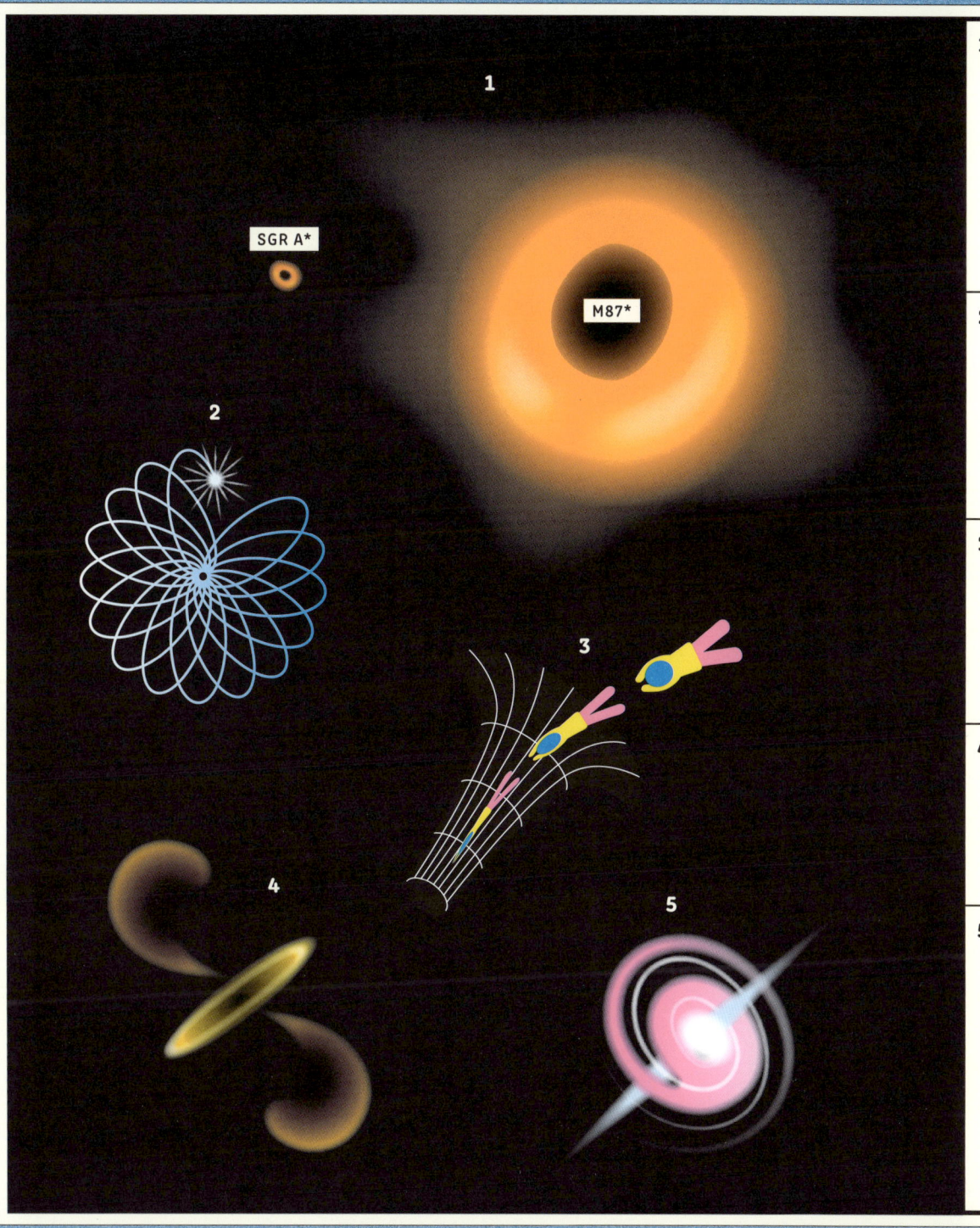

#	
1	**MONSTER MASS** At 24 million miles across, M87* is one of the largest black holes ever detected. It is billions of times more massive than our Sun, and lies 55,000 light-years from Earth. Photos of M87*'s glowing accretion disc capture the shadow of the black hole itself. It is shown here next to a similar image of Sagittarius (Sgr A*).
2	**COSMIC SPIROGRAPH** A supermassive black hole with the mass of 4.3 million Suns lies at the heart of the Milky Way. The bright star S2 has an elliptical orbit around the black hole, but its position changes with each orbit, drawing a flower around the black hole.
3	**COSMIC SPAGHETTI** Supermassive black holes gobble up stars, planets, gas, dust, and anything else that gets too close. As matter falls in, the black hole's immense gravity stretches it into long, thin strands. This is known as spaghettification.
4	**BLOWING BUBBLES** As supermassive black holes feed, powerful jets of hot gas are expelled at close to the speed of light. These jets carve out bubble-shaped cavities in the plasma that fills the spaces between galaxies.
5	**QUASARS** Quasars are the most high-energy objects in the universe, found at the center of the most active galaxies. They are formed by vast amounts of material falling into a supermassive black hole. Quasars are the size of our solar system, and can emit as much energy as hundreds or thousands of Milky Ways put together.

HIGH-ENERGY ASTRONOMY

IN THE LAST 50 YEARS WE HAVE LEARNED TO DETECT THE HIGH-ENERGY RADIATION AND PARTICLES RELEASED BY THE HOTTEST, MOST EXTREME OBJECTS AND EVENTS IN THE UNIVERSE—FROM COLLAPSING STARS TO COLLIDING GALAXIES.

Very hot objects in space emit ultraviolet (UV) light, X-rays, and gamma rays. These high-energy forms of light have very short wavelengths, and are easily absorbed and scattered by gas and dust. This means very little high-energy radiation passes through Earth's atmosphere. This is good news for living things, but means we have to detect high-energy light using telescopes in space.

Telescopes need incredibly smooth mirrors to reflect high-energy light without scattering it. The Hubble Space Telescope's well-polished mirrors can detect the UV light from young stars, hot white dwarfs, and the interstellar medium. X-ray telescopes can help identify even hotter objects, including black holes, neutron stars, supernova remnants, and quasars. They can also detect the superheated gas in galaxy clusters, helping astrophysicists to calculate the proportion of dark matter.

Gamma rays pass straight through a telescope. They are detected in a different way, by observing their effects on certain materials. Sudden bursts of gamma rays can mean a supernova or neutron star collision.

SHORT WAVELENGTHS

UV, X-ray, and gamma rays are high-energy forms of light with wavelengths much shorter than visible light.

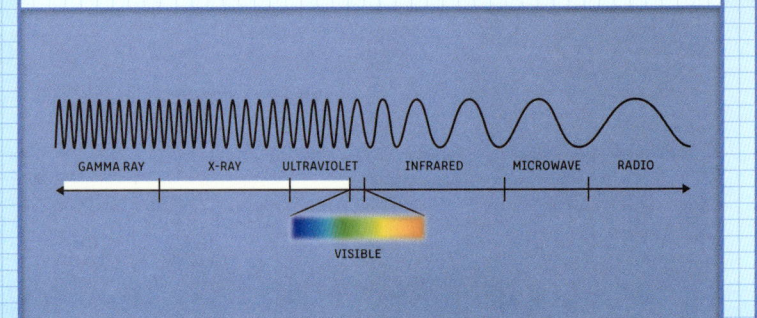

GAMMA RAY | X-RAY | ULTRAVIOLET | INFRARED | MICROWAVE | RADIO

VISIBLE

X-RAY BINARIES

The brightest sources of X-rays in the Milky Way are known as X-ray binaries. They are made up of a normal star and a very dense collapsed star orbiting one another. The collapsed star (a black hole, neutron star, or white dwarf) pulls in material from the normal star, forming a swirling disc of superheated matter.

CHANDRA X-RAY TELESCOPE

The mirrors in X-ray telescopes have to be perfectly smooth. A bump just a few atoms high will scatter X-rays, making them impossible to focus on the telescope's detector. The Chandra X-ray Observatory (NASA) is named after Indian American physicist Subrahmanyan Chandrasekhar (see page 151). It has the smoothest mirrors ever made, and the sharpest X-ray vision of all.

Chandra's surveys of the sky help us see the shock waves rippling through space when clusters of galaxies collide. They have even helped us indirectly image dark matter (see page 204)!

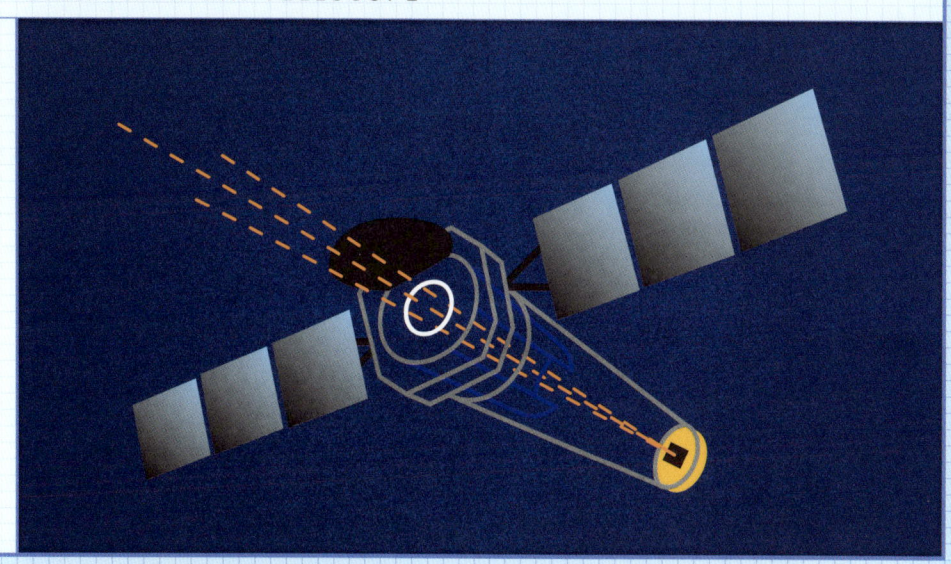

FERMI BUBBLES

NASA's Fermi Gamma-ray Space Telescope is our best tool for watching the gamma ray universe. It has helped to detect blazars, pulsars, supermassive black holes, and supernova remnants. It has also found some intriguing sources of gamma rays in the Milky Way, including the two gigantic bubbles of hot gas known as Fermi bubbles (see page 173).

DETECTING NEUTRINOS

A supernova explosion happens every few seconds, somewhere in the universe. How can astronomers know where to point telescopes to see one? One clue comes from high-energy **neutrinos**—tiny particles of matter thrown out across the universe by supernovae, at close to the speed of light. While gamma rays are blocked by our atmosphere, neutrinos pass straight through. They keep going even after reaching the ground! This is why neutrino detectors are placed deep underground Because neutrinos don't get blocked or scattered, their path can easily be traced back to pinpoint their source in the sky, and point other telescopes in the right direction.

EXPLORING INTERACTING GALAXIES

GALAXIES DON'T DEVELOP AS LONELY ISLANDS, BUT CHANGE AND GROW AS A RESULT OF VIOLENT COLLISIONS. GALACTIC ARCHAEOLOGISTS ARE UNCOVERING THE HISTORY OF COLLISIONS AND MERGERS THAT SHAPED OUR MILKY WAY.

ALL ABOUT

Some of the most exciting galaxies to gaze at through a telescope are those with unusual shapes, strange dusty features, or extreme activity. They are known as peculiar galaxies. Their distorted shapes are thought to be caused by galaxy–galaxy interaction.

This can be as simple as two galaxies moving past one another. During a flyby, the immense gravity of each galaxy tugs on and distorts the stars and interstellar gas and dust of the other from as far as 100,000 light-years away. The denser a galaxy cluster is, the more interactions there are—and the fewer "normal" spiral galaxies remain.

However, most peculiar galaxies are products of more dramatic collisions and mergers. Colliding galaxies might punch holes in each other as they pass through, or lead to mergers as the larger galaxy rips apart and gobbles up the smaller one, mingling its stars, gas, and dust with its own.

This galactic cannibalism is thought to be how monster galaxies grow. By sending pressure waves rippling through the interstellar gas and dust, galactic collisions and mergers trigger the birth of billions of new stars, forming brightly glowing star clusters. Astronomers have detected plenty of signs of past cannibalism by our own galaxy, the Milky Way.

Elsewhere in the universe, gobbling up smaller galaxies is probably what turns supermassive black holes into quasars (see page 182), providing an influx of new material that falls into the black hole, with chaotic consequences. It can even lead to the collision and merger of two giant black holes—an event so dramatic it causes ripples in the fabric of the universe itself.

EXPLORATION TIMELINE

1781	Charles Messier's catalog of "fuzzy objects" includes peculiar galaxies, such as M64 (the Black-eye galaxy), M51, and M82.
1941	Erik Holmberg simulates the changes in a pair of interacting galaxies by sliding lightbulbs across a table.
1966	Halton Arp produces *The Atlas of Peculiar Galaxies*, with 338 entries.
1995	The first Hubble Deep Field image peers back in time at distant galaxies, revealing how different the universe looked 12 billion years ago.
2007	The Galaxy Evolution Explorer telescope proves that galaxies evolve as a result of interactions.
2008	59 images of colliding galaxies taken by Hubble are published to celebrate the telescope's 18th birthday.

ARE WE THERE YET?

- Arp 220 is one of Earth's closest merging galaxies, located 250 million light-years away.
- This means our latest pictures of the galaxy are already 250 million years out of date!

HELPING HUMANS

In around four billion years, the Milky Way will begin to collide with the huge Andromeda galaxy. They are currently moving toward each other at around 250,000 mi/h. Rather than ripping each other apart, the two spiral galaxies will likely merge to create a large new elliptical galaxy.

SUPERCOMPUTERS HELP MODEL THESE GRAVITATIONAL DANCES (PAGE 206)

#		
1	**LOOKALIKES**	In 2024, the Webb Space Telescope captured an incredible image of Arp 142, a pair of interacting galaxies that look like a penguin guarding its egg.
2	**CAUGHT IN ACTION**	Peering far across the universe, the Hubble and Webb telescopes have caught many galaxies in the process of colliding and merging. The colliding galaxies of Arp 148 look like an arrow hitting a bullseye.
3	**SUN STORY**	The Milky Way is currently polishing off another small galaxy, called Sagittarius. Over the past 7 billion years, Sagittarius has passed through the Milky Way's disc several times. Each time, the shock waves triggered star formation in the Milky Way—including the formation of our own Sun and solar system.
4	**GREEDY GALAXY**	Data collected by the Gaia mission suggests some of the Milky Way's stars were once part of a different galaxy. Objects in space follow predictable paths, so astronomers can rewind these paths by billions of years. This has revealed that our galaxy pulled in a dwarf galaxy around 10 billion years ago.
5	**PECULIAR GALAXIES**	Peculiar galaxies have distorted and unusual shapes, caused by collisions, mergers, and other galaxy–galaxy interactions (see page 176). The ring-like Cartwheel Galaxy, for example, was probably shaped by a galaxy punching a hole straight through another, pushing its stars, gas, and dust outward in a ring.

THE UNIVERSE

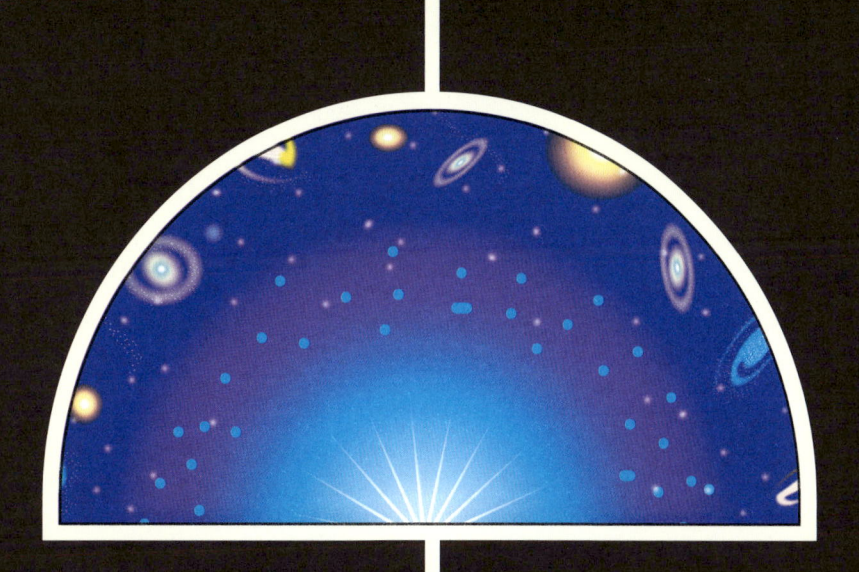

HOW DID EVERYTHING BEGIN? IT'S ONE OF THE BIGGEST QUESTIONS HUMANS ASK, AND FOR TENS OF THOUSANDS OF YEARS, WE HAVE GAZED AT THE SKIES TO TRY AND FIND ANSWERS.

Today's cosmologists are trying to answer the same question. In order to do so, they start with two smaller questions: what is out there? And what is it made of?

The biggest breakthroughs came in the last 100 years, with the discovery that the universe extends far beyond the Milky Way, and the even more remarkable discovery that it's still expanding.

Our view will always be limited by how far we can see—an area known as the observable universe. The actual universe is likely to be much larger, possibly even infinite. We will never be able to see everything that is out there, but with 200 billion or so galaxies in the observable universe there is plenty to look at.

As for the second question, we are still figuring out what the observable universe is made of. We know it includes space, time, matter, and energy—but that only makes up four percent of everything that exists! Most of the universe consists of dark energy and matter that we haven't yet learned to detect.

The clues we've collected so far are just the beginning but are already helping generate answers about how the universe began, and how it will end.

THE OBSERVABLE UNIVERSE

CATEGORY	AGE
OBSERVABLE UNIVERSE	13.8 BILLION YEARS

WHEN WE LOOK OUT ACROSS THE UNIVERSE, WE CAN SEE 46 BILLION LIGHT-YEARS IN EACH DIRECTION. IT'S IMPOSSIBLE TO SEE BEYOND THIS, BECAUSE THE LIGHT FROM MORE DISTANT SOURCES HASN'T HAD TIME TO REACH US.

ALL ABOUT

The 60 million or so galaxies surrounding our Milky Way make up our cosmic neighborhood, the local universe. But we can see far beyond this. Telescopes have detected light from distant galaxies that has been traveling toward Earth for almost 13.8 billion years—the time that has elapsed since the universe began.

Soon after proving that there are galaxies outside our own (see page 180), Edwin Hubble used spectroscopy to make another amazing discovery: the universe is expanding. This means that in the time the light from distant objects takes to reach Earth, those objects have moved even farther away. Astronomers have calculated the current distance of the most distant galaxies to be 46 billion light-years. This means that we can technically see 46 billion light-years in each direction—a bubble 92 billion light-years across, with Earth at its center.

Everything that lies within this bubble is part of the observable universe. It includes an estimated 200 billion galaxies! Because the light from distant objects takes so long to reach us, we see those objects as they were in the past, when the light began its journey, and not as they are now.

Every year, the light from even more distant objects reaches Earth, and the size of the observable universe increases by one light-year. At the same time the universe continues to expand, carrying those distant objects farther out of reach.

KEY FACTS

- Every square foot of the universe contains an average of just one particle of matter.
- Multiplied by the volume of the observable universe, this adds up to a whopping 8.8×10^{54} (8.8 followed by 54 zeros!) lbs of matter.

NAMED AFTER

The word universe comes from old French and Latin words meaning "all things turned into one." It is used to describe everything that exists, from the light and matter we can detect, to the dark energy and matter we can't.

WHAT IS IT MADE OF?

The observable universe is the region of the universe visible from Earth. We can see objects that lie 46 billion light-years away in each direction, so the observable universe is a sphere 92 billion light-years across with Earth at its center. Of course, Earth is not at the center of the universe as a whole. It's just where we happen to be looking from.

PAST, PRESENT, FUTURE

When looking at objects in space, we see them as they were when the light arriving at our eyes left their surface. The most distant galaxies are seen as they were when they were in the process of forming, just 300 million years after the Big Bang. This helps us learn how galaxies change over time.

★ DISCOVER THE "DARK ENERGY" THOUGHT TO BE PUSHING GALAXIES AWAY FROM ONE ANOTHER ON PAGE 202 ★

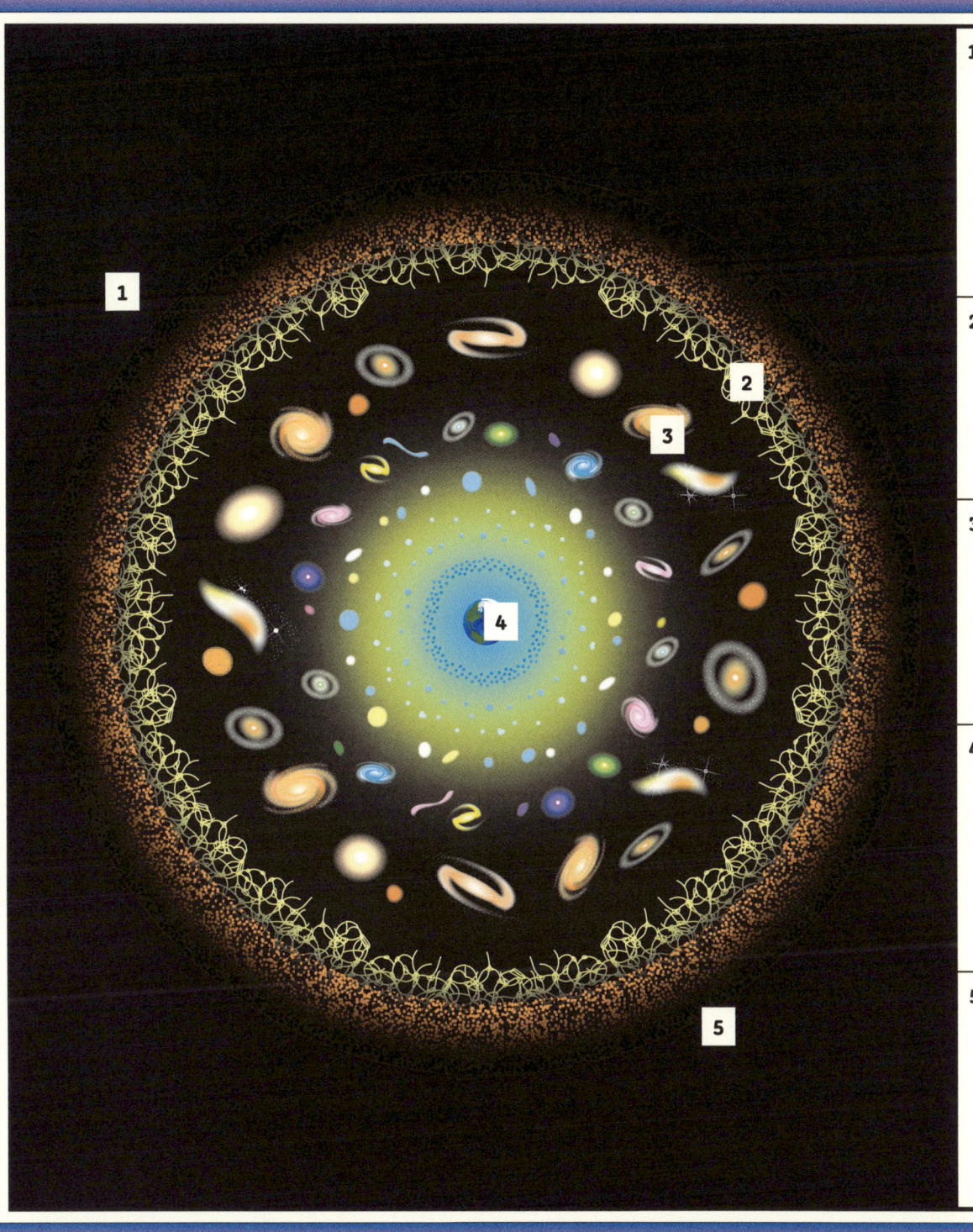

#	
1	**DEEP FIELD** Our deepest view of the universe so far comes from space telescopes that capture the light streaming toward Earth from a tiny patch of sky, over the course of many hours. These deep-field images look flat, but include objects at all distances from Earth, from nearby stars to galaxies more than 40 million light-years away.
2	**SUPERCLUSTERS** Looking at distant objects is a chance to see the largest structures in the universe—superclusters of tens of thousands of galaxies. They form in flat sheets and threads, separated by huge empty spaces known as voids.
3	**DISTANT GALAXIES** The light from the most distant galaxies we can see has been traveling for about 13.8 billion years—the age of the universe. As it traveled through expanding space, the light has been stretched and redshifted toward the infrared end of the spectrum.
4	**EARTH AT CENTER** Earth lies at the center of the observable universe, simply because that is where we are looking from. If we stood elsewhere in the universe, we'd also be able to see objects 46 billion light-years in each direction, and those objects would also be moving away, as space itself expands.
5	**COSMIC HORIZON** The limit of the observable universe is known as the cosmic horizon. Just like the horizons on sea and land, we know there is more universe beyond the cosmic horizon, but its light hasn't had time to reach us yet.

EXPLORING THE OBSERVABLE UNIVERSE

ASTRONOMERS HAVE LEARNED TO DETECT LIGHT AND PARTICLES FROM ACROSS THE OBSERVABLE UNIVERSE, INCLUDING THE COSMIC HORIZON ITSELF. THEY'VE ALSO DISCOVERED THAT THE UNIVERSE IS FULL OF ENERGY AND MATTER THAT *CAN'T* BE DETECTED.

ALL ABOUT

Just over a century ago, most scientists still assumed that the universe was a large but fixed area, made up of the stars of the Milky Way. During the 1920s, this view changed completely. American astronomer Edwin Hubble proved that there are galaxies outside our own, and that they appear to be moving away from us. The universe is vaster than anyone had imagined—and getting bigger still.

If the universe is expanding, it must have been smaller in the past. By observing the movements of galaxies, cosmologists have been able to create models that "rewind" time back to the moment that the expansion—and the universe itself—began. This moment is known as the Big Bang, but it was not an explosion. It is the idea that the universe began small and hot, and is cooling as it expands.

Key evidence for the Big Bang arrived in 1964, when astronomers detected the **Cosmic Microwave Background (CMB)**—ancient light leftover from a very hot, young universe. The CMB can be detected from every direction in the sky.

NASA's world-famous Hubble Space Telescope provided the next key pieces of evidence. It allowed astronomers to see more than ten times farther across the universe than the telescope Edwin Hubble himself used. Deep-field images revealed very distant (and therefore very young) galaxies, still in the process of forming.

Most important, data collected by the Hubble Space Telescope allowed astrophysicists to more accurately figure out the rate at which the universe is expanding, known as the Hubble constant. This was key to calculating the true age of the universe: 13.8 billion years old.

EXPLORATION TIMELINE

1924	Edwin Hubble discovers that "spiral nebulae" are actually galaxies outside the Milky Way.
1929	Edwin Hubble discovers the universe is expanding.
1931	Georges Lemaître puts forward ideas now known as the Big Bang theory.
1940s	Existence of leftover radiation from Big Bang predicted.
1966	CMB detected by chance by Arno Penzias and Robert Wilson using a radio telescope.
1989	Cosmic Background Explorer is the first space mission designed to study the CMB.
1995	Hubble Ultra Deep Field provides the most detailed images of the universe yet.
2022	The Webb Space Telescope captures its first deep-field image.

ARE WE THERE YET?

- The edge of the observable universe is thought to lie 46 billion light-years from Earth. The world's fastest spacecraft would take 120 trillion years to go that far.
- The universe is expanding, so by the time the spacecraft arrived, the galaxy it had been aiming at would have moved even farther away!

HELPING HUMANS

Today, deep-field images taken by the Webb Space Telescope are helping astronomers peer even farther across the universe, and even deeper into the past. NASA's Roman Space Telescope promises to shed more light on dark energy.

★ EXPLORE THE BIG BANG THEORY AND THE EVIDENCE FOR IT ON PAGE 194 ★

1	**REDSHIFT** We know the universe is expanding because we can detect redshift in light from distant galaxies. As light travels from a galaxy toward us, the space it is traveling through expands. When the light arrives, it looks redder than it did when it left the galaxy.
2	**THEORETICAL TOOLS** Albert Einstein was the first physicist to try and produce a mathematical description of the entire universe, with his general theory of relativity. It's the basis for how we think about space, time, and gravity.
3	**ANCIENT AFTERGLOW** CMB was once visible light, but has traveled for so long across expanding space that it has redshifted beyond the infrared spectrum, to become microwaves. It is responsible for some of the "static" heard when tuning analog radios, and was first detected using a radio receiver (initially, a pair of pigeons got the blame!).
4	**WARPED LIGHT** In deep-field images, distant galaxies (such as the small red object in this image) can look larger and brighter than they really are, because their light has been distorted by the gravity of galaxies closer to Earth (such as the small blue object in this image). The solid yellow lines show the curved path of light from the red galaxy, and the right-hand image shows both galaxies as seen from Earth. Known as gravitational lensing, this effect was predicted by Einstein's general theory of relativity.

THE ORIGINS OF THE UNIVERSE

BY ASKING WHAT IS OUT THERE, AND WHAT IT'S MADE OF, COSMOLOGISTS ARE AIMING TO ANSWER AN EVEN BIGGER QUESTION: HOW DID THE UNIVERSE BEGIN?

The leading theory for the origin of the universe is known as the Standard Model of Cosmology. It assumes that everything in the universe—including space, time, matter, and energy—began with a sudden expansion known as the Big Bang (see page 192). The universe has been expanding and cooling ever since.

At first, the universe was pure energy. Within a few seconds, it had cooled enough for most of this energy to become tiny particles of matter. Within 300,000 years, these had clumped together to form atoms. Within 200 million years, atoms had clumped together to form stars and galaxies.

According to this model, the rate at which the universe is expanding is controlled by two things: gravity and dark matter, which tend to pull things together; and mysterious dark energy, which tends to push things apart.

Although there is some very complex math behind this model—including Einstein's general relativity (see page 198)—the model itself is quite simple. It's also good at explaining most of the things we see in the universe, from the mixture of elements, to the way galaxies can be seen speeding away from us. The best evidence for the Big Bang is the Cosmic Microwave Background (CMB), thought to be the afterglow from a very, very hot young universe.

Despite this evidence, the Standard Model will always be impossible to prove, and there are certain things it can't explain. Like all scientific theories, it is constantly being revised as new evidence is gathered. Some scientists have put forward completely different theories about how the universe began.

WHAT'S NEXT?

Just as there are different theories for the beginning of the universe, there are different ideas about how it will end. The Big Freeze model predicts that the expanding universe will eventually cool down so much that new stars will no longer form, and the universe will just be thin, cold gas doing nothing. The Big Rip model predicts a more dramatic end, as the expanding universe tears everything apart, from atoms to time itself.

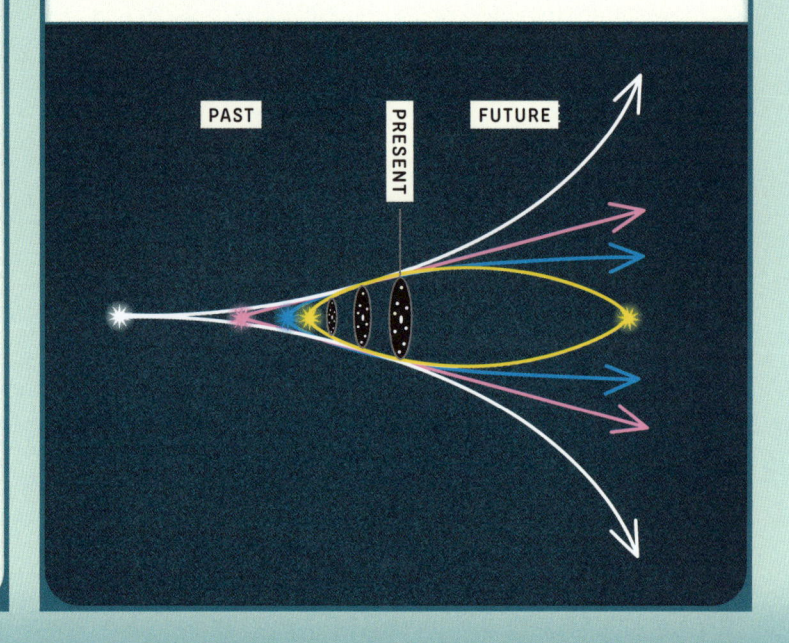

AFTERGLOW

CMB radiation can be detected from every direction in space. It is thought to be the afterglow from a very hot young universe, soon after the Big Bang. It was once visible light, but during 13.8 billion years of travel through expanding space, it has redshifted down to microwave wavelengths (see page 174).

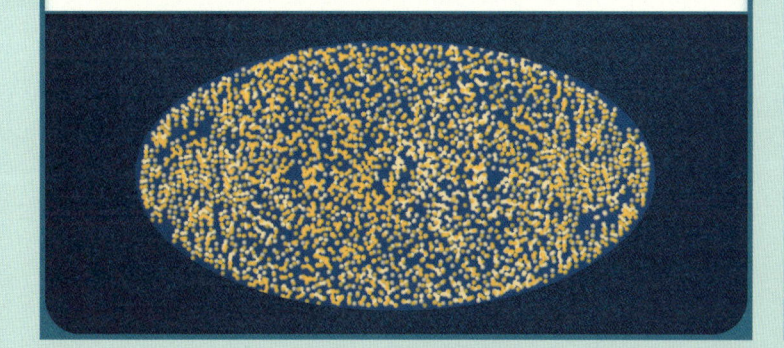

BIG BOUNCE

One problem with the Standard Model is that it assumes before the Big Bang there was nothing at all. However, physicists know that energy cannot be created or destroyed. Where did the heat in the very early universe come from? One idea is that a previous universe collapsed down to a tiny point, then began to expand again in a "Big Bounce."

EXOTIC THEORIES

Some alternatives to the Big Bang theory sound like movie plots, but are the result of mathematical models. Black hole cosmology sees our entire observable universe as being inside a supermassive black hole in a much bigger parent universe! Multiverse theory suggests that our universe is just one among many, while the simulation hypothesis suggests that our universe is just a very good computer simulation.

ULTRA-DEEP FIELD

Deep-field images taken by the Hubble Space Telescope and the Webb Space Telescope support the Big Bang theory. They allow us to look back in time and see that the most distant (and therefore youngest) galaxies are much more densely packed than older, nearby regions of space. In the billions of years since this light left their surface, the space between galaxies has expanded.

THE COSMIC WEB

CATEGORY	AGE
LARGE-SCALE STRUCTURES	13.5 BILLION YEARS

OVER THE LAST FEW DECADES, ASTRONOMERS HAVE GATHERED GLIMPSES OF THE UNDERLYING STRUCTURE OF THE UNIVERSE ITSELF—KNOWN AS THE COSMIC WEB.

ALL ABOUT

As astronomers built up a better picture of what's out there, the next challenge was figuring out how it all fits together. In 1986, astrophysicists proposed that galaxy clusters and superclusters are connected by long, thin bands of gas and plasma. This vast spider web of interconnected matter arranges itself around large holes or voids in space, like the film on soap bubbles, or the material of a sponge.

A few years later in 1989, astronomers detected a piece of this "cosmic web" for the first time—a sheet or filament of galaxies that is about 500 million light-years long, but very thin. It became known as a "great wall." At first astronomers could only detect sheets and filaments that had been heated by a nearby quasar (see page 182). But we can now see fainter filaments, too, and have learned they are mainly made of hydrogen gas.

The Cosmic Microwave Background (CMB) offers clues to why the universe is structured in this way. When it was first detected, the CMB signal seemed to be the same across the entire sky. But in 1989, NASA's Cosmic Background Explorer satellite began to notice tiny temperature differences. Turning these into a picture that we can see is like making a map of the very early universe, just 300 million years after the Big Bang.

In this "baby photo" of the universe, slightly hotter spots in the CMB reveal where the ancient light has traveled through clumps of slightly denser matter in the early universe, picking up a little extra energy. Astrophysicists reason that these clumps eventually became today's galaxy clusters, and the two maps match up well.

The next step in understanding the cosmic web will be to figure out what role dark matter and dark energy have played in shaping its structure.

KEY FACTS

- The temperature of the CMB is around -454 °F (just above absolute zero—the coldest temperature possible).
- Tiny temperature variations of just a few millionths of a degree are enough to reveal the hidden structure of the young universe.

NAMED AFTER

The term cosmic web was first used in 1996, to describe the web of filaments connecting matter across the entire universe.

COSMIC STRUCTURES

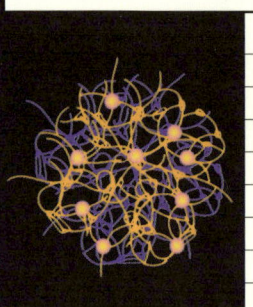

The large-scale structure of the universe is made up of superclusters of galaxies, linked by filaments of gas and plasma. These areas of high-density matter form interconnected threads and sheets surrounding enormous voids in space.

PAST, PRESENT, FUTURE

Scientists have used computer simulations to predict how dark matter (see page 206) is distributed. The pattern matches models of the large-scale structure of the universe, the cosmic web. In 2024, scientists even found indirect evidence of dark matter "dangling" from a filament of the cosmic web.

★ THE STRUCTURE OF THE UNIVERSE HAS ALSO BEEN INFLUENCED BY DARK ENERGY (PAGE 202) ★

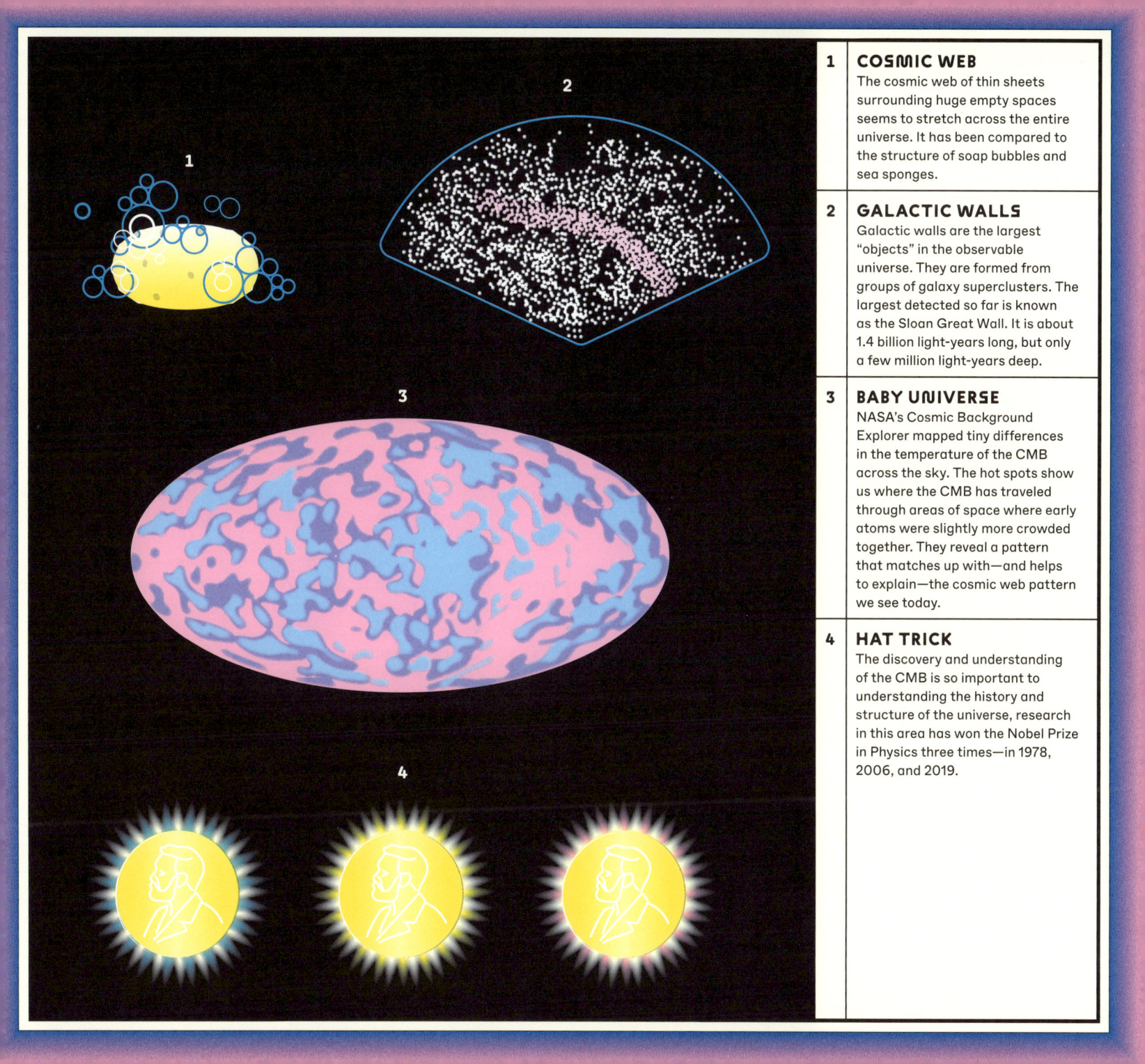

1	**COSMIC WEB**	The cosmic web of thin sheets surrounding huge empty spaces seems to stretch across the entire universe. It has been compared to the structure of soap bubbles and sea sponges.
2	**GALACTIC WALLS**	Galactic walls are the largest "objects" in the observable universe. They are formed from groups of galaxy superclusters. The largest detected so far is known as the Sloan Great Wall. It is about 1.4 billion light-years long, but only a few million light-years deep.
3	**BABY UNIVERSE**	NASA's Cosmic Background Explorer mapped tiny differences in the temperature of the CMB across the sky. The hot spots show us where the CMB has traveled through areas of space where early atoms were slightly more crowded together. They reveal a pattern that matches up with—and helps to explain—the cosmic web pattern we see today.
4	**HAT TRICK**	The discovery and understanding of the CMB is so important to understanding the history and structure of the universe, research in this area has won the Nobel Prize in Physics three times—in 1978, 2006, and 2019.

A THEORY OF EVERYTHING

IN THE QUEST TO UNDERSTAND THE UNIVERSE, THEORY HAS BEEN JUST AS IMPORTANT AS OBSERVATION. THE ULTIMATE GOAL OF PHYSICS IS A "UNIFIED THEORY" THAT CAN EXPLAIN EVERYTHING WE SEE IN THE UNIVERSE.

Theories are explanations based on or backed up by evidence. They can be tested by using the ideas to make predictions. If the results of observations or experiments agree with the predictions, the theory gains support. If not, the theory might have to be adapted—or abandoned.

At the moment, two famous theories—general relativity and quantum physics—are needed to explain different aspects of the universe.

General relativity is great at explaining the effects we call gravity. Many of its predictions—from gravitational lensing (see page 193) to gravitational waves (see page 200) have been confirmed by astronomers. However, the math of general relativity can't predict or explain the behavior of the smallest things in the universe—the subatomic particles inside atoms. To do this, physicists rely on quantum theory.

Quantum theory is brilliant at explaining the behavior of atoms and their building blocks. It tells us how nuclear fusion happens at the core of stars, how their energy radiates across space, and even the color of their light. But it can't explain the gravity that holds stars together in the first place!

Although both theories work well, at the back of every physicist's mind is that when a theory can't explain something, a new and better theory is needed. The ultimate quest is a unified theory—a theory of everything, that can describe the large-scale structure of the universe just as well as the events inside a single atom.

GENERAL RELATIVITY

In 1905, Einstein's special theory of relativity introduced the idea that nothing except the speed of light is "fixed." Everything we observe is experienced in a way that is relative to where we are, and how we are moving, as we observe it. Even space and time can be stretched or bent. For the next decade, Einstein explored what this theory means in different, real-life situations, to set out a general theory of relativity. In doing so, he changed the way we understand gravity, explaining that it is not an invisible force pulling objects toward each other, but a result of space-time itself being distorted by objects. The more mass an object has, the more it warps space-time around it—causing the effects we call gravity.

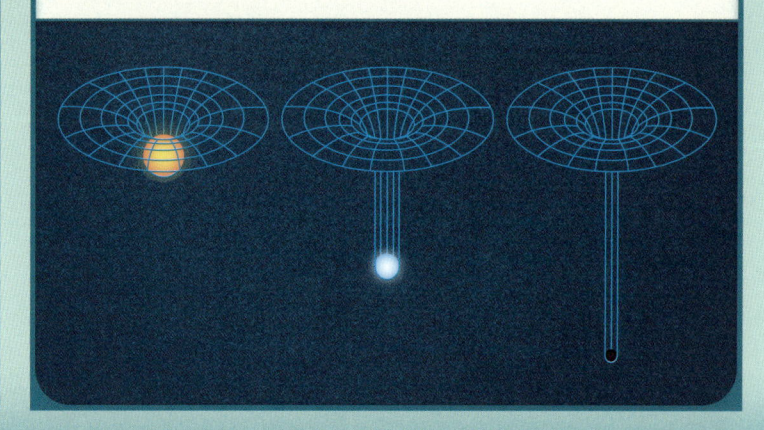

$E = mc^2$

Einstein's most famous equation tells us about the relationship between the energy of an object (E) and its mass (m). The constant c is the speed of light, which never changes. It tells us that mass and energy are interchangeable—in other words, we can think of matter as simply a different form of energy. Stars themselves convert matter (hydrogen atoms) into energy that shines out across the universe.

SHAPE OF THE UNIVERSE

According to Einstein's math, the universe goes on forever. This could mean the universe is flat or nearly flat, and infinite, but other shapes are also possible: a sphere, for example, where you can keep going forever by looping back on yourself. Or a doughnut shape, which is one way to explain the patterns seen in the Cosmic Microwave Background.

QUANTUM THEORY

Quantum theory began with Einstein's realization that light is given out (by things like stars) and absorbed (by things like atoms) in little packets of energy, as photons. If energy can be thought of as both waves AND particles, then surely matter can too. This idea turned out to work well, but only for the very smallest things: particles that are smaller than atoms.

Quantum theory has helped us to figure out what atoms are made from, and how these particles interact with each other, governed by four basic forces. This is known as the Standard Model of particle physics.

PARTICLES PREDICTED TO EXIST BY THE STANDARD MODEL OF PARTICLE PHYSICS

I	II	III
u (up quark)	c (charm quark)	t (top quark)
d (down quark)	s (strange quark)	b (bottom quark)
e (electron)	μ (muon)	τ (tau)
V_e (electron neutrino)	$V_μ$ (muon neutrino)	$V_τ$ (tau neutrino)

g (gluon), γ (photon), Z (Z boson), W (W boson), H (higgs)

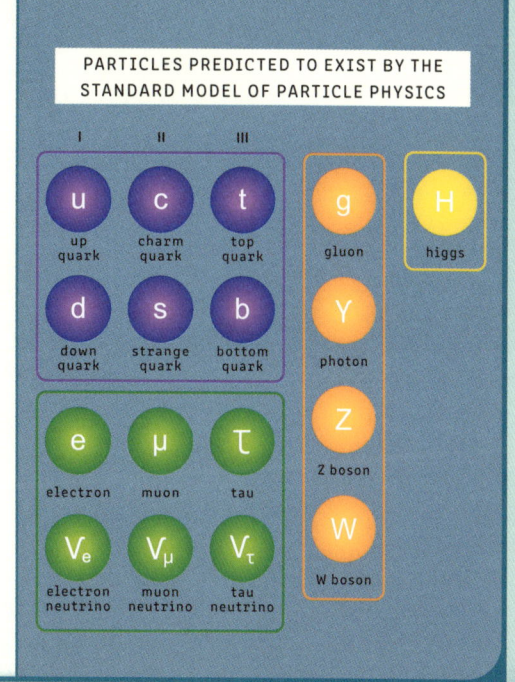

WORMHOLES

Not everything predicted by general relativity has been observed yet. Most famous are Einstein-Rosen bridges, better known as wormholes. They would form when extreme distortions of space-time bring together two points in space and time that were previously very distant from one another. Black holes are the only objects massive enough to bend space-time this much.

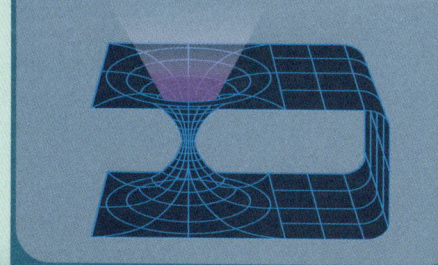

DETECTING GRAVITATIONAL WAVES

SOME OF TODAY'S MOST EXCITING DISCOVERIES ARE COMING NOT FROM TELESCOPES THAT DETECT DIFFERENT FORMS OF LIGHT, BUT FROM EQUIPMENT THAT DETECTS COMPLETELY DIFFERENT KINDS OF WAVES.

Gravitational waves were predicted by Albert Einstein more than a hundred years ago. His general theory of relativity allowed him to calculate what would happen during collisions between the most massive objects in the universe—objects such as neutron stars or black holes.

Einstein's mathematics showed that in order to move closer together, these massive objects must lose some of the energy that keeps them apart and orbiting each other. Energy cannot be destroyed. Instead, it is carried away by gravitational waves. These ripples would spread outward like sound waves traveling through air, but gravitational waves travel through the fabric of space-time itself.

In the 1970s, astronomers found the first indirect proof that gravitational waves really do exist. Using a giant radio telescope, they detected two pulsars orbiting one another. Over four years, they watched as the stars gradually moved closer together, at exactly the rate predicted by Einstein's theory if they were emitting gravitational waves.

The next challenge was to build a detector that could measure gravitational waves directly, by detecting some of these distortions in space-time as they rippled through Earth. The Laser Interferometer Gravitational-Wave Observatory (LIGO) opened in 2015, and quickly detected its first gravitational wave, beginning a brand-new type of astronomy.

A NEW ASTRONOMY

Gravitational waves pass through everything in the universe without being scattered or absorbed. This means they can bring us information from parts of space we can't see with telescopes—such as the area hidden behind the dense, dusty disc of the Milky Way.

LASER INTERFEROMETER GRAVITATIONAL-WAVE OBSERVATORY (LIGO)

1. Gravitational waves travel through space-time like sound waves travel through air, by stretching and squeezing the medium they are traveling through. This medium is space-time—the fabric of the universe itself!

2. The only thing that can't be stretched or squeezed is light. LIGO splits a light beam from a laser, and measures the time taken by the light to travel down two long arms and back again.

3. Each arm is 2.5 miles long.

4. Mirrors are used to bounce the light down the arms and back again. They are designed so that they don't wobble due to tiny vibrations in Earth's crust.

5. Normally, the two beams of light would arrive back at the detector at exactly the same time. If they don't, it means that the beams have traveled through space-time that was being stretched and squeezed by a gravitational wave.

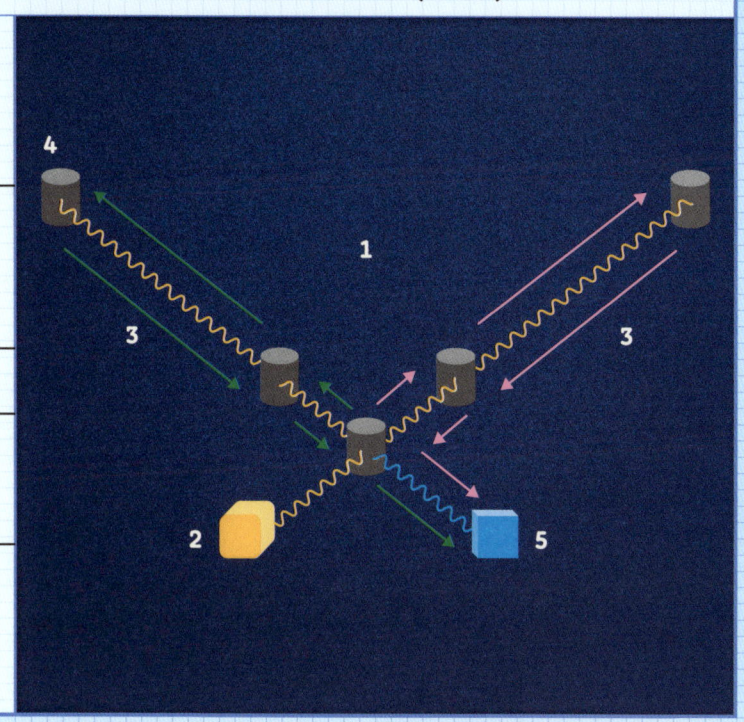

A FAIR TEST

To be completely sure of the result, LIGO has two identical detectors, built 1,864 miles apart. If they measure the same result, it must be due to gravitational waves. These traces show the first gravitational waves detected at each site.

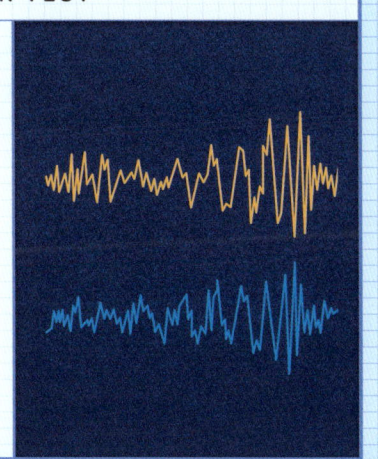

VIOLENT COLLISIONS

Using Einstein's math and supercomputers, astrophysicists can even figure out the source of each set of gravitational waves that are detected (see page 206). The first gravitational waves detected in 2015 were produced by the merger of two black holes, 1.3 billion light-years from Earth.

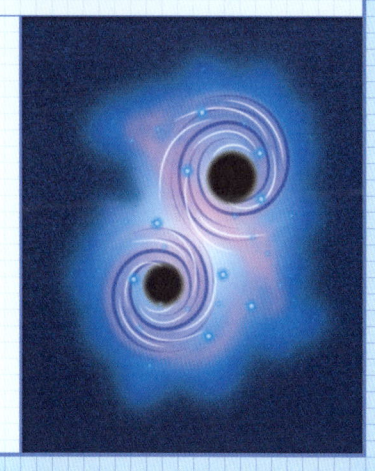

THE DARK UNIVERSE

CATEGORY	AGE
DARK ENERGY AND DARK MATTER	UNKNOWN

MOST OF THE UNIVERSE CONSISTS OF DARK ENERGY AND MATTER THAT WE CAN'T DETECT WITH ANY OF OUR EXISTING INSTRUMENTS OR METHODS.

ALL ABOUT

After Edwin Hubble discovered that galaxies are moving apart from one another, a new question emerged. What is causing the universe to expand?

In 1998, astronomers investigating this question used the powerful Hubble Space Telescope to repeat Edwin Hubble's measurements for much more distant galaxies. They made a shocking discovery. Instead of slowing down after the Big Bang, as gravity pulled galaxies together, the universe is expanding faster now than it did in the past! This was impossible to explain using existing ideas. It's like the sparkles from a firework continuing to speed up forever after exploding from the shell.

The only possible explanation is that something completely new—something no one had detected or even guessed at—must be acting against gravity, pushing galaxies apart. This mysterious phenomenon is now known as dark energy. We don't yet understand dark energy, but by building it into their models, scientists have used it to figure out that the observable universe is much larger than the starlight reaching us suggests.

Meanwhile, astronomers studying the orbit of stars around galaxies had noticed something else that was puzzling. Galaxies have a greater gravitational force than expected from counting their stars, planets, gas, and dust. This means they contain more matter than we can see. This invisible dark matter makes up about 85 percent of all matter there is. It does not give out or reflect light of any kind, so it must be very different from the matter that makes up stars and planets.

KEY FACTS

- Cold dark matter may have been produced in the very early universe.
- It accounts for around a quarter of the mass of the universe.
- Around 90 percent of the mass of the Milky Way is thought to be dark matter.

NAMED AFTER

Dark matter and dark energy get their name simply because they are not visible—they don't emit light, absorb light, or reflect light of any kind. Ordinary matter—made up of atoms—is known as baryonic matter by astronomers.

COSMIC PROPORTIONS

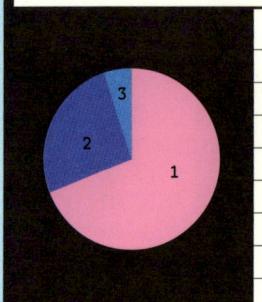

No one is able to observe, measure, or detect dark energy (1) or dark matter (2). However, we know they exist and how much of them there is, because of their effects on the things we can detect (3). Those things—the ones covered in the rest of this book—make up just four to five percent of the universe!

PAST, PRESENT, FUTURE

Dark energy and dark matter are not the only things in the universe we can't see. There is also ordinary matter and energy that is simply too far away from Earth to detect. Because of the expansion of the universe, light from these objects will never reach Earth, no matter how long we wait.

★ EXPLORE EDWIN HUBBLE'S DISCOVERIES ON PAGE 190 ★

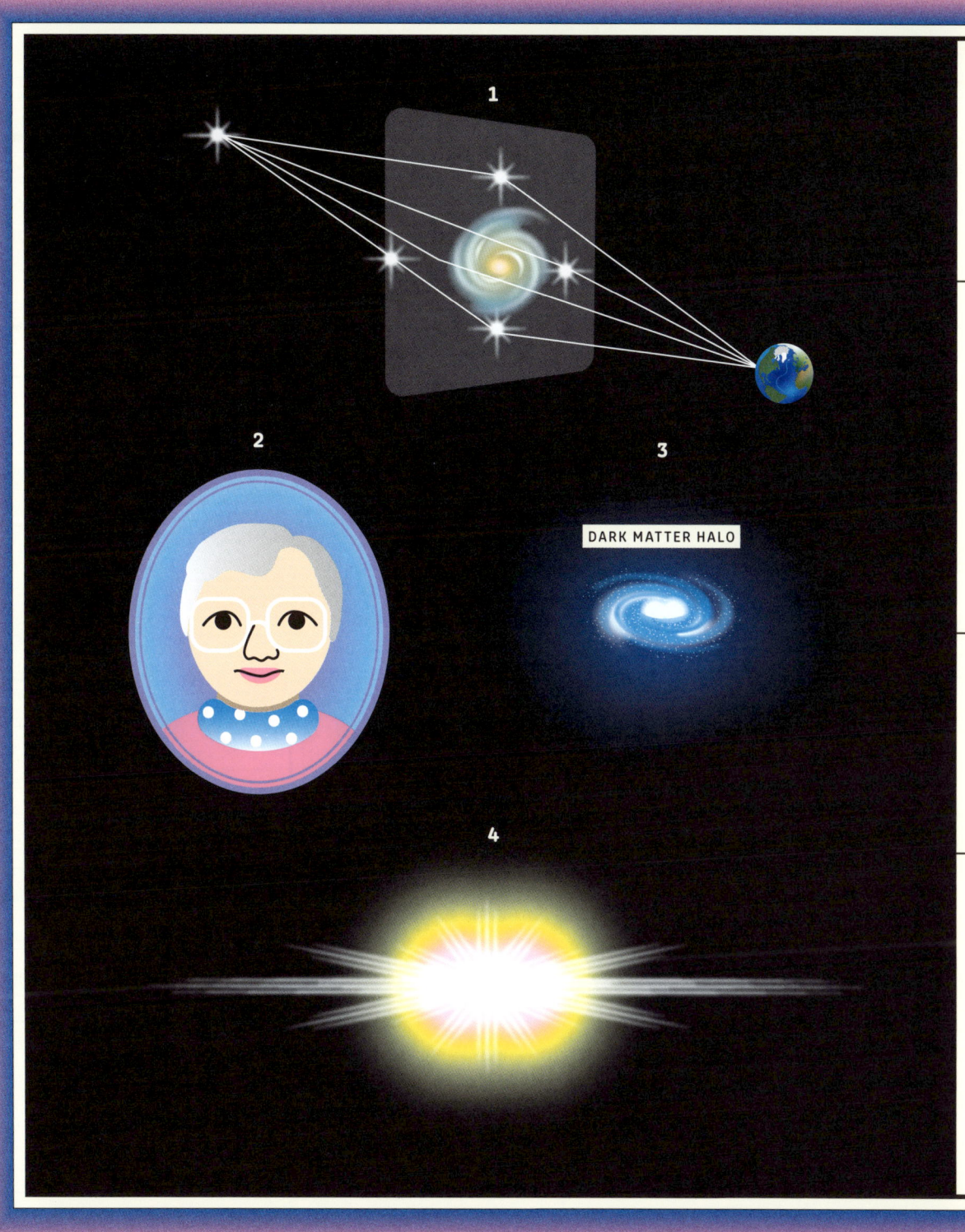

1	**BENDING LIGHT**	The dark matter in a galaxy cluster helps to hold everything together. It is also thought to be responsible for the gravitational bending, or lensing, of light that passes by a cluster on its way to Earth. This can lead to us seeing a single star multiple times in the sky, for example!
2	**VERA RUBIN**	American astronomer Vera Rubin found the key piece of evidence for dark matter when she discovered that stars and star clusters far from the center of a galaxy move just as quickly as those farther in. The visible stars and planets in a galaxy do not have enough gravity to hold these fast-moving outer stars in orbit. This means galaxies must contain lots of additional, invisible dark matter that holds each galaxy together and stops it from flying apart.
3	**ON OUR DOORSTEP**	Dark matter forms an invisible halo around galaxies, meaning the gravitational force of a galaxy is much more evenly spread out than it looks. Almost 90 percent of matter in the Milky Way is dark matter. Its gravitational force helps to shape the spiral arms.
4	**DARK ENERGY**	By measuring the brightness of supernova explosions in very distant galaxies, scientists realized the expansion of the universe is speeding up. Dark energy is our best way to explain this. Dark energy is even less well understood than dark matter, but it seems to have the opposite effect to gravity—driving objects apart instead of bringing them together.

EXPLORING DARK MATTER

DARK MATTER IS THE ULTIMATE MYSTERY. SCIENTISTS KNOW IT MUST EXIST, BECAUSE ITS GRAVITY SHAPES GALAXIES, BUT WE STILL DON'T KNOW EXACTLY WHAT DARK MATTER IS.

ALL ABOUT

The idea that the universe contains matter we can't detect was first suggested almost a century ago, but it wasn't until the 1970s that American astronomer Vera Rubin found evidence to support this theory.

Rubin was studying stars in the Andromeda Galaxy, measuring how quickly they move in their long orbits around the galactic center. She expected to see a pattern similar to the one in our solar system, where objects farther from the center orbit far more slowly. She was shocked to discover that star clusters near Andromeda's edge were moving just as quickly as the ones near the center. The only way they could move so quickly without tearing the galaxy apart is if the galaxy's gravity—and therefore mass—was ten times greater than scientists had predicted by counting its stars. This was indirect evidence for the missing matter that scientists had predicted. Rather than being concentrated at the center, this dark matter seemed to be spread throughout galaxies in a giant invisible halo.

Over the last 50 years, scientists have detected the effects of dark matter on other things we can see, including the Cosmic Microwave Background (CMB). Physicists are also searching for direct evidence using new types of detectors, and even trying to create dark matter particles themselves. These hypothetical particles are known as WIMPs, which stands for Weakly Interacting Massive Particles. "Massive" means they have mass, and "Weakly Interacting" describes how they pass straight through normal matter instead of interacting. There are probably WIMPs passing unnoticed through your body right now!

EXPLORATION TIMELINE

1933	Fritz Zwicky is first to suggest the universe contains unseen dark matter.
1970s	Vera Rubin finds evidence of dark matter in the rotation curves of distant galaxies.
1986	First experiment to detect the effects of dark matter particles, at the Homestake Mine in South Dakota, USA.
2013	Details of fluctuations in the CMB collected by the Planck observatory help scientists calculate that dark matter makes up 27 percent of the universe.
2021	The world's most sensitive dark matter detector, the LZ detector, begins operating.
2024	The Keck Cosmic Web Imager, at the top of a volcano in Hawaii, indirectly detects dark matter dangling from a strand of the cosmic web.

ARE WE THERE YET?

- You don't have to travel far to encounter dark matter. It is spread throughout the universe, and in our galaxy outweighs normal matter by nine to one.
- Every second, up to trillions of dark matter particles pass through your body without a trace.

HELPING HUMANS

Although we know very little about dark matter, people have speculated that it could lead to new technologies beyond our imagination. This might include ways to travel farther across the universe at close to the speed of light.

★ FIND OUT MORE ABOUT NORMAL MATTER ON PAGE 156 ★

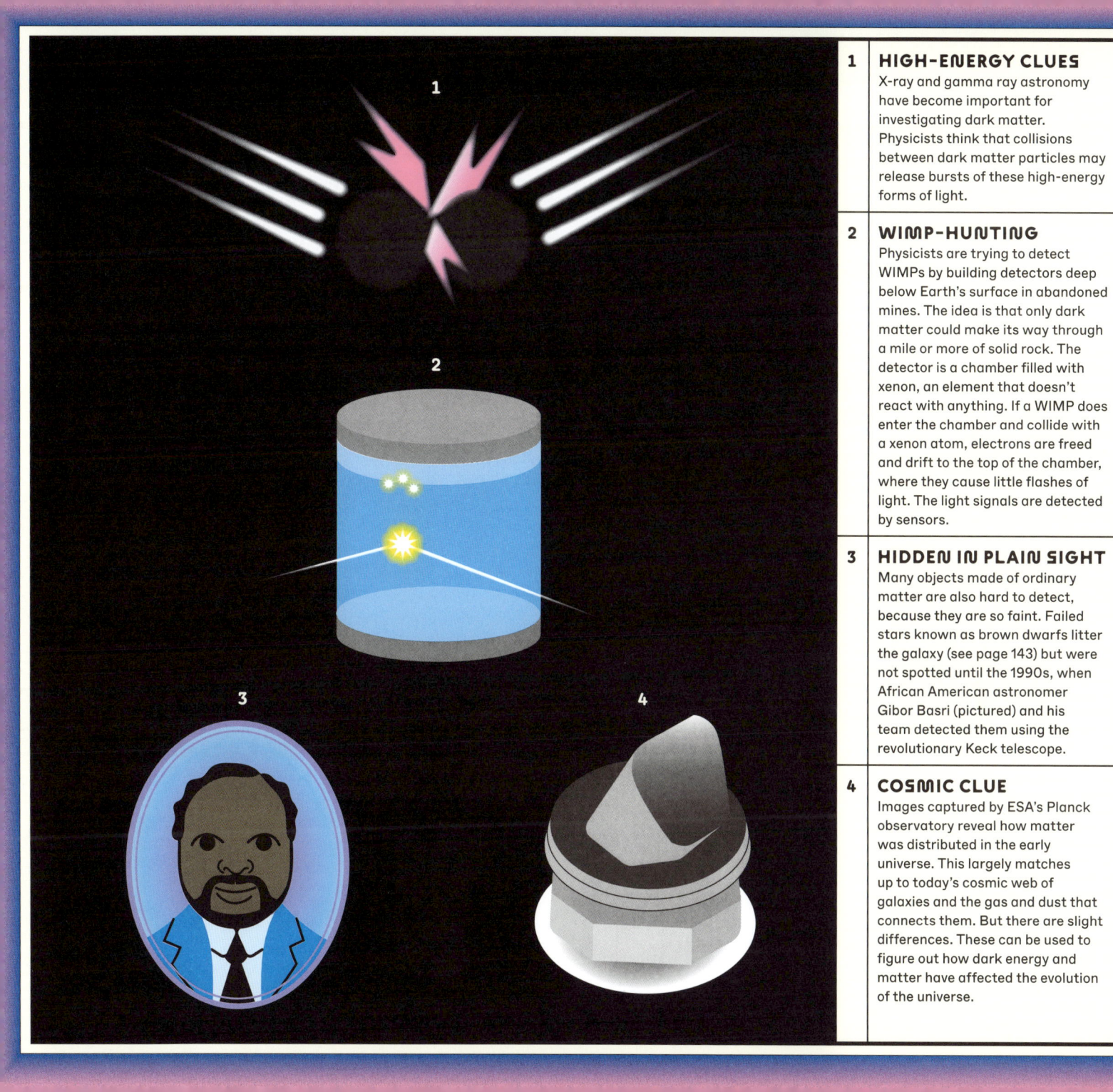

#		
1	**HIGH-ENERGY CLUES**	X-ray and gamma ray astronomy have become important for investigating dark matter. Physicists think that collisions between dark matter particles may release bursts of these high-energy forms of light.
2	**WIMP-HUNTING**	Physicists are trying to detect WIMPs by building detectors deep below Earth's surface in abandoned mines. The idea is that only dark matter could make its way through a mile or more of solid rock. The detector is a chamber filled with xenon, an element that doesn't react with anything. If a WIMP does enter the chamber and collide with a xenon atom, electrons are freed and drift to the top of the chamber, where they cause little flashes of light. The light signals are detected by sensors.
3	**HIDDEN IN PLAIN SIGHT**	Many objects made of ordinary matter are also hard to detect, because they are so faint. Failed stars known as brown dwarfs litter the galaxy (see page 143) but were not spotted until the 1990s, when African American astronomer Gibor Basri (pictured) and his team detected them using the revolutionary Keck telescope.
4	**COSMIC CLUE**	Images captured by ESA's Planck observatory reveal how matter was distributed in the early universe. This largely matches up to today's cosmic web of galaxies and the gas and dust that connects them. But there are slight differences. These can be used to figure out how dark energy and matter have affected the evolution of the universe.

SUPERCOMPUTERS & AI

OVER THE LAST 75 YEARS, COMPUTERS HAVE PLAYED A CENTRAL ROLE IN ASTRONOMY, **ASTROPHYSICS**, AND SPACE EXPLORATION. WITH ARTIFICIAL INTELLIGENCE, THEY HAVE BECOME INDISPENSABLE.

From the very first star catalog, astronomy has always been about collecting and analyzing data, to discover patterns in nature and figure out their meaning. Since electronic computers were invented in the 1940s, they have been used to help with these tasks.

Telescopes rely on computing power to process raw data collected using digital cameras, removing noise (random signals that aren't from the source being studied) and turning the digital data into information such as pictures that we can understand. Space probes, landers, and rovers are controlled by onboard computers, programmed with the instructions for each mission.

Back on Earth, supercomputers are used to sift through mind-boggling amounts of data at incredible speed. They can be programmed to spot patterns—such as the signs of a dangerous asteroid, or an alien planet. Artificial intelligence can also be trained to spot unexpected and unique patterns in data—things the computer *hasn't* been told to look for. By revealing the unexpected, this will bring exciting new discoveries.

Computer simulations are used to model events, based on the mathematical rules that govern the universe. They can be used to speed up astronomical events that happen over millennia, or to rewind time and figure out how stars, galaxies, or the universe itself formed.

Simulations are also used to test new ideas and theories about the universe. A simulation can be run a million different times, using different starting points or variables each time. The results can then be compared with real-life observations, to figure out which theories are on the right track.

PRACTICE RUN

The Webb Space Telescope is so large, it had to be partly constructed in space. There was only one chance to get it right, as repair missions were impossible. Because it was also impossible to re-create conditions in space on the ground, the engineers relied on computer modelling to perfect the sequence of 50 deployments needed to unfold the telescope in space.

HUMAN COMPUTERS

The first "computers" in space exploration were human mathematicians, hired to do the calculations needed to get spacecraft into Earth's orbit and beyond. One of the most famous is Katherine Johnson, an African American mathematician whose calculations helped to launch the first US astronauts into space and land the first humans on the Moon.

SEEING THE UNSEEABLE

Since the 1970s, computers have been used to turn data collected by X-ray, infrared, radio, and gamma-ray telescopes into images that we can see with our eyes. Often, data from several telescopes is combined to create the most spectacular images in astronomy. They include planetary nebulae, star nurseries, and supernova remnants.

DATA TSUNAMI

The Rubin Observatory Legacy Survey of Space and Time (LSST) collects around 20 terabytes of data and detects 10 million interesting events *every night*. It would be impossible for humans to look through all this raw data, so the first sifts will be carried out by computer algorithms trained to alert scientists to interesting things.

ALL POSSIBILITIES

When gravitational waves were detected, supercomputers were used to help deduce their original source. They used Einstein's equations to model the type of gravitational waves that would be formed by a million different possible events in space. The one that best fit the waves actually seen was the merger of two supermassive black holes, 1.3 billion years ago.

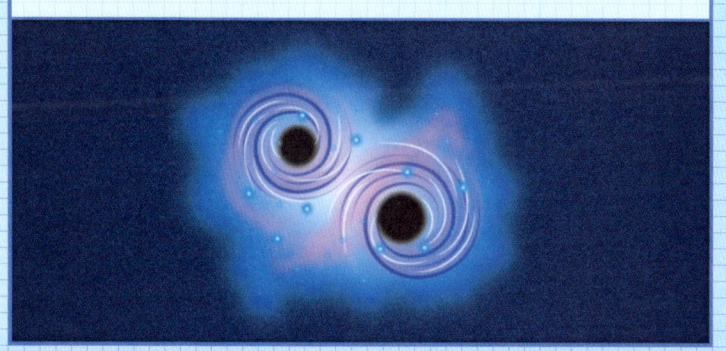

ASTRONOMICAL DATA AND OTHER RESOURCES

YOUR JOURNEY THROUGH THE UNIVERSE IS JUST BEGINNING.

Cosmology (the study of the universe as a whole) is a young science. We have only suspected the true scale of the universe for around a century, and many of the key discoveries and ideas in cosmology are just a few decades old. Many of the objects and phenomena in this book will become better understood as new evidence is found. Some of the facts may change altogether.

There are still plenty of mysteries to solve and discoveries to make, both within and outside our solar system. If you keep studying mathematics and science, you could be among the future astronomers, cosmologists, engineers, and astronauts who will help to find answers.

Space begins 60 miles above your head, but you can start exploring the universe from the Earth's surface. Here are some things to try.

STARGAZING

On dark nights, try identifying constellations of stars. You can borrow a **planisphere** from a library, or download a star map or stargazing app to help (see page 219 for ideas). Stand away from artificial lights and give your eyes about 20 minutes to adjust to the dark.

SPOTTING OTHER OBJECTS

Learning to spot constellations can help you to locate other astronomical objects more easily—for example, the planets in our solar system. Mercury, Venus, Mars, Jupiter, and Saturn can all be seen with the naked eye, but their position changes throughout the year. A star chart or app can tell you where to look at any particular time.

You don't need a telescope to start taking a closer look at the universe. With a pair of binoculars you can see hundreds of thousands more stars, the rings around Saturn, and even

Jupiter's largest moons. Some amazing discoveries—including comets and asteroids—have been made this way.

Many observatories open their powerful telescopes to the public, giving you the chance to see nebulae, galaxies, and other extraordinary sights for yourself. Search "Where is my nearest observatory" on a web browser, and look out for events open to the public. Events run by amateur astronomers are often free of charge. You can also visit planetariums, where images and videos of the cosmos are projected onto a giant dome, so you can lie back and journey through the universe.

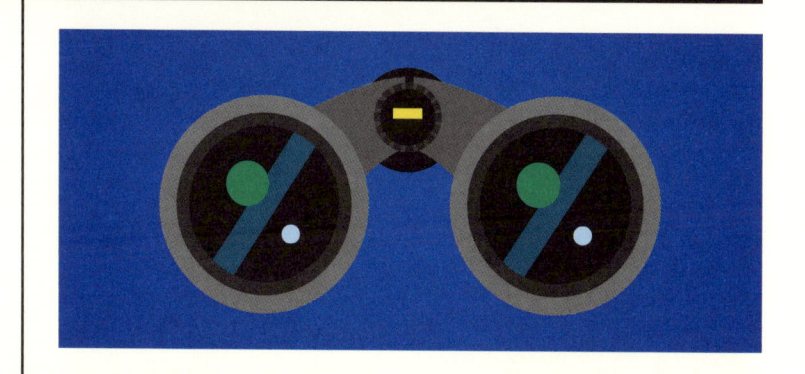

COSMIC CALENDAR

The universe has celebrated an estimated 13.8 billion birthdays. This is an enormous stretch of time compared to a human lifespan. To make it easier to visualize, this cosmic calendar condenses key events in the 13.8-billion-year history of the universe into one year. Each month represents just over a billion years.

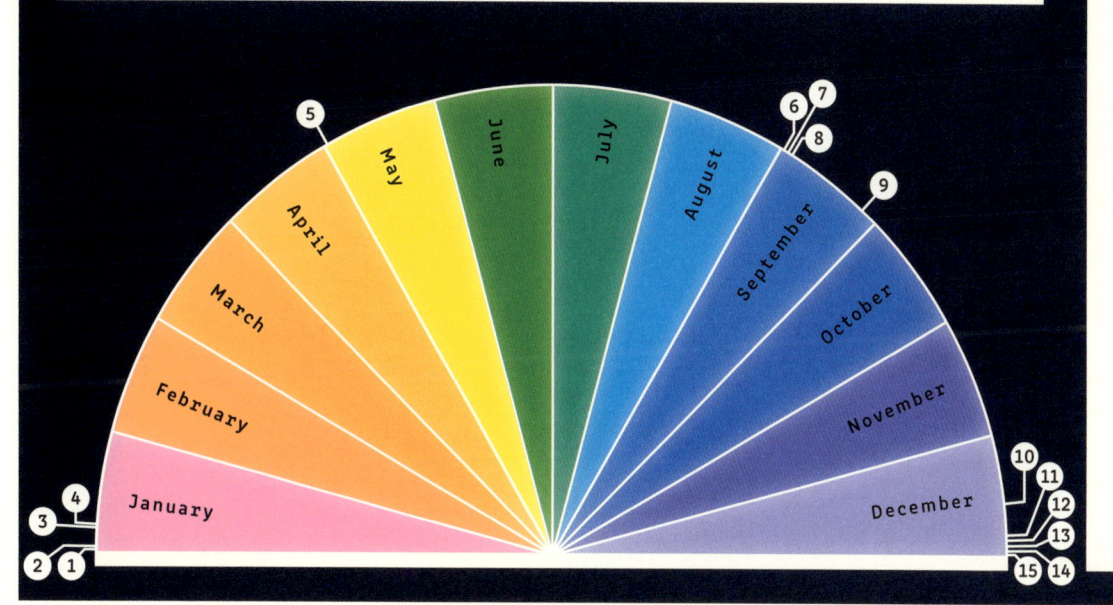

1. The Big Bang
2. The first atoms form
3. The first stars and galaxies form
4. Light leaves the galaxy JADES-GS-z14-0*
5. Milky Way begins to form
6. The Sun forms
7. Earth forms
8. The Moon forms
9. Earliest life on Earth
10. The first vertebrates
11. Dinosaurs appear
12. The first mammals
13. Dinosaurs die out
14. The first humans
15. Light from JADES-GS-z14-0 strikes the Webb Space Telescope's infrared detector

*the most distant and earliest galaxy spotted at the time of writing, forming just 300 million years after the Big Bang

CONCLUSION: ASTRONOMICAL DATA AND OTHER RESOURCES

COMPARING COSMIC TEMPERATURES

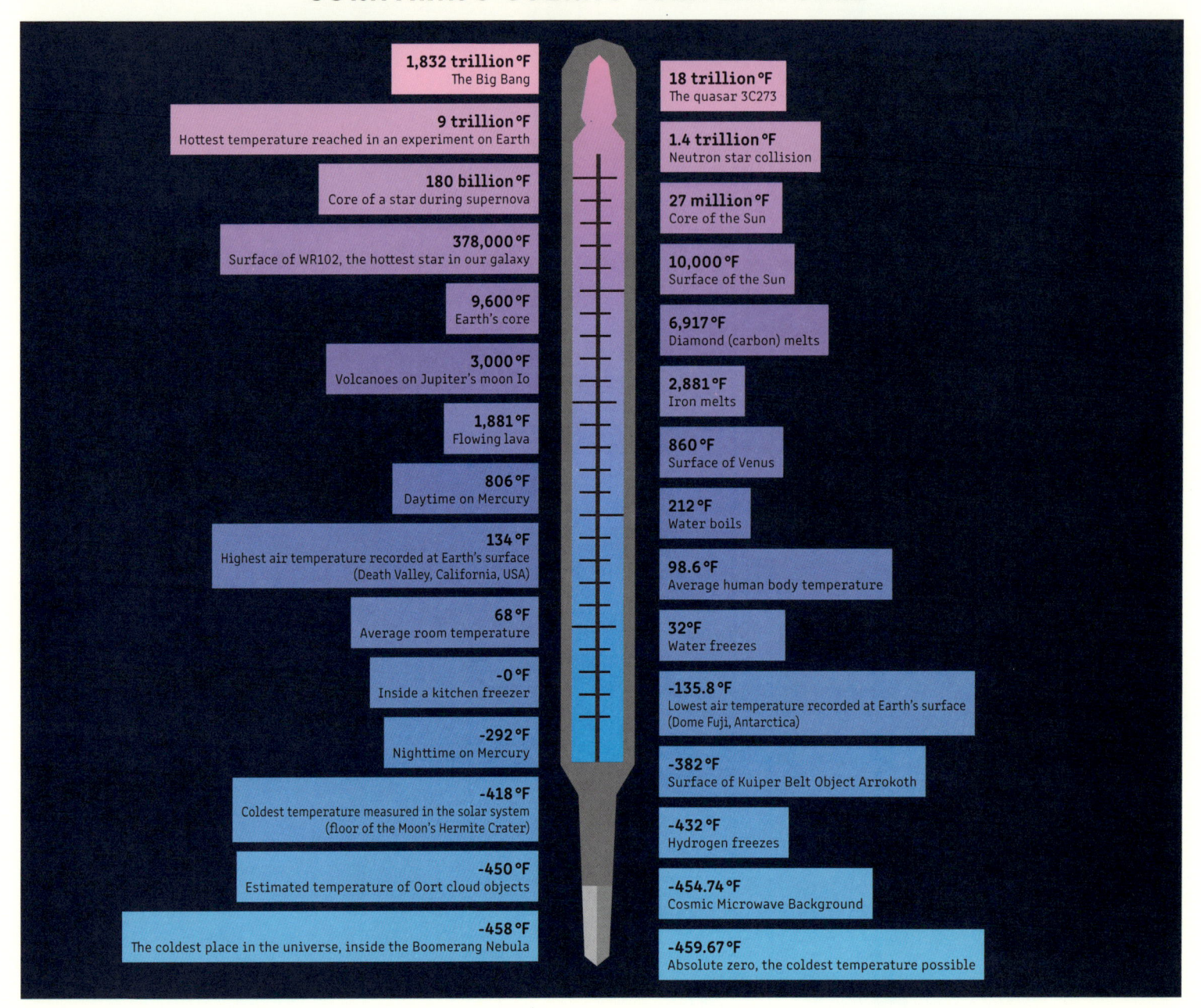

1,832 trillion °F	The Big Bang
18 trillion °F	The quasar 3C273
9 trillion °F	Hottest temperature reached in an experiment on Earth
1.4 trillion °F	Neutron star collision
180 billion °F	Core of a star during supernova
27 million °F	Core of the Sun
378,000 °F	Surface of WR102, the hottest star in our galaxy
10,000 °F	Surface of the Sun
9,600 °F	Earth's core
6,917 °F	Diamond (carbon) melts
3,000 °F	Volcanoes on Jupiter's moon Io
2,881 °F	Iron melts
1,881 °F	Flowing lava
860 °F	Surface of Venus
806 °F	Daytime on Mercury
212 °F	Water boils
134 °F	Highest air temperature recorded at Earth's surface (Death Valley, California, USA)
98.6 °F	Average human body temperature
68 °F	Average room temperature
32 °F	Water freezes
-0 °F	Inside a kitchen freezer
-135.8 °F	Lowest air temperature recorded at Earth's surface (Dome Fuji, Antarctica)
-292 °F	Nighttime on Mercury
-382 °F	Surface of Kuiper Belt Object Arrokoth
-418 °F	Coldest temperature measured in the solar system (floor of the Moon's Hermite Crater)
-432 °F	Hydrogen freezes
-450 °F	Estimated temperature of Oort cloud objects
-454.74 °F	Cosmic Microwave Background
-458 °F	The coldest place in the universe, inside the Boomerang Nebula
-459.67 °F	Absolute zero, the coldest temperature possible

CONCLUSION: ASTRONOMICAL DATA AND OTHER RESOURCES

PLANETS OF OUR SOLAR SYSTEM

These tables will help you compare key features of the eight planets of our Solar System, as well as the dwarf planet Pluto. New features are discovered all the time, so categories such as surface temperatures and number of moons are likely to change.

	Mercury	Venus	Earth	Mars	Jupiter	Saturn	Uranus	Neptune	Pluto
Average distance from Sun (mi)	36 million	67 million	93 million	142 million	484 million	890 million	1,781 million	2,805 million	3,670 million
Diameter at equator (mi)	3,032	7,521	7,926	4,220	88,846	74,897	31,763	30,775	1,476
Average surface temperature (°F)	333	867	59	-85	-166	-220	-319	-328	-373
Time to orbit the Sun (days)	88	224.7	365.2	687	4,331	10,747	30,589	59,800	90,560
Time to spin on axis (hours)	1,407.6	5,832.5	23.9	24.6	9.9	10.7	17.2	16.1	153.3
Surface gravity (ft/s^2)	12.1	29	32	12.1	75.7	29.5	28.5	36	2.3
Orbital speed (mi/s)	29.5	22	18.5	14.9	8.1	6	4.2	3.4	2.9
Moons	0	0	1	2	95	146	28	16	5
Rings	✗	✗	✗	✗	✓	✓	✓	✓	✗
Magnetosphere	✓	✗	✓	✗	✓	✓	✓	✓	Unknown

Astronomical data often involves very large numbers that are hard to imagine. To help you visualize the scale and conditions of other planets and the dwarf planet Pluto, this table converts their data into direct comparisons with Earth.

	Mercury	Venus	Earth	Mars	Jupiter	Saturn	Uranus	Neptune	Pluto
Average distance from Sun (AUs)	0.387	0.723	1	1.52	5.20	9.57	19.17	30.18	39.48
Diameter compared to Earth	0.383	0.949	1	0.532	11.21	9.45	4.01	3.88	0.187
Mass compared to Earth	18 Mercurys = mass of Earth	1.2 Venuses = mass of Earth	1	9.3 Marses = mass of Earth	317.8 Earths = mass of Jupiter	95.2 Earths = mass of Saturn	14.5 Earths = mass of Uranus	17.1 Earths = mass of Neptune	454.5 Plutos = mass of Earth
Volume compared to Earth	Would fit inside Earth 17.8 times	Would fit inside Earth 1.2 times	1	Would fit inside Earth 6.6 times	1,321 Earths would fit inside	763.6 Earths would fit inside	63 Earths would fit inside	57.7 Earths would fit inside	Would fit inside Earth 170 times
Atmospheric pressure at surface	0	92	1	0.01	-	-	-	-	0.00001
Weight of a 154-lb human on the surface	58.4 lbs	139.9 lbs	154 lbs	58.2 lbs	390 lbs	164.2 lbs	137.1 lbs	173.7 lbs	10.4 lbs

CONCLUSION: ASTRONOMICAL DATA AND OTHER RESOURCES

ARTIFICIAL SATELLITES

Near-Earth space is becoming increasingly crowded with active and inactive artificial satellites and the debris produced by launching missions into space. Find out more on pages 52 to 55 and page 62.

COUNTING SATELLITES

SOLAR SYSTEM PLANETS TO SCALE

NEPTUNE — URANUS — SATURN — JUPITER — MARS — EARTH — VENUS — MERCURY — SUN

CONCLUSION: ASTRONOMICAL DATA AND OTHER RESOURCES

HOW BIG WOULD THE SUN LOOK FROM DIFFERENT PLANETS?

Objects in space look smaller the farther away they are. This is what the Sun would look like in the sky of each planet at its closest approach, compared to its size in Earth's sky.

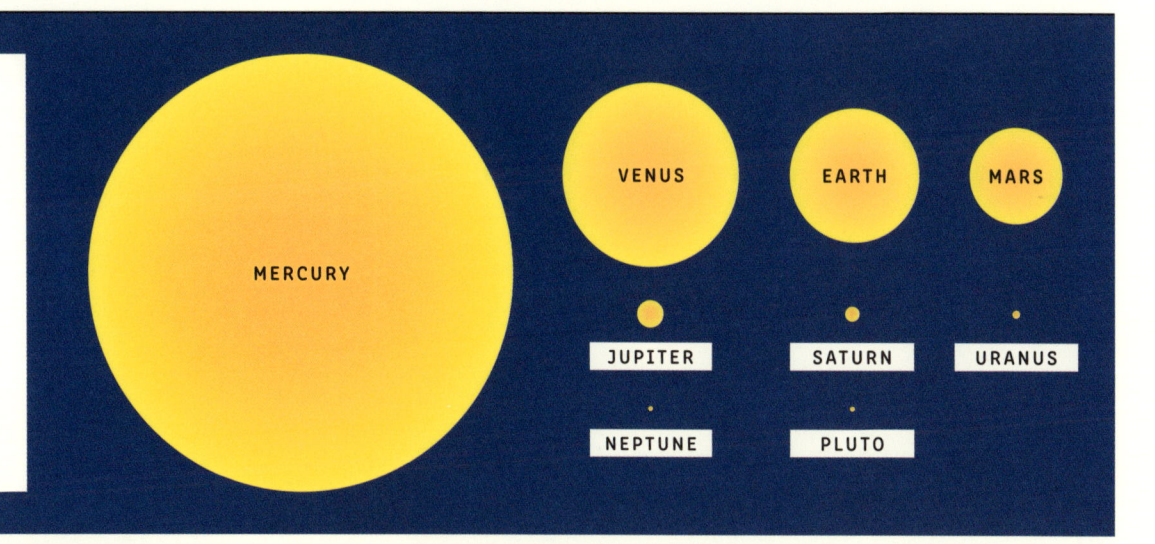

MERCURY

VENUS

EARTH

MARS

JUPITER

SATURN

URANUS

NEPTUNE

PLUTO

COULD WE BREATHE ON MERCURY?

All the planets in our solar system have an atmosphere. These charts show the mixture of gases that make up the "air" on each planet. Although Mercury has life-giving oxygen, its atmosphere is far too thin to breathe.

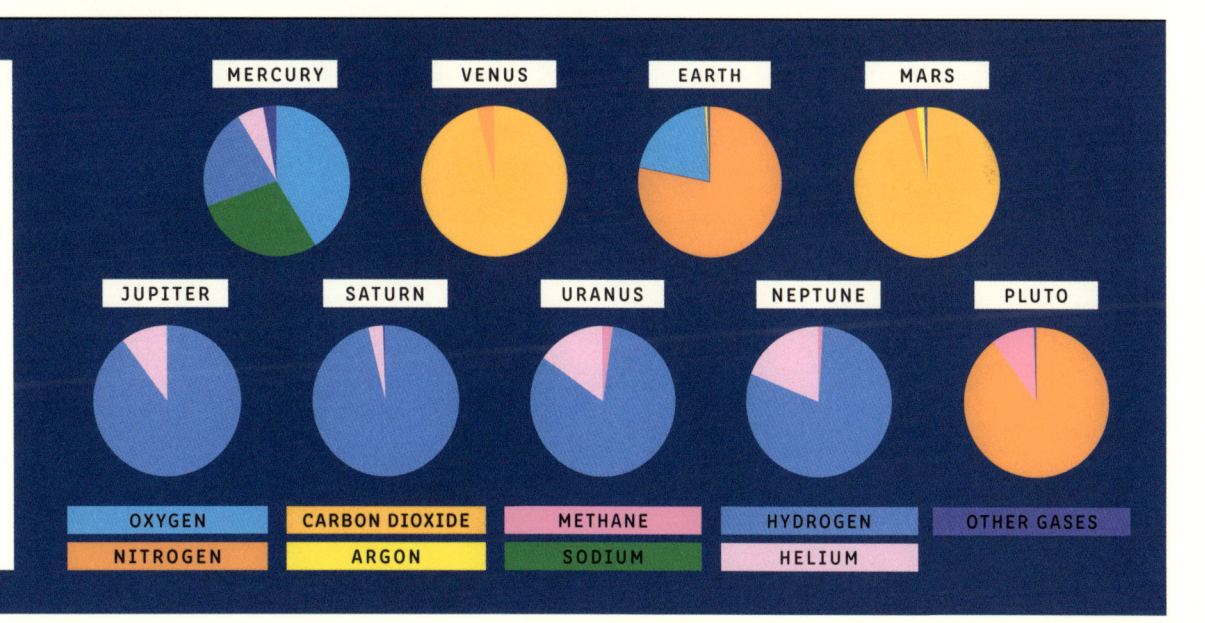

MERCURY · VENUS · EARTH · MARS

JUPITER · SATURN · URANUS · NEPTUNE · PLUTO

OXYGEN · CARBON DIOXIDE · METHANE · HYDROGEN · OTHER GASES
NITROGEN · ARGON · SODIUM · HELIUM

CONCLUSION: ASTRONOMICAL DATA AND OTHER RESOURCES

COMPARING BRIGHTNESS

The brightness of a star in Earth's sky is known as its **apparent magnitude**. This scale was first devised by an astronomer in ancient Greece, long before telescopes were invented. At that time, the brightest stars in the sky were recorded as magnitude 1. Today, even brighter objects have been added (such as the planet Venus, magnitude -4.2), so they have negative numbers on the scale. The faintest objects visible with our eyes are around magnitude 6, but dimmer objects only visible through binoculars or a telescope have also been added using the same rules, with each step representing a 2.5 x decrease in brightness.

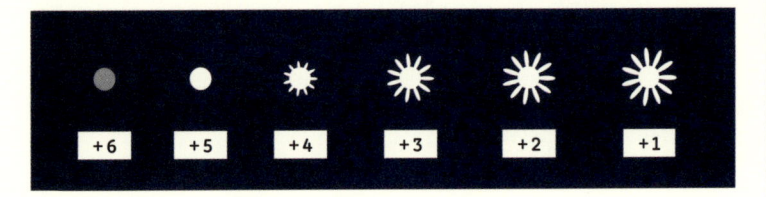

COMPARING TEMPERATURE

Astronomers use spectroscopy to split a star's light into its different wavelengths. This reveals the color of the light in a way that our eyes can't, and in turn this tells us a star's surface temperature. Astronomers sort stars into seven spectral types based on their color and temperature.

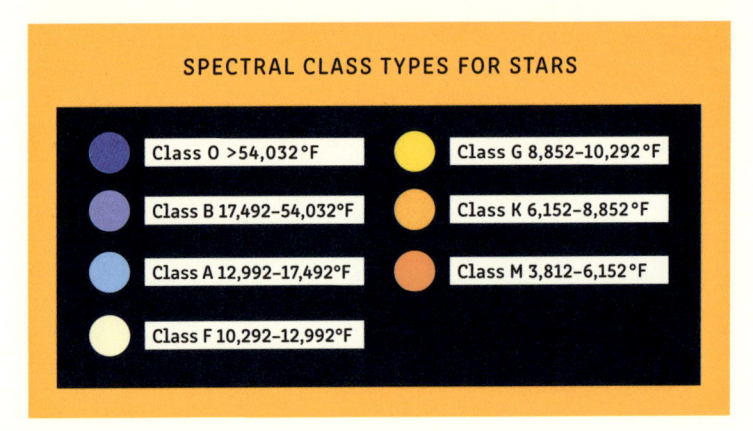

SPECTRAL CLASS TYPES FOR STARS

Class O >54,032 °F	Class G 8,852–10,292 °F
Class B 17,492–54,032 °F	Class K 6,152–8,852 °F
Class A 12,992–17,492 °F	Class M 3,812–6,152 °F
Class F 10,292–12,992 °F	

THE HERTZSPRUNG-RUSSELL DIAGRAM

The Hertzsprung-Russell diagram is a chart that plots stars by their brightness (compared to the Sun) and surface temperature (as measured by the color of their light). Stars move to different positions on the diagram during different stages of their life. The Sun is steadily burning hydrogen, and sits on the main sequence. As it runs out of hydrogen and starts to burn helium instead, the Sun will swell into a cool but bright red giant and move to the top right of the diagram. At the end of its life, it will lose its outer layers and collapse to become a hot but dim white dwarf star, appearing on the bottom left of the diagram.

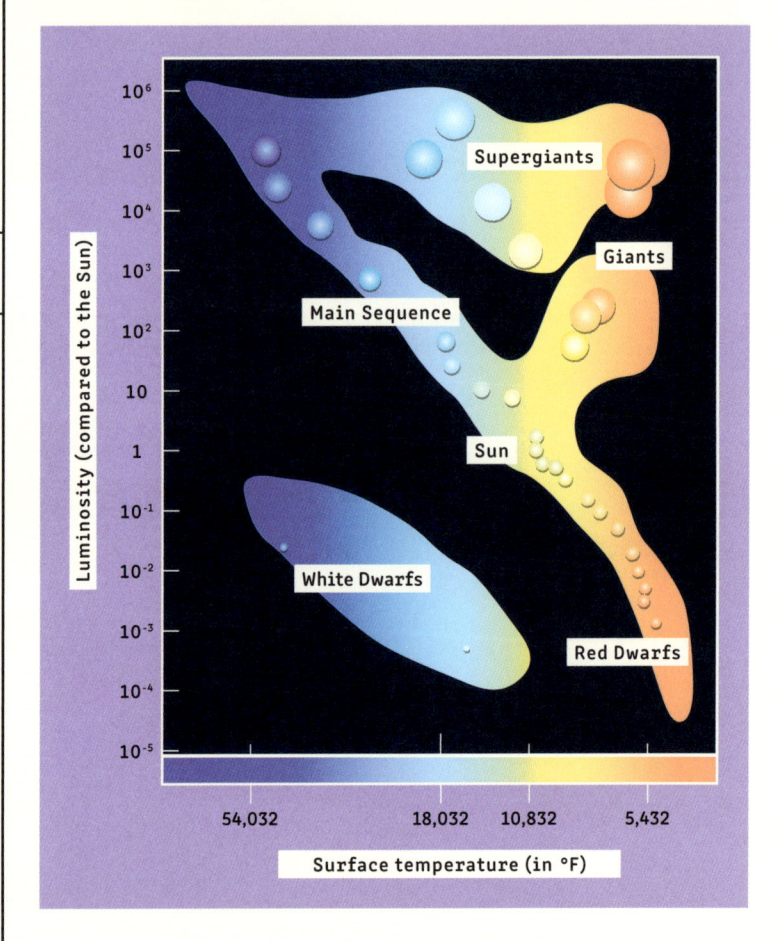

CONCLUSION: ASTRONOMICAL DATA AND OTHER RESOURCES

MAPPING STARS

From Earth, stars look like pinpricks of light on a "shell" around our planet. We can imagine that these dots are all the same distance from Earth, and join them to create shapes, called constellations. In reality, space is three-dimensional, and some stars in a constellation are much farther from Earth than others. But constellations are still useful tools. They help astronomers to divide the vast sky up into 88 areas, which is helpful for locating familiar objects and recording new discoveries.

Stars in a constellation are not actually close together in space. They simply lie in the same direction when seen from Earth.

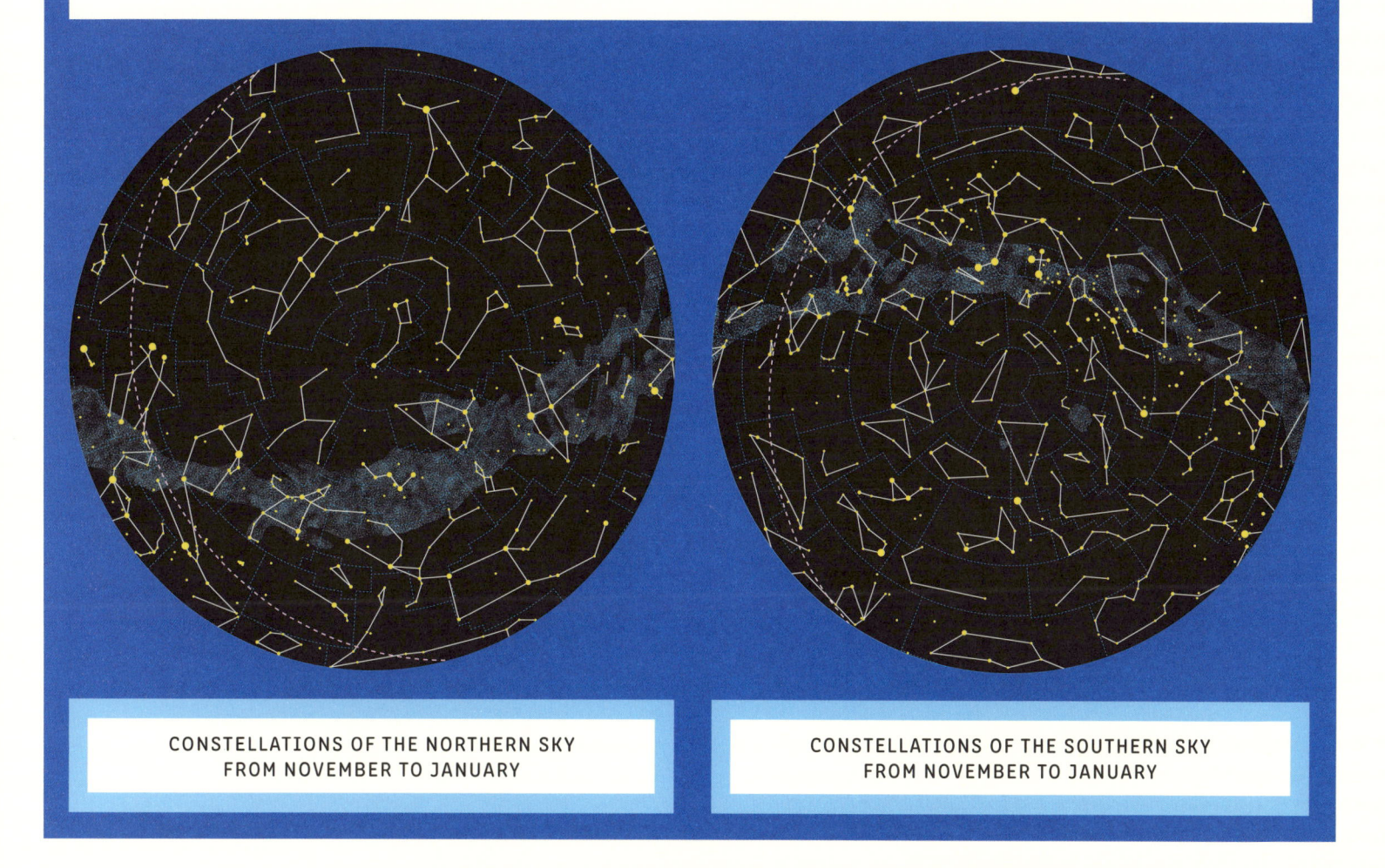

CONSTELLATIONS OF THE NORTHERN SKY FROM NOVEMBER TO JANUARY

CONSTELLATIONS OF THE SOUTHERN SKY FROM NOVEMBER TO JANUARY

CONCLUSION: ASTRONOMICAL DATA AND OTHER RESOURCES

GLOSSARY

A list of acronyms used to identify space agencies can be found on page 11.

absolute magnitude: A measure of how bright an object in space really is, as seen at a standard distance (rather than from Earth).

accelerate: Undergo a change in speed.

accretion disc: A rotating disc of **matter** that is swirling toward a **massive** object in space (such as a **black hole**) due to **gravity**.

altitude: The height of an object or a point (usually above sea level or ground level).

apparent magnitude: A measure of how bright an object in space looks from Earth. This depends on both its **absolute magnitude** and its distance from Earth.

asteroid: A small rocky object that **orbits** the Sun, typically found in the **asteroid belt** between Mars and Jupiter.

asteroid belt: A region between the **orbits** of Mars and Jupiter, where most **asteroids** in our solar system are located.

astronomer: A scientist who studies celestial objects, space, and the universe as a whole.

astronomical unit (AU): A unit of length equal to the average distance between Earth and the Sun, effectively 93 **million** mi.

astronomy: The scientific study of celestial objects, space, and the universe beyond Earth's **atmosphere**.

astrophysicist: A scientist who studies the nature of **stars** and other objects in space, using the laws and theories of physics to understand their properties and interactions.

astrophysics: The branch of **astronomy** that uses the laws and theories of physics to interpret astronomical observations and understand **stars** and other objects in space.

atmosphere: The layer of gases surrounding an object in space, held in place by **gravity**.

atom: The smallest possible **particle** of a chemical element; the fundamental building blocks of **matter**.

Big Bang: A **theory** that describes how the universe began as a hot, **dense** speck that began to expand.

billion: 1,000,000,000 (a number followed by nine zeros).

binary star: A system of two **stars** that **orbit** around a common center of **mass**.

binoculars: A pair of telescopic lenses mounted side by side, used for viewing distant objects with both eyes.

black hole: A region in space around an extremely **dense** object, known as a singularity, where the **gravitational force** of the singularity is so strong that not even **light** can escape.

Ceres: The largest object in the **asteroid belt** between Mars and Jupiter; classified as a **dwarf planet**.

comet: A small icy body that **orbits** the Sun, developing a bright coma and tails of gas and dust when close to the Sun.

corona: The outermost part of a **star's atmosphere**, visible as a halo of **light** during a solar eclipse.

Cosmic Microwave Background (CMB): Faint radiation (**light**) from the **Big Bang**, detected across the universe as microwaves.

cosmic web: The large-scale structure of the universe, consisting of an interconnected web of **galaxy** clusters, surrounding vast voids in space.

cosmologist: A scientist who studies the origins, structure, and evolution of the universe.

cosmology: The scientific study of the origin, structure, and evolution of the universe as a whole.

dark energy: A mysterious form of energy that can't be detected directly but is believed to be responsible for the expansion of the universe.

dark matter: A mysterious form of **matter** that can't be detected directly, because it does not emit **light** or interact with normal matter or energy. Its presence is predicted from its **gravitational** effects on visible matter.

density: A measure of the **mass** (how much of) a substance that is packed into a certain volume (or region of space).

dwarf planet: A celestial body that **orbits** the Sun, is **spherical** in shape, but has not cleared its orbit of other objects.

electromagnetic radiation: A form of energy that includes **visible light**, **radio waves**, microwaves, **infrared**, **ultraviolet** light, **X-rays**, and **gamma rays**.

electron: A **particle** much smaller than an **atom**, with a negative electrical charge; one of the building blocks of atoms.

exoplanet: A **planet** that **orbits** a star outside our solar system.

fusion (nuclear): A reaction in which the nuclei (center) of **atoms** combine to form a larger atom, releasing energy in the process.

---

216   GLOSSARY AND FIND OUT MORE

galaxy: A large system of stars, gas, dust, and **dark matter** bound together by **gravity**.

gamma (radiation/rays): A type of high-energy **electromagnetic radiation** (light), often emitted by **radioactive** substances or cosmic events.

gravitational force (gravity): A force of attraction that exists between any two objects, proportional to their **masses** and inversely proportional to the square of the distance between them.

gravitational wave: A ripple in **space-time** caused by some of the most violent and energetic processes in the universe.

habitable zone: The region around a **star** where conditions might be right for liquid water to exist on a **planet's** surface.

infrared (radiation): A type of **electromagnetic radiation (light)** with wavelengths longer than **visible light** but shorter than microwaves. We feel infrared radiation as heat.

ion: An **atom** or **molecule** that has lost or gained one or more **electrons**, and so now has an electrical charge.

Kuiper Belt: A region of our solar system beyond Neptune's **orbit**, populated with icy bodies, **dwarf planets**, and **comets**.

Kuiper Belt Object (KBO): An object **orbiting** in the **Kuiper Belt**.

lander: A spacecraft designed to land on the surface of a **planet** or moon, with instruments to make observations and conduct scientific experiments.

light: Electromagnetic radiation. We also use the word light or **visible light** to describe the type of electromagnetic radiation that can be detected by the human eye.

magnetic field: The area around a magnetic object where its magnetic effects are felt by other magnetic materials.

magnetosphere: The region around a **star**, **planet**, or moon where its **magnetic field** is the dominant magnetic field.

main-sequence star: A **star** in the stable phase of its life cycle, fusing hydrogen into helium in its core. Its combination of **absolute magnitude** and surface temperature means it would be plotted on the main sequence of the Hertzsprung-Russell diagram (see page 214).

mass: The amount of **matter** in an object, typically measured in kilograms or grams.

massive: Has a large **mass**.

matter: Any substance that has **mass** and takes up space, from a **subatomic particle** to a **star**.

meteor: An **asteroid** or **meteoroid** that has entered Earth's **atmosphere** and is burning up, often creating a streak of **light** in the sky, known as a "shooting **star**."

meteorite: A **meteor** that survives its passage through Earth's **atmosphere** and lands on the surface.

meteoroid: A small rocky or metallic body traveling through space, smaller than an **asteroid**.

million: 1,000,000 (a number followed by six zeros).

mineral: A naturally occurring, nonliving solid with a specific chemical composition.

molecular cloud: A cold, **dense** cloud of gas and dust in space, where new **stars** and **planets** are formed.

molecule: The smallest unit of a chemical compound, consisting of two or more **atoms** bonded together.

nebula: A large, glowing cloud of gas and dust in space. There are several types of nebulae, including emission nebulae that release their own **electromagnetic radiation**, reflection nebulae that reflect or scatter **light** from other sources, planetary nebulae that form around dying **stars**, dark nebulae (also known as **molecular clouds**), and **supernova** remnants. Certain **galaxies** were also known as nebulae before **astronomers** realized they are galaxies outside our own.

neutrino: A **subatomic particle** with no electrical charge and a **mass** close to zero that rarely interacts with normal **matter**.

neutron: A **subatomic particle** with no electrical charge, found in the nuclei (central core) of most **atoms**.

neutron star: A type of **stellar** remnant created after a **massive star** explodes in a **supernova**, leaving behind a **dense** core rich in **neutrons**.

Northern Hemisphere: The half of a **planet** or moon located north of its equator.

observable universe: The portion of the universe that can be observed from Earth.

optical telescope: A **telescope** that gathers **visible light** (the range of **electromagnetic radiation** we can see with our eyes).

orbit: The curved path of an object as it moves around another object in space.

orbital period: The time it takes for a celestial body to complete one full **orbit** around another object.

orbiter/orbital probe: A spacecraft designed to **orbit** a **planet**, moon, or other celestial body, carrying instruments to make observations.

particle: A tiny piece of **matter**, such as an **atom**, **proton**, or **electron**.

particle accelerator: A large machine that uses strong magnets and electrical currents to get **particles** traveling at very high speeds, before smashing them into other particles. They are used for research, to create conditions and particles that don't exist naturally on Earth.

planet: A large celestial body that **orbits** a **star**, is **massive** enough for **gravity** to pull it into a **spherical** shape, and has cleared its orbit of other objects.

planisphere: A handheld map that shows you which **stars** are visible in the night sky at any particular time.

probe: An uncrewed spacecraft designed to explore space.

proton: A **subatomic particle** with a positive electrical charge, found in the nucleus (central core) of every **atom**.

protostar: A young **star** still in the process of forming, before **nuclear fusion** begins in its core.

quasar: An extremely energetic and distant active **galactic** nucleus (central core), powered by a **supermassive black hole**.

radiation: Energy in the form of electromagnetic waves or **particles**, including **visible light**, **infrared** (heat) energy, **ultraviolet** light, **X-rays**, **gamma rays**, and **radio waves**.

radioactive: Naturally gives out certain types of **radiation** or **particles**.

radio waves: A type of low-energy **electromagnetic radiation (light)**. Microwaves are a certain set of radiowave frequency.

red giant: A large, luminous **star** in the late stages of its life, expanding and cooling after using up most of the hydrogen in its core.

rover: A robotic vehicle designed to explore the surface of a **planet** or moon.

satellite: A natural or artificial object that **orbits** an object in space.

space-time: The four-dimensional fabric of the universe.

spectroscopy: Analyzing objects and substances by measuring the types of **radiation** that they absorb, emit, or scatter.

spectrum: A range of different colors or types of **light** produced when light from a source is passed through a prism; or the range of **radiation** from a source.

spherical: Shaped like a sphere, or ball.

star: A **massive**, glowing ball of gas, that generates energy through **nuclear fusion**. The term is also used to describe very young and very old stars that are not actively fusing elements.

stellar: To do with **stars**.

stellar wind: A flow of charged **particles** released from a **star's** outer layers into space.

subatomic: A **particle** of **matter** smaller than an **atom**.

supergiant: An extremely large and bright **star**, much more **massive** than the Sun.

supermassive: Referring to a **black hole** or object with a **mass millions** to **billions** of times that of the Sun.

supernova: A powerful and bright **stellar** explosion that marks the death of a **massive star**.

telescope: An instrument used to make distant objects look larger and brighter. The first telescopes gathered **visible light**, but the term is now used to describe instruments designed to collect any type of **electromagnetic radiation**.

theory: A well-substantiated explanation of some aspect of the natural world that is based on a body of evidence.

trillion: 1,000,000,000,000 (a number followed by 12 zeros).

ultraviolet (UV): A type of **electromagnetic radiation (light)** that we can't see, with wavelengths shorter than **visible light**.

variable star: A **star** whose brightness changes over time, sometimes in a very regular way.

visible light: The form of **electromagnetic radiation (light)** that can be detected by the human eye.

weight: The force exerted on an object by the **gravity** of another object, usually measured in newtons (N).

X-ray (radiation): A very high-energy form of **electromagnetic radiation (light)**.

young stellar object: A **star** in the early stages of its development, which isn't yet carrying out steady **nuclear fusion** at its core.

FIND OUT MORE

Hundreds of sources were consulted to write and illustrate this book. It is impossible to list them all here, but the author recommends the following books and websites to readers who would like to continue exploring the universe.

BOOKS

Astronomical!: An awesome encounter with the wonders of the Universe, DK, 2025

Astrophysics for Young People in a Hurry, Neil DeGrasse Tyson and Gregory Mone, W. W. Norton & Company, 2019

Exploring the Elements: A Complete Guide to the Periodic Table, Isabel Thomas and Sara Gillingham, Phaidon, 2020

Full of Life: Exploring Earth's Biodiversity, Isabel Thomas and Sara Gillingham, Phaidon, 2022

Seeing Stars: A Complete Guide to the 88 Constellations, Sara Gillingham, Phaidon, 2018

Seven Brief Lessons on Physics, Carlo Rovelli, Erica Segre, and Simon Carnell, Penguin, 2016

Universe: Exploring the Astronomical World, Phaidon, 2017

The Universe: The Book of the BBC TV Series, Andrew Cohen and Brian Cox, William Collins, 2021

WEBSITES AND APPS

Extraordinary images captured by the Webb Space Telescope:
https://science.nasa.gov/mission/webb/multimedia/images/

Get involved in citizen space science projects:
https://www.esa.int/Enabling_Support/Preparing_for_the_Future/Space_for_Earth/Citizen_science and https://www.skao.int/en/resources/outreach-education/citizen-science

Find your nearest Dark Sky Place:
https://darksky.org/what-we-do/international-dark-sky-places/all-places/

International Astronomical Union Office of Astronomy for Education:
https://astro4edu.org/

NASA: https://www.nasa.gov/

NASA Solar System Exploration:
https://science.nasa.gov/solar-system/

Speak with astronauts on the International Space Station:
https://www.ariss.org/

Stargazing mobile apps:
https://www.space.com/best-stargazing-apps

Stellarium Web (online star maps): https://stellarium-web.org/

The European Space Agency: https://www.esa.int/

The Sky Live (online planetarium):
https://theskylive.com/planetarium

URLs were accurate at the time of going to press. Please note that due to the dynamic nature of the internet, some of the URLs listed in this book may change or become unavailable after publication. The author and publisher are not responsible nor liable for the content or correctness of the URLs provided.

INDEX

Page numbers in **bold** refer to main entries

A
absolute magnitude 136
accretion discs 159, 160, 161, 180, 182
Aglaonice of Thessaly 21
AI (artificial intelligence) 90, **206–7**
Akatsuki probe 79
Allen Telescope Array 166
ALMA telescope 143
Alpha Centauri 146
Anaxagoras 20
Andromeda 33, 176, 179, 180, 181, 186, 204
animals in space **58–9**
Antares 153
Apollo missions 48, 49, 58
apparent magnitude 214
Aristarchus 8, 28
Aristotle 7, 28, 29
Armstrong, Neil 49, 58
Arrokoth 118, 119, 210
asteroid belt 11, **86–7**, 88, 116, 118
asteroids 10, 69, 76, **88–91**, 94, 106, 206, 209
astronauts 58, 60, 61, 64
astronomy 11, 22
atoms 156, 157, 194, 197, 198, 199
aurorae 33, 39, 101

B
Bennu 89
BepiColombo 74, 75
Betelgeuse 152, 153
Big Bang 156, 157, 174, 192, 194, 195, 210
Big Freeze model 194
Big Rip model 194

binary systems 162, 163
binoculars **25**
black dwarfs 151
black holes 9, 13, 57, 127, 137, 154, **160–1**, 162, 163, 172, 180, 184, 199, 201
  supermassive black holes 169, 170, 171, 173, 174, 175, **182–3**, 185, 186, 195
blue supergiants 153, 155
Boeing CST-100 Starliner **65**
Brahe, Tycho 28
brown dwarfs 142, 143, 144, 205
Burnell, Jocelyn Bell 159
Burney, Venetia 117

C
Callisto 94, 95
Calypso 102
Cannon, Annie Jump 147
capsules, reusable **65**
Cassini **73**, 96, 99, 104, 105, **106**
Cassini, Giovanni 92, 105
Cavendish, Henry 28
Centaurs 86
Cepheids 179, 180
Ceres **86–7**, 88, 89
Chandra X-ray Observatory 57, **185**
Chandrasekhar, Subrahmanyan 151, 185
Chang'e 4 rover 59
Characterising ExOPlanet Satellite (CHEOPS) 164
Charon 107, 116, 119
CHIME satellites 55
climate change 42, 46, 54, **132**
clouds 39, 54
collapsars 160
comets 10, 11, 25, 32, 33, 66, 69, 106, 119, 209

Comet 1P/Halley 33, 119, **122–3**, 124
Comet 9P/Tempel 1 73, 124
Comet 67P 124, 125
Comet Shoemaker-Levy 97, 125
exploring **124–5**
long-period 120, 124, 125
Copernicus, Nicolaus 18, 26, 28, 29
coral reefs 43
Cosmic Background Explorer 196, 197
cosmic calendar 209
cosmic horizon 191
Cosmic Microwave Background (CMB) 192, 193, 194, 195, 196, 204, 210
cosmic rays 127, 136, 141
cosmic web 13, **196–7**
Crab Nebula 154, 163
Curiosity rover 84

D
Dactyl 88
dark energy 13, 56, 189, 194, 196, **202–3**, 205
dark matter 13, 172, 180, 181, 184, 185, 189, 194, 196, **202–5**
DART (Double Asteroid Redirection Test) mission 88, **90–1**
Dawn mission 11, 87, 88, 89
Deep Impact **73**, 125
Deep Space Network 85
Deimos 81
Didymos 91
dinosaurs 59, 88, 162, 170
Dione 102
dogs in space 58
Doppler effect 179
Dragon spacecraft **65**
Dragonfly 105

Drake equation **166**
Dream Chaser (Sierra Space) **65**
dwarf planets 10, 26, 69, 86, 106, 107, 116, 121

E
Earendel 136
the Earth **36–43**, 46, 124, 191
  astronomical data 211, 212, 213
  atmosphere **9**, 23, 35, **38–9**, 56, 63, 66, 175
  gravity on 9, 31, 35, 46
  life on 36, **42–3**, 46, 98
  measuring **8**
  and the Moon 44, 45, **46–7**, 52, 54
  Sun-Earth system 7, 8, 18, 28, 29, 82, 128, **132–3**
  water 37, **40–1**
Einstein, Albert 30, 74, 139
  general theory of relativity 158, 161, 193, 194, **198–9**, 200, 201
electromagnetic radiation 138, 144, 174
electromagnetic waves **138**
electrons 156
elements 42, 153, 155, 156, **157**, 159
Enceladus 99, 102, 103, 104, 105, 106
Eratosthenes 8
Eris 116, 118, 119
Europa 94, 95, 99
Europa Clipper 96
Event Horizon Telescope **175**
exoplanets 12, 158, **164–5**, 166, 167
exosphere 9, 39
Extremely Large Telescope (ELT) **25**
extremophiles 43

F
faculae 87
Falcon 9 booster **65**

220 | INDEX

FAST (Five-hundred-metre Aperture Spherical Telescope) **175**
Fermi bubbles 173, 185
Fermi Gamma-ray Space Telescope 173, **185**
forces 50, 51
4 Vesta 86, 88, 89
fruit flies 58

G

Gacrux 148, 149
Gagarin, Yuri 58
Gaia-BH3 160, 161
Gaia satellite 137, 161, 172, 173, 179, 187
galactic walls 196, 197
galaxies 12, 13, 142, **168–87**, 190, 191, 192, 194, 202
   cosmic web **196–7**
   exploring **180–1, 186–7**
Galilean moons 27
Galilei, Galileo 20, 25, 28, 74, 94, 136, 172
   planets 26, 27, 78, 82, 96, 97, 104
   telescopes 24, 48
Galileo probe 64, 88, 96
gamma rays 56, 136, 138, 139, 155, 159, 184, 185, 205
Ganymede 94, 95, 96
Genesis space probe 130
geocentric model 8, 28, 29
Gilbert, William 29
Giotto mission 124
Golden Record **167**
gravitational lensing 193, 198, 203
gravitational waves 13, 158, 198, **200–1**
gravity 11, **30–1**, 35, 74, 128, 150, 182, 194
   Earth and 9, 28, 46
   galaxies 12, 202, 203, 204
   Galilean moons 94, 95

general theory of relativity 193, 198
gravity well 161
Isaac Newton's theory of 7
Lagrange points 47
on Mercury 70, 71
the Moon 46
multiple star systems 162
neutron stars 158
orbits and 52
planet formation 29
rockets and 50, 51
the Sun's 74
water and 41
greenhouse effect **132**

H

Habitable Worlds Observatory **167**
Halley, Edmond 27, 32, 122
Halley's comet 33, 119, **122–3**, 124
Hawking, Stephen 161
Hayabusa probe 88
heliocentric model 28, 29
heliopause 107
Hera mission **91**
Herbig Ae/Be stars 142, 143
Herbig-Haro objects 142, 143
Herschel, William 110, 130, 136, 139, 144, 172
Hertzsprung-Russell diagram 146, **214**
high-energy radiation **184–5**
Hipparchus 22
Hipparcos mission 172
Hooker Telescope **25**
Horsehead Nebula 141
Hubble, Edwin 25, 172, 176, 179, 180, 181, 190, 192, 202
Hubble constant 192
Hubble Space Telescope 56, 57, 64, 110, 114, 142, 148, 181, 184, 186, 187, 192, 195, 202

Huygens, Christiaan 104
Huygens probe **73**, 104, 105
Hyperion 103

I

Iapetus 102, 105
impactors **73**, 106
infrared light 56, 57, 136, 138, 139, **144–5**
Ingenuity Mars Helicopter 82, **85**
Inouye Solar Telescope 131
International Space Station (ISS) 31, 55, 58, **60–1**, 63, 64, 65
Io 94, 95, 210

J

Johnson, Katherine 207
Juno mission 96, 97
Jupiter 24, 26, 86, **92–7**, 100, 101, 108, 109, 113, 149, 208
   astronomical data 211, 212, 213
   exploring 74, **96–7**, 104, 107
   moons 26, 93, **94–5**, 96, 99, 102, 208–9, 210
Jupiter Icy Moons Explorer (JUICE) 96, 97, 106

K

Kármán line 38, 58
Kepler, Johannes 26, 27, 28
Kepler space telescope 114, 149, 164, 165
Kordylewski clouds 47
Kuiper Belt 107, 110, 112, **116–19**, 120, 179
Kuiper Belt Objects (KBOs) 116, 118, 122

L

Lagrange points 47
landers 10, **72–3**, 206
Laplace, Pierre-Simon 29

Laser Interferometer Gravitational-Wave Observatory (LIGO) 200, **201**
Leavitt, Henrietta Swan 179
Leonids 32, 33
LICIACube 91
life: on Earth 36, **42–3**, 46, 98
   in our solar system **98–9**
   outside our solar system **166–7**
   in space **58–9**
light 9, 12, 47, 56, **138–9**, 199
   infrared light 56, 57, 136, 138, 139, **144–5**
   moonlight 20, 21, 32
   speed of light 13, **139**
   starlight 22, 23, 56, 179
   sunlight 18, 19, 26, 32, 36, 56, 128, 129
   supernovae 154
   ultraviolet (UV) light 38, 56, 57, 136, 138, 139, 184
light-years 13
Local Group 176
Low Earth Orbit (LEO) 53, 54, 55, 58, 63
Luna missions 48, 49, 106
Lunar Reconnaissance Orbiter 49
Lunar Rover Vehicles 84
Lunokhod lunar rovers **84**

M

M-type asteroids 89
M87* 182, 183
Magellan 78
magnetars 159
magnetic fields 36, 70, 93, 95, 101, 113, 129, 131, 141
magnetosphere 36
main-sequence stars **146–7**, 148, 149, 157, 170
Mariner missions 74, 75, 78, 79, 82, 83

INDEX
221

Mars 26, 67, **80–5**, 98, 153, 208
  astronomical data 211, 212, 213
  exploring 73, **82–5**
mass 9, 31
matter 9, **156–7**, 190
Maxwell, James Clerk 139
Mercury 26, 36, **70–1**, 149, 208
  astronomical data 210, 211, 212, 213
  exploring Mercury **74–5**
mesosphere 9, 39
MESSENGER 74, 75
Messier, Charles 32, 180, 181, 186
meteorites 44, 45, **66–7**, 75, 77, 83, 88, 94
meteoroids **66–7**, 69
meteors 32, 33, 39, 42, **66–7**, 70, 71
  meteor showers 66, 67, 123
Milky Way 25, 32, 141, 154, 158, 160, 165, 166, 169, **170–3**, 176, 177, 182, 183, 186, 187, 202, 203
Mimas 102, 193
Mir Space Station 59
molecular clouds 140, 141
the Moon 19, 24, 44–9
  and the Earth 44, 45, **46–7**, 52, 54
  exploring the 9, 46, **48–9**, 58, 59, 73, 84
  lunar eclipses 7, 8, 21
  lunar meteorites 44, 67
  moonlight 20, 21, 32
  our view of the moon **20–1**
  phases of the moon 17, 20, 21
moons 10, 27, 69, 73, 111
  Jupiter 93, **94–5**, 96, 99, 102, 208–9, 210
  landers on 73
  Neptune 112, 113, 114, 115
  Pluto 107, 116, 119
  Saturn 99, **102–3**, 104, 106
  Uranus 111

N
Near-Earth Objects 66, 88, 89, 90
NEAR Shoemaker 88
nebulae 12, 33, 141, 142, 144, 154, 169, 172
Nemesis 162
Neptune 29, 108, **112–15**, 118
  astronomical data 211, 212, 213
  exploring **114–15**
  moons 112, 113, 114, 115
neutrinos **185**
neutron stars 127, 137, 154, 156, 157, **158–9**, 162, 163, 174, 184, 210
neutrons 156
New Horizons 48, 96, **107**, 110, 117, 118, 119, 179
Newton, Isaac 7, 24, 28, 30, 32, 50, 51, 52, 128, 138

O
O-type stars 147
Oort, Jan 120, 173
Oort cloud **120–1**, 173
Opportunity rover 84
orbital velocity 51
orbiters 10, 106
  see also individual orbiters
Orbiting Astronomical Observatory 136
Orbiting Solar Observatory (OSO 1) 130
orbits **52–3**, 54
Orion 23
OSIRIS-REx 88
oxygen 42, 43
ozone layer 38

P
parallax **178–9**
Parker Solar Probe 130, 131, **134–5**, 172, 180
particle accelerators 101

payloads 50, 51, 64
peculiar galaxies 186, 187
penguins 43
Perseverance rover 83, 84, **85**, 98
Philae 124, 125
Phobos 80, 81, 83
photons 199
photosphere 128, 129
photosynthesis 19, 132
phytoplankton 42, 43
Pillars of Creation 141
Pioneer missions 72, 96, 104, 130
Planck Observatory 205
planetary nebulae 150, 151
planets 10, **26–7**, 28, 29, 54, 69, **211**, 212
  see also individual planets
Pluto 26, 48, 107, 112, **116–17**, 118
  astronomical data 211, 212, 213
  moons 107, 116, 119
Polaris 23, 147, 162
Potentially Hazardous Asteroids (PHAs) 90
probes 10, 11, 50, 58, **106–7**, 206
  see also individual probes
propellants 50, 51
protons 156
protostars 127, 140, 142, 143, 170
Proxima Centauri 136, 137, 162, 167, 170
Ptolemy 8, 18, 28, 29
pulsars 154, **158–9**, 185, 200
Pythagoras 26

Q
quantum physics 198, 199
quasars 159, 182, 183, 184, 186, 210

R
radio telescopes 141, 166, 173, **174–5**, 179, 182, 192, 200
radio waves 78, 136, 138, 139, 141, 158, 171, 172, **174**, 175, 182
red dwarfs 146, 147
red giants 102, **148–9**, 150, 151, 163, 170, 171, 179
red supergiants **152–3**
redshift **179**, 193, 195
Ring Nebula 151
robotic landers **72–3**
robotic rovers **84–5**
rockets 38, **50–1**, 52, 56, 62, 63, 64, **65**, 130
rogue planets 165
Roman, Nancy Grace 56
Roman Space Telescope 56
Rosetta probe 124, 125
rovers 10, 49, 59, 82, 83, 206
  see also individual rovers
Rubin, Vera 180, 203, 204
Rubin Observatory Legacy Survey of Space and Time (LSST) 207

S
Sagittarius A* 170, 173, 182, 183
satellites 35, 38, 39, 50, 52, 53, **54–5**, 58, 62, 63, 137, **212**
Saturn 26, **100–5**, 108, 109, 149, 208
  astronomical data 211, 212, 213
  exploring **104–5**, 106, 107
  moons 73, 99, **102–3**, 104, 106
seasons 17, 18
Sedna 121
Shoemaker, Carolyn and Gene 125
shooting stars 32, 33, 39, **66–7**, 69
Sirius 22, 23, 147, 162
Sloan Digital Sky Survey 179
Sojourner 82, 83, 84
Solar and Heliospheric Observatory (SOHO) 57, 131
Solar Orbiter **134**
solar system 8, 10, **68–125**
solar wind 107, 129, 130, 135

Soyuz spacecraft 60, 61
space debris 35, **62–3**, 83
Space Rider **65**
Space Shuttle System 59, 60, **64**
space stations 31, 35, 55, 58, 59, **60–1**, 62, 63, 64
space weather 36, 130, 133
spacecraft 10, **64–5**
spacetime 198, 199
SpaceX 65
species 42
spectroscopy 22, 130, 131, 136, **139**, 156, 190, 214
spiders 59
Spirit rover 84
Sputnik missions 55, 58, 62
Square Kilometre Array Observatory (SKAO) **174**
standard candles 154, **179**
Standard Model of Cosmology 194, 195, 199
Starliner **65**
stars 11–12, 24, **126–67**, 179, 184, 194, 203, 210
   astronomical data 214
   comparing brightness 214
   constellations 6, 17, 22, 23, 208, **215**
   exploring **136–7**, **142–3**
   galaxies **168–87**
   main-sequence stars **146–7**
   multiple star systems **162–3**
   neutron stars and pulsars **158–9**
   our view of the **22–3**, 208
   red giants **148–9**
   red supergiants **152–3**
   starlight 23, 56, 179
   stellar nurseries **140–1**
   supernovae **154–5**
   white dwarf stars **150–1**
   see also Sun
states of matter **40**

stellar-mass black holes 160, 161, 170
stellar parallax **178**, 179
stellar winds 127
stratosphere 9, 39
the Sun 8, 11, 17, 20, 29, 57, 102, 127, **128–35**, 146, 149, 169, 170, 210
   exploring the **130–1**
   heliopause 107
   heliosphere 121
   Oort cloud 120, 121
   Parker Solar Probe 130, 131, **134–5**
   proximity to Mercury and Venus 74, 78
   size 21
   solar eclipses 19, 21, 131
   solar energy 18, 19, 39, 132, 133
   solar flares 133
   solar wind 107, 129, 130, 135
   Sun-Earth system 7, 8, **18–19**, 27, 28, 29, 82, 128, **132–3**
   sunlight 18, 26, 32, 36, 56, 128, 129
super-Earths 165
supercomputers 90, **206–7**
supermassive black holes 169, 170, 171, 173, 174, 175, **182–3**, 185, 186, 195
supernovae 17, 32, 33, 140, **154–5**, 158, 160, 174, 179, 184, 185, 203

T
T Tauri stars 142, 143
tardigrades 59
telescopes 9, 18, 22, **24–5**, 26, 28, 48, 131, 136, 178, 180, 184, 206
   see also individual telescopes
temperature 210, 214
Tethys 102
Theia 44
thermosphere 9, 38, 39

Tiangong space station (CNSA) 55
tides 46, 47, 94
time travel 7, 13
Titan 73, 99, 102, 103, 104, 105
Titania 111
Trans-Neptunian Objects 116
Transiting Exoplanet Survey Satellite (TESS) 164, 165
Triton 112, 115
troposphere 9, 39

U
ultraviolet (UV) light 38, 56, 57, 136, 138, 139, 184
the Universe **188–215**
   dark universe **202–3**
   measuring & mapping **178–9**
   observable universe **190–3**
   origins of the **194–5**
Uranus 29, **108–11**, 112, 114, 211, 212, 213

V
variable stars 137, 152
Vega probes 72
Venera missions **72**, 78, 79
Venus 24, 26, 27, 74, **76–9**, 98, 99, 134, 148, 208
   astronomical data 210, 211, 212, 213
   exploring 72, **78–9**, 104
Venus Express 78, 79
Voyager missions 88, 94, 96, 104, 107, 110, 114, 115, 120, 136, 167
VY Canis Majoris 153

W
water 37, **40–1**, 48, 76, 79, 94, 98, 99, 133
weather 37, 38, 39, 54, 132
   space weather 36, 130, 133
   weather balloons 38, 39

Webb Space Telescope 57, 110, 111, 114, 142, 144, **145**, 155, 180, 187, 192, 195, 206
weight 31
white dwarf stars 137, **150–1**, 155, 163, 170, 184
WIMPS (Weakly Interactive Massive Particles) 204, 205
wormholes 199

X
X-rays 56, 57, 136, 138, 159, 182, 205
   X-ray binaries 163, **184**
   X-ray telescopes 184, **185**, 207

Z
Zoozve 76

Thank you to Kate Shaw for all your support, and to Sara Gillingham and the Phaidon creative and editorial team behind this book, in particular Meagan Bennett, Maya Gartner, and Alice-May Bermingham. A huge thank-you to Robin Pridy for helping me to wrangle everything in the universe into 224 pages—you have been my lifeboat! Thank you to the thousands of astronomers, astrophysicists, cosmologists, and engineers whose discoveries and inventions allow us to leave our home planet and travel in time and space, to worlds stranger than imagination. I am grateful to the UK Association for Science and Discovery Centres (ASDC), whose Space Community Calls gave me the opportunity to hear directly from scientists working on wonders such as the Webb Space Telescope, Mars Perseverance, and the Artemis program. Also, to the American Association for the Advancement of Science (AAAS) for supporting me to attend two inspiring annual meetings where I had the chance to hear firsthand from people like Dr. Jane Rigby, Senior Project Scientist for the Webb Space telescope. Her poetic description of the mission was a huge inspiration for a book that combines art and cosmology. Most of all, thank you to my family for bearing with me while I spent a year exploring the universe.

—Isabel Thomas

ACKNOWLEDGMENTS:
The graph of satellite launches on page 212 is based on data and charts from ESA's Annual Space Environment Report, July 2024.

The Hertzsprung-Russell diagram on page 214 is based on an ESO image, and used under a Creative Commons Attribution 4.0 International License.

The image of the observable universe on page 191 is based on an image by Pablo Carlos Budassi/thecelestialzoo.

Photographic elements in planet images on pages 7, 9, 18, 20, 36–39, 45, 48, 69–71, 74–78, 80–82, 86–8, 92–93, 96–97, 100–101, 104–105, 107–114, 116–118, 125, 128–130, 212, and back of jacket are courtesy of NASA.

Special thanks to the brilliant star system that pulled together to make this book: to Meagan Bennett for pulling a million parts of the cosmos together with such mastery and grace; to Isabel Thomas and Robin Pridy for your illuminating words and wisdom and guidance with the visuals; to Alice-May Bermingham and Maya Gartner for your patience, vision, and championing of this book; and to Michelle Clement and Nora Aoyagi for your impeccable production assistance and support.

—Sara Gillingham

Phaidon Press Limited
2 Cooperage Yard
London E15 2QR

Phaidon Press Inc.
111 Broadway
New York, NY 10006

Phaidon SARL
55, rue Traversière
75012 Paris

phaidon.com

First published 2025
© 2025 Phaidon Press Limited
Text © Isabel Thomas 2025
Illustrations © Sara Gillingham 2025

Text set in ABC Whyte and ABC Maxi Round
978 1 83729 063 5 (US edition)
004-0825

A CIP catalog record for this book is available from the Library of Congress. All rights reserved. No part of this publication may be reproduced, stored in a retrieval system, or transmitted, in any form or by any means, electronic, mechanical, photocopying, recording, or otherwise, without the written permission of Phaidon Press Limited.

Printed in China

Commissioning Editor: Maya Gartner
Project Editor: Alice-May Bermingham
Editor: Robin Pridy
Assistant Editor: Rachel Craig-McFeely
Production Controller: Rebecca Price
Design: Meagan Bennett